Contents

KT-497-786

Part Three: **Supercharging Your Blog**

The Missing Credits

About the Author

 Matthew MacDonald is a science and technology writer with well over a dozen books to his name. Web novices can tiptoe out onto the Internet with him in *Creating a Website: The Missing Manual*. HTML fans can learn about the cutting edge of web design in *HTML5: The Missing Manual*. And human beings of all description can discover just how strange they really are in the quirky handbooks *Your Brain: The Missing Manual* and *Your Body: The Missing Manual*.

About the Creative Team

Peter McKie (editor) graduated from Boston University's School of Journalism and lives in New York City. He archives material chronicling the history of his summer beach community. Email: *pmckie@oreilly.com*.

Holly Bauer (production editor) lives in Ye Olde Cambridge, MA, where she is an avid home cook, prolific DIYer, and mid-century modern furniture design enthusiast. Email: *holly@oreilly.com*.

Ron Strauss (indexer) specializes in the indexing of information technology publications of all kinds. Ron is also an accomplished classical violist and lives in northern California with his wife and fellow indexer, Annie, and his miniature pinscher, Kanga. Email: *rstrauss@mchsi.com*.

Nancy Reinhardt (proofreader) lives in the Midwest, where she enjoys summer weekends at the lake, boating, swimming, and reading voraciously. Nan is not only a freelance copyeditor and proofreader, but she's also a published romance novelist. Check out her work at *www.nanreinhardt.com*. Email: *nanleigh1@gmail.com*.

Sallie Goetsch (technical reviewer) (rhymes with 'sketch') hand-coded her first website in HTML in 1995, but hasn't looked back since discovering WordPress in 2005. She works as an independent consultant and organizes the East Bay WordPress Meetup in Oakland, California. You can reach her at *www.wpfangirl.com*.

Christian Michael (technical reviewer) is an experienced public communicator for the US Air Force and owner of Scroll Media. He performs professional voice work and is currently writing his sixth novel, in addition to authoring a weeknight blog at *www.Rechabite.com*. Email: *cmichael.public@gmail.com*.

Acknowledgments

No author could complete a book without a small army of helpful individuals. I'm deeply indebted to the whole Missing Manual team, including my editor Peter McKie, expert tech reviewers Sallie Goetsch and Christian Michael, and numerous others who've toiled behind the scenes indexing pages, drawing figures, and proofreading the final copy.

Finally, for the parts of my life that exist outside this book, I'd like to thank all my family members. They include my parents Nora and Paul, my extended parents Razia and Hamid, my wife Faria, and my daughters, Maya and Brenna. Thanks everyone!

The Missing Manual Series

Missing Manuals are witty, superbly written guides to computer products that don't come with printed manuals (which is just about all of them). Each book features a handcrafted index and cross-references to specific pages (not just chapters). Recent and upcoming titles include:

Access 2010: The Missing Manual by Matthew MacDonald

Adobe Edge Preview 7: The Missing Manual by Chris Grover

Buying a Home: The Missing Manual by Nancy Conner

Creating a Website: The Missing Manual, Third Edition, by Matthew MacDonald

CSS: The Missing Manual, Second Edition, by David Sawyer McFarland

David Pogue's Digital Photography: The Missing Manual by David Pogue

Dreamweaver CS6: The Missing Manual by David Sawyer McFarland

Droid 2: The Missing Manual by Preston Gralla

Droid X2: The Missing Manual by Preston Gralla

Excel 2010: The Missing Manual by Matthew MacDonald

FileMaker Pro 12: The Missing Manual by Susan Prosser and Stuart Gripman

Flash CS6: The Missing Manual by Chris Grover

Galaxy S II: The Missing Manual by Preston Gralla

Galaxy Tab: The Missing Manual by Preston Gralla

Google+: The Missing Manual by Kevin Purdy

HTML5: The Missing Manual by Matthew MacDonald

iMovie '11 & iDVD: The Missing Manual by David Pogue and Aaron Miller

iPad: The Missing Manual, Fourth Edition by J.D. Biersdorfer

iPhone: The Missing Manual, Fifth Edition by David Pogue

iPhone App Development: The Missing Manual by Craig Hockenberry

iPhoto '11: The Missing Manual by David Pogue and Lesa Snider

iPod: The Missing Manual, Tenth Edition by J.D. Biersdorfer and David Pogue

JavaScript & jQuery: The Missing Manual, Second Edition by David Sawyer McFarland

Kindle Fire: The Missing Manual by Peter Meyers

Living Green: The Missing Manual by Nancy Conner

Mac OS X Mountain Lion: The Missing Manual by David Pogue

Microsoft Project 2010: The Missing Manual by Bonnie Biafore

Motorola Xoom: The Missing Manual by Preston Gralla

Netbooks: The Missing Manual by J.D. Biersdorfer

NOOK Tablet: The Missing Manual by Preston Gralla

Office 2010: The Missing Manual by Nancy Connor, Chris Grover, and Matthew MacDonald

Office 2011 for Macintosh: The Missing Manual by Chris Grover

Personal Investing: The Missing Manual by Bonnie Biafore

Photoshop CS6: The Missing Manual by Lesa Snider

Photoshop Elements 10: The Missing Manual by Barbara Brundage

PHP & MySQL: The Missing Manual by Brett McLaughlin

QuickBooks 2012: The Missing Manual by Bonnie Biafore

Switching to the Mac: The Missing Manual, Lion Edition by David Pogue

Windows 7: The Missing Manual by David Pogue

Windows 8: The Missing Manual by David Pogue

Your Body: The Missing Manual by Matthew MacDonald

Your Brain: The Missing Manual by Matthew MacDonald

Your Money: The Missing Manual by J.D. Roth

For a full list of all Missing Manuals in print, go to *www.missingmanuals.com/library .html.*

Introduction

Throughout history, people have searched for new places to vent their opinions, sell their products, and just chat it up. The World Wide Web is the culmination of this trend—the best and biggest soapbox, marketplace, and meeting spot ever created.

But there's a problem. If you want a website that's taken seriously, you need first-rate content, a dash of good style, and the *functionality* that ties everything together. The first two items require some hard work. But the third element—the industrial-strength web plumbing that powers your site—is a whole lot trickier. Overlook that, and you've got a broken mess of pages that even your mom can't love.

This is where the ridiculously popular web publishing tool named WordPress comes in. WordPress makes you a basic deal: You write the content, and WordPress takes care of the rest.

The services that WordPress provides are no small potatoes. First, WordPress puts every page of your content into a nicely formatted, consistent layout. It provides the links and menus that help visitors get around, and the search box that lets people dig through your archives. WordPress also lets your readers add comments with their Facebook or Twitter identities, so they don't need to create a new account on your site. And if you add a few community-created plug-ins (from the vast library that currently tops 20,000 items), there's no limit to the challenges you can tackle. Selling products? Check. Setting up a membership site? No problem. Building forums and collaborative workspaces? There's a plug-in for that, too. And while it's true that WordPress isn't the best tool for *every* type of website, it's also true that wherever you find a gap in the WordPress framework, you'll find some sort of plug-in that attempts to fill it.

WordPress is stunningly popular, too—it's responsible for roughly one-sixth of the world's websites, according to the web statistics company W3Techs (see *http://tinyurl.com/3438rb6*). And one out of every five new sites runs on WordPress, so you're in good company.

■ The Very Basics of Reading This Book

You'll find very little jargon or nerd terminology in this book. You will, however, encounter a few terms and concepts you'll come across frequently in your computing life:

- **Clicking**. This book gives you three kinds of instructions that require you to use your computer's mouse or trackpad. You already know how to *click*—that is, point the mouse cursor at something and press the button on your mouse (or laptop trackpad). You also know how to *double-click*—just point and click twice in rapid succession. And hopefully you remember that to *drag* means to move the mouse cursor while holding down the mouse button.

- **Keyboard shortcuts**. Every time you take your hand off the keyboard to move the mouse, you lose time and potentially disrupt your creative flow. That's why many experienced computer fans use keystroke combinations instead of menu commands wherever possible. Ctrl+B (⌘-B for Mac folks), for example, gives you boldface type in most programs.

   When you see a shortcut like Ctrl+S (⌘-S), it's telling you to hold down the Ctrl or ⌘ key and type the letter S, and then release both keys. (This command, by the way, saves changes to the current document in most programs.)

About→These→Arrows

Throughout this book, and throughout the Missing Manual series, you'll find sentences like this one: "Choose Appearance→Themes in the dashboard menu." That's shorthand for a longer series of instructions that go something like this: "Go to the dashboard in WordPress, click the Appearance menu item, and then select the Themes entry underneath." Our shorthand system keep things more snappy than these long, drawn-out instructions.

■ About WordPress

This book provides a thorough soup-to-nuts look at WordPress. You'll learn everything you need to know, including how to create, manage, maintain, and extend a WordPress site.

Notice, we haven't yet used the word *blog*. Although WordPress is the world's premiere blogging tool, it's also a great way to create other types of websites, like those that promote products, people, or things (say, your thrash-metal chamber-music band), sites that share stuff (for example, a family travelogue), and even sites that let people get together and collaborate (say, a short-story writing club for vampire fans). And if you're not quite sure whether the site you have in mind is a good fit for WordPress, the discussion on page 15 will help you decide.

What You Need to Know

If you're planning to make the world's most awesome blog, you don't need a stitch of experience. Chapters 1 to 12 will cover everything you need to know. However, you will come across some examples that feature *HTML* (the language of the Web), and any HTML knowledge you already have will pay off handsomely.

If you're planning to create a website that *isn't* a blog (like a catalog of products for your handmade jewelry business), you need to step up your game. You'll still start with the WordPress basics in Chapters 1 through 12, but you'll also need to learn the advanced customization skills you'll find in Chapters 13 and 14. How much customization you do depends on the type of site you plan to build, and whether you can find a theme that already does most of the work for you. But sooner or later, you'll probably decide to crack open one of the WordPress template files that controls your site and edit it.

When you do that, you'll encounter two more web standards: *CSS*, the style sheet language that sets the layout and formatting for your site; and *PHP*, the web programming language up on which WordPress is built. But don't panic—we'll go gently and introduce the essentials from the ground up. You *won't* learn enough to write your own web programs, but you *will* pick up the skills you need to customize a WordPress theme so you can build the kind of site you want.

Your Computer

WordPress has no special hardware requirements. As long as you have an Internet connection and a web browser, you're good to go. Because WordPress (and its design tools) live on the Web, you can use a computer running Windows, Mac OS, Linux, or something more exotic; it really doesn't matter. In fact, WordPress even gives you tools for quick-and-convenient blog posting through a smartphone or tablet computer (see page 177 for the scoop).

Hosting WordPress

There are two ways to host WordPress: you can use the free *WordPress.com* hosting service, or you can install WordPress on a hosting company's web server and run the whole show yourself, which is called *self-hosting*. Page 25 has much more about the difference.

But that's for the future. For now, all you need to know is that you can use the information in this book no matter which approach you use. Chapter 2 explains how to sign up with WordPress.com, Chapter 3 details self-hosting, and the chapters that follow try to pay as little attention to your hosting decision as possible.

That said, it's worth noting that you'll come across some features, particularly later in the book, that work only with self-hosted installations of WordPress. Examples include sites that use plug-ins and those that need heavy customization. But, happily, the features that *do* work on both WordPress.com-hosted sites and self-hosted sites work in almost exactly the same way.

■ About this Book

This book is divided into five parts, each with several chapters:

- **Part One: Starting Out with WordPress.** In this part of the book, you'll start planning your path to WordPress web domination. In Chapter 1, you'll plan the type of website you want, decide how to host it, and think hard about its *domain name*, the unique address that visitors type in to find your site on the Web. Then you'll see how to get a basic blog up and running, either on WordPress.com (Chapter 2) or on your own web host (Chapter 3).

- **Part Two: Building a WordPress Blog.** This part explains everything you need to know to create a respectable blog. You'll learn how to add posts (Chapter 4), pick a stylish theme (Chapter 5), make your posts look fancier (Chapter 6), add pages and menus (Chapter 7), and manage comments (Chapter 8). Even if you're planning something more exotic than JAWB (Just Another WordPress Blog), don't skip this section. The key skills you'll learn here also underpin custom sites, like the kind you'll learn to build in Part Four of the book.

- **Part Three: Supercharging Your Blog.** If all you want is a simple, classy blog, you can stop now—your job is done. But if you're hoping to add more glam to your site, this part will help you out. First, you'll learn that plug-ins can add thousands of new features to self-hosted sites (Chapter 9). Next, you'll see how to put video, music, and photo galleries on any WordPress site (Chapter 10). You'll also learn how to collaborate with a whole group of authors (Chapter 11), and how to attract boatloads of web visitors (Chapter 12).

- **Part Four: From Blog to Website.** In this part, you'll take your WordPress skills beyond the blog and learn to craft a custom website. First, you'll crack open a WordPress theme and learn to change the way your site works by adding, inserting, or modifying the CSS styles and PHP commands embedded inside (Chapter 13). Next, in Chapter 14, you'll apply this knowledge to create a WordPress product-catalog site that doesn't look anything like a typical blog.

- **Part Five: Appendixes.** At the end of this book, you'll find two appendixes. The first (Appendix A) explains how to take a website you created on the free WordPress.com hosting service and move it to another web host to get more features. The second (Appendix B) lists some useful web links culled from the chapters in this book. Don't worry—you don't need to type these into your browser by hand. It's all waiting for you on the Missing CD page for this book at *http://missingmanuals.com/cds/wpmm/*.

About the Online Resources

As the owner of a Missing Manual, you've got more than just a book to read. Online, you'll find example files as well as tips, articles, and maybe even a video or two. You can also communicate with the Missing Manual team and tell us what you love (or hate) about the book. Head over to *www.missingmanuals.com*, or go directly to one of the following sections.

Web Links

Often, this book will point you to a place on the Web. It might be to learn more about a specialized WordPress feature, or to get background information on another topic, or to download a super-cool plug-in. To save your fingers from the wear and tear of typing in all these long web addresses, you can visit the clickable list of links on the Missing CD page at *http://missingmanuals.com/cds/wpmm/* .

Living Examples

This book is packed full of examples. But unlike many other types of computer books, we don't encourage you to try and download them to your own computer. That's because once you place WordPress files on a local computer, they lose their magic. In fact, without the WordPress software running on a web server, your website loses all its abilities. You won't be able to try out even a single page.

To get around this limitation, many of the finished examples from this book are available for you to play around with at *www.prosetech.com/wordpress*. Although you won't be able to actually take charge of the example site (modify it, manage comments, or do any other sort of administrative task), you can take a peek and see what it looks like. This is a handy way to witness some features that are hard to experience in print—say, playing an embedded video or reviewing pictures in an image gallery.

Registration

If you register this book at oreilly.com, you'll be eligible for special offers—like discounts on future editions of *WordPress: The Missing Manual*. If you buy the ebook from oreilly.com and register your purchase, you get free lifetime updates for this edition of the ebook; we'll notify you by email when updates become available. Registering takes only a few clicks. Type *www.oreilly.com/register* into your browser to hop directly to the Registration page.

Feedback

Got questions? Need more information? Fancy yourself a book reviewer? On our Feedback page, you can get expert answers to questions that come to you while reading, share your thoughts on this Missing Manual, and find groups for folks who share your interest in creating their own sites. To have your say, go to *www.missing manuals.com/feedback*.

Errata

To keep this book as up-to-date and accurate as possible, each time we print more copies, we'll make any confirmed corrections you suggest. We also note such changes on the book's website, so you can mark important corrections in your own copy of the book, if you like. Go to *http://tinyurl.com/7mujhnx* to report an error and view existing corrections.

■ Using Code Examples

In general, you may use the code in this book in your programs and documentation. You don't need to contact us for permission unless you're reproducing a significant portion of the code. For example, writing a program that uses several chunks of code from this book does not require permission. Selling or distributing a CD of examples from O'Reilly books does require permission. Answering a question by citing this book and quoting example code does not require permission. Incorporating a significant amount of example code from this book into your product's documentation does require permission.

We appreciate, but do not require, attribution. An attribution usually includes the source book's title, author, publisher, and ISBN. For example: *"WordPress: The Missing Manual* by Matthew MacDonald (O'Reilly). Copyright 2012, 978-1-4493-0984-8."

If you feel your use of code examples falls outside fair use or the permission given above, feel free to contact us at *permissions@oreilly.com*.

■ Safari® Books Online

Safari® Books Online is an on-demand digital library that lets you search over 7,500 technology books and videos.

With a subscription, you can read any page and watch any video from our library. Access new titles before they're available in print. Copy and paste code samples, organize your favorites, download chapters, bookmark key sections, create notes, print out pages, and benefit from tons of other timesaving features.

O'Reilly Media has uploaded this book to the Safari Books Online service. To have full digital access to this book and others on similar topics from O'Reilly and other publishers, sign up for free at *http://my.safaribooksonline.com*.

Starting Out with WordPress

The WordPress Landscape

Since you picked up this book, it's likely that you already know at least a bit about WordPress. You probably realize that it's a brilliant tool for creating a huge variety of websites, from gossipy blogs to serious business sites. However, you might be a bit fuzzy on the rest of the equation—how WordPress actually works its magic, and how you can use WordPress to achieve your own website vision.

In this chapter, you'll get acquainted with life the WordPress way. First, you'll take a peek at the inner machinery that makes WordPress tick. If you're not already clear on why WordPress is so wonderful—and how it's going to save you days of work, years of programming experience, and a headful of gray hairs—this discussion will fill you in.

Next, you'll consider the types of sites you can build with WordPress, and how much work they need. As you'll see, WordPress began life as a premiere blogging environment, but has since mutated into a flexible, easy-to-use tool for creating virtually any sort of website.

Finally, you'll face your first WordPress decision: choosing a home for your WordPress site. You'll discover you have two options, you have two options. You can use WordPress's free hosting service (called *WordPress.com*), or you can install the WordPress software on another web host, for a monthly fee. Both approaches work, but the choice to use WordPress.com imposes a few limitations you should understand before you decide.

How WordPress Works

You probably already realize that WordPress isn't just a tool to build web pages. After all, anybody can create a web page—you just need to know a bit about HTML (the language that web pages are written in) and a bit about CSS (the language that formats web pages so they look beautiful). It also helps to have a first-class web page editor like Adobe Dreamweaver at your fingertips. Meet these requirements, and you'll be able build a *static* website—one that looks nice enough, but doesn't actually *do* anything (Figure 1-1).

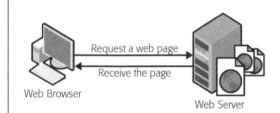

FIGURE 1-1

In an old-fashioned static website, a web designer creates a bunch of HTML files and drops them into a folder on a web server. When someone visits one of those pages, they see the exact HTML file that the web designer created. WordPress works a little differently—it builds its pages in real time, as you'll see next.

NOTE Just in case your webmaster skills are a bit rusty, remember that a *web server* is the high-powered computer that runs your website (and, usually, hundreds of other people's websites, too).

With WordPress, you strike up a different sort of partnership. Instead of creating a web page, you give WordPress your raw content—that's the text and pictures that make up an article, a product listing, a blog post, or some other type of content. And when a visitor surfs to your site, WordPress assembles the content that person wants into a made-to-measure web page.

Because WordPress is a *dynamic* website—it creates web pages on the fly—it provides some useful interactive features. For example, when visitors arrive at a WordPress blog, they can browse through the content in different ways—looking for posts from a certain month, for example, or on a certain topic, or tagged with a certain keyword. Although this seems simple enough, it requires a live program that runs on a web server and assembles the relevant content. For example, if a visitor searches a blog for the words "tripe soup," WordPress needs to find all the appropriate posts, stitch them together into a web page, and then send the result back to the web browser. More impressively, WordPress lets visitors write comments and leave other types of feedback, all of which become part of the site's ongoing conversation.

WordPress Behind the Scenes

In a very real sense, WordPress is the brain of your website. When someone visits a WordPress-powered site, the web server fires up the WordPress software and tells it to get busy. A blink of an eye later, a new web page is delivered to your visitor.

Two crucial ingredients allow WordPress to work the way it does:

- **A database.** This is an industrial-strength storage system that sits on a web server; think of it as a giant, electronic filing cabinet where you can search and retrieve any piece of content in an instant. In a WordPress website, the database stores all the content for its pages, the category and tag labels for those pages, and all the comments that people have added. WordPress uses the MySQL database engine, because it's a high-quality, free, open-source product, much like WordPress is.

- **Programming code.** When someone requests a web page on a WordPress site, the web server loads up a template and runs some code. It's the code that does all the real work—fetching information from different parts of the database, creating the page, and so on.

Figure 1-2 shows how these two pieces come together.

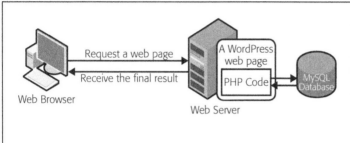

FIGURE 1-2

When a browser sends a request to a dynamic website, that request kicks off some programming code that runs on the web server. In the case of WordPress, that code is known as PHP, and it spends most of its time pulling information out of a database (for example, retrieving info on a product you want to see). The PHP then inserts the information into a regular-seeming HTML page, which it sends back to the browser.

The Evolution of Dynamic Sites

Dynamic websites are nothing new; they existed long before WordPress hit the scene. In fact, modern, successful websites are almost always dynamic, and almost all of them use databases and programming code behind the scenes. The difference is who's in charge. If you don't use WordPress (or a site-building tool like it), it's up to you to write the code that powers your website. Some web developers do exactly that, but they generally work with a whole team of experienced coders. But if you use WordPress to build your site, you don't need to touch a line of code or worry about defining a single database table. Instead, you supply the content and WordPress takes care of everything from storing the content in a database to inserting it into a web page when it's needed.

Even if you *do* have mad coding skills, WordPress remains a great choice for site development. That's because using WordPress is a lot easier than writing your own software. It's also a lot more reliable and a lot safer, because every line of logic has been tested by a legion of genius-level computer nerds—and it's been firing away for years on millions of WordPress sites. Of course, if you know your way around PHP, the programming language that runs WordPress, you'll have a head start when it comes to tweaking certain aspects of your site's behavior, as you'll see in Chapter 13.

In short, the revolutionary part of WordPress isn't that it lets you build dynamic websites. It's that WordPress pairs its smarts with site-creation and site-maintenance tools that ordinary people can use.

WordPress Themes

There's one more guiding principle that shapes WordPress—its built-in *flexibility*. WordPress wants to adapt itself to whatever design you have in mind, and it achieves that through a feature called *themes*.

Basically, themes let WordPress separate your content (which it stores in a database) from the layout and formatting details of your site (which it stores in a theme). Thanks to this system, you can tweak the theme settings—or even swap in a whole new theme—without disturbing any of your content. Figure 1-3 shows how this works.

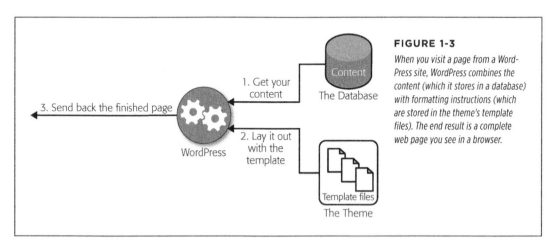

FIGURE 1-3

When you visit a page from a WordPress site, WordPress combines the content (which it stores in a database) with formatting instructions (which are stored in the theme's template files). The end result is a complete web page you see in a browser.

If you're still not quite sure how WordPress helps you with themes, consider an example. Imagine Jan decides to create a website so he can show off his custom cake designs. He decides to do the work himself, so he not only has to supply the content (the pictures and descriptions of his cakes), he also has to format each page the same way, because each page has two parts—a description of the cake and a picture of it—and he wants his pages to be consistent. But, as so often happens, a week after he releases his site, Jan realizes it could be better. He decides to revamp his web pages with a fresh, new color scheme and add a calorie-counting calculator in the sidebar.

Applying these changes to a non-WordPress website is no small amount of work. It involves changing the website's style sheet (which is relatively easy) and modifying every single cake page, being careful to make *exactly the same change* on each (which is much more tedious). If Jan's lucky, he'll own a design tool that has its own template feature (like Dreamweaver), which will save editing time. However, he'll still need to rebuild his entire website and upload all the new web pages.

With WordPress, these problems disappear. To get new formatting, you tweak the style settings, either using WordPress's administrative hub (called the *dashboard*), or by editing the styles by hand. To get the calorie counter, you simply drop the corresponding widget (and yes, WordPress *does* have a a calorie-counting widget plug-in) into the current theme's layout. And that's it. You don't need to rebuild or regenerate anything, go through dozens of pages by hand, or check each page to try to figure out which detail you missed when you copied HTML from one page to another.

■ What You Can Build with WordPress

There are many flavors of website, and many ways to create them. But if you want something reasonably sophisticated and you don't have a crack team of web programmers to make that happen, WordPress is almost always a great choice.

That said, some types of WordPress websites require more work than others. For example, if you want to create an e-commerce site complete with a shopping cart and checkout process, you need to ditch WordPress or rely heavily on someone else's WordPress plug-ins. This doesn't necessarily mean that WordPress is a poor choice for e-commerce websites, but it does present an extra challenge. (In Chapter 14, you'll take a closer look at what it takes to make a basic e-commerce site that uses a plug-in to go beyond WordPress's standard features.)

In the following sections, you'll see some examples of WordPress in action. You'll consider the types of sites that use WordPress most easily and most commonly. Along the way, you should get a feel for how WordPress suits your very own website-to-be.

Blogs

As you probably know, a blog is a wildly popular type of site that consists of separate, dated entries called *posts* (see Figure 1-4). Good blogs reflect the author's personality, and are informal and overflowing with content.

When you write a blog, you invite readers to see the world from your viewpoint, whether the subject is work, art, politics, technology, or your personal experience. Blogs are sometimes described as online journals, but most blogs are closer to old-school newspaper editorials or magazine commentary. That's because a journal writer is usually talking to himself, while a half-decent blogger unabashedly addresses the reader.

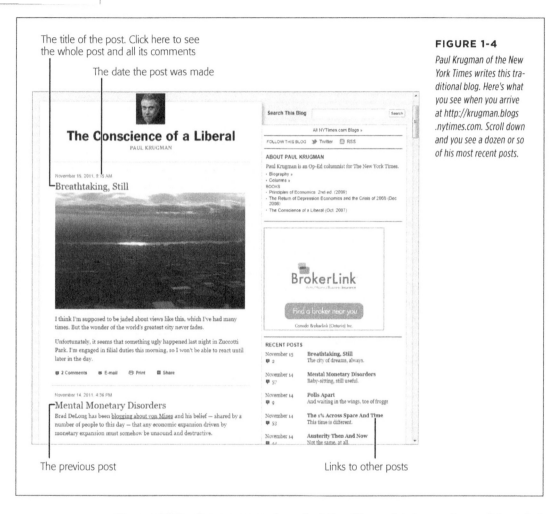

The title of the post. Click here to see the whole post and all its comments

The date the post was made

FIGURE 1-4

Paul Krugman of the New York Times writes this traditional blog. Here's what you see when you arrive at http://krugman.blogs .nytimes.com. Scroll down and you see a dozen or so of his most recent posts.

The previous post

Links to other posts

Blogs exhibit a few common characteristics. These details aren't mandatory, but most blogs share them. They include:

- **A personal, conversational tone.** Usually, you write blogs in the first person ("*I* bought an Hermes Birkin bag today" or "Readers emailed *me* to point out an error in yesterday's post"). Even if you blog on a serious topic—you might be a high-powered executive promoting your company, for example—the style remains informal. This gives blogs an immediacy and connection to you that readers love.

- **Dated entries.** Usually, blog posts appear in reverse-chronological order, so the most recent post takes center stage. Often, readers can browse archives of old posts by day, month, or year (see "Recent Posts" in Figure 1-4). This emphasis on dates makes blogs seem current and relevant, assuming you post regularly. But miss a few months, and your neglected blog will seem old, stale, and seriously out of touch—and even faithful readers will drift away.

- **Interaction through comments.** Blogs aren't just written in a conversational way, they also "feel" like a conversation. Loyal readers add their feedback to your thoughts, usually in the form of comments appended to the end of your post (but sometimes through a ratings system or an online poll). Think of it this way: your post gets people interested, but their comments get them *invested*, which makes them much more likely to come back and check out new posts.

However, some WordPress blogs challenge the traditional expectations of what a blog should be. One wildly popular example is a *photo blog*, which ditches text in favor of pictures (see Figure 1-5).

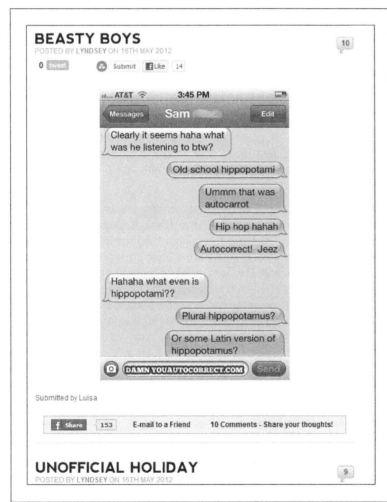

FIGURE 1-5

You can put photo blogs to a wide variety of uses—everything from serious photography to lowbrow fun. Examples of the latter include sites like http://failblog.org or http://damnyouautocorrect.com (shown here), where each page is a screen capture from an iPhone conversation gone horribly wrong.

Who's Blogging?

Technorati, a popular blog search engine, maintains a list of the most popular blogs at *http://technorati.com/blogs/top100* and compiles statistics about the blog universe. Their 2011 report found the following:

- **60%** of bloggers write for the sense of personal satisfaction they get by sharing their world view with readers.

- **18%** of people blog professionally. They're compensated for their work, although for many it's a supplementary source of income, not their livelihood. Professional bloggers may be part-time or full-time, and they usually blog about technology or their own personal musings.

- **13%** of bloggers are considered entrepreneurs. Their goals are similar to those of corporate bloggers (see next), but they blog for a company they own.

- **8%** of bloggers work for and write under the imprimatur of a company. They generally talk about business or technology, and their goals are to share expertise, gain professional recognition, and lure new clients.

Equally interesting is the question of what bloggers blog about. The answer is *everything*, from travel and music to finance and real estate, from parenting and relationships to celebrities and current events. To see the full stats about popular blog topics, tone, and style, check out the relevant slides in Technorati's State of the Blogosphere report (*http://bit.ly/rqGfCs*).

Other types of non-traditional blogs include video blogs that feature regular clips; microblogs that use tiny, frequent posts (like Twitter messages); and business blogs that launch company promotions, offer free samples for feedback, or solicit potential employees.

Blogging with WordPress is a slam-dunk. After all, WordPress was created as a blogging tool (in 2003), and has since exploded into the most popular blogging software on the planet. In fact, if you're planning to create a blog, there's really no good reason *not* to use WordPress. Although there are several other blogging platforms out there, and they all work reasonably well, none of them has the near-fanatical WordPress community behind it, which is responsible for thousands of themes and plug-ins, and might even help you solve hosting and configuration problems (just ask your questions in the forums at *http://wordpress.org/support*).

Creating a Modern Blog

Perhaps the idea of writing a blog seems a bit boring to you. If so, you're probably locked into an old-fashioned idea about what a blog *is*.

Today's blogs aren't glorified online diaries. In fact, the best way to create an *un*successful blog is to chronicle your meandering, unfiltered thoughts on everything from the Tea Party to toe jam. Even your friends won't want to sift through that. Instead, follow these tips to make your blog truly legit:

- **Pick a topic and focus relentlessly.** People will seek out your blog if it's based on a shared interest or experience. For example, create a blog about your dining experiences around town, and foodies will flock to your pages. Talk up the challenges of taking care of a baby, and other new parents will come by and commiserate. If you're having trouble deciding exactly what you want to accomplish with your blog and what topics are truly blog-worthy, WordPress has a great article with blog brainstorming tips at *http://learn.wordpress.com/get-focused.*

- **Add a title.** Once you choose your topic, give your blog a name that reinforces it, which will also help you stay on-topic. Paul Krugman, for example, calls his blog The Conscience of a Liberal (Figure 1-4), despite the fact that his name is well-recognized among his target audience.

- **Find a new perspective.** It's a rule of the Web that everything has been blogged before, so find a unique angle from which to attack your topic. For example, when Scott Schuman began his now blazingly popular blog The Sartorialist (*www.thesartorialist.com*), he didn't just slap together an ordinary fashion blog. Instead, he created a unique commentary on real-life fashion by using pictures he snapped strolling the streets of New York.

- **Don't be afraid to specialize.** You won't pique anyone's interest with yet another movie review site called My Favorite Movies. But throw a different spin on the subject with a blog that finds film flaws (In Search of Movie Mistakes) or combines your experience from your day job as a high-school science teacher (The Physics of Vampire Movies), and you just might attract a crowd.

- **Don't forget pictures, audio, and video.** Bloggers shouldn't restrict themselves to text. At a bare minimum, blogs need pictures, diagrams, comics, or some other visual element to capture the reader's eye. Even better, you can weave in audio or video clips of performances, interviews, tutorials, or related material. They don't even need to be your own work—for example, if you're discussing the avant-garde classical composer Grigori Ligeti, it's worth the extra five minutes to dig up a performance on YouTube and embed that into your post. (You'll learn how to do that in Chapter 10.)

Other Types of WordPress Sites

Blogs are fantastic, exciting things, but they're not for everyone, even if you have a streamlined tool like WordPress at your disposal. The good news is that, because of its inherent flexibility, WordPress makes an excellent program for building more traditional websites, too. In fact, as long as you're willing to do a little theme customization, you can convert your WordPress pages into something that doesn't look one whit like a traditional blog. When you do, you'll still be relying on the same WordPress technology, which runs on a web server working the same database-contacting and theme-processing magic it does with blogs. But now, instead of spitting out an ordinary blog, WordPress will produce the custom pages you want.

If you're interested in taking the WordPress engine beyond a blogging tool, the following sections will show you some of the types of sites you can create.

■ STORIES AND ARTICLES

WordPress makes a great home for personal, blog-style writing, but it's an equally good way to showcase the more polished writing of a news site, Web magazine, short-story collection, scholarly textbook, and so on. WordPress also allows multiple authors to work together, each adding content and managing the site (as you'll discover in Chapter 11).

Consider, for example, the Internet Encyclopedia of Philosophy shown in Figure 1-6 (and located at *www.iep.utm.edu*). It's a sprawling catalog of philosophy topics amassed from about 300 authors and maintained by 25 editors, all with heavyweight academic credentials. Created in 1995, the site moved to WordPress in 2009 to make everyone's life a whole lot easier.

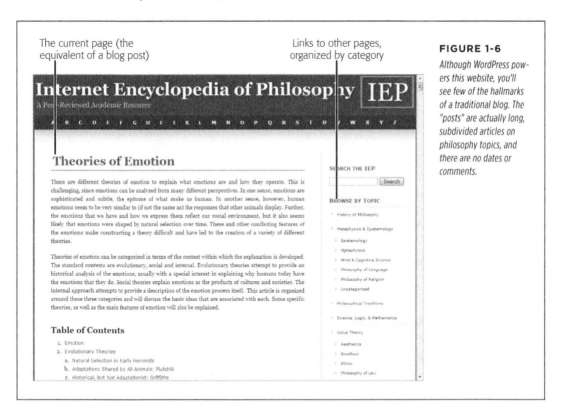

The current page (the equivalent of a blog post)

Links to other pages, organized by category

FIGURE 1-6

Although WordPress powers this website, you'll see few of the hallmarks of a traditional blog. The "posts" are actually long, subdivided articles on philosophy topics, and there are no dates or comments.

The Internet Encyclopedia of Philosophy is an interesting example for the sheer number and size of the articles it hosts. However, you'll also find WordPress at work in massive news sites, including TechCrunch, TMZ.com, Salon, Boing Boing, Think Progress, and the CNN site Political Ticker.

How to Find Out If a Website Uses WordPress

There are plenty of websites built with WordPress, even if it's not always apparent. So what can you do if you simply *must* know whether your favorite site is one of them?

You could ask the website administrator. But if you're in a hurry, there are two easier ways. The first is the quick-and-dirty approach: right-click the page in your browser, choose View Source to bring up the page's raw HTML, and then hit Ctrl+F to launch your browser's search feature. Hunt for text starting with "wp-". If you find *wp-content* or *wp-includes*

somewhere in the mass of markup, you're almost certainly looking at a WordPress site.

Another approach is to use a browser plug-in, called a *sniffer*, that analyzes the markup. The advantage of this approach is that most sniffers detect other types of web-creation tools and programming platforms, so if the site's not in WordPress you might still find out a bit more about how it works. One of the most popular sniffers is Wappalyzer (*http://wappalyzer.com*), which works with the Firefox and Chrome browsers.

▩ CATALOGS

WordPress is particularly well-suited to websites that are stuffed full of organized content. For example, think of a website that has a huge archive of ready-to-make recipes (Figure 1-7). Or consider a website that collects classified ads, movie critiques, restaurant reviews, custom products, or something else.

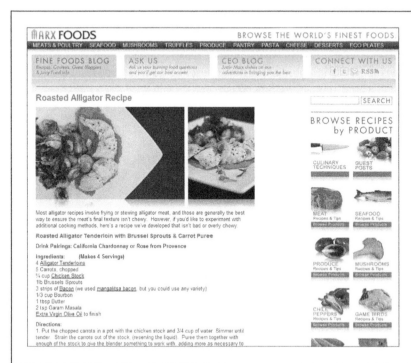

FIGURE 1-7

This WordPress site features a huge catalog of recipes and articles with cooking tips. What makes this site distinctly different from a blog is the fact that the recipes aren't categorized by date and displayed in a single listing in reverse-chronological order. Instead, its recipes are organized into common-sense categories like Meat, Seafood, Mushrooms, and so on.

Because WordPress relies on a database, it's a wizard at organizing massive amounts of content. In a properly designed catalog site, people can find a review, product, or whatever else they want in a number of ways, such as searching by keyword or browsing by category.

Catalog sites are also known by many other names. Some people describe them as content-based sites, others call them CMS sites (for "content management system," a term explained in the box on page 23). No matter what you call them, the sites share a few key characteristics:

- **They include a large volume of content.** If you want to create a recipe site with just four recipes, it probably wouldn't be worth the WordPress treatment.

- **The content can be divided into separate pages.** With a blog, the "pages" are actually blog posts. In the recipe site, each page is a recipe. (And in the Encyclopedia of Philosophy shown on page 20, each page is a lengthy scholarly article.)

- **Each page consists of text, images, and/or video.** Usually, pages are stuffed with text. Often, they're enriched with pictures and video. That's where Word-Press shines. It's less adept at displaying reams of numeric data, like the last 12 years' worth of sales at your chain of mattress superstores.

- **Visitors browse the content by category.** You categorize pages by their subject matter. Visitors use those categories to find exactly what they want—like a recipe for a specific ingredient. Often, guests get to what they want by clicking through a slick, multilayered menu.

These criteria encompass a surprisingly huge range of modern-day websites. Examples include event listings for festivals, a portfolio of your work, a list of products you sell, and so on. Pretty much everywhere there's a mass of text or pictures that needs to be categorized and presented to the world, WordPress is there, making itself useful.

The WordPress CMS Smackdown

What's the difference between WordPress and an official content-management system?

In the not-so-distant past, site-development tools like WordPress were just about blogs. Webmasters who wanted to create content-focused websites (like the kind described on page 22) would usually turn to a piece of software called a *content-management system* (CMS), which stores pieces of content, like articles, as discreet units and then inserts them into web pages it builds on the fly.

Today, WordPress has grown into a capable CMS itself. In fact, some web designers build *every* sort of site in WordPress. However, other CMS tools are out there (two popular examples are Joomla and Drupal), so it's natural to ask why a web designer should choose WordPress over another CMS.

The primary reason is simplicity. Not only does WordPress make it relatively easy to create a good-looking site, it also makes it easy to *manage* the site. That's important if the person who ends up managing the site isn't the person who created it. For example, a knowledgeable WordPress developer (like you, once you finish this book) can create a perfectly tailored website for a client (and be paid handsomely for the effort).

With just a little training, the client can handle the necessary day-to-day tasks, like monitoring site traffic, reviewing comments, adding new content, and making backups. Theoretically, other CMS products should work as simply this, but they seldom do. Instead, newly trained users end up overwhelmed and intimidated, and they need outside help to keep their site current.

At the same time, WordPress isn't the CMS for everyone. It lacks some of the high-powered features that big corporate outfits may expect. There's no version control, for example, which means you can't see a log of the changes you make to the design of the site and roll back mistakes; and there's no workflow management, where you route work from one person to another in a team. And if you want to connect your website to a back-end system running on your company's computers (for example, you want to link your site to a company database that has inventory information), WordPress probably isn't the ticket.

Overall, it's best to think of WordPress as a *lightweight* CMS. If you can live with its limitations, WordPress will prove itself flexible, powerful, and easy to use. It's also a "safe" platform—because of its wild popularity, the WordPress community is certain to thrive for many years.

■ BUSINESS SITES

WordPress isn't just a great tool for self-expression, it's also an excellent way to do business. The only challenge is deciding exactly *how* you want to use WordPress to help you out.

The first, and simplest, option is to take your existing business website and augment it with WordPress. For example, Ford uses WordPress for its news site *http:// social.ford.com*, which invites customers to post feedback and share the hype about their new vehicles on Facebook and Twitter. But if you head to Ford's main site, *www .ford.com*, and you search for a local dealer or ask for a price quote, you'll be entirely WordPress-free. These parts of Ford's site rely on custom web applications, which web developers working for Ford created.

Other companies *do* use WordPress to take charge of their entire websites. Usually, they're smaller sites, and often the goal is simply to promote a business and share its latest news. For example, you could use WordPress to advertise the key details about your new restaurant, including its location, menu, and recent reviews. Or imagine you need more detailed information for a tourist attraction, like the detailed website for Perth Zoo (Figure 1-8).

FIGURE 1-8

The Perth Zoo website has it all—detailed menus, information about animals, a review of the zoo's policies, and up-to-date news. But there's a catch: To make this website look as beautiful as it does here, the designers needed to combine Word-Press knowledge with some traditional web design skills (including a good knowledge of HTML and CSS).

A greater challenge is when a business doesn't just want to advertise or inform with its website, but it also wants to *do* business over the Web. For example, imagine you create a website for your family-run furniture store, like the one shown Figure 1-9. But you don't just want to advertise the pieces you offer, you want to take orders for them, too, complete with all the typical trappings of an e-commerce website (such as a shopping cart, checkout page, email confirmation, and so on). In this situation, you need to go beyond WordPress's native features and add a plug-in to handle the checkout process.

FIGURE 1-9

On this furniture website, you can view the chairs for sale, their prices, and their dimensions. All this is possible with WordPress's standard features and a heavily customized theme. But if you want to allow online ordering, you need to add a plug-in developed by a third party.

For some small businesses, an e-commerce plug-in offers a practical solution. But for many others, this approach just isn't flexible enough. Instead, most e-commerce sites need a custom-tailored transaction-processing system that integrates with other parts of their business (like their inventory records or their customer database). This functionality is beyond the scope of WordPress and its plug-ins.

> **TIP** To see more examples of what you can do with WordPress, including plenty of business sites, visit the WordPress showcase at *http://wordpress.org/showcase*.

■ WordPress Hosting

If you've reached this point, it's safe to say you're on board with WordPress. Now you need to decide exactly where you'll put your WordPress site.

The simplest (and cheapest) option is to sign up for the free WordPress.com service, which is run by the fine folk at Automattic (founded by a guy named Matt Mullenweg, hence the "matt" in the company name). The deal is simple: they give your website a home, some exposure, and a free web address that ends in *.wordpress .com* (although you can buy a custom domain name if you want), and you accept a few limitations—most notably, your website can't show ads or use other people's plug-ins, and you can't edit your theme by hand.

NOTE The people at Automattic are also largely responsible for (but not completely in control of) the development of the WordPress software. That's because Automattic employs many of WordPress's lead developers, but the program is still a community-driven, open-source project.

Your other hosting option is to install WordPress on your web host's server and build your site there. The drawback here is that you need to pay your web host. And although you won't be on the hook for much coin—good plans run a few dollars a month—you still need to open your wallet. Generally, WordPressers call this approach *self-hosting*, although someone else actually does the hosting. In other words, you're not running a web server in your basement; you're contracting with a web hosting company for some space on *their* servers.

NOTE Although the WordPress nomenclature is a bit confusing, the real story is simple. *WordPress* is the software that powers all WordPress sites. (Sometimes, people call the software *WordPress.org*, because that's the web address where you download the program.) On the other hand, *WordPress.com* is a free web hosting service that uses the WordPress software. So no matter where you decide to host your site—through WordPress. com or on your own web host—you'll be using the WordPress software.

Choosing Where to Host Your Site

If WordPress.com is so eager to give you a free, reliable web host, why *wouldn't* you use it? Here are a few good reasons to consider self-hosting instead:

- **You want to create a site that isn't a blog.** In this chapter, you've seen plenty of examples of websites, from webzines to recipe catalogs to slick business sites. Many of those sites are more difficult to create with WordPress.com (if not impossible). That's because WordPress.com prevents you from editing the code in your theme, or from using a theme that isn't in WordPress.com's pre-approved list of about 200 themes.

- **You already have a website.** With most third-party web hosts, you won't have to pay extra to add a WordPress site. And if you already have a web presence, it makes sense to capitalize on the *domain name* (that's your web address, like *www.PajamaDjs.com*) and the web space you already have.

- **You want complete control over your site's appearance**. If you're the sort of person who can't sleep at night unless you get the chance to tweak every last WordPress setting, you definitely want the free reign of a self-hosted site. With it, you can choose from thousands of site-enhancing plug-ins and a universe of custom themes.

- **You want to make money advertising.** Ordinarily, WordPress.com doesn't allow its sites to display ads or participate in affiliate programs. However, WordPress. com is in the midst of a pilot program called WordAds, which allows a limited type of advertising, provided your site is accepted into the program. You can learn more and apply at *http://wordpress.com/apply-for-wordads*.

> **NOTE** Even though you can't run standard ads on WordPress.com, you can still make money there. WordPress.com is perfectly fine with a website that promotes a particular product or business, includes a PayPal-powered Donate button, or advertises your own personal fee-based services.

- **You don't want your readers to see ads, ever.** WordPress.com is a bit sneaky in this regard. In some cases, it will insert an ad into one of your pages. This usually happens when someone stumbles across your site from a search engine. It doesn't happen if a visitor surfs from one WordPress.com site to another, or if a visitor is logged in with a WordPress.com account. For these reasons, you might never notice the ads that other people could see. If this behavior bothers you, you can remove the ads from your site, but you need to pay a yearly fee (currently, $30 per year).

> **NOTE** WordPress.com isn't necessarily as free as you think. In addition to paying for ad-free pages, you can opt (and pay) for a personalized web address, the ability to edit the fonts in your theme, and extra space for big files and hosted video. You can get information about all these upgrades at *http://support.wordpress.com/upgrades*. It's worth noting that self-hosters get virtually all these features through their own web hosts, so if you plan to buy several upgrades, you should at least consider getting your own web host instead—it may end up costing you less.

In general, self-hosting is a slightly more powerful and more expensive strategy than hosting with WordPress.com. But there are reasons why people actually prefer to use WordPress.com rather than self-host:

- **No-headache maintenance.** If WordPress.com hosts your site, all the website maintenance is taken care of. You don't need to think about installing patches or WordPress updates, or making backups of your site.

- **Better discoverability.** If your site is on WordPress.com, people can stumble across it two ways. First, they can browse the giant index of popular subject tags at *http://wordpress.com/tags*, and pick one you use in your posts. Second, if you write a particularly popular post, your site may appear in the "Blog of the Day" list that WordPress.com features prominently on its front page (*http://wordpress.com*), and attract a click-storm of new traffic.

- **Reliability.** It's not hard to find a good web host that has solid WordPress support. That said, no one serves as many WordPress sites as WordPress.com—they use over a thousand web servers to hand out *billions* of WordPress pages every month. That means that if a page on your WordPress site suddenly gets a burst of popularity—for example, it gets noticed on a social news site like Digg (*http://digg.com*)—WordPress.com will handle the challenge, while a less able web-hosting service could buckle.

What WordPress.com Won't Allow

It probably comes as little surprise that there are some types of websites that WordPress.com doesn't welcome. Here are the problem areas:

- **Spam.** If you create a website for the sole purpose of attracting clicks for another site, artificially inflating another site's Google search ranking with spurious links, promoting "get rich quick" schemes, or showing ads, WordPress will wipe it off the Web in minutes.

- **Copyright violation.** If you create a site that includes content owned by someone else and you don't have permission to use it, WordPress has the power to yank your site. Copyright (and other) complaints are made at

http://wordpress.com/complaints.

- **Masquerading.** It's not acceptable to create a blog where you pretend to be someone else.

- **Threats or criminality.** If your blog threatens another real-life person, incites violence, or promotes an illegal scheme, you obviously aren't a nice person, and WordPress won't want you.

You'll notice that there's one oft-censored site type missing from this list: namely, those that include sex, erotica, or pornography. It turns out that WordPress.com is mostly OK with that, but it will slap "mature" blogs with an adults-only warning, and it won't include them in its home page or tag directory.

WordPress.com Sites vs. Self-Hosted Sites

Struggling to keep all the details about WordPress.com and WordPress.org in mind at once? Table 1-1 summarizes the key differences. Remember that the WordPress program is packed with functionality, and the table leaves out the long list of features that work equally well in WordPress.com and on self-hosted WordPress sites.

TABLE 1-1 *Comparing WordPress.com and Self-Hosted Sites*

YOU WANT TO...	WITH WORDPRESS.COM	WITH A SELF-HOSTED SITE
Pay as little as possible	The starting cost is free, but various enhancements cost money	You pay the cost of web hosting (typically $5 to $10 per month, unless your site is wildly popular, in which case you need to pay your host more for the high traffic)
Forget all about web server maintenance	Yes	No, you need to back up your content regularly, and update WordPress with new versions (but fortunately both jobs are pretty easy)
Use a custom website address (like *www.myName.com*)	Yes, but it requires an upgrade ($17 to $24 per year)	Yes, but you must buy it through your web host or a domain registrar

YOU WANT TO...	WITH WORDPRESS.COM	WITH A SELF-HOSTED SITE
Get good-looking, ready-made themes	Yes, you can choose from about 200 themes (and the list is growing)	Yes, you can choose from roughly 1,600 themes (and the list is growing)
Change the layout of your theme and add new widgets	Yes (although you're limited to the widgets that WordPress.com includes)	Yes (and you can get more widgets by installing plug-ins)
Edit the styles (fonts and formatting) in your theme	Yes, but it requires an upgrade ($30 per year)	Yes
Change the code in your theme files	No	Yes
Create a non-blog site	Yes, if you can find a suitable theme, but there are many limitations	Yes
Show pictures and videos	Yes, but it costs extra if you want to host the video files on your website, instead of through a service like YouTube or Vimeo	Yes, but you'll probably still need a hosting service like YouTube or Vimeo for your videos
Make money with ads	No, unless you're accepted to WordPress's WordAds program (which has its own restrictions)	Yes
Keep ads off your site	Yes, but it requires an upgrade ($30 per year)	Yes (there are no ads, unless you put them there)
Let multiple people post on the same site	Yes	Yes
Create multiple sites	Yes	Yes
Create a multisite network that allows other people to create their own personal sub-sites	No	Yes
Use WordPress plug-ins to get even more features	No	Yes, you can choose from a staggeringly large and ever-expanding collection of over 20,000 plug-ins.
Get help with your problems	Yes, through the forums at http://forums.wordpress.com	Yes, through the forums at http://wordpress.org/support

Overall, the best advice is this: if you're a keen WordPress fan with a bit of curiosity, a smattering of computer experience, and a willingness to experiment (and if you've picked up this book, you almost certainly fit that description), you'll be happiest self-hosting WordPress.

However, if you don't have a web host and you're a bit overwhelmed, it's a perfectly good idea to *start* with WordPress.com. You can always migrate to a self-hosted WordPress site later on, and Appendix A describes exactly how to do that. The only recommendation with this strategy is that you buy your own domain name, as described on page 32. That way, should you move to a self-hosted WordPress site, you can keep the address you used when you when you were at WordPress.com, and you won't lose the audience you spent so long building up.

> **NOTE** There's one very special exception to the rules listed in Table 1-1. WordPress.com offers a VIP hosting program for heavily trafficked websites (current clients include CNN, Time, and TechCrunch). These sites aren't bound by the same limitations you are, if you sign up for WordPress.com. For example, VIP customers have unlimited freedom to change or customize WordPress themes and display ads. However, the cost is *at least* $2,500 per month, with a $1,500 one-time setup fee. You can learn more at *http://vip.wordpress.com*.

UP TO SPEED

Managed Hosting

There is one other, relatively new type of WordPress hosting that's geared to less experienced site developers who don't want to mess with WordPress administration, but want more features and flexibility than WordPress.com offers. It's called *managed hosting*.

If you sign up for a managed hosting plan, your web hosting company provides you with a domain name and some web hosting space, just like you'd get with a self-hosted site. However, managed hosting companies also add WordPress-specific services like automatic updates, daily backups, caching, and site recovery (repairing your site after a spammer hijacks it). You might even get a techy support person to install your plug-ins for you. Plans for small- to medium-sized sites start at around $30 per month, but heavily trafficked sites can pay hundreds of dollars per month.

You can learn more about managed hosting by checking out some of the web hosts that provide it, such as WP Engine (*http://wpengine.com*) and Synthesis (*http://websynthesis.com*).

Signing Up with WordPress.com

In Chapter 1, you took a big-picture look at WordPress and the sites it can build. Now, you're ready to partner with WordPress and start building your own web masterpiece.

But not so fast. Before you can create even a single WordPress-powered page, you need to decide where to *put* it. This is the challenge of WordPress hosting, and as you found out in Chapter 1, WordPress gives you two perfectly good choices:

- **The WordPress.com hosting service.** This is a wonderfully free and supremely convenient service for web authors who want to build an ordinary blog and can live with a few limitations (described on page 26).

- **Self-hosting.** This option requires you to install the free WordPress software on your own web host, which is a little bit more work (but still not much hassle). Self-hosted sites are more powerful and flexible than WordPress.com-hosted sites—they let you show ads, use plug-ins, and create completely customized pages that go far beyond ordinary blogs.

In this chapter, you'll get started with WordPress.com. But if you want to give self-hosting a whirl, skip this chapter and jump straight to Chapter 3. No matter which route you take, the paths converge in Chapter 4, where you'll begin adding content, refining your site, and developing the skills of a true WordPress wizard.

TIP If you're still divided between the convenience of WordPress.com and the flexibility of a self-hosted site, you can review the key differences on page 25. Or you can leave both doors open: Start with a WordPress. com website, but buy a domain name (your own custom web address) so you can switch to a self-hosted site in the future. The first section of this chapter explains how.

◼ Choosing a Web Address

As you already know, a web address is a short bit of text, like *SuperStyleFreak.com*, that someone types into a browser to get to your site.

The most essential part of a web address is the *domain name* (often shortened to just *domain*), which points to the web server where your website exists. For example, in the website URL *http://WineSnobs.com/exotic-cocktails*, the domain is *WineSnobs.com*. The first part of the URL, *http://*, simply indicates that the URL points to a location on the Internet, which uses a networking technology called HTTP. The last part of the URL, */exotic-cocktails*, points to a specific page on the *WineSnobs.com* domain. Clearly, the domain name is the most important part of the equation, because it identifies the central hub for all your pages.

Before you sign up with WordPress.com, you need to give some serious thought to the web address you want to use. That's because WordPress.com gives you a choice: you can buy your own domain name, or you can use a WordPress.com freebie domain name.

Here's the catch: If you get a free domain name from WordPress.com, it will have *.wordpress.com* appended to the end of it. That means you'll end up with an address like *WineSnobs.wordpress.com*. But if you pay WordPress.com a small yearly fee of about $18, you can buy a custom domain name that doesn't have this limitation—say, *WineSnobs.com*. And while there's nothing wrong with a web address that ends in *.wordpress.com*, a custom domain name can be beneficial for several reasons.

- **Names matter.** A catchy web address is easier for visitors to remember, and a clever name can attract more visitors to your site. If you're willing to buy a custom domain name, you'll have more naming choices, and your web address will probably be shorter and snappier.

- **You may not want to advertise WordPress.** In some circles, using WordPress is a badge of honor. But in other fields, it could make your site seem less professional. For example, *victoriassecret.wordpress.com* doesn't leave quite the same impression as the real site address.

- **Custom domain names are more portable.** This is usually the most important consideration. If you go with a free name and decide later to move your WordPress site to a different host, you'll need to change your domain name. (For example, you might go from *WineSnobs.wordpress.com* to *www.WineSnobs.com*, assuming *www.WineSnobs.com* is even available when you make the move.) Changing your domain name risks severing all the relationships you built up through your original *.wordpress.com* address. It also breaks any links on other sites that point to your site, and it confuses the visitors who have bookmarked your old site. And if all that's not bad enough, you'll lose the hard-earned Google search ranking that helps your site show up in web searches, too.

When you're just starting out, it's easy to underestimate the likelihood of migrating to a custom web host and the headache of changing your domain name. But life happens, people change, and many die-hard WordPress.com bloggers eventually move to a do-it-yourself web host so they have more flexibility in what they can do on their site. For all these reasons, we strongly suggest that you buy a custom domain name for your WordPress.com blog at the outset. If you do, you'll be able to keep your domain name forever, even if you switch to a different web host. You'll simply need to transfer your domain to your new host (page 521).

Assuming you do want a custom domain name, you can get one in several ways. The most common method is to simply buy your domain name when you sign up with WordPress.com, as you'll learn to do in the next section. At the time of this writing, WordPress.com charges $18 per year for custom domains, except for domains that end in *.me*, which it sells for $25 per year (without really explaining the price difference).

Another option is to use a domain name you bought from a domain registrar or a different web hosting company. For example, you might have registered a domain name in the past, just to make sure no one else got hold of it. Or, you might have bought a domain when you signed up to host your site with another company. For instance, if you bought the domain *SuperStyleFreak.com* a few months back, you can ask WordPress.com to use this web address when you create your blog. From a technical standpoint, WordPress.com does all the grunt work on your blog—storing your content, managing it, and so on. But the company that originally registered the name remains the registrar for that name. So what's the bottom line? You need to pay your original web host to maintain the address (which typically costs about $10 a year) and you need to pay WordPress.com to use the domain (currently $13 per year). You also need to perform a bit of extra setup after you sign up with WordPress.com, which is described on page 43.

NOTE Keep in mind that using a custom domain name or a domain name that you own doesn't avoid any of the other limitations that WordPress.com hosting imposes (see page 26). For example, you still won't be allowed to place ads on your site or use plug-ins.

Before you continue, take a moment to determine your domain name strategy. If you're a technophobic sort and you positively, absolutely don't plan to move to a self-hosted site—ever—you can choose a good *.wordpress.com* address and forget about the rest. However, paying a little extra for a custom domain name is almost always worth the trouble. Think of it as a bit of added insurance for whatever the future might hold.

If you don't already own a domain, think of a few potential names for your new WordPress site. Then carry on to the next section.

■ Creating Your WordPress.com Account

Once you've got a basic idea about the identity of your blog and some potential names you can use for the website address, you're ready to create your site. Here's how:

1. **In your browser, travel to** *http://wordpress.com,* **and click the "Sign up now" link.** (Or, for a shortcut, head straight to the sign-up page at *http://wordpress .com/signup.*)

   The all-in-one signup form appears (Figure 2-1).

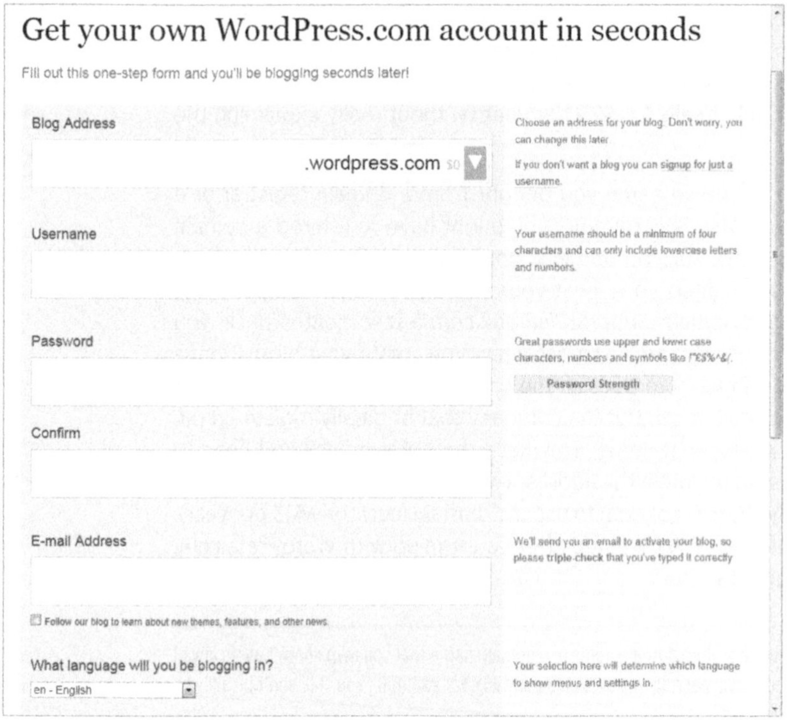

Get your own WordPress.com account in seconds

Fill out this one-step form and you'll be blogging seconds later!

Blog Address

.wordpress.com ▼

Username

Password

Password Strength

Confirm

E-mail Address

☐ Follow our blog to learn about new themes, features, and other news.

What language will you be blogging in?

en - English

Choose an address for your blog. Don't worry, you can change this later.

If you don't want a blog you can signup for just a username.

Your username should be a minimum of four characters and can only include lowercase letters and numbers.

Great passwords use upper and lower case characters, numbers and symbols like !"£$%^&/.

We'll send you an email to activate your blog, so please triple-check that you've typed it correctly.

Your selection here will determine which language to show menus and settings in.

FIGURE 2-1

If you've ever stumbled through 13 pages of forms to buy something online, you'll appreciate WordPress.com's single-page sign-up. You need to supply just four critical pieces of information: a website address and your user name, password, and email address.

2. **Type the website address you want into the Blog Address box.**

   If you want to use a free *.wordpress.com* domain, type in the first part of the name (for example, "RebelPastryChef" if you want the domain *RebelPastryChef .wordpress.com*).

   If you want to buy a custom domain, which gives you the flexibility to move to a self-hosted site later, click the drop-down arrow at the right of the Blog Address box. Then pick the *top-level domain*—that's the final part of your domain name after the period, such as *.me, .com, .net,* or *.org.* Once you pick the top-level domain, type in the first part of the domain name, like "RebelPastryChef" to get the domain *RebelPastryChef.me.* (As you probably already know, capitalization is unimportant in a domain name, so there's no difference between *RebelPastry Chef.me* and *REBELpastrychef.ME,* for instance.)

As explained earlier, if you already own a custom domain name, you can use that for your new WordPress blog. To make this work, you need to go through a process called *mapping*. The first step is to pick an ordinary *.wordpress.com* website address. You then connect this to your custom domain after you finish the sign-up process, by following the steps on page 43. In this situation, the *.wordpress.com* website address that you pick isn't terribly important, but you may as well try to get one that's similar to your domain name.

NOTE For almost all websites, the *www* prefix is an acceptable but optional part of the domain name. In other words, *RebelPastryChef.me* and *www.RebelPastryChef.me* are equivalent. Some people think that it's simpler, cleaner, and more modern to leave out the extra letters at the beginning, and WordPress.com agrees. As a result, if you register a domain through WordPress.com, the *www* prefix never appears. If you insist on typing the *www* part into a browser, you'll get to the right site, but WordPress will strip the prefix out of the browser's address bar (changing *www.RebelPastryChef.me* to *RebelPastryChef.me*, for example).

WORD TO THE WISE

Domain Name Frustration

The only disadvantage to buying your own domain name is that it can be hard to find one that's both good and available. You may think that most of the best *.wordpress.com* addresses have been snapped up already, but that's nothing compared to the competition for top-level *.com* domains. So while it's easy enough to decide to buy your own domain name (which is always a good idea), it's a bit harder to actually find one.

Here are some tips that can help:

Incorporate your business name. Domains that are just combinations of popular words ending in *.com* (like *Delicious-Chocolate.com, ThoroughbredHorses.com*) are almost certainly taken. Mix it up with your business name (*DelilasChocolates.com, AcmeThroughbredHorses.com*), and you stand a much better chance.

Think quirky. If you're creating a new blog, you can afford to try out unusual-yet-catchy word combinations that capture the spirit of your writing, but have been overlooked by the rapacious domain name sharks. Possibilities include *ThatThing-IsWeird.com, WhyCantISpell.com*, and *DieAutoTuneDie.com*. They may be a bit odd and a bit long, but they're catchy choices, for the right site.

Settle for a less common top-level domain. The top-level domain is the final few letters of a domain name, after the last period. The most popular top-level domain is *.com*, but it's also the most competitive. You'll find many more options if you're willing to settle for *.org* (which was originally intended for non-commercial websites, but no longer has any restriction), *.net*, or the relatively new and catchy *.me*. For example, at the time of this writing, *wickedcode.com* is taken, but *wickedcode.me* is available. But be careful—the last think you want is a potential visitor accidentally adding *.com* to the end of your address and ending up at your competitor's site.

3. **Wait while WordPress.com checks to see if your domain name is available.**
   A few seconds later, it reports the answer (Figure 2-2). If your first choice isn't free, try a variation or change the top-level domain using the drop-down list on the right. Finding a good domain name requires equal parts effort, creativity, and compromise.

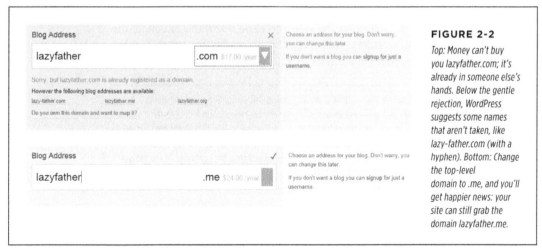

FIGURE 2-2

*Top: Money can't buy
you lazyfather.com; it's
already in someone else's
hands. Below the gentle
rejection, WordPress
suggests some names
that aren't taken, like
lazy-father.com (with a
hyphen). Bottom: Change
the top-level
domain to .me, and you'll
get happier news: your
site can still grab the
domain lazyfather.me.*

4. **Choose a user name.**

   You use your user name and password to log into WordPress when you want
   to add new posts or manage your site. Ordinarily, WordPress uses the first part
   of your blog address as your user name, so if you create a blog at *lazyfather
   .wordpress.com*, WordPress suggests the user name *lazyfather*. This is fine,
   unless someone already has that user name, in which case you'll see the same
   red warning box you get when you pick an already-occupied domain, and you'll
   need to change it to something else.

   Not only does your user name become part of the login process, it's also the
   name WordPress uses as your *display name*, which is the name that appears
   at the end of your blog posts and in the comments you leave (among other
   places). However, you can easily change your display name to something more
   suitable, as described on page 101.

5. **Choose a password.**

   Take the time to pick a password that's different from the passwords you use
   on other sites, not found in the dictionary, and difficult to guess. If you're not
   sure how to do that—or why you should bother—check out the box on page 37.

A WordPress Password is More Than a Formality

WordPress websites are commonly attacked by hackers looking to steal traffic or to stuff in some highly objectionable ads. The best way to avoid this danger is with a strong password.

With enough tries, web evildoers can guess any password using an automated program. But most human WordPress hackers look for common words and patterns. If you use your first name (*ashley*), a string of close-together letters on the keyboard (*qwerty, qazwsx*), or a single word with a few number-fied or symbol-fied characters (like *passw0rd* and *pa$$word*), be afraid. These passwords aren't just a little bit insecure, they regularly make the list of the world's 25 *most stolen* passwords. (For the complete list of bad passwords, check out *http://onforb.es/v2rdOb*.)

That doesn't mean you need a string of complete gibberish to protect your site. Instead, you can deter casual hackers (who are responsible for almost all WordPress attacks) by taking a reasonably unique piece of information and scrambling it lightly. For example, you can use a favorite musician (*HERBeeHANcock88*), a movie title (*dr.strangel*ve*), or a short sentence with some vowels missing (*IThinkThrforIM*). As you type in a potential password, WordPress assesses its strength. For example, type in a "qwerty" and WordPress rates your password "Bad." Add a few more letters and some symbols, and you'll get a more encouraging rating of "Good" (which means the password is passable) or "Strong" (which is even better).

It's acceptable to write your password down on paper and tuck it in a desk drawer—after all, you're not worried about family members or office colleagues, but international spammers, who certainly won't walk into your office and rifle through your belongings. (However, it's still a bad idea to put your password in an email or text message.)

6. **Fill in your email address.**

   You need a valid email address to activate your account. You can also decide whether you want to receive WordPress.com news—if so, turn on the "Follow our blog" checkbox.

7. **Pick your language.**

   If you're creating an English-language website, you don't need to make a change here. If you're writing in another language, choose it from the list. WordPress uses this information when it lists your website and submits it to search engines like Google. That way, blog readers can hunt down websites in their preferred language.

8. **Click the Create Blog button. Or, if you're buying the WordPress Value Bundle (see the box on page 38), click Upgrade instead.**

   If you chose a custom domain name in step 2, you now need to register that name so that any web browser will recognize it. To do so, continue with step 9.

   If you chose a *.wordpress.com* domain in step 2, WordPress displays a page where you can update your profile if you like (Figure 2-3). Once you do that, skip to step 11.

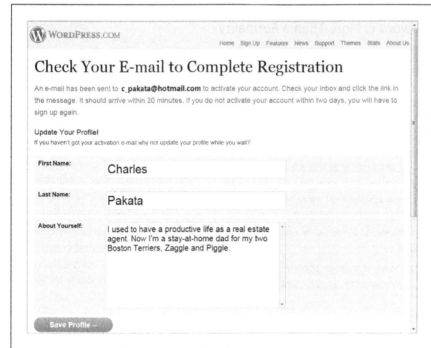

FIGURE 2-3

You may as well fill in some basic profile information before you forget. This info doesn't appear directly on your site, but other WordPress-ers can read some of it if they browse your profile on Automattic's Gravatar site (page 258).

WORD TO THE WISE

The WordPress Value Bundle

Just before you sign up, WordPress may attempt to seduce you with something called the WordPress Value Bundle. It folds several WordPress upgrades, each of which normally costs a yearly fee, into one cheaper-priced package (typically, about $100 per year).

Even if you aren't offered the value bundle when you sign up, you may see it later in the WordPress.com store. Before you plunk down any cash, you need to review whether the bundle is worthwhile to you. The answer is "Probably not," unless you want to host video on your WordPress site.

The most useful WordPress upgrades give you a custom domain name, prevent the display of ads, and give you the ability to edit the styles in your chosen theme. All of these are included in the value bundle, but they don't quite come to $100 per year (the current total is $78 a year).

The other two upgrades in the value bundle are additional space (for hosting very big files) and VideoPress support (for video files). Usually, the only people who need these features are those who want to show videos on their sites. However, most people find it cheaper and easier to host videos with a free service like YouTube, and simply embed a YouTube video window on their WordPress pages (see page 336 to learn how). VideoPress is a more specialized (and appealing) option if you plan to show content that isn't suitable for YouTube—for example, videos that run longer than YouTube's 15-minute limit, or ones that a visitor can download.

You'll learn more about VideoPress on page 342. In the meantime, you probably want to hold off on the value bundle, unless you're fairly certain you want all these features.

9. **If you picked a custom domain name, WordPress shows you a new domain registration form (Figure 2-4) .Fill in your contact details and click Register Domain.**

   This registration information includes your name, postal address, and email address. WordPress submits this information, on your behalf, to the Domain Name System (DNS)—a key part of Internet bookkeeping that tracks who owns each piece of web real estate.

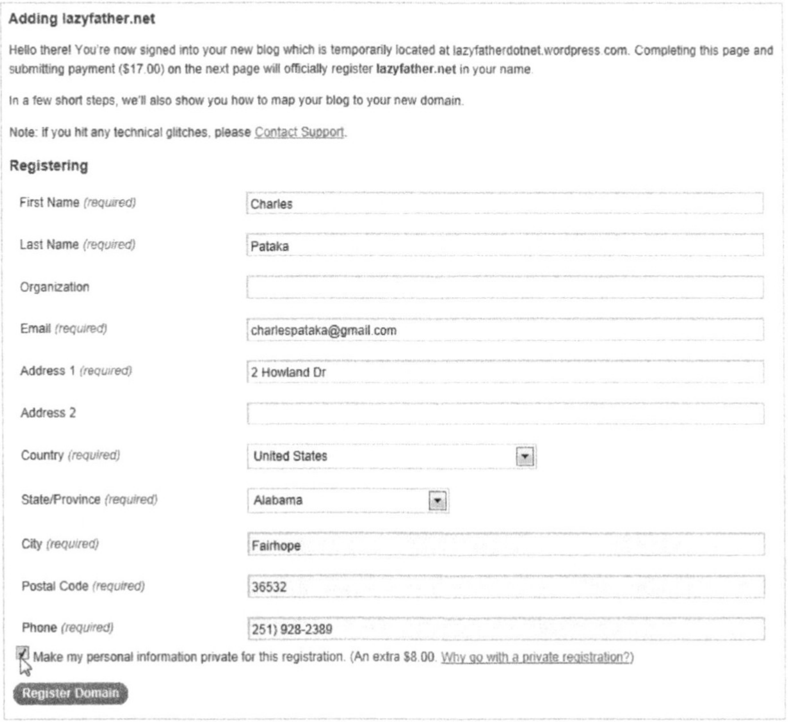

Adding lazyfather.net

Hello there! You're now signed into your new blog which is temporarily located at lazyfatherdotnet.wordpress.com. Completing this page and submitting payment ($17.00) on the next page will officially register **lazyfather.net** in your name.

In a few short steps, we'll also show you how to map your blog to your new domain.

Note: If you hit any technical glitches, please Contact Support.

Registering

First Name *(required)* Charles

Last Name *(required)* Pataka

Organization

Email *(required)* charlespataka@gmail.com

Address 1 *(required)* 2 Howland Dr

Address 2

Country *(required)* United States

State/Province *(required)* Alabama

City *(required)* Fairhope

Postal Code *(required)* 36532

Phone *(required)* 251) 928-2389

Make my personal information private for this registration. (An extra $8.00. Why go with a private registration?)

Register Domain

FIGURE 2-4

Here's the information you need to register lazyfather.net. Use the checkbox at the bottom of the screen to keep this information hidden from spammers' prying eyes, a good use of the $8 it costs.

   Domain name registration is public, which means that anyone with an Internet connection can look up your domain and find out that you own it. (They also get your phone number and email address.) Usually, this isn't a problem, but it does provide an opening for spammers to hassle you. If you don't want your public details exposed, *don't* try to fake them with incorrect information. Instead, tick the box that says "Make my personal information private for this registration." It costs an extra $8, but it gives you guaranteed anonymity—at least until you start posting.

10. **Now WordPress asks you to pay up.** Fill out your payment information and click the "Purchase and Register Domain" button.

WordPress makes it easy to pay for a custom domain name with either a credit card or through the popular PayPal service. Either way, once you fill in the necessary details, scroll down and click the "Purchase and Register Domain" button to finish the job.

11. **Check your email for an activation message from WordPress.** When you find it, click the Activate Blog button (or copy the URL shown underneath and paste it into your browser's address bar).

    Clicking the activation button launches your web browser, and sends you to the "dashboard"—the WordPress management screen—for your new site (described in Chapter 4). You'll get a second email summarizing the key details of your site, including your user name and password, and quick links you can follow to create a new post, change your site settings, read useful tutorials, and more. Save this message for future reference. And if you bought a custom domain name, WordPress will email you a receipt for that as well.

After you create a WordPress site, you can visit it any time by typing the address you picked in step 2 into your web browser. In this example, if you type *lazyfather .wordpress.com* into your browser's address bar, you go to a site like the one pictured in Figure 2-5.

FIGURE 2-5

When you create a new site, WordPress.com adds a single dummy post with some basic instructions in it. Although it doesn't look like much, this shell of a site has all the infrastructure you need to build a genuinely useful WordPress site, which you'll learn to do starting in Chapter 4.

This shortcut takes you to the dashboard at lazyfather.wordpress.com/wp-admin.

You can type *wp-admin* at the end of the address to go right to the dashboard to manage your site. WordPress will ask you to sign in with your user name and password if you aren't already logged in. For example, you manage *lazyfather.wordpress.com* at *lazyfather.wordpress.com/wp-admin* (Figure 2-6). WordPress will have sent you an email with these details.

Buying a Domain Name After Sign-Up

As you've already seen, you can buy a custom domain name when you create your WordPress.com site. But what happens if you already built a thriving blog using a *.wordpress.com* address?

For example, say you've been blogging for some time on *HelloPickles.wordpress.com*. But, after reading the domain name discussion on page 32, you decide that you really want the custom domain *HelloPickles.net*. Happily, WordPress can help you realize your dream. It lets you buy a custom domain name for an existing blog, rather than force you create a whole new blog under the new name.

To change your site name, follow these steps:

1. **Go to the dashboard.**

   That's your website address, with *wp-admin* tacked onto the end.

2. **In the menu on the left, click Store.**

WordPress shows a list of all the upgrades you can buy.

3. **In the "Add a Domain" box, click Buy Now.**

WordPress displays a list of all the domains your site currently uses. Unless you already bought a custom domain name through WordPress.com, the list includes just one address: the *.wordpress.com* address you picked when you created your site (Figure 2-7).

FIGURE 2-7

Currently, this site uses the domain lazyfather .wordpress.com. Here, you're about to request the more memorable domain lazyfather.me.

4. **Type the domain you want into the Add a Domain box, and click the "Add domain to blog" button.**

If someone already owns the domain, WordPress prompts you to try something else.

If the domain is available, you'll see the standard domain registration page (Figure 2-4), where you need to fill in your personal details.

5. **When you finish, click Register Domain and follow the instructions to pay.**

When you add a custom domain name, WordPress won't leave your current audience in the cold. Instead, it's smart enough to reroute people visiting your old *.wordpress.com* address to your new domain. That means that if you started with *HelloPickles.wordpress.com*, and then you buy the custom domain *HelloPickles.net*, WordPress will automatically redirect people who type in *HelloPickles.wordpress.com* to your blog's new domain, *HelloPickles.net*, just as you would want. (Really, there's no difference between the two addresses. They are simply two names that point to the same site—your blog.)

Using a Domain Name You Already Own

Life is easiest if you buy your custom domain name from WordPress.com, but sometimes that isn't possible. For example, you might have already bought the domain name you want from a domain registrar. (You may have even bought it years ago.) Because it isn't currently possible to transfer a domain you own from another web host to WordPress.com, you need to use another trick, called *mapping*.

Technically, mapping is a technique that, in this case, connects your custom domain name to your WordPress.com blog. That way, when someone types in the custom domain name (say *HelloPickles.net*), that person ends up at your WordPress.com blog. And if that person types in your former *.wordpress.com* address (say, *HelloPickles .wordpress.com*), they're redirected to your custom domain, which is what you want. It's exactly as if you had bought the custom domain name from WordPress.com when you signed up.

Mapping is relatively easy, but not free. WordPress charges a mapping fee (currently $13 a year), which you pay in addition to the annual fee you pay to keep the domain name registered through your original domain registrar.

Mapping requires you to complete two setup operations: one with the web host that owns the domain name, and one with WordPress. But before you get started with either operation, you need to decide exactly how you want to link your custom domain name with your WordPress site. You have two options:

- **Use your whole domain.** For example, you might create a blog at *www.Wine Snobs.com*. If you map this address to a WordPress.com address, you need to keep your entire website on WordPress.com. This makes sense if you purchased a domain name from another company, but you haven't actually bought any web *space* from that company.

- **Use a subdomain.** Technically, a subdomain takes your domain name (say, *www.WineSnobs.com*), removes the optional *www* part, and adds a different prefix (like *blog.WineSnobs.com*). The goal is to create a separate web address for your WordPress site, so you can put something else at your main domain name (in this case, *www.WineSnobs.com*). Of course, your main site won't be a WordPress site, and you'll need to pay your web host for some web space.

There's also third option—use a *subdirectory* in your domain (for example, *www.WineSnobs.com/blog*)—but WordPress.com doesn't currently support that technique.

Before you can map your domain, you have to do a little extra configuration with your web host. These setup steps differ depending on whether you want to map the full domain name or you want to map just a subdomain, so follow the instructions in the appropriate section below.

■ MAPPING AN ENTIRE DOMAIN NAME

If you're mapping an entire domain name, you simply have to change your web domain's *name servers*. These are the high-powered computers that direct traffic on the Internet, and that tell browsers where to go to find your site. Right now, your domain name uses the name servers from your domain registrar or your original web host (not WordPress.com). You need to change that, so your domain uses the WordPress.com name servers.

The change is simple enough—it usually involves changing just two pieces of text—the *name server addresses*. However, you may need to dig around on your web host's administration page before you find exactly where these settings are (they're usually in a section called "Domain Name Servers" or "DNS Settings"). If in doubt, contact your web host.

For example, if you're using the web host *www.brinkster.com*, the name servers would be set to this:

```
NS1.BRINKSTER.COM

NS2.BRINKSTER.COM
```

No matter what web host you're using, you must change the name servers to this:

```
NS1.WORDPRESS.COM

NS2.WORDPRESS.COM
```

These are the two computers that direct your visitors to the WordPress.com site they want to read.

■ MAPPING A SUBDOMAIN

If you're mapping a subdomain, you need a slightly different configuration. Instead of changing your name servers, you must add a *CNAME record*. Although it sounds intimidatingly techy, all a CNAME record does is redirect traffic from your subdomain to your WordPress.com blog.

Every web host has a different process for defining a CNAME record, but it usually involves logging in, heading to an administration section with a name like "DNS Management" or "Name Server Management," and then adding the CNAME record. Each record requires two pieces of information. The first is the subdomain prefix (for example, that's *blog* if you're creating the subdomain *blog.WineSnobs.com*). The second is your current WordPress.com address, like *WineSnobs.wordpress.com*, which is often called the *destination*.

NOTE If you can't find or figure out your web host's domain management tools, make time for a quick support call. Changing name servers and adding subdomains are two common tasks that domain registrars and web hosts deal with every day.

■ FINISHING THE JOB: SETTING UP THE WORDPRESS.COM MAPPING

Name server changes require time to take effect. Once you make your changes, the settings need to be spread to various traffic-directing computers across the Internet. It will take at least 24 hours, and possibly two or three days, before the change takes effect and you can tell WordPress.com to start using your domain. Unfortunately, there's no high-tech way to monitor the process.

Once your name server changes have taken effect, you can add the domain by following the next set of steps. If you're not sure whether you've waited long enough, don't worry—there's no harm in trying. If the name server changes haven't taken effect, WordPress will let you know about the problem when you get to step 4 below, and you'll need try again later.

1. **Go to the dashboard.**

   Type your website address, with */wp-admin* tacked on the end.

2. **In the menu on the left, click Store.**

   WordPress shows a list of all the upgrades you can buy.

3. **In the "Add a Domain" box, click Buy Now.**

   WordPress shows a list of all the domains your site currently uses.

4. **Type the domain you already own into the Add a Domain box, and click the "Add domain to blog" button.**

   If the domain isn't pointing to WordPress yet (either because you didn't complete the configuration steps, or they still haven't spread over the Internet), WordPress warns you about the problem (Figure 2-8).

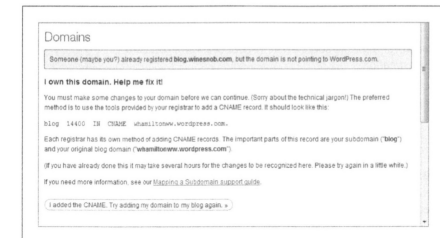

If the domain is reconfigured and ready to use, WordPress will ask you for your payment details. Once that's done, the mapping is complete. Congratulations—you can now get to your WordPress site by using your custom domain name.

The WordPress.com Community

Once you have your very own WordPress site, you're also a member of the WordPress.com *community*. Warm and fuzzy feelings aside, the connections and exposure you get through the community can have real benefits, particularly if your WordPress.com site is a straight-up, traditional blog. These benefits include:

- **Ideas.** No site exists in a vacuum, especially not a blog. By looking at other people's work, you can tune into a powerful source of inspiration for both content and style. On the *content* side, you can discover trending topics and popular subjects (using the Freshly Pressed tab and Popular Topics link described in the next section, for example). Then, you can join in on the conversation by giving your own spin on hot topics on your blog. On the *style* side, you can see how other people polish themes and perfect their layouts, and you can use that insight to improve your own site.

- **Promotion.** As in the real word, one of the most successful ways to make friends, attract attention, and score a new job is by networking with other, like-minded people. When you find other blogs that tackle the same issues yours does, you can exchange links and create a blogroll that connects their sites to yours (page 150). Or, you can increase your exposure by commenting on someone else's posts (on their blog) or publishing a full reply post (on your blog). Eventually, these practices can attract many more visitors to your site.

With that in mind, you're ready to survey the field. Start at the WordPress.com front page (*http://wordpress.com*). If you aren't already logged in, fill in your user name and password in the boxes at the top of the page and then click Log In.

TIP Once you log in, WordPress displays a dark-gray toolbar at the top of the browser window while you visit other sites. This makes it particularly easy to create a list of posts you like and blogs you follow, which WordPress.com stores in your user account (see page 48).

Browsing Other WordPress.com Sites

The first place you should go to get a sense of the chatter on WordPress.com is the Freshly Pressed tab on the WordPress.com front page (*http://wordpress.com*). It shows a cross-section of the day's most attention-grabbing posts (Figure 2-9).

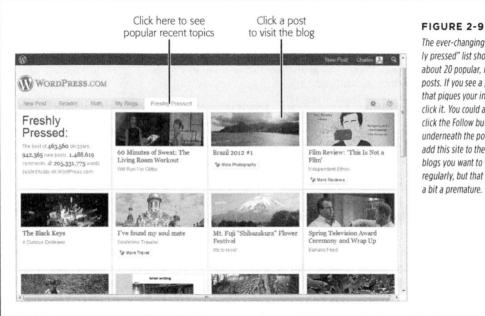

FIGURE 2-9

The ever-changing "freshly pressed" list shows about 20 popular, recent posts. If you see a post that piques your interest, click it. You could also click the Follow button underneath the post to add this site to the list of blogs you want to watch regularly, but that seems a bit a premature.

Another way to find an interesting new WordPress.com sites is to go *tag surfing*. When WordPress users create a new post, they add a few descriptive words, called *tags*, to classify it. Tags give you a way to home in on posts that interest you in a specific site (as you'll see on page 113, when you start posting). Tags also give you a way to find blogs that discuss your favorite topics.

To go tag surfing, start at the *http://wordpress.com* main page, scroll down past the tabs to the links at the bottom of the page, and click Popular Tags. You'll see a page similar to the one shown in Figure 2-10.

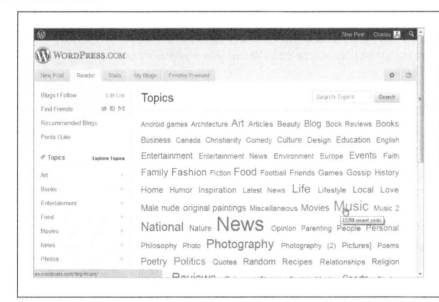

FIGURE 2-10

The tag list reflects recent posts. The bigger tags (like Music and News) have more recent posts. To browse these posts, click the tag that interests you, and then click a post to continue on to the blog.

> **TIP** When you browse through WordPress.com, you don't see the many sites created with WordPress software but hosted on sites other than WordPress.com. Although there's no central repository of self-hosted WordPress sites, you can browse a showcase with some examples at *http://wordpress.org/showcase.*

Liking Posts and Following Blogs

When you navigate to a WordPress.com blog and you're signed in as a WordPress.com user, a dark-gray toolbar appears at the top of the page (Figure 2-11). On the left side is the name of the blog you're currently viewing, and two important buttons: Follow and Like. If you like the post you're reading, you can click the Like button (which adds it to a list of your favorite posts). Or, if you decide the content is so good that you want to come back to this site and read more, you can click the Follow button (which adds the site to your personal watch list of blogs).

Usually, you'll choose to click Like on a post if you want to refer to it later—perhaps to follow an ongoing conversation in the Comments section. You'll choose Follow to keep watching the blog for new content. Less commonly, you can use the Reblog link to copy the post to your blog and, optionally, add your comments. This is a fairly heavy-handed way to join in on a conversation, because it lifts a sizeable chunk of someone else's work. Most top-tier bloggers refrain from posting someone else's content on their site without explicit permission (even though WordPress ensures that each reblogged post is fully credited with a link to the original blog).

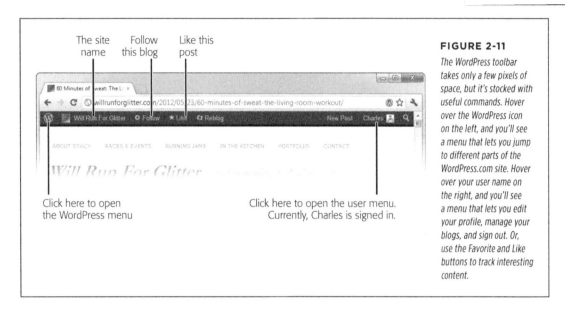

The site   Follow   Like this
name   this blog   post

Click here to open
the WordPress menu

Click here to open the user menu.
Currently, Charles is signed in.

FIGURE 2-11

*The WordPress toolbar
takes only a few pixels of
space, but it's stocked with
useful commands. Hover
over the WordPress icon
on the left, and you'll see
a menu that lets you jump
to different parts of the
WordPress.com site. Hover
over your user name on
the right, and you'll see
a menu that lets you edit
your profile, manage your
blogs, and sign out. Or,
use the Favorite and Like
buttons to track interesting
content.*

To review your liked posts and read your followed blogs, return to *http://wordpress
.com* and click the Reader tab (Figure 2-12). Or, use the handy toolbar—just click the
WordPress "W" icon (on the far left of the toolbar) and then choose Reader→Blogs
I Follow from the menu that appears.

FIGURE 2-12

*As you scroll down the
list of options under the
Reader tab, you'll see the
most recent posts from
all the sites you follow,
amalgamated into a single
reverse-chronological list.
(Here, you can see the
first two posts, one from
The Spiral Staircase and
the other from The Green
Geek.) To read the full post
(and its comments), click
the title, or click the "Posts
I Like" link in the sidebar
on the left to revisit your
favorite posts.*

This brings you to the end of this chapter's WordPress.com exploration. To start adding posts, jump ahead to Chapter 4. Or, read Chapter 3 to compare the setup process required to get WordPress up and running on your own web host.

Adding More Sites

There's no need to limit yourself to a single WordPress.com site. In fact, every WordPress.com user is allowed to create an *unlimited* number of sites.

The easiest way to add a new site is to visit the *http://wordpress.com* home page, log in with your user account, and click the My Blogs tab. This shows a list of all the WordPress sites you've created so far. To add a new one, click the "Create a New Blog" link at the bottom of the list. You'll have to supply the same information you entered when you created your first blog, including a website address and blog name. You won't need to supply a new user name or password, because you already have a WordPress.com account.

You can't delete any of your WordPress.com sites from the My Blogs tab. Instead, you need to visit the dashboard, the administrative hub you'll explore in Chapter 4. Once you're in the dashboard, you can remove the current site by choosing Tools→Delete Blog from the left-side menu.

Installing WordPress on Your Web Host

There's nothing wrong with WordPress.com—it's cheap, relatively powerful, and has a thriving community of blogs. But the most serious WordPress users aren't satisfied unless they can run WordPress on their own web host.

This approach, called *self-hosting*, gives you a world of new opportunities. For example, WordPress self-hosters can choose from a dizzying range of plug-ins to add new features to their sites. They can put a WordPress blog in the same domain as a traditional website (for example, they can have a site at *www.HandMadePaintBrushes .com* and a blog at *www.HandMadePaintBrushes.com/news*). They can slap ads on their blogs, and—most usefully of all—create sites that don't look like blogs at all.

This chapter assumes you know, deep down in your heart, that you are a WordPress self-hoster. You aren't willing to settle for a merely convenient WordPress.com blog when you can design exactly what you want with a self-hosted WordPress site. In the following pages, you'll learn how to get started.

■ Preparing for WordPress

Before you dive into a self-hosted WordPress setup, you need to tick off a few requirements. The first is setting up an account with a web host. (If you've already done that, you can safely skip ahead to the next section, starting on page 52.)

If you're just starting out, choosing a good web host can seem daunting. Technically, your web host needs to meet two requirements to run WordPress: First, it needs to support PHP (version 5.2.4 or greater), which is the programming language that powers WordPress. And second, it needs to support MySQL (version 5.0 or greater), which is the database that stores WordPress content. Virtually every web host supports these requirements. In fact, choosing a WordPress-friendly host is hard simply because so many hosts offer essentially the same thing. Other selling points that hosts advertise—the amount of disk space or bandwidth you get, for example—are largely unimportant for self-hosters. Even popular WordPress sites are unlikely to approach anywhere near the limits offered, unless you're planning to host huge video files (and even then, you'll probably find it far easier to host your videos with a paid video hosting service like Vimeo, or a free one like YouTube).

Fortunately, WordPress has become so super-popular that the vast majority of web hosts support it, even with the cheapest web hosting plans they offer. And because WordPress is so popular, many hosts specifically advertise "WordPress support" or "one-click WordPress installation" (which allows you to use an autoinstaller, as described on page 57).

> **NOTE** There are a few rare web hosts who don't support WordPress at all. Most notably, free web hosts—the ones that don't charge anything for the web space they provide—sometimes forbid WordPress. If you're in any doubt, contact your web hosting company or search their website support section for information about WordPress compatibility.

The most important considerations in choosing a host isn't the amount of web space or bandwidth you get. Instead, it's reliability, security, and support—in other words, how often your website will be down due to technical troubles, how quickly you can get an answer to your questions, and whether your host will be in business several years into the future. These attributes are more difficult to assess, but before you sign up with a host, you should try contacting their support office (both by email and phone). Don't trust website reviews (which are usually paid for), but do look up what other people say about the hosts you're considering on the popular forum Web Hosting Talk (*http://bit.ly/vQ7tkH*). Hawk Host, StableHost, SpeedySparrow, and MDD Hosting are just four examples of web hosts who are frequently praised on these boards.

You can also choose a WordPress-recommended host (see the short list at *http://wordpress.org/hosting*), but keep in mind that hosts pay to be on this exclusive list. They're perfectly good hosts, but you can find equally excellent options on your own, and possibly save a few dollars.

> **TIP** To budget for WordPress, assume you'll pay $6 to $10 a month for web hosting. Then add the cost of a custom domain name (that's the snazzy web address that leads to your site), which you can typically find for a paltry $12 or so per year.

Where to Put WordPress

When you sign up for a web hosting account, you typically get a domain name (that's the web address a visitor types into a browser to get to your site) and some space for your web pages. But before you can create your first WordPress site, you need to think a bit about how your web hosting account and your WordPress site will fit together.

NOTE You don't need to actually do anything yet. You'll learn how to configure WordPress when you set it up on your host's server. However, before you get to that point, you need to make a decision about exactly where you'll put the WordPress files and how your visitors will access them. By making this decision before you get started, you reduce the chance that you'll be stopped cold in the middle of the installation.

You can choose one of three basic strategies for installing WordPress on your host's server:

- **Put WordPress in the root folder of your site. This is the best approach if you want to let WordPress run your entire site.** For example, imagine you sign up for a site with the domain *www.BananaRepublican.org* and you put WordPress in the root folder of that site. Now, when visitors type that address into their browsers, they'll go straight to your WordPress home page. (As you'll learn below, you can also create a hybrid website, one that uses WordPress on part of the site, like community news, and traditional HTML programming on other parts of the site).

- **Put WordPress in a subfolder of your site.** This is the choice for you if your web presence will include both traditional web pages (for example, something you've handcrafted in a web editor like Dreamweaver) and a WordPress site. Often, people use this choice to add a WordPress blog to an existing website. For example, if you bought the domain *www.BananaRepublican.org*, you might direct blog readers to the subfolder *www.BananaRepublican.org/blog* to see your WordPress masterpiece. To set this up, you need to create a subfolder (in the web address above, it's named *blog*) and put WordPress *there*.

- **Put WordPress in a subdomain of your site.** This is another way to handle websites that have a WordPress section and a non-WordPress section. The difference is that instead of using a subfolder for the WordPress part of your site, you use a *subdomain*. To create a subdomain, you take your domain (say, *www.BananaReublican.org*), remove the www part, if it has one (now you've got *BananaReublican.org*), and then put a different bit of text at the front, separated by a period (as in *social.BananaReublican.org*). For example, you could have a traditional website at *www.BananaRepublican.org* and a news-style WordPress site with user feedback at *social.BananaRepublican.org*, just like the automotive giant Ford does (page 23).

The first option is easy enough—you simply don't specify a subfolder when you install WordPress.

The second option is just as easy. If you use an autoinstaller (and most web hosts provide one, so you probably will), you simply need to pick a folder name. The autoinstaller will create the folder automatically.

The third option requires a bit more prep work. Before you can install WordPress to a subdomain, you need to create the subdomain you want. The following section explains how.

TIP You can learn much more about web hosting and the basics of traditional website design in *Creating a Website: The Missing Manual.*

Multiply the Fun with Multiple WordPress Sites

Most of the time, you'll install WordPress once. But you don't need to stop there. You can create multiple WordPress websites that live side-by-side, sharing your web hosting account.

The most logical way to do this is to buy additional web domains. For example, when you first sign up with a web hosting company, you might buy the domain *www.patricks-tattoos .com* to advertise your tattoo parlor. You would then install WordPress in the root folder on that domain. Sometime later, you might buy a second domain, *www.patrickmahoney.me*, through the same web hosting account. Now you can install WordPress there, too. (It's easy—as you'll see when you install WordPress, it asks you what domain you want to use.) By the end of this process, you'll have two distinct WordPress websites, two yearly domain name charges, but only one monthly web hosting fee.

Interestingly, you don't actually need to have two domains to have two WordPress sites. You could install separate WordPress sites in separate folders on the *same* domain. For example, you could have a WordPress site at *www.patrickmahoney.me/blog* and another at *www.patrickmahoney.me/tattoos*. This is a relatively uncommon setup (unless you're creating a bunch of WordPress test sites, like we do for this book at *www.prosetech .com/wordpress*). However, it is possible, and there's no limit. That means no one's stopping you if you decide to create several dozen WordPress websites, all on the same domain. But if that's what you want, you should probably use the WordPress multisite feature, which lets you set up a network of WordPress sites that share a common home but have separate settings (and can even be run by different people). Page 375 explains how that feature works.

Creating a Subdomain

Creating a subdomain is a task that's quick and relatively straightforward. Unfortunately, the process isn't the same on all web hosts, so you may need to contact your host's support department to get help. If your host uses the popular cPanel administrative interface (and many do), the process goes like this:

1. **Using your browser, log into the control panel for your web host.**

   Look for the Subdomains icon (usually, you'll find it in a box named "Domains."

   If you can't find the Subdomains box, try searching with the cPanel's Find box. Type in the first few characters (that's "subd") and it should appear at the top of the page.

2. **When you find the Subdomains icon, click it.**

   This loads the Subdomains page (Figure 3-1).

You create a subdomain here

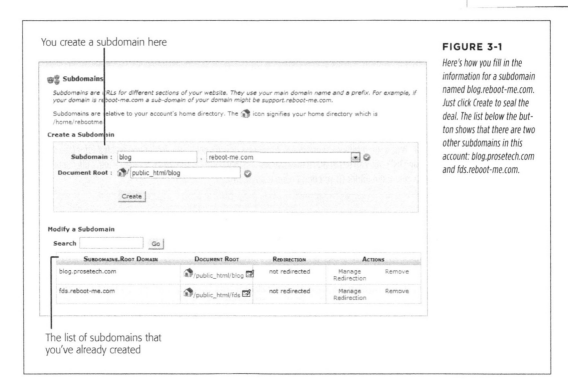

FIGURE 3-1

*Here's how you fill in the
information for a subdomain
named blog.reboot-me.com.
Just click Create to seal the
deal. The list below the button shows that there are two
other subdomains in this
account: blog.prosetech.com
and fds.reboot-me.com.*

The list of subdomains that
you've already created

3. **Choose the domain you want from a list of all the domains you own.**

   Some people have a web hosting account with just one domain, but others
   own dozens.

4. **In the Subdomain box, type in the prefix you want to use for the subdomain.**

   For example, if you want to create the subdomain *blog.reboot-me.com* on the
   domain *reboot-me.com*, you need to type *blog* in the Subdomain box.

5. **In the Document Root box, pick the folder where you want to store the files
   for this domain.**

   Your web host will suggest something based on your subdomain (for example,
   public_html/blog if you named the subdomain *blog*). You can use that if you're
   not sure what you want, or you can edit it to something you like better.

6. **Click the Create button to create your subdomain.**

   After a brief pause, you'll be directed to a new page that tells you your subdomain
   has been created. Click Go Back to return to the Subdomains page.

You'll see your new subdomain in the list on the Subdomains page. Right now, it has no web files, so there's no point in typing the address into a browser. However, when you install WordPress, you'll put its files in that subdomain.

After you finished admiring your work, look for a Home button to take you back to cPanel's main page.

To delete a subdomain, find it in the list and click the Remove link. Now, if you try to access your site by typing the subdomain into a web browser, you'll get an error message.

NOTE When you remove a subdomain, WordPress doesn't delete the folder you created for it (see step 5 in the preceding list). You can either add a new subdomain that points to this folder, or use cPanel's file management features to delete the folder (if you don't need it anymore).

The Administrator Account

Before you install WordPress, you need to decide what user name and password you'll use to manage your website. When you self-host, you're responsible for every file and folder on the site, and you have the ability to do anything from adding new posts to deleting the entire site. You do all this through an all-powerful *administrator account*.

Hackers, spammers, and other shady characters are very interested in your WordPress administrator account. If they get hold of it, they're likely to sully it with lurid ads (see Figure 3-2), phony software offers, or spyware.

FIGURE 3-2

If you don't look twice, you could almost miss it. This church runs a WordPress blog that's been hacked by spammers. In a Google search result page, the site title and description promotes cheap Viagra. Awkward.

Your best protection against these attacks is to follow two rules when you create your administrator account:

- Make your user name non-obvious (that means you should prefer *AngryUnicorn* to *admin*, *user*, or *wordpress*).

- Choose a strong, non-obvious password that includes a combination of letters and numbers (like *bg8212beauty* rather than *bigbeauty*). For guidelines on creating a secure password, see the box on page 37.

Once you settle on where you want to install WordPress and you've picked a good user name and password for your administrator account, you're ready to press on.

■ Installing WordPress with an Autoinstaller

Here's good news: installing WordPress for the site you created when you signed up with your web host is nearly as easy as signing up for a WordPress.com account. The only catch is that the process you follow depends on the web host you use. That's because every host uses a different administrative interface—that's the control panel you use to manage your site—so installing WordPress is never quite the same on each host. But it's almost always very similar. With that in mind, the following sections explain the steps you need to follow to get WordPress up and running.

The easiest way to install WordPress is to use an *autoinstaller,* a special tool that installs programs on your site. Most web hosts offer an autoinstaller as part of their service.

There are several autoinstallers in the world. Two of the most popular are Fantastico and Softaculous, both of which you'll learn to use in this section. Other autoinstallers you might come across include Installatron and the less extravagantly named SimpleScripts.

> **NOTE**   In an effort to please everyone, some web hosts support more than one autoinstaller. If that's the case for you, you can use either one. However, we prefer Softaculous, because at the time of this writing Softaculous offers a handy backup feature that Fantastico doesn't. Page 78 has the scoop.

All autoinstallers work in more or less the same way: you sign in to your web hosting account and click the autoinstaller icon to see a catalog of the add-on software your host offers. Look for WordPress, and then start the installation. You need to supply the same basic pieces of information during the installation—most significantly, the website folder where you want to install WordPress, and the user name and password you want to use for the WordPress administrator account (which your autoinstaller will create).

The following sections explain how to use Fantastico (first) and Softcaulous (second). If your web host uses another autoinstaller, the steps are similar and you can follow along with a few adjustments.

> **NOTE**   Once you finish installing WordPress, you can safely skip the rest of the setup-oriented discussion in this chapter and go straight to the final section on page 75, "Maintaining Your Site," which will explain how to keep your site rigorously up-to-date.

Installing WordPress with Fantastico

How do you know if your host offers Fantastico? You could ask, but it's probably quicker to look for yourself:

1. **Log into the control panel for your web host.**

2. **Look for a Fantastico icon.**

    Some control panels pile dozens of icons onto the same page. To look for Fantastico, you can use your browser's Find feature. Just press Ctrl+F (Command+F on a Mac) and type in "Fantastico." Figure 3-3 shows a successful search.

    If you can't find a Fantastico icon, you might luck out with one of the autoinstallers listed above. Try searching for a Softaculous, Installatron, or SimpleScripts icon. If you find Softaculous, you can use the steps on page 61. If you find another autoinstaller, try following the steps listed here—just mentally replace "Fantastico" with the name of your autoinstaller.

> **TIP** If you're super-savvy, you may already know that some control panels have their own Find feature, which is even more convenient than your browser's Find function. To use it, look for a Find box on the web page itself (not in your browser's toolbar or menus). If you find one, type in the autoinstaller's name (for example, "Fantastico"). And if you can't find any autoinstaller, try typing in "WordPress." Sometimes, this finds the autoinstaller's setup script even if you don't know the autoinstaller's name.

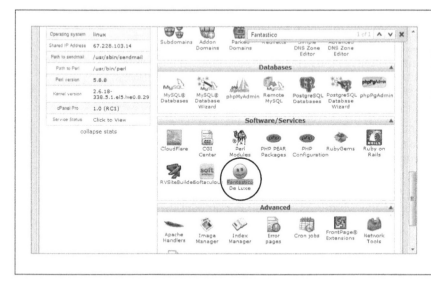

FIGURE 3-3

Here, the Google Chrome browser matches your search term by highlighting the Fantastico icon.

3. **Click the Fantastico icon.**

    Fantastico's menu page appears, with a list of all the software it can install. Usually, you'll find WordPress near the top of the list, along with other site-building tools (Figure 3-4).

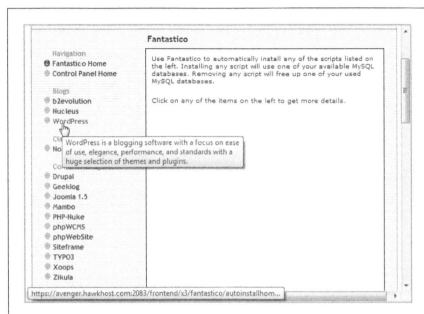

FIGURE 3-4

WordPress is just one of many programs an autoinstaller like Fantastico can install.

4. Click WordPress.

Fantastico displays basic information about WordPress, including the version you're about to install and the space it will take up. Autoinstallers always use the latest stable version of WordPress, so you don't need to worry about these details.

5. Click the "New Installation" link.

Now Fantastico starts a three-step installation process.

6. Pick a domain name and a directory (Figure 3-5).

This is where you decide where to put WordPress and all its files. As you learned earlier (page 53), you have three basic options:

If you want to make WordPress run your entire website, you must install it in the root folder of your web hosting account. To do that, choose the domain name you registered for your website (in the first box) and leave the directory box blank.

If you want to install WordPress in a subfolder, choose your domain name in the first box, and then fill in the name of the subfolder. The example in Figure 3-5 uses the domain *reboot-me.com* and a folder named *blog*. Remember, the autoinstaller will automatically create the folder you specify here. (And if there's already a WordPress site in that folder, you'll overwrite the old site with the new one.)

To install WordPress in a subdomain, you must have already created the subdomain (by following the steps on page 54). If you have, you can choose the subdomain name from the first box, and leave the directory box blank.

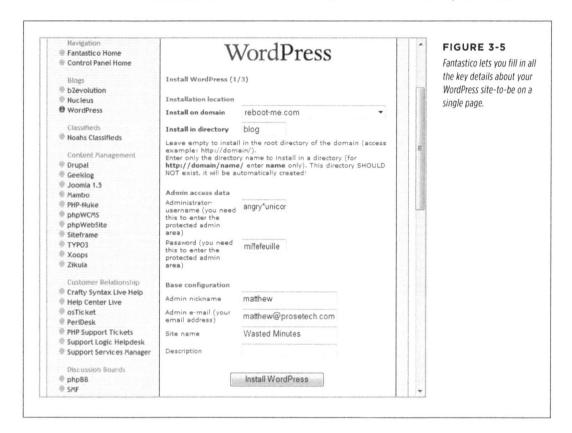

FIGURE 3-5

Fantastico lets you fill in all the key details about your WordPress site-to-be on a single page.

7. **Choose a user name and password for your administrator account.**

   Pick a name that's not obvious and a password that's difficult to crack (page 37). Doing otherwise invites spammers to hijack your blog.

8. **Fill in the remaining details in the "Base configuration" section.**

   The administrator nickname is the name that WordPress displays at the end of all the posts and comments you write. You can change it later if you like.

   The administrator email address is *your* email address, which becomes part of your WordPress user profile. It's also the email address that you'll use for administration—for example, if you forget your administrator password and you need WordPress to email you a password reset link.

   The site name is the title you want to give to your WordPress site ("Wasted Minutes" per Figure 3-5 here). It shows prominently on every page of your site.

The description is a short, one-sentence summary of your site. WordPress displays it in smaller text just underneath the title on every page of your site.

9. **Click the Install WordPress button.**

The next screen summarizes the information you just typed in (Figure 3-6). For example, it displays the exact location of your new site and the name of the MySQL database that will hold all its content. You might want to double-check this info for accuracy, and then write down the details for safekeeping.

FIGURE 3-6

Here, Fantastico tells you what it's about to do. To hold all the data for this WordPress site, Fantastico will create a MySQL database named rebootme_wrdp1 (the name is based on the domain name www.reboot-me. com), and it will create the site at www.reboot-me .com/blog.

10. **Click "Finish installation" to move to the final step.**

Now Fantastico does its job—creating the folder you picked (in this case, *blog*), copying the WordPress files to it, and creating the MySQL database. When it finishes, you'll see a confirmation message. This message reminds you of your administrator user name and password you supplied, and lists the administration URL—the address you type into your browser to get to the dashboard that controls your site. As with all WordPress sites, the administration page is your WordPress site's address with */wp-admin* tacked onto the end (for example, *www.reboot-me.com/blog/wp-admin*. You can visit the dashboard now, or wait to explore it in the next chapter.

Installing WordPress with Softaculous

Softaculous is another popular autoinstaller. Like Fantastico, it replaces the aggravating manual installation process WordPress users once had to endure (in the brutish dark ages of a few years back) with a painless click-click-done setup wizard. Here's how to use it:

1. **Log into the control panel for your web host.**

2. **Look for a Softaculous icon.**

Remember, many control panels have a search feature that lets you type in the name of the feature you want, rather than forcing you to hunt through dozens of icons.

3. **Click the Softaculous icon.**

   Softaculous shows a large, colorful tab for each program it can install using a *setup script* (Figure 3-7).

FIGURE 3-7

Along the left, Softaculous lists all the scripts it supports. But you won't need to hunt for the script that installs WordPress, because it usually appears in the top position on the Softaculous home page, due to its popularity.

4. **Hover over the WordPress box and click Install.**

   This takes you to an all-in-one installation page that collects all the information WordPress needs (Figure 3-8).

5. **Pick a domain name and a directory.**

   You can choose from any of the domain names you registered with your web host or any subdomain you created within that domain (page 54). This example uses *prosetech.com*.

   If you want to put your WordPress installation at the root of the domain (or in an existing subdomain), leave the directory box blank. If you want to create a subdomain, here's where you fill in the name of the folder for Softaculous to create. This example uses a folder named magicteahouse, which means the WordPress site will be created at *http://prosetech.com/magicteahouse*. Remember, it doesn't matter that the folder doesn't exist yet, because Softaculous will create it.

FIGURE 3-8

Here's the full page of information Softaculous needs before it installs WordPress. If you're not ready to install it just yet, you can click one of the commands that run across the top of the page. For example, Overview tells you the specific WordPress version Softaculous uses and its space requirements, Screenshots and Demo show you what a basic WordPress blog looks like, Reviews and Ratings tell you what other people think about WordPress, and so on.

6. **Optionally, change your database name and prefix.**

   The database name is the name of the MySQL database that stores all the content for your WordPress site. The actual name doesn't matter much, as long as it's different from any other database you've already created. You can name the database after your site (like *magicteahousedb*) or use the autogenerated name Softaculous suggests (like *wp224*).

   The database prefix is a short bit of text that's added to the beginning of the name of every table inside your database. Some people believe that by changing this prefix, you can get a little bit of extra security, because some WordPress attackers assume you're using the standard *wp_* prefix. Other than that, it's not important.

7. **Choose a site name and description.**

   The site name is the title you want to give your WordPress site (like "Magic Tea Emporium"). It shows prominently on every page of your site.

   The description is a short, one-sentence profile of your site. It appears in smaller text, just underneath the title on every page of your site.

   Don't worry about the Multisite feature just yet—you'll consider that in Chapter 11.

8. **Choose a user name, password, and email address for your administrator account.**

   Remember, a good password is all that stands between you and a compromised WordPress site that's showing banner ads for timeshares. Here, Softaculous's neglect is nearly criminal. The default administrator name it plops in (*admin*) is a bad choice because it's obvious and therefore open to attack, and the password it suggests (*pass*) is downright dangerous. Do yourself a favor and follow the rules set out in the box on page 37 to defend your site properly.

   The administrator email address is your email address. When you finish the install, Softaculous emails you a page with all the important details, including the administrator user name and password you picked.

9. **Click Install to finish the job.**

   Softaculous creates the folder you picked, copies the WordPress files there, and creates the MySQL database. After a few seconds, its work is done and you see a confirmation message (Figure 3-9).

FIGURE 3-9

When Softaculous finishes creating your WordPress site, it gives you the address of your site and the address of its administration page—the latter's the address you type into your browser to get to the dashboard that controls your site. (You'll explore the dashboard in Chapter 4.)

Installing WordPress by Hand

If you don't have the help of an autoinstaller like Fantastico or Softaculous, don't panic. Before these tools were widespread, WordPress was known for a relatively easy installation process. In fact, WordPress promoted it—heavily—as the "famous five-minute install." And while that's wildly optimistic (unless you're a seasoned webmaster, it'll take far longer), WordPress is still known for being easier to set up than most other blog software and content-management systems.

Here's an overview of what you need to do to get WordPress up and running the old-fashioned way:

1. **Create a MySQL database for WordPress to use.**

2. **Upload the WordPress files to your web host.**

3. **Run the installation script to get everything set up.**

In the following sections, you'll tackle each of these tasks.

NOTE Before you go down the WordPress self-installation route, make sure that it's truly necessary. The overwhelming majority of web hosts now provide some sort of WordPress installation feature that you can use instead. And although installing WordPress by hand isn't a Mensa-level challenge, it's an unnecessary slog if your web host provides an easier approach.

Create a MySQL Database

As you learned on page 13, WordPress stores all the details of your website—from your posts to your comments—in a database. MySQL is the name of the database software that manages your WordPress content, storing and fetching it. In fact, before you can install WordPress, you need to have a blank MySQL database waiting for it. Here's how to create one:

1. **Use your browser, to log into the control panel for your web host.**

2. **Look for an icon that has something to do with databases or MySQL.** Examples include "MySQL Administration," "MySQL Databases," or "Database Manager." When you find it, click it.

   You'll see a new page with information about all the MySQL databases currently stored on your site, if any. Figure 3-10 shows an example.

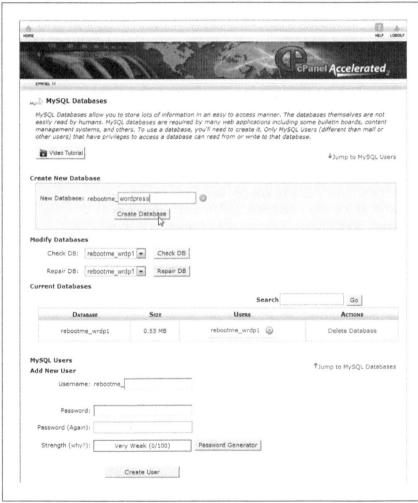

FIGURE 3-10

If your web host uses the cPanel interface, you'll manage databases in a page like this. It's divided into several sections. For a WordPress installation, the three important sections are "Create New Database" (shown here at the top), "Add New User" (lower down), and "Add User to Database" (all the way at the bottom of the page, and not shown here).

3. **Create a new database.**

    You need to choose an appropriate name for your database. Most people use a name that has some variation of "WordPress" in it, like *MagicTeaHouse_wp*. Often, your web host will automatically add the domain name to the beginning of the database name you specify. So if you type in "wordpress" as the name of the database, you actually get a database named "rebootme_wordpress" (see Figure 3-10).

TIP Make a note of the exact name you use for the database, because you'll need to tell WordPress about it when you run the WordPress installation script.

    Once you type in a name, click a button that's named something like Create Database or New. If your web host runs the standardized cPanel control panel, the next step is to click the Go Back button to return to the database management page. (If your host uses a different control panel, look for similarly named commands.)

4. **Add a new database user.**

    Right now, no one has control over your database. To be able to use it, you need to appoint yourself its administrator by creating an administrator account. You do that by adding a new user (you) and giving yourself across-the-board permission to manage the database. That way, you can log into the database and have free rein to store and retrieve information.

    To add a new user in cPanel, scroll down the page to the "Add New User" section and type in a user name and password for yourself. Click the Create User button to make it official. Then click Go Back to return to the database management page.

NOTE Many web hosts automatically insert the site name before your user name. So if you type in the user name *dbadmin* for the *reboot-me.com* site, you end up with something like *rebootme_dbadmin* as your user name. Although the database administrator account is harder for hackers to get at than the WordPress admin account, it's still worth some time picking a difficult-to-guess password.

5. **Register your user name with the database.**

    Although it may sound strange, you, as the new database user, can't do anything yet, because you haven't given yourself permission to use the database. To fix this, you need to give yourself access to the WordPress database you created in step 3.

    In a cPanel control panel, scroll to the bottom of the page, to the "Add User to Database" section, which contains two drop-down lists. In the first one, pick the user name you just added; in the second, pick the name of the database you created. Then click Add to seal the deal.

This is also the point where you tell the database exactly what this user is allowed to do. Because you're the uber-powerful database administrator, this account should be able to do everything, from adding and deleting tables to searching and changing the data inside them. To make that happen, pick All Privileges and then click Make Changes (Figure 3-11). Now you can have your way with your brand-new database.

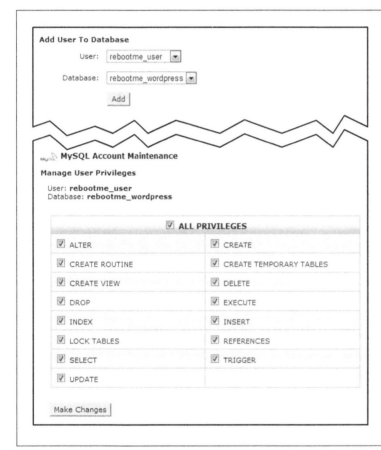

FIGURE 3-11

Here, the user rebootme_user is linked to the rebootme_wordpress database (top). After clicking Add, you need to set the user's security privileges. Checking the topmost "All Privileges" box is a quick way to check all the boxes.

Uploading the WordPress Files

Now you have a perfectly configured MySQL database waiting for someone to come along and use it. But before you can get WordPress up and running, you need to transfer the program to your website. This is a two-step process: first you download the latest version of WordPress, and then you upload it to your site. Here's how:

1. **In your browser, go to *http://wordpress.org/download*, and click the Download WordPress button.**

This downloads the latest version of WordPress as a compressed ZIP file, which virtually all computers support. (If you look closely, you'll see an alternate link for downloading WordPress as a compressed .tar.gz file, but you don't need that.)

2. **Inside the ZIP file is a folder named "wordpress."** You need to extract that folder to a convenient place on your hard drive, like the desktop.

For example, on a Windows computer you can drag the *wordpress* folder out of the ZIP file and onto the desktop, automatically unzipping its contents in the process. (You don't need much free space. Altogether, the WordPress files take up only a few megabytes of storage.) On Mac OS X, double-click the ZIP file to extract its contents.

Using either method, you end up with a folder named *wordpress*, which will have several subfolders and several dozen files in it, but you don't need to worry about those.

NOTE No matter where you put the *wordpress* folder, it will be a temporary storage location. After all, the WordPress files can't do much trapped on your computer. Your ultimate goal is to upload all these files to your website, where they can work their magic. Once you do that, you can delete the WordPress files from your desktop.

---

3. **Figure out the FTP address you need to use.**

You could ask your web host, but the address is almost always *ftp://* followed by your domain name, as in *ftp://reboot-me.com*. The initial *ftp://* is critical—it indicates that you're making a connection for transferring files, not visiting a website (in which case you'd use an address starting with *http://*).

4. **Load your FTP program and navigate to your site.**

FTP is a standard that lets computers pass files from one to the other. You'll use it to upload the WordPress files to your website.

In the old days of the Web, uploaders used specialized FTP programs to transfer files. Many people still use dedicated FTP programs, and you can, too. However, the latest versions of Windows and Mac OS X have built-in FTP functionality, so you don't need a separate program.

NOTE Depending on your web host, you may be able to upload files from your browser by using your site's control panel. However, browser-based file management is usually awkward and can trigger a triple-Tylenol headache if you need to upload a large batch of files, like the contents of the wordpress folder and its subfolders. FTP is easier.

To open an FTP connection in any modern version of Windows, start by firing up the Windows Explorer file manager. (Right-click the Start button, and click a menu command that has a name like Open Windows Explorer.) Then, type the FTP address into the Windows Explorer address bar.

To open an FTP connection in Mac OS X, start out at the desktop and hit Command+K to launch the Connect to Server window. Then, type in the FTP address and click Connect.

5. **When your FTP program asks, enter your user name and password in the boxes provided.**

This is the same user name and password you use to connect to your host's control panel to manage your website.

> **NOTE** Having trouble keeping track of all the different login identities you need to self-host WordPress? There are three altogether: one for your web host's control panel, one for your database, and one for your WordPress administrator account.

Once you log in through the FTP panel, you'll see your site's folders and files—the ones on your web server—listed; you can copy, delete, rename, and move them in much the same way you can for local folders and files.

6. **Browse to the root folder of your website.**

This is the heart of your site—the place people go when they type in your web address. It may be a folder named *public_html* or *webroot*. Or, you may start off in the right place when you log in. If you already have a traditional website on your domain, you'll know you're in the root folder when you see your web pages there. And if you're still in doubt, it may be worth a quick call to your web host's support center to make sure you're in the right spot.

7. **Open another file-browsing window to view the wordpress folder on your computer.**

This is the place where you unzipped the WordPress files in step 2.

8. **Copy the files from the wordpress folder to your website.**

There are two ways to do this. If you want WordPress to take over your entire site (see page 53), you must select all the files in the wordpress folder (including subfolders). Then, copy all these files over to your root web folder. This is the strategy to use if you want people to go straight to your WordPress content when they type in your domain name (like *www.reboot-me.com*).

> **NOTE** If you're putting WordPress in your root web folder, make sure you don't have another default page there. A *default page* is the page your website sends to a visitor when he types in your domain name (for example, *www.reboot-me.com*) rather than specifying a site page (like *www.reboot-me.com/mypage.html*). WordPress has its own default page, *index.php*, but you don't want another default page trying to take over. Possible default pages include anything that starts with "index" (*index.html, index.shtml, index.html*) and "default" (*default.asp, default.aspx*).

If you want to create a subfolder on your website for WordPress, you follow a slightly different procedure. First, rename the wordpress folder on your computer to the name of the folder you want to create on your website. For example, if you want to create a subfolder named *blog*, rename the wordpress folder *blog*. Now you simply need to select and copy a single item—the blog folder that holds all the WordPress files.

Either way, you upload the files in the same way you copy them on your computer. For example, you can drag the selected files from your computer and drop them on the FTP window (Figure 3-12). Or, you can copy the selected files (that's Ctrl+C on Windows and Command+C on a Mac), switch to the FTP window, and then paste them (with Ctrl+V or Command+V).

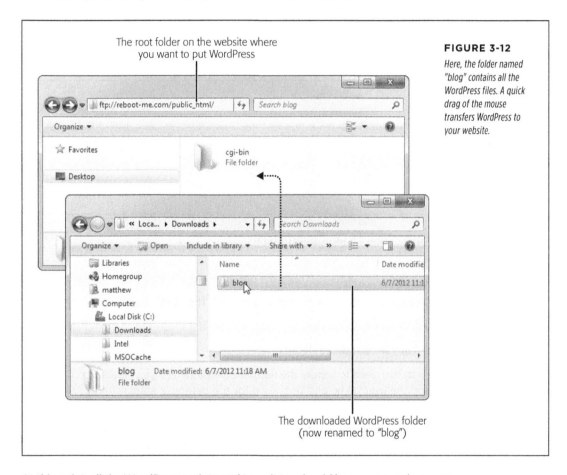

The root folder on the website where you want to put WordPress

FIGURE 3-12

Here, the folder named "blog" contains all the WordPress files. A quick drag of the mouse transfers WordPress to your website.

The downloaded WordPress folder (now renamed to "blog")

At this point, all the WordPress scripts and templates should be on your web server, although they aren't actually switched on yet. Before you continue to the final step, it's a good idea to make sure you uploaded the software successfully. To do that, try requesting WordPress's *readme.html* file, which should be in the folder you just uploaded. For example, if you put WordPress at *www.reboot-me.com/blog* you can request *www.reboot-me.com/blog/readme.html*. When you do, you'll see a WordPress page with some very basic information about the setup process. If you get a "webpage not found" error, you've accidentally uploaded your files to a different location, so you need to take some time to sort it all out.

Running the Install Script

This is the final set of steps. Think of it as *activating* the WordPress site you just created.

1. **To start the installation, type the web address where you installed Word-Press into your browser, and then add */wp-admin/install.php* to the end.**

   So if you installed WordPress at *www.reboot-me.com/blog*, you would request *www.reboot-me.com/blog/wp-admin/install.php*. At this point, WordPress warns you that it can't find a configuration file (Figure 3-13). Don't worry, you'll create one.

FIGURE 3-13

There's no configuration file, so you need to create one and provide all the configuration details.

---

2. **Click "Create a Configuration File."**

   On the next page, WordPress reminds you about the information you'll need to complete this process (that's the database details from the previous section).

3. **Once you work up your confidence, click the "Let's go" button.**

   WordPress displays a page requesting your database information (Figure 3-14).

4. **Fill in your database details.**

   First, you need to supply the database name (which you created on page 67), and the user name and password for the database administrator (which you picked on page 67).

   You also need to supply the location of the database. The default value, *localhost*, indicates that it's on the same server as the WordPress installation file, which is almost always what you want.

   Lastly, you need to pick a table prefix—a few characters that WordPress will add to the name of every table it creates in the database. The standard prefix, *wp_*, is perfectly fine, but you may get marginally better security by choosing something less common.

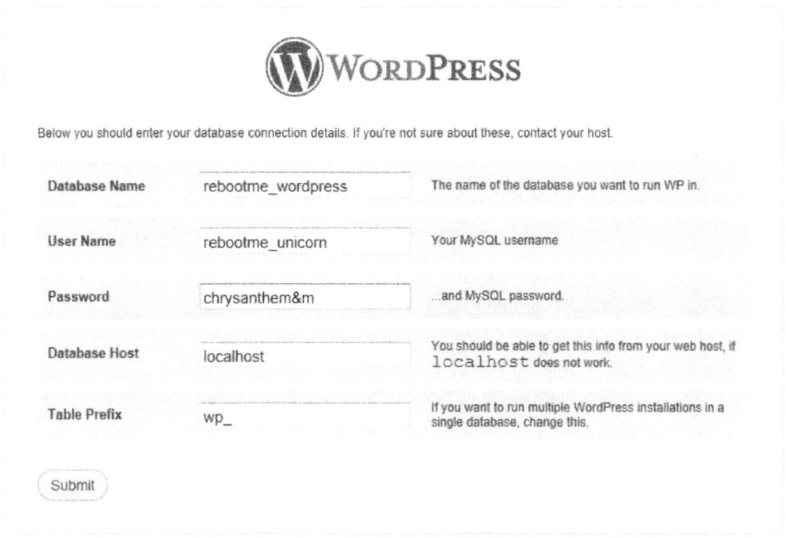

FIGURE 3-14

WordPress needs to know where your database is, and what user name and password it should use to access it. You need to fill in this information (Database Name, User Name, and Password). You can leave the other settings (Database Host and Table Prefix) with their standard values.

5. **Once you enter all these details, click Submit.**

   If WordPress manages to contact your database, it gives you a virtual thumbs up, and offers to start the installation.

6. **Click "Run the install" to start the WordPress installation.**

   The next page collects some essential information about your WordPress site.

7. **Fill in your site's particulars (Figure 3-15).**

   The site title is the heading that crowns your WordPress site.

   The user name and password is what you use to log in to the WordPress dashboard, configure things, and write new posts. Choose a not-so-obvious user name and a crack-resistant password (page 37).

   The email address you type in will appear in your WordPress profile, and WordPress uses it if you forget your password and need to reset it.

   Leave the "Allow my site to appear in search engines" checkbox turned on, unless you're trying to keep a low profile. (But keep in mind that even if your site isn't listed in a Google search, there are still plenty of ways for people to stumble across it. The only way to keep out strangers is to create a private site, as discussed on page 373.)

FIGURE 3-15

This WordPress site is named Wasted Minutes. The administrator's user name, angry_unicorn, is far less predictable than common (but less secure) choices like admin, user, wp, wp_admin, and so on.

8. **Click Install WordPress to finish the job.**

   This is the point where the WordPress installation script really gets to work, configuring your database and loading it up with its first bits of WordPress content. When the process is finished, you'll see a confirmation page (Figure 3-16).

   Before you close the page, why not visit your site and verify that it's working? As always, you can add */wp-admin* to the end of your site address to get to the administration dashboard.

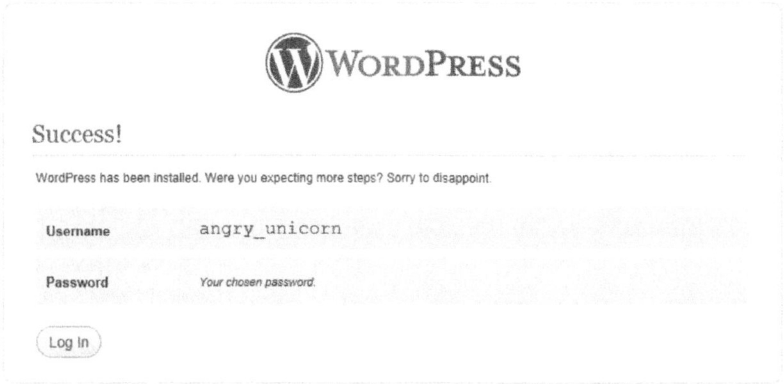

FIGURE 3-16

WordPress has finished installing your site. This confirmation screen reminds you of the user name you picked as the administrator, but it doesn't repeat your password. Click Log In to go the dashboard and start managing your site.

Maintaining Your Site

As a self-hoster, your WordPress responsibilities don't end after you install the software. You also need to keep WordPress up-to-date, by installing the latest patches and fixes as they become available. And like every good website administrator, you need to perform regular backups, so you can recover from unexpected catastrophes (like the sudden bankruptcy of your web hosting company, or a spammer who defaces your site). In the following sections, you'll quickly consider both tasks.

Updating WordPress

No WordPress website should be left unprotected. If you don't install the latest WordPress updates, you could be running a website with known security vulnerabilities. Do that, and you'll attract the interest of plenty of hackers and spammers looking to show their ads or otherwise tamper with your site.

NOTE Don't underestimate the threat of a WordPress attack. Even though your site may not be large enough to attract a hacker's personal attention, hackers run automated tools that can launch attacks against thousands of WordPress blogs at a time. These attacks are relatively simple—usually, they use brute force attempts to crack the administrator password (so make sure yours is strong; see page 37), or they attempt to capitalize on a known flaw in an old version of WordPress or a WordPress plug-in (so make sure your site is always up-to-date).

Fortunately, WordPress is aware of the threat of old software, and is quick to alert you to new updates as they become available. Whenever you travel to the dashboard—the administrative interface described in the next chapter—WordPress checks for new versions.

To get to the dashboard, take your WordPress site address (like *www.prosetech* *.com/magicteahouse* and add */wp-admin* on the end (as in *www.prosetech.com/* *magicteahouse/wp-admin*). Initially, you start at the dashboard home page. If Word-Press detects that there's a newer version available, it tries to grab your attention by adding a yellow box to the top of this page (Figure 3-17).

FIGURE 3-17

There's a new version of WordPress available, and your site isn't using it. To keep yourself secure, click the "Please update now" link immediately. This takes you to the Updates section of the dashboard (Figure 3-18).

The Updates page is an all-in-one glance at everything that's potentially old and out-of-date in your site. Usually, the Updates page will simply tell you that all's well. But when updates are available, you'll see something else. First, WordPress adds a black number-in-a-circle icon to the Updates command in the dashboard menu. The actual number reflects the number of website components that need updating. In Figure 3-18 that number is 3, because you need to update WordPress and two themes.

NOTE Themes and plug-ins are two ways you can enhance and extend your site. But if they contain flaws, hackers can use those flaws to attack your site. You'll learn more about themes in Chapter 5 and plug-ins in Chapter 9.

To install an update, use the buttons on the Updates page. If there's a new WordPress update, click the Update WordPress button. If there's a newer theme or plug-in, turn on the checkbox next to that theme or plug-in, and then click Update Themes or Update Plugins.

WordPress updates are impressively easy. There's no need to enter more information or suffer through a long wait. Instead, you'll see a brief summary that tells you what happened (Figure 3-19). Your site will carry on functioning exactly as it had before.

FIGURE 3-18

The Update page explains that three components need updating: the WordPress software and two themes that you installed on your site.

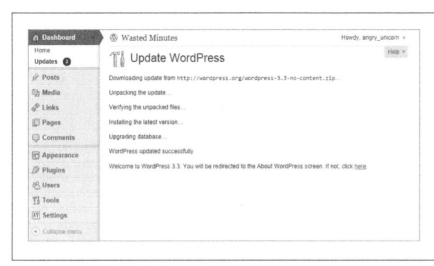

FIGURE 3-19

Breathe easy: WordPress is up-to-date once more.

Backing Up Your Site

Along with updating your website, you should back up your WordPress files periodically. Should you be unlucky enough to be hacked, you can often recover by reverting back to a slightly older version of your site.

Unfortunately, the WordPress backup procedure can be tedious. The problem is that WordPress uses both files and a database, and these two components have different backup requirements. As a result, backing up a WordPress site by hand is time-consuming and more than a little intimidating for anyone who doesn't fancy himself a seasoned web administrator. This is a problem, because a backup isn't a one-time process (like setting up WordPress)—it's a job you need to carry out monthly, weekly, or even daily, depending on how fast your site changes.

Fortunately, there are two good options that save you the hassle of a manual backup:

- **Use your autoinstaller.** Some autoinstallers, such as Softaculous, have integrated backup features. Others, such as Fantastico, do not.

- **Use a plug-in.** You'll consider how plug-ins work and learn about plug-in-powered backup options in Chapter 9.

To see if your autoinstaller has a backup feature, launch it, and click over to the WordPress section. You should be able to find a list of all the WordPress installations on your web hosting account. (Remember, you can install multiple WordPress sites in different folders or domains, as described in the box on page 54.) In both Fantastico and Softaculous, this list appears under the heading "Current Installations" (Figure 3-20).

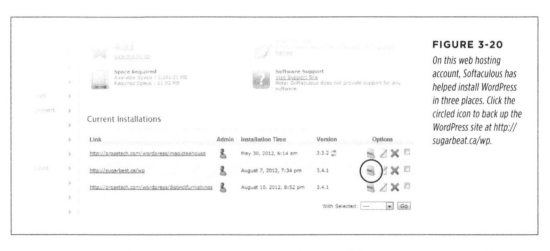

FIGURE 3-20

On this web hosting account, Softaculous has helped install WordPress in three places. Click the circled icon to back up the WordPress site at http://sugarbeat.ca/wp.

Most autoinstallers have some sort of button or link that lets you remove a WordPress installation. Often, that's about the only feature you'll get. But Softaculous gives you three options. You can delete the WordPress files, edit the installation details (which can cause configuration problems, so don't try it unless you know exactly what you're doing), or back up your site (which is by far the most useful feature).

To back up your files in Softaculous, start by clicking the Backup icon next to your site address (It looks like a yellow file folder with a band around it). When you do, Softaculous asks you what you want to back up (Figure 3-21)

FIGURE 3-21

WordPress sites store their content in a database, and stash other supporting resources (like pictures) in separate files. To create a full backup, you need to create a copy of both your website directory and your database. Page 299 has more about WordPress backups, but for now make sure you turn on both checkboxes shown here.

Once you select what you want to backup (usually, that's everything), click the Backup Installation button. The backup takes place on your web host's web server, in the background. Softaculous won't show you the progress as the backup unfolds, but it will send you an email when it's finished (using the administrative email address you supplied when you first installed the WordPress site).

Softaculous creates a single large zip file that has all your backed-up data in it. The file name includes the backup date (like *wp.1.2013-08-20_05-30-16.zip*). Softaculous stores the backup file in a separate, private section of your web hosting account. Usually, it's in a folder named *softaculous_backups*, but you'll see the exact details in the email you get when Softaculous finishes the backup.

To make sure your backup is safe, you should follow up by downloading it to your computer. To do that, head back to Softaculous and click the large backup icon top-right corner (Figure 3-22), which takes you to the backup section (Figure 3-23).

FIGURE 3-22

Click here to see all the backups Softaculous has made at your behest.

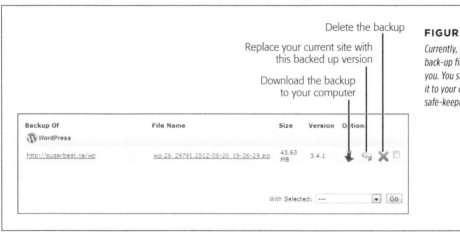

Delete the backup

Replace your current site with
this backed up version

Download the backup
to your computer

FIGURE 3-23

Currently, there's one back-up file waiting for you. You should download it to your computer for safe-keeping.

If your backup is extremely large (for example, your website has hundreds of high-resolution pictures on it), you may consider deleting the backup from your web hosting account to free up more space. If you don't need the space, don't delete the backup. (The backup shown in Figure 3-23 uses 43 MB, which is trivial.)

If disaster strikes, you can restore your site using the backup. To do that, head back to the Softaculous backups section, find the most recent backup, and click the restore icon that appears next to it, and looks like a curved, up-pointing arrow (see Figure 3-23).

To restore your site on a new web server—one that has Softaculous, but doesn't have your backup file—you can do that too. First, upload your ZIP backup file to the *softaculous_backups* folder using an FTP program. (Ask your web hosting company if you have trouble finding that folder.) Then, when you launch Softaculous and go to the backups section, you'll see your backup file waiting there, ready to be restored.

Building a WordPress Blog

4

Creating Posts

Now that you've signed up for a WordPress.com account (Chapter 2), or installed the WordPress software on your web host (Chapter 3), you're ready to get started publishing on the Web. In this chapter, you'll go to your fledgling WordPress site and start posting *content*, which can be anything from bracing political commentary to juvenile jokes. Along, the way you'll learn several key WordPress concepts.

First, you'll get comfortable in WordPress's *dashboard*—the administrative cockpit from which you pilot your site. Using the dashboard, you'll create, edit, and delete posts, all without touching a single HTML tag (unless you really want to).

Next, you'll learn how to classify your posts by using categories and tags, so you can group them in meaningful ways. WordPress calls this art of organization *taxonomy*, and if you do it right, it can help your readers find exactly the content they want.

You'll also take a hard look at the web address (URL) that WordPress generates for every new post. You'll learn how to take control of your URLs, making sure they're meaningful, memorable, and accessible to search engines. You'll also learn how to shorten the URL of any post, which is handy if you need to wedge a link to your post into a small place (like a Twitter message, Facebook post, or a bit of bathroom graffiti).

Introducing the Dashboard

The dashboard is the nerve-center of WordPress administration. When you want to add a new post, tweak your site's theme, or review other people's inflammatory comments, this is the place to go.

The easiest way to get to the dashboard is to take your WordPress website address and add */wp-admin* (short for "WordPress administration") to the end. For example, if you're hosting your site at *http://magicteahouse.net*, you can reach the site's dashboard at *http://magicteahouse.net/wp-admin*. When you do, WordPress will ask for your user name and password. Once you supply the right information, you'll see a page like the one in Figure 4-1.

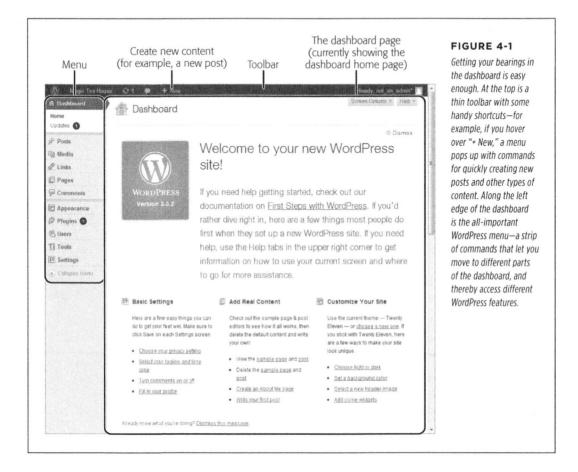

Menu

Create new content
(for example, a new post)

Toolbar

The dashboard page
(currently showing the
dashboard home page)

FIGURE 4-1

Getting your bearings in the dashboard is easy enough. At the top is a thin toolbar with some handy shortcuts—for example, if you hover over "+ New," a menu pops up with commands for quickly creating new posts and other types of content. Along the left edge of the dashboard is the all-important WordPress menu—a strip of commands that let you move to different parts of the dashboard, and thereby access different WordPress features.

The Dashboard in WordPress.com

WordPress.com sites and self-hosted sites share a very similar dashboard. Most of the commands (in the menu on the left) are identical. In the rare cases that they aren't, this book makes a note of the discrepancy.

The toolbar at the top of the dashboard is less consistent. WordPress.com sites have a set of shortcuts similar to what's in Figure 4-1, but in a completely different arrangement from a self-hosted WordPress installation. This isn't a problem either, because the toolbar simply duplicates some of the features already in the WordPress menu. It's up to you to discover these shortcuts and decide whether you want to use them from the toolbar at all.

When you finish working at the dashboard, it's a good idea to log out. That way, you don't need to worry about a smart-alecky friend hijacking your site and adding humiliating posts or pictures while you're away from your computer. To log out, click your user name in the top-right corner of the toolbar, and then click Log Out.

There's another way to go backstage with your site. When WordPress creates a new site, it adds a sidebar that sits on the right side of its home page. In that sidebar are links for reading recent posts and a section named "Meta," which contains a "Log in" link. Click it, and you'll go directly to the dashboard. (If you're already logged in, you'll see a "Site Admin" link instead of a "Log in" link.)

NOTE Although the Meta section is helpful when you first start out, you won't want administrative links in a finished site. Page 144 explains how to remove the Meta section.

The Menu

A link to every administrative feature WordPress offers appears somewhere in the menu—the panel that runs down the left side of the dashboard.

WordPress groups the commands in the menu into submenus. To see a submenu, hover over one of menu headings (like "Posts") and you'll see it pop open (Figure 4-2).

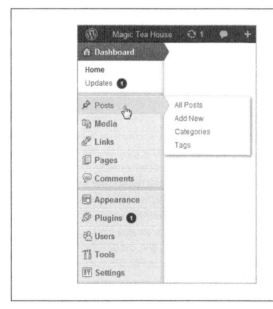

FIGURE 4-2

WordPress's menu packs a lot of features into a small strip of web-page real estate. Initially, all you see is the first level of menu headings. But hover over one of the items, and a submenu appears. (The exception is Comments, which doesn't have a submenu. You just click it to review comments.)

When you click a menu command, the rest of the dashboard changes to reflect the task you picked. For example, say you choose Posts→Add New. (In other words, you mouse over to the left-side menu, hover over "Posts" until its submenu appears, and then click the "Add New" command.) Now, the dashboard shows an HTML-savvy post editor where you can write your post.

You can also click a menu heading directly (for example, "Posts"). If you do, you go to the first item in the corresponding submenu, as shown in Figure 4-3.

FIGURE 4-3

If you click the heading Posts, you actually go to the submenu item Posts→All Posts. And if you lose your bearings in the dashboard, just look for the bold, black text in the menu to find out where you are. In this example, that's "All Posts" (though it's harder to tell in a black-and-white book). The other entries, which correspond to pages you aren't currently viewing, have blue text.

NOTE If you resize your web browser window to be very narrow, the menu shrinks itself to free up more space, removing the menu names (like Posts, Media, and Links), and leaving just the tiny menu icons. Hover over one of these icons, and the submenu appears, but with a helpful difference: now WordPress displays the menu name as a title at the top.

FREQUENTLY ASKED QUESTION

WordPress Update Notifications

What are those numbers that appear in the dashboard?

If you're running a self-hosted WordPress site, your dashboard menu may sometimes include a large black number-in-a-circle. See, for example, the number "1" in Figure 4-2. This difficult-to-ignore signal tells you there's an update waiting for you. It could be for core WordPress software, for one of your plug-ins (as is the case in Figure 4-2), or for one of your themes.

Because updates often correct security vulnerabilities, and because there are legions of cyber-attackers ready to attack any chink in the armor of a WordPress site as soon as it's discovered, you should always update your site as soon as possible. In fact, if you see the numbers, you should probably stop everything you're currently doing, and update your site immediately. Typically, updates take just a few seconds, so you won't be stalled for long.

To perform an update, choose Dashboard→Updates or click the Update icon in the toolbar at the top of the page. (It's a circle made up of two arrows, sort of like the recycling symbol.) Either way, you'll get to the WordPress Updates page, which tells you the status of the WordPress software, plug-ins, and themes on your site. If there's a new WordPress update, click the Update WordPress button. If there's a new plug-in or theme, check the box next to that theme or plug-in, and click Update Themes or Update Plugins. Blink twice, and WordPress will let you know that everything is up-to-date.

If you're using WordPress.com, you won't see any WordPress update notifications. That's because Automattic, WordPress's parent company, always installs the latest WordPress software when it's ready.

The Home Page

Your starting place in the dashboard is a densely packed home page. You can get back to this page any time by choosing Dashboard→Home from the menu.

If you just created your WordPress site, a welcome box fills the top part of the dashboard (Figure 4-4). It provides links that lead to some of the more important parts of the dashboard, where you can edit settings and add new posts.

FIGURE 4-4

Although the links in the welcome box work perfectly well, it's probably a better idea to get used to finding what you need in the dashboard menu. Before you continue, scroll down past the welcome box or click "Dismiss this message" to remove it altogether, so you can see the rest of the home page. (If you want it back later on, you can use the Screen Options button that's described on page 123.)

The dashboard home page may seem like a slightly overwhelming starting point, because it's crowded with gray boxes. Each one handles a separate task, as detailed in Figure 4-5. Sometimes, you'll also see yellow boxes with important news (for example, an announcement about an update of the WordPress software).

FIGURE 4-5

At the top of the dashboard home page, you'll see a Right Now box that shows the vital signs for your site—including how many posts, pages, and comments it has. To the right of that is a QuickPress box that lets you create a new post in a hurry. Below that, you'll find additional boxes with information about recent comments (that other people have left on your posts), recent drafts (posts you started but haven't yet finished), and links to WordPress news.

Don't be surprised to find that your brand-new WordPress site has some content in it. WordPress starts off every new site with one blog post, one page, and one comment, all of which are dutifully recorded in the "Right Now" box. Once you learn to create your own posts, you'll see how to delete these initial examples (page 103).

NOTE WordPress continually evolves. When you use the latest and greatest version, you may find that minor details have changed, such as the exact wording of links or the placement of boxes. But don't let these details throw you, because the underlying WordPress concepts and procedures have been surprisingly steady for years.

Dashboard Practice: Changing Basic Settings

Now that you understand how the dashboard works, why not try out a basic task? The following steps show you how to change a few useful WordPress settings, which are worth reviewing before you start posting. And best of all, they'll help you get used to clicking your way through the dashboard menu to find what you need.

1. **In the dashboard menu, choose Settings→General.**

   The rest of the dashboard loads up a page of tweakable settings (Figure 4-6).

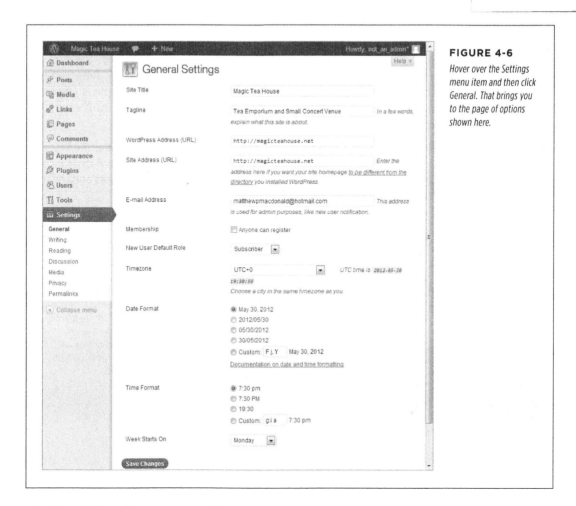

Hover over the Settings menu item and then click General. That brings you to the page of options shown here.

2. **If you'd like, change some settings.**

   Here are some suggestions:

   - **Site Title and Tagline.** In a basic WordPress site, every page has a header section at the top. WordPress puts the site title and tagline in the header (Figure 4-7). The site title also shows up at the top of the browser window (or tab), and, if a visitor decides to bookmark your site, the browser uses the site title as the bookmark text. You shouldn't change these details often, so it's worthwhile to double-check that you've got a clear title and catchy tagline right now.

   - **Timezone.** This tells WordPress where you are, globally speaking. (For example, UTC-5 is the time zone for New York.) If WordPress doesn't have the right time zone, it will give posts and comments the wrong timestamp. For example, it might tell the world that a comment you left at 8:49 PM was actually recorded at 3:49 AM. If you're not sure what your time zone offset is, you can use a website like *www.timeanddate.com/worldclock* to search for your home city and figure it out.

- **Date Format and Time Format.** Ordinarily, WordPress displays the date for every post you add and the time for every comment made. These settings control how WordPress displays the date and time. For example, if you want dates to be short—like "2012/12/18" rather than "December 18, 2012"—the Date Format setting is the one to tweak.

- **Week Starts On.** This tells WordPress what day it should consider the first day of the week in your country (typically, that's Saturday, Sunday, or Monday). This setting changes the way WordPress groups posts into weeks and the way it displays events in calendars.

Magic Tea House
Tea Emporium and Small Concert Venue

 Search

Home   Sample Page

FIGURE 4-7

The header includes the title of the site and the tag line. The title (in this case, "Magic Tea House") is shown in a large font. The tag line, a one-sentence description ("Tea Emporium and Small Concert Venue"), sits underneath.

3. **Click Save Changes to make your changes official.**

WordPress takes a fraction of a second to commit your changes, and then shows a "Settings saved" message at the top of the page. You can now move to a different part of the dashboard.

NOTE There are plenty more WordPress settings to play around with in the Settings submenu. As you explore various WordPress features in this book, you'll return to these settings to customize them.

■ Adding Your First Post

Comfortable yet? As you've seen, the WordPress dashboard gives you a set of relatively simple and anxiety-free tools to manage your website. In fact, a good part of
the reason that WordPress is so popular is because it's so easy to take care of. (And
as any pet owner knows, the most exotic animal in the world isn't worth owning if
it won't stop peeing on the floor.)

But to really get going with your website, you need to put some content on it. So
it makes perfect sense that one of the first dashboard tasks that every WordPress
administrator learns is *posting*.

Creating a New Post

To create a new post, follow these steps:

1. **In the dashboard menu, choose Posts→Add New.**

   The Add New Post page appears, complete with a big fat box where you can
   type in your content (Figure 4-8).

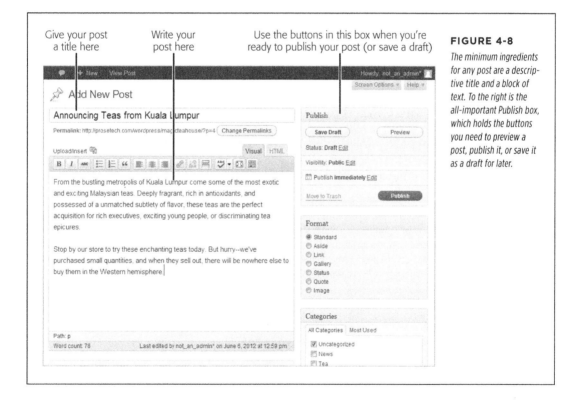

Give your post a title here   Write your post here   Use the buttons in this box when you're ready to publish your post (or save a draft)

FIGURE 4-8

The minimum ingredients for any post are a descrip-tive title and a block of text. To the right is the all-important Publish box, which holds the buttons you need to preview a post, publish it, or save it as a draft for later.

You can save time by using the toolbar at the top of the WordPress screen. If you're running WordPress on your own web host, click New→Post. If you're signed up with WordPress.com, click the WordPress "W" icon (in the corner on the left) and then click New Post.

2. **Start by typing a post title into the blank box at the top of the page (right under "Edit Post").**

A good post title clearly announces what you're going to discuss. Often, visitors will come across your post title before getting to your post text. For example, they might see the title in a list of posts or a search engine results page. A good title communicates your subject and entices the reader to continue on to the post. A lousy title might be cute, clever, or funny, but fail to reflect what the post is about.

Here are some good post titles: "Obama Struggles in Recent Poll," "Mad Men Is Officially Off the Rails," and "My Attempt to Make a Chocolate-Bacon Soufflé." And here are weaker titles for exactly the same content: "Polls, Polls, and More Polls," "Mad Men Recap," and "My Latest Kitchen Experiment."

3. **Click in the big box under the post title (or just press the Tab key).** Now, type in the content for your post (Figure 4-8).

A basic blog post consists of one or more paragraphs. After each paragraph, press the Enter key (once) to start the next paragraph. WordPress automatically adds a bit of white space between paragraphs, so they don't feel too crowded. Resist the urge to sign your name at the end, because WordPress automatically adds this information to the post.

TIP Paragraphs and line breaks give your web page two different looks. When you start a new paragraph by pressing Enter, WordPress includes some extra blank space between paragraphs. When you add a *line break*, the adjacent lines remain relatively close together. (For example, you'd use line breaks to separate lines in a mailing address or a poem.) When you want a line break instead of a new paragraph (to avoid getting the space between paragraphs), hold down the Shift key while you press Enter.

If you want fancier formatting for your post, the toolbar that sits above the content box lets you add lists, subheadings, pictures, and more. You'll take a closer look at these features on page 168.

NOTE Don't worry if you're not yet feeling inspired. It's exceptionally easy to delete blog posts, so you can add a simple post just for practice and then remove it later (see page 103).

4. **Check your spelling.**

   A post with typographic errors or clumsy spelling mistakes is as embarrassing as a pair of pants with a faulty elastic band. Before you inadvertently reveal yourself to the world, it's a good idea to double-check your writing.

   If you're using a browser with a built-in spell-checker, which includes Internet Explorer 10, most versions of Firefox, and Chrome, spell checking is automatic. You'll see red squiggly lines under your mistakes, and you can right-click misspelled words to choose the right spelling from a pop-up menu.

   If you're using a browser that doesn't do spell-checking (like IE 9 or earlier), you need to ask WordPress to do the work for you. When you finish your post, click the Proofread Writing button in the WordPress editing toolbar, which sits at the top of the box that has your post text. (This button looks like a checkmark with the letters ABC shown above it; if you don't see it, make sure you selected the Visual tab, not the HTML tab above the editing box. You'll learn what these two tabs do on page 175.) WordPress underlines all potentially problematic words in red, and you can edit them or right-click to use a suggested correction. But remember, if you type in any new words, they won't be spell-checked until you click the Proofread Writing button again.

5. **When you finish writing and editing, click Preview.**

   Your post preview opens in a new browser tab or new browser window. It shows you a perfect rendition of what the post will look like on your site, with the current theme.

> **NOTE** In some cases, your browser may block the preview because this feature uses a pop-up window. If your browser displays a warning message and no preview window, you may need to lower the pop-up security settings for your site. Although every browser is different, you usually accomplish that by clicking the pop-up warning icon and choosing an "Allow pop-ups" option.

6. **If you like what you saw in the preview window, click Publish.**

   In a self-hosted site, a yellow message box will appear at the top of the page, confirming that your post has been published. In a WordPress.com site, a side panel pops into view, with a message that tells you how many posts you've written to date.

   The moment you publish a post, it becomes live on your site and visible to the world. WordPress.com shows you the result right away; if you're running a self-hosted WordPress site, you need to click the "View post" link to see the published post (Figure 4-9).

If you're not quite done but you need to take a break, click Save Draft instead of Publish. WordPress holds onto your post so you can edit and publish it later. Returning to a draft is easy—in the dashboard home page (that's Dashboard→Home), find the Recent Drafts box, and click your post in the list to resume editing it. After, you can continue postponing the moment of publication (click Save Draft again), you can publish it like a normal post (click Publish), or you can discard it altogether (click Move to Trash).

FIGURE 4-9

Here's the finished post, transplanted into the stock layout of your WordPress site. The circled section is the content you contributed. WordPress has added plenty of details, like the date above your post and the author byline below it. You'll learn to take charge of these details in this chapter and the next.

Magic Tea House

Tea Emporium and Small Concert Venue

🔎 Search

Home   Sample Page

Posted on June 6, 2012   ← Previous

Announcing Teas from Kuala Lumpur

From the bustling metropolis of Kuala Lumpur come some of the most exotic and exciting Malaysian teas. Deeply fragrant, rich in antioxidants, and possessed of a unmatched subtlety of flavor, these teas are the perfect acquisition for rich executives, exciting young people, or discriminating tea epicures.

Stop by our store to try these enchanting teas today. But hurry—we've purchased small quantities, and when they sell out, there will be nowhere else to buy them in the Western hemisphere.

This entry was posted in Uncategorized by not_an_admin*. Bookmark the permalink.

Why Your Post Might Look a Little Different

If you try out these steps on your own WordPress site (and you should), you might not get exactly the same page as shown in Figure 4-9. For example, the date information, the author byline, and the Previous link (which lets you jump to the post that was published just before this one), may be positioned in different spots or have slightly different wording. If you created your site on WordPress.com, you'll get social media sharing buttons at the bottom of your post, which make it easier for your readers to talk about you on Facebook and Twitter. And there are other differences in the formatting and arrangement of your site, if you care to dig around.

You might assume that these alterations represent feature differences—for example, things that WordPress.com sites can do that self-hosted WordPress sites can't. But that isn't the case. Instead, this variability is the result of different themes, plug-ins, and WordPress settings.

The best advice is this: don't get hung up on these differences. Right now, the content of your site is in your hands, but the other details (like the placement of the sidebar and the font used for the post text) are beyond your control. But in Chapter 5, when you learn how to change to a new theme or customize a current one, these differences will begin to evaporate. And by the time you reach the end of Part Two in this book, you'll be able to customize a self-hosted WordPress site or a WordPress.com site to look the way you want it to.

Browsing Your Posts

Adding a single post is easy. But to get a feel for what a real, thriving blog looks like, you need to add several new posts. When you do, you'll find that WordPress arranges your posts in the traditional way: one after the other, in reverse chronological order.

To take a look, head to the home page of your blog (Figure 4-10). To get there, just enter your WordPress site address, without any extra information tacked onto the end of the URL. Or, if you're currently viewing a post, click the Home button in the menu bar (just under the header section and the stock picture).

The number of posts you see on the home page depends on your WordPress settings. Ordinarily, you get a batch of 10 posts at a time. If you scroll to the bottom of the home page, you can click the "Older posts" link to load up the next 10. If you want to show more or fewer posts at once, choose Settings→Reading and change the "Blog pages show at most" setting to the number you want.

WordPress.com sites include an infinite scroll feature. When it's switched on, you won't see the "Older posts" link. Instead, WordPress loads new posts as you scroll down, creating an ever-expanding page (until you reach the very first post on the site). To turn this feature off, choose Settings→Reading and then turn off the checkbox next to "Scroll Infinitely."

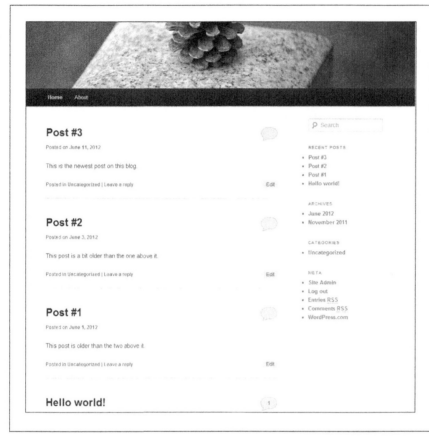

FIGURE 4-10

When you visit the home page of a blog, you start out with a reverse chronological view that puts the most recent post first. If you don't like to scroll, the sidebar on the right gives you several more ways to browse through posts.

You don't need to read every post in a WordPress site from newest to oldest. Instead, you can use one of the many other ways WordPress gives you to browse posts:

- **By most recent.** The Recent Posts list lets you quickly jump to one of the five most recently created posts. It's the first set of links in the sidebar on the right.

- **By month.** Using the Archives list, you can see a month's worth of posts. For example, click "June 2012" to see all the posts published that month, in reverse chronological order. Some WordPress blogs also include a calendar for post browsing, but if you want that you'll need to add it yourself (see page 149 to learn how).

- **By category or tag.** Later in this chapter, you'll learn how to place your posts in categories and add descriptive tags. Once you take these steps, you'll have another way to hunt through your content, using either the Categories list in the sidebar or the category and tag links that WordPress adds to the end of every post.

- **By author.** Click the name at the bottom of the post, and you'll see all the posts that person has created for this site, in reverse chronological order (as always). This isn't terribly useful right now, but it makes more sense when you create a blog that has multiple authors, as you'll learn to do in Chapter 11.

- **Using a search.** Just type in a keyword or two you'd like to find in the search box, which appears at the top-right of your site, and then press Enter. WordPress will search the title and body of each post, and show you a list of matching posts.

FREQUENTLY ASKED QUESTION

How Do I Change My Home Page?

I don't like the look of my home page. Is there anything I can do to change it?

The home page is the first thing visitors see on your website. For that reason, it's no surprise that it's one of the things WordPress authors want to tweak first. Here are some of your options:

- **Change the number of posts.** Want to see more (or fewer) than 10 posts at a time? On the dashboard, choose Settings→Reading. In the "Blog pages show at most" box, type in a different number, and then click Save Changes.

- **Show post summaries.** Ordinarily, WordPress shows the entire post on the home page. If you like to write thorough, detailed posts with plenty of text and pictures

(or if you're just incurably long-winded), you would probably prefer to show a brief summary instead. You'll learn how to pull off this trick on page 192.

- **Show a static page.** If you'd rather show a custom home page that you've designed, instead of a list of recent posts, you need to create a *static page*. You'll learn how to do that—and use it for your home page—in Chapter 7.

These are just a few examples. As you read this book, many more options will open up. For example, in Chapter 10 you'll learn how to create a home page that uses image thumbnails (page 330). And when you consider the advanced theme-editing techniques in Chapter 14, you'll see how to create a home page that displays a list of categorized links to just the posts you want.

Delayed Publishing

Sometimes, you might decide your post is ready to go, but you want to wait a little before putting it on the Web. For example, you might want your post to coincide with an event or product announcement. Or maybe you want your post to appear at a certain time of day, rather than the 2:00 AM time you wrote it. Or maybe you simply want to add a bit of a buffer in case you get new information or have a last-minute change of heart.

In all these situations, you can choose to save your post as a draft (page 96) and then publish it later. That gives you complete control over when the post appears, but it also forces you to make a return trip to your computer. A different approach is to use *delayed publishing*, which allows you to specify a future publication time. Before that time arrives, you may return and edit your post (or even cancel your upcoming post publication plan). But if you do nothing, the post will magically appear, at exactly the time you specified.

To use delayed publishing, follow these steps:

1. **Before you start, make sure WordPress has the right time settings (page 91).**

   If WordPress thinks you're in a different time zone, its clock won't match yours, and when you tell it to publish a post at a certain time, it will actually appear a few hours before or after you expect.

2. **To write your post, choose Posts→Add New in the dashboard.**

   Write your post in the usual way.

3. **In the Publish box, click the Edit link next to "Publish immediately."**

   A new group of settings drops into view (Figure 4-11).

4. **Use the provided boxes to pick a forthcoming date and the exact time when the post should go live.**

   Here, WordPress uses a 24-hour clock, so put in 14:00 for 2:00 PM.

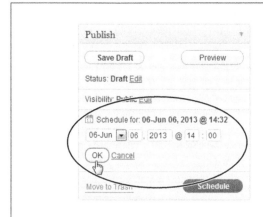

FIGURE 4-11

WordPress lets you schedule publication down to the minute.

5. **Click OK to apply your changes.**

   At this point, the Publish button turns into a Schedule button.

6. **Click the Schedule button to commit to publishing the post.**

   WordPress will wait until the time you specify, and then publish your work.

   If you decide you don't actually want to publish the post at the time you set, you can edit the post (as described on page 102) and put the scheduled time to a very distant future date. Or, you can delete the post altogether (page 103).

Changing Your Nickname

If you're running a self-hosted site, you'll notice that after every post you publish, WordPress adds a link with text like this:

This entry was posted in Uncategorized by not_an_admin.* Bookmark the permalink.

You'll learn how to give your post a category—and what a permalink is—in the following sections. But now it's time to focus on a different detail: your *nickname*. By default, WordPress uses your user name as your nickname. That's the name you chose for the administrator account when you created your WordPress site in Chapter 3. If you followed best security practices, your user name will combine letters with numbers or symbols. It won't be obviously guessable—like your real first name.

All this makes for good security but a distinctly lousy byline after your posts. Fortunately, you can easily add a more meaningful and readable nickname (Figure 4-12). In fact, it's even a good practice, because it keeps the name of your administrator account out of the public eye.

FIGURE 4-12

Top: By default, your user name signs every post. Bottom: A nickname makes more sense.

To change your nickname on a self-hosted WordPress site, follow these steps:

1. **From the dashboard, choose Users→My Profile.**

2. **Enter your new name in the Nickname box, in exactly the way you want it to appear.** It's perfectly valid to use just a first name ("Bob"), a first and last name separated by a space ("Bob Jones"), or a made up handle ("SuperEater").

3. **Make sure WordPress has your nickname selected in the "Display name publicly as" box.**

4. **Click Update Profile.**

If you're using the default Twenty Eleven theme on a WordPress.com site, your user name doesn't appear unless your site has multiple authors. However, as you'll discover in Chapter 5, many other themes *do* display an author byline, so it's worth setting a good display name. Here's how:

1. **On the dashboard, choose Users→My Profile.**

2. **Enter your new name in the "Display name publicly as" box, exactly the way you want it to appear.**

3. **Click Update Profile.**

> **NOTE** You can change your nickname any time. WordPress will use your new name for every new post you write and will change the byline for every post you've already written. This is one of the benefits of dynamic websites like the ones you create with WordPress—they're intelligent enough to keep everything up-to-date.

Editing a Post

Many people assume that posting on a blog is like sending an email message: you compose your thoughts, write your content as best you can, and then send it out to meet the world. But the truth is that you can tinker with your posts long after you've published them.

WordPress gives you two easy ways to edit a post. If you're logged in as the site administrator and you're viewing a post, you'll see an Edit button or an Edit link somewhere on the page (its exact position depends on your theme). Click that link, and WordPress takes you to the Edit Post page, which looks almost identical to the Add New Post page. In fact, the only difference is that the Publish button has been renamed "Update." Using the Edit Post page, you can change any detail you want, from correcting a single typo to replacing the entire post. When you finish making changes, click the Update button to commit your edit.

Another way to pick a post for editing is to use the dashboard. First, choose Posts→All Posts, which shows you a list of all the posts you've published (Figure 4-13). Find the post you want to edit, hover over it, and then click the Edit link to get to the Edit Post page, where you can make your changes.

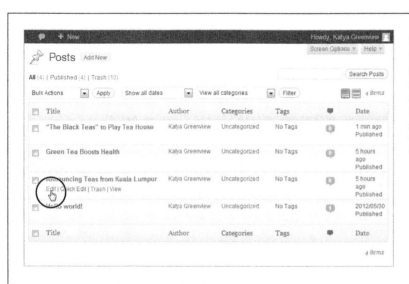

FIGURE 4-13

The Posts page lists your posts in reverse chronological order, starting with the most recent, and including any drafts (page 96). When you hover over a post, you'll see several additional links that let you edit, delete, or view the post.

Along with the Edit link, the Posts page includes a Quick Edit link. Unlike Edit, Quick Edit keeps you in the Posts page, but pops open a panel that lets you edit some of the post details. For example, you can use Quick Edit to change a post's title, but you can't use it to change the actual post text.

Being able to edit in WordPress is a nearly essential feature. Eventually, even the best site will get something wrong. There's no shame in opening up an old post to correct an error, clean up a typing mistake, or even scrub out a bad joke.

NOTE Unlike some blogging and content management systems, WordPress doesn't display any sort of timestamp or message about when you last edited a post. If you want that, you'll need to add it as part of your edit. For example, you might tack an italicized paragraph (page 169) onto the bottom of a post that says "This post edited to include the full list of names" or "Updated on January 25th with the latest survey numbers."

Deleting a Post

As you've just seen, you can edit anything you've ever written on your WordPress website, at any time, without leaving any obvious fingerprints. You can even remove posts altogether.

The trick to deleting posts is to use the Posts page (Figure 4-13). Find the post you want to vaporize, and then click Trash. Or, in the Edit Post page, click the "Move to Trash" link that appears in the Publish box.

TIP Now that you know how to remove a post, try out your new skill with the "Hello world!" example post that WordPress adds to every new blog. There's really no reason to keep it.

Trashed posts aren't completely gone. If you discover you removed a post that you actually want, don't panic. WordPress gives you two ways to get your post back.

If you realize your mistake immediately after you trash the post, look for the message "Item moved to Trash. Undo." It appears in a yellow box at the top of the Posts page. Click the Undo link, and your post returns immediately to both the Posts list and your site.

If you want to restore a slightly older trashed post, you need to dive into the Trash. Fortunately, it's easy (and not at all messy). First, click Posts→All Posts to get to the Posts page. Then click the Trash link that appears just above the list of posts (Figure 4-14). You'll see every post that's currently in the trash. Find the one you want, hover over it, and then click Restore to resurrect it (or click Delete Permanently to make sure no one will find it again, ever).

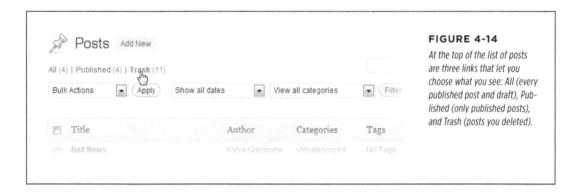

FIGURE 4-14

At the top of the list of posts are three links that let you choose what you see: All (every published post and draft), Published (only published posts), and Trash (posts you deleted).

NOTE Of course, removing posts from your blog and scrubbing content from the Web are two vastly different things. For example, if you post something impolite about your boss and remove it a month later, the content can live on in the cache that search engines keep and in Internet archival sites like the Wayback Machine (*http:// web.archive.org*). So always think before you post, because WordPress doesn't include tools to reclaim your job or repair your online reputation.

Creating a Sticky Post

As you know, WordPress orders posts by date on the home page, with the most recent post occupying the top spot. But you might create an important post that you want to feature at the top of the list, regardless of its date. For example, you might write up a bulletin that announces that your business is temporarily closing for renovations, or answer a frequently asked questions ("No, there are no more seatings available for this Sunday's Lobster Fest"). To keep your post at the top of the list so it can catch your readers' eyes, you need to turn it into a *sticky post*.

NOTE WordPress displays all your sticky posts before all your normal posts. If you have more than one sticky post, it lists the most recent one first.

You can designate a post as a sticky when you first write it (in the Add New Post page) or when you edit it later (in the Edit Post page). Either way, you use the Publish box. Next to the label "Visibility: Public," click Edit. A few more options will drop into view (including the private post options you'll explore on page 371). To make your post sticky, turn on the checkbox next to "Stick this post to the front page," and then click Publish or Update to confirm your changes.

The only caveat with sticky posts is that they stay sticky forever—or until you "unstick" them. The quickest way to do that is to choose Posts→All Posts, find the sticky post in the list, and then click the Quick Edit link underneath it. Finally, turn off the "Make this post sticky" checkbox and then click Update.

The Path to Blogging Success

There's no secret trick to building a successful blog. Whether you're recording your thoughts or promoting a business, you should follow a few basic guidelines:

- **Make sure your content is worth reading.** As the oft-reported slogan states, *content is king*. The best way to attract new readers, lure them in for repeat visits, and inspire them to tell their friends about you, is to write something worth reading. If you're creating a topical blog (say, putting your thoughts down about politics, literature, or gourmet marshmallows), your content needs to be genuinely *interesting*. If you're creating a business blog (for example, promoting your indie record store or selling your real estate services), it helps to have content that's truly *useful* (say, "How to Clean Old Records" or "The

Best Chicago Neighborhoods to Buy In").

- **Add new content regularly.** Nothing kills a site like stale content. Blogs are particularly susceptible to this problem because posts are listed in chronological order, and each post prominently displays the date you wrote it (unless you remove the dates by editing your theme files; see Chapter 13).

- **Keep your content organized.** Even the best content can get buried in the dozens (or hundreds) of posts you'll write. Readers can browse through your monthly archives or search for keywords in a post, but neither approach is convenient. Instead, a good blog is ruthlessly arranged using *categories* and *tags* (see the next section).

Organizing Your Posts

WordPress gives you two complementary tools for organizing your posts: *categories* and *tags*. Both work by grouping related posts together. In the following sections, you'll learn about both, and how to use them effectively.

Understanding Categories

A category is a short text description that describes the topic of a group of posts. For example, the Magic Tea House uses categories like *Tea* (posts about teas for sale), *Events* (posts about concert events at the tea house), and *News* (posts about other developments, like renovations or updated business hours).

Categories are really just text labels, and you can pick any category names you want. For example, the categories Tea, Events, and News could just as easily have been named Teas for Sale, Concerts, and Miscellaneous, without changing the way the categories work.

In a respectable WordPress site, every post has a category. (If you don't assign a category, WordPress automatically puts your post in a category named Uncat-egorized, which presents a bit of a logical paradox.) Most of the time, posts should have just one category. Putting a post in more than one category is a quick way to clutter up the structure of your site, and confuse anyone who's browsing your posts one category at a time.

You don't need to create all your categories at once. Instead, you can add them as needed (for example, when you create a new post that needs a new category). Of course, you'll have an easier time organizing your site if you identify your main categories early on.

It's up to you to decide how to categorize posts and how many categories you want. For example, the Magic Tea House site could just as easily have divided the same posts into more categories, or into different criteria, as shown in Figure 4-15. The box on page 107 has some tips for choosing good categories.

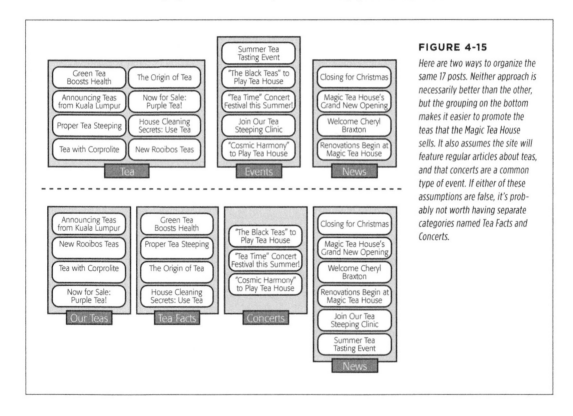

FIGURE 4-15

Here are two ways to organize the same 17 posts. Neither approach is necessarily better than the other, but the grouping on the bottom makes it easier to promote the teas that the Magic Tea House sells. It also assumes the site will feature regular articles about teas, and that concerts are a common type of event. If either of these assumptions are false, it's probably not worth having separate categories named Tea Facts and Concerts.

How to Choose Good Categories

To choose the right categories, you need to imagine your site, up and running, several months down the road. What posts does it have? How do people find the content they want? If you can answer these questions, you're well on the way to choosing the best categories.

First, you need to choose categories that distribute your posts *well.* If a single category has 90 percent of your posts, you probably need new—or different—categories. Similarly, if a category accounts for less than 2 percent of your posts, you may have too many categories. (Although there are exceptions—perhaps you're planning to write more on that topic later, or you want to separate a very small section of special-interest posts from the rest of your content.)

You may also want to factor in the sheer number of posts you plan to write. If your site is big and you post often, you may want to consider more categories. For example, assuming the Magic Tea House has a couple of dozen posts, a category split like this works fine: Tea (70%), Concerts (20%), News (10%). But if you have hundreds of posts, you'll probably want to subdivide the big Tea group into smaller groups.

It also makes sense to create categories that highlight the content you want to promote. For example, if you're creating a site for a furniture store, you'll probably create categories based on your products (Couches, Sofas, Dining Room Tables, and so on). Similarly, the Magic Tea House can split its Tea category into Our Teas and Tea Facts to better highlight the teas they sell (Figure 4-15).

Finally, it's important to consider how your readers will want to browse your information. If you're a lifestyle coach writing articles about personal health, you might decide to add categories like Good Diet, Strength Training, and Weight Loss, because you assume that your readers will zero in on one of these subjects and eagerly devour all the content there. Be careful that you don't split post categories too small, however, because readers could miss content they might otherwise enjoy. For example, if you have both a Good Diet Tips and Superfoods category, a reader might explore one category without noticing the similar content in the other. This is a good place to apply the size rule again—if you can't stuff both categories full of good content, consider collapsing them into one group or using subcategories (page 109).

Categorizing Posts

You can easily assign a category to a post when you first add the post. Here's how:

1. **Choose Posts→Add New to start a new post.**

   Or, you can start editing an existing post (page 102), and change its category. The Add New Post and Edit Post pages work the same way, so it's easy.

2. **Look for the Categories box.**

   You'll find it near the bottom-right corner of the page, under the Publish and Format boxes (Figure 4-16).

   If the category you want exists, skip to step 5.

   If your post needs a new category, one that you haven't created yet, continue on to step 3.

FIGURE 4-16

The Categories box has two tabs. The default tab (All Categories), lists all your categories in alphabetical order. If you've created quite a few categories, you might find it faster to choose your category from the Most Used tab, which lists the categories you use most often.

3. **At the bottom of the Categories box, click Add New Category.**

   This expands the Categories box, so you can enter your category information.

4. **Enter the category name in the box underneath the Add New Category link, and then click Add New Category.**

   Don't worry about the Parent Category box underneath—you'll learn to use that on page 109, when you create subcategories.

   Once you add your category, you see it appear in the Categories box.

5. **Find the category you want to use in the list, and then turn on the checkbox next to it.**

   When you add a new category, WordPress automatically turns on its checkbox, because it assumes this is the category you want to assign to your post. If it isn't, simply turn off the checkbox and pick something else.

You can add a post to more than one category, but it's best not to unless you're a pro. Doing so is likely to mask a poor choice of categories, and it makes it hard to change your categories later on.

6. **Carry on editing your post.**

   That's it. When you publish your post, WordPress assigns it the category you chose (Figure 4-17). If you didn't choose any category, WordPress automatically puts it in a category named (paradoxically) Uncategorized.

TIP Ordinarily, the category named Uncategorized is WordPress's *default category*—that means WordPress uses it for new posts unless you specify otherwise. However, you can tell WordPress to use a different default category. Simply choose Settings→Writing, and pick one of your categories in the Default Post Category list.

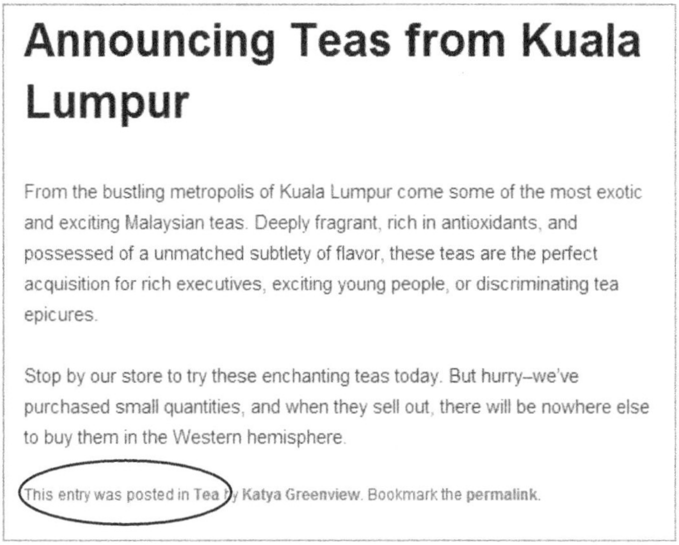

Announcing Teas from Kuala Lumpur

From the bustling metropolis of Kuala Lumpur come some of the most exotic and exciting Malaysian teas. Deeply fragrant, rich in antioxidants, and possessed of a unmatched subtlety of flavor, these teas are the perfect acquisition for rich executives, exciting young people, or discriminating tea epicures.

Stop by our store to try these enchanting teas today. But hurry—we've purchased small quantities, and when they sell out, there will be nowhere else to buy them in the Western hemisphere.

 This entry was posted in Tea by Katya Greenview. Bookmark the permalink.

FIGURE 4-17

This post is in the Tea category. Click the link, and you'll see all the posts in the Tea category. (You get the same effect if you click Tea in the Categories list in the sidebar.)

Using Subcategories

If you have a huge site with plenty of posts and no shortage of categories, you may find that you can organize your content better with *subcategories*.

The idea behind subcategories is to take a large category and split it into two or more smaller groups. However, rather than make these new categories completely separate, WordPress keeps them as subcategories of the original category, which it calls the *parent category*. For example, the Magic Tea House site could make Tea a parent category, and create subcategories named Black Tea, Green Tea, Rooibos, and Herbal Tea.

Done right, subcategories have two potential benefits:

- **You can show a category tree.** A category tree arranges the list of your categories in multiple levels, to show their hierarchy. In a complex site with lots of categories, most readers find that this makes it easier to browse the categories and understand how the different topics you cover are related. You'll learn how to build a category tree in just a moment.

- **Visitors can browse posts by subcategory or parent category.** That means that people using the Magic Tea House site can see all the tea posts at once (by browsing the Tea category) or they can drill down to the subcategory of tea that interests them the most.

You can create subcategories using the Categories box—in fact, it's just as easy as creating ordinary categories (Figure 4-18). The only requirement is that you create the parent category first. Then, enter the subcategory name, pick the parent category in the Parent Category list, and click Add New Category.

NOTE Yes, you can create subcategories inside of subcategories. But doing so can complicate life, and make it more difficult to fit a proper category tree in your sidebar. If possible, stick with one level of subcategories.

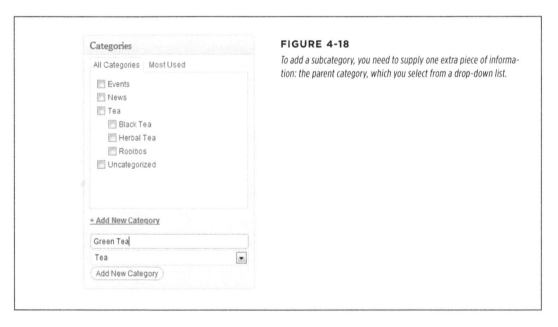

FIGURE 4-18

To add a subcategory, you need to supply one extra piece of information: the parent category, which you select from a drop-down list.

WordPress displays categories hierarchically in the Categories box. That means that you'll see your subcategories (like Green Tea) displayed underneath the parent category (Tea). However, there's an exception—when you first add a new subcategory, WordPress puts it at the top of the list, and it stays there until you refresh the page or add a new category. Don't let this quirk worry you; your new category is still properly attached to its parent.

NOTE When you assign a subcategory to a post, make sure you pick the subcategory only, *not* the parent category. That means that if you want to add a post about green tea, you should turn on the checkbox next to the Green Tea box, but *not* the Tea box. Because Tea is the parent category, people who browse the Tea category will automatically see your Green Tea posts.

When you start adding subcategories to your site, you'll probably be disappointed by how they appear in the Categories list, the category-browsing links that appear in the sidebar alongside your posts. The standard list of categories is a flat, one-dimensional list in alphabetical order. You can't see the relationships between parent categories and subcategories (Figure 4-19, left).

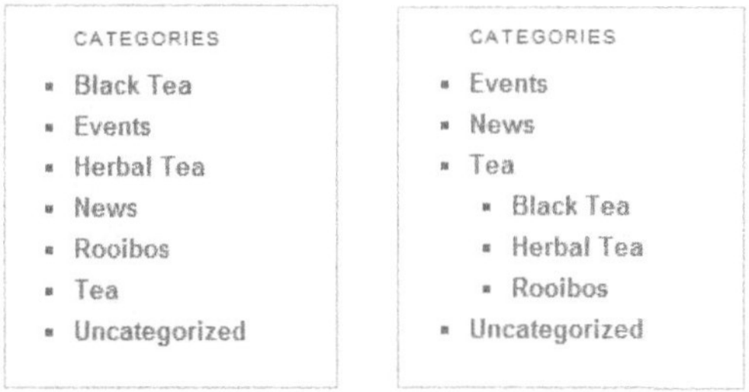
CATEGORIES
Black Tea
Events
Herbal Tea
News
Rooibos
Tea
Uncategorized
CATEGORIES
Events
News
Tea
Black Tea
Herbal Tea
Rooibos
Uncategorized

FIGURE 4-19

Ordinarily, the Categories list ignores subgroups (left). But fear not, with a simple configuration change you can get a more readable tree (right).

NOTE The Categories list shows only the categories you currently use. So if you create a new category but don't assign it to a post, you won't see it in the Categories list.

Fortunately, it's easy to change the standard list of categories into a tree of categories, by borrowing a theme-altering trick you'll explore in more detail in the next chapter. Technically, the Categories list is known as a *widget*. Like all widgets, it can be moved, removed, and reconfigured. Here's how:

1. **On the dashboard, choose Appearance→Widgets.**

   The Widgets page shows you all the individual ingredients that WordPress puts into the sidebar on your site.

2. **In the Main Sidebar box, find the Categories widget.**

   This is the widget that creates the list of categories that appears next to your posts.

3. **Click the down-pointing arrow on the right-side of the widget.**

   This expands the Categories widget, so you can see its settings.

4. **Turn on the checkbox in the "Show hierarchy" settings and then click Save.**

   Now return to your site and admire the result (Figure 4-19, right).

NOTE   No matter what setting you tweak, WordPress always orders categories alphabetically. If you want to put a specific category on top, you need to put in some extra work and create a menu (page 210).

Managing Categories

As you've seen, you can create a category whenever you need, right from the Add New Post or Edit Post page. However, the WordPress dashboard also includes a page for managing categories. To get there, choose Posts→Categories and you'll see a split page that lets you add to or edit your categories (Figure 4-20).

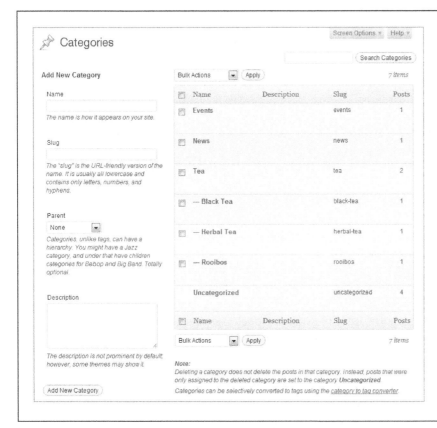

FIGURE 4-20

The Categories page includes a section on the left for adding new categories, and a detailed list of all your categories on the right. The categories list works in much the same way as the list of posts on the Posts page. Hover over a category that interests you, and you can choose to edit or delete it.

The Categories page lets you perform a few tasks that aren't possible from the lowly Categories box:

- **Delete categories you don't use.** When you take this step, WordPress reassigns any posts in the category to the default category, which is Uncategorized (unless you've changed it in the Settings→Writing page).

- **Edit a category.** For example, you might want to take an existing category and rename it, or make it a subcategory by giving it a parent.

- **Enter extra category information.** You already know that every category has a name and, optionally, a parent. In addition, categories have room for two pieces of information that you haven't used yet: a slug and a description. The *slug* is a simplified version of the category name that appears in the URL when a visitor browses posts by category (see the box on this page). The *description* explains what the category is all about. Some themes display category descriptions in their category-browsing pages. You'll see this feature in action on page 480.

UP TO SPEED

Browsing Categories with a URL

The category slug is the key to a nifty WordPress feature. Using your website address with the slug, you can easily call up a list of posts in any category.

For example, imagine you create a category named Herbal Tea. If you don't specify a slug, WordPress will cook one up based on your category name. First it replaces every uppercase letter with a lowercase one, and then it replaces spaces with hyphens (-), and lastly it strips out unsupported special characters, if you used them. As a result, the slug name for the Herbal Tea category becomes *herbal-tea*.

To use the slug name, you need to start out with site address (*http://magicteahouse.net*) and then add */category/* to the end, like this:

http://magicteahouse.net/category/

Then you add the category slug:

http://magicteahouse.net/category/herbal-tea

Type this into your browser, and you'll see all the posts in the Herbal Tea category.

Incidentally, this is exactly what happens when you click the Herbal Tea category name at the bottom of a post or in the Categories widget. But now that you understand how Word-Press structures category URLs, you can use them anywhere you need them. You can also see why you might customize the category slug. Usually, it's to further simplify the URL—for example, by replacing *herbal-tea* with *herbal*.

Understanding Tags

Like categories, tags are text labels that add bits of information to a post. But unlike categories, a post can (and should) have multiple tags. For that reason, the process of applying to tags is less strict than the process of putting your post in the right category.

Tags are often more specific than categories. For example, if you're writing a review of a movie, you might use Movie Reviews as your category and the movie and director's name as tags.

Follow these guidelines when you use tags:

- **Don't over-tag.** Instead, choose the best 5 to 10 tags for your content. If you're using WordPress.com and you create a post with 15 tags or more, it's much less likely to appear in the WordPress.com tag cloud (page 48), which means new visitors are less likely to stumble across your blog.

- **Keep your tags short and precise.** Pick "Grateful Dead" over "Grateful Dead Concerts."

- **Reuse your tags on different posts.** Once you pick a good tag, put it to work wherever it applies. After all, tags are designed to help people find related posts. And never create a similarly named tag for the same topic. For example, if you decide to add the tag "New York Condos," and then you use the tag "NY Condos" and "Condo Market," you've created three completely separate tags that won't share the same posts.

- **Consider using popular tags.** If you're on WordPress.com, check out popularly used tags (page 48) and consider using them in your posts, when they apply. If you're trying to attract search engine traffic, you might consider using hot search keywords for your tags (page 422).

- **Don't duplicate your category with a tag of the same name.** That's because WordPress treats categories and tags in a similar way, as bits of information that describe a post. Duplicating a category with a tag is just a waste of a tag.

TIP Here's some advice to help you get straight about categories and tags. Think of the category as the *fundamental grouping* that tells WordPress how a post fits into the structure of your site. Think of a tag as a *searching convenience* that helps readers hunt for content or find a related post.

Tagging Posts

Adding a tag to a post is even easier than giving it a category. When creating a post (in the Add New Post page) or editing a post (in the Edit Post page), look for the Tags box, which appears just under the Categories box.

The Tag box gives you three ways to add tags:

- Type a tag into the text box, and then click the Add button. Repeat.

- Type all your tags at once into the tag text box. Make sure you place a comma between each tag, as shown in Figure 4-21.

- Click the "Choose from the most used tags" link and pick from the tags you've used for other posts.

FIGURE 4-21

Left: Right now, this post has one tag, Kuala Lumpur. It's about to get three more. Right: Now the post has four tags. If you change your mind, you can remove a tag by clicking the tiny X icon that appears next to it.

When you publish a post, the byline will list the post's category and all its tags (Figure 4-22). You can follow these links to browse similarly-tagged posts. Many blogs also use a *tag cloud*, a cluster of tag links, sized in proportion to how often you use them (in other words, in proportion to how many posts feature that tag). The default WordPress site layout doesn't use a tag cloud, but you can add one easily using the Tag Cloud widget. You learn how on page 154.

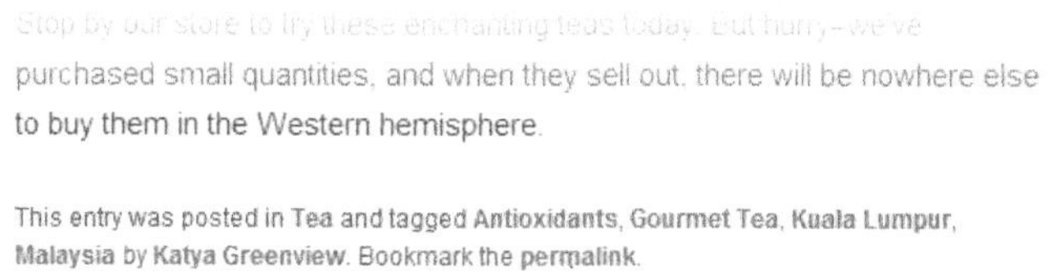

Stop by our store to try these enchanting teas today. But hurry—we've purchased small quantities, and when they sell out, there will be nowhere else to buy them in the Western hemisphere.

This entry was posted in Tea and tagged Antioxidants, Gourmet Tea, Kuala Lumpur, Malaysia by Katya Greenview. Bookmark the permalink.

FIGURE 4-22

The exact post byline depends on your theme, but most list the categories and tags used in a post.

As with categories, tags have their own management page, which you can see by choosing Posts→Tags. However, there's only one additional piece of information you can edit for a tag: its slug. And just like categories, you can browse all the posts that use a specific tag using a URL like *http://magicteahouse.net/tags/kuala-lumpur*.

How to Get High-Quality URLs

Every post you put on a WordPress site has its own unique web address, or URL. So far, you haven't really thought about what those URLs look like. After all, nobody *needs* to type in a URL to read a post. Instead, people can simply visit the front page of your site and click through to whatever content interests them.

However, seasoned web designers know that URLs matter—not just for the front page of your site, but for each distinct bit of content. One reason is that search engines pay attention to the keywords in a URL, so they treat something like *http://wastedminutes.com/best_time_wasters* differently from *http://wastedminutes.com/post/viewer.php?postid=3980&cat=83*. All other factors being equal, if someone searches for "time wasters" in Google, the search engine is more likely to suggest the first page than the second.

Another important detail is the *lifetime* of your URLs. Ideally, a good URL never changes. Think of a URL as a contract between you and your readers. The promise is that if they bookmark a post, the URL will still work when they return to read it, even months or years later (assuming your entire site hasn't gone belly-up in the interim). WordPress takes this principle to heart. In fact, it calls the unique URL that's assigned to every post a *permalink*, emphasizing its permanent nature.

As you'll soon see, WordPress will happily give your posts meaningful URLs that last forever, but you might need to help it out a bit. Before you can do that, you need to understand a bit more about how the WordPress permalink system works. The details differ depending on whether you're using WordPress.com or you've installed WordPress on your web host. The following sections lay out the essentials.

Permalinks in WordPress.com

On a WordPress.com site, permalinks always follow this structure:

```
http://site/year/month/day/post-name
```

For example, if you create a blog named *lazyfather.wordpress.com* on November 27, 2012, WordPress will automatically create a post named "Hello world!" that has a permalink like this:

```
http://lazyfather.wordpress.com/2012/11/27/hello-world
```

The year, month, and day numbers are set when you create the post. The last part—the post name—is based on the title of the post. WordPress changes spaces to hyphens and ignores funky characters (like @, #, and $). If you create two posts with the same name on the same day, WordPress adds a number to the end of the second post title. (If you create a post with the same name but on a different day, there's no problem, because the first part of the URL is already different.)

WordPress's URL-generating strategy is a pretty good starting point. However, you can change the URL for any post when you create it. This is a great feature if you think your post title is ridiculously long or you think you have an idea for a clearer URL that's more likely to net you some serious search engine traffic. Page 119 explains how to change a post's permalink.

Permalinks on a Self-Hosted Site

Here's the good news: If you have a self-hosted version of WordPress, you can choose the permalink style. And here's the bad news: If you don't change it yourself, you'll be stuck with distinctly old-fashioned URLs.

The default permalink style is created by a self-hosted site and are short but rather cryptic URLs that use the post ID. They follow this structure:

```
http://site/?p=id
```

For example, if you create a WordPress blog at *lazyfather.com/blog*, the first "Hello world!" post gets a permalink like this:

```
http://lazyfather.com/blog/?p=1
```

The *post ID* is a unique, sequential number that WordPress gives to every new post. So it's no surprise that the first post has a post ID of 1.

This permalink style is short, but it has no other benefits. The permalinks are meaningless to other people and search engines, because it's impossible to tell what a given post is about. Can you tell the difference between *http://lazyfather.com/blog/?p=13* (a post about cute family pets) and *http://lazyfather.com/blog/?p=26* (a post about the coming Mayan apocalypse)? The post ID is essentially a secret code that doesn't mean anything to anyone except the web server database that holds the collection of correspondingly numbered posts.

Even if you love the convenience of short URLs (and who doesn't?) you'll almost certainly want to pick a more descriptive permalink structure. Fortunately, WordPress makes it easy. Just follow these steps:

1. **In the dashboard, choose Settings→Permalinks.**

   The Permalinks Setting page appears.

2. **Choose a new permalink style.**

   Your choices are listed under the "Common Settings" heading. Your options include:

- **Default.** This is the WordPress.org standard: brief but obscure permalinks that use the post ID, like *http://magicteahouse.net/?p=13.*

- **Day and name.** This style is the same as the WordPress.com standard. Permalinks include several pieces of information, including the year, month, and date, separated by slashes. At the end is the much more descriptive post name (a simplified version of the post title), as in *http://magicteahouse.net/2013/07/28/announcing-teas-from-kuala-lumpur.*

- **Month and name.** This style is similar to "Day and name," except that it leaves out the date number, giving you a slightly more concise permalink, like *http://magicteahouse.net/2013/07/announcing-teas-from-kuala-lumpur.*

- **Numeric.** This is a nicer looking version of the default style. It uses the post ID, but without including the *?p=* characters. Instead, it adds the text */archives,* as in *http://magicteahouse.net/archives/13.* However, this type of permalink is still as clear as mud.

- **Post name.** This style omits all the date information, and uses just the post name, as in *http://magicteahouse.net/announcing-teas-from-kuala-lumpur.* The advantages of this system are that the permalinks it creates are concise and easy to remember and understand. They don't emphasize the date the content was created, which is important if you have timeless content that you want to refer to months or years later. One disadvantage is that if you give more than one post the same name, WordPress needs to tack a number onto the end of the permalink to make it unique.

- **Custom structure.** This is an advanced option that lets you tell WordPress exactly how it should cook up post permalinks. The most common reason to use a custom structure is because you want the post category to appear in your permalink (as explained in the box on page 119).

TIP If you don't want to emphasize dates and you're willing to put in a bit of extra work to avoid duplicate titles, the "Post name" style is a great choice. If you're concerned about clashing titles, "Month and name" is safer, and if you want to emphasize the exact date of your posts—for example, you're writing time-sensitive or news-like content, "Day and name" is a good choice.

UP TO SPEED

Understanding Permalink Codes

When you choose a permalink style other than Default, you'll notice that WordPress automatically inserts the matching codes in the "Custom structure" box. For example, if you choose "Day and name," these codes appear:

    %year%/%monthnum%/%day%/%postname%

Think of this as a recipe that tells WordPress how to build the permalink. Each code (that's the bit of text between percentage signs, like *%year%* and *%monthnum%*) corresponds to a piece of information that WordPress will stick into the URL.

In this example, four codes are separated by three slashes. When WordPress uses this format, it starts with the site address (as always) and then adds the requested pieces of information, one by one. First, it replaces the %year% code with the four-digit year number:

    http://magicteahouse.net/**2013**/
    %monthnum%/%day%/%postname%

Then it replaces the %monthnum% code with the two-digit month number:

    http://magicteahouse.net/
    2013/**07**/%day%/%postname%

It carries on until the permalink is complete:

    http://magicteahouse.net/2013/07/28/
    the-origin-of-tea

You don't need to understand WordPress's permalink codes in order to use different permalink styles. However, you do need to understand them if you want to create your own recipe for generating permalinks, as described in the box on page 119.

3. **Click Save Changes.**

   WordPress applies the permalink change to your entire site. That means that WordPress will update any posts you already published to the new style. If you're switching from the default style to another style, this never causes a problem, because the ID-based links continue to work. (That's because no matter what permalink style you use, WordPress continues to give each post a unique post ID, which it stores in its database.) However, if you switch to a second permalink style (for example, "Day and name") and then to a third style (say, "Month and name"), the outlook isn't so rosy. Anyone who bookmarked a "Day and name"–style URL will find that it no longer works.

TIP If you want to tweak the way your WordPress site generates permalinks (and if you're using the self-hosted version of WordPress, you almost certainly do), it's best to make that change as soon as possible. Otherwise, changing the permalink style can break the URLs for old posts, frustrating readers who have bookmarked posts on your site. Think twice before tampering with the URL structure of an established site.

Create Permalinks that Include the Category

If you're ambitious, you can make deeper customizations to the way WordPress generates post permalinks. To do that, you need to choose the Custom Structure permalink type, and then fill in your permalink "recipe" with the right codes.

WordPress recognizes 10 codes. More than half are date-related: `%year%` `%monthnum%` `%day%` `%hour%` `%minute%` `%second%`. Additionally, there's a code for the category slug (`%category%`) and the author (`%author%`). Finally, every permalink must end with either the numeric post ID (represented by `%post_id%`) or post name (`%postname%`), because this is the unique detail that identifies the post.

Often, WordPress gurus use a custom permalink structure that adds category information. They do so because they feel that the permalinks are aesthetically nicer—in other words, clearer or more meaningful—or because they think that this increases the chance that search engines will match their post with a related search query.

Here's an example of a custom permalink structure that creates category-specific permalinks:

```
%category%/%postname%
```

Now WordPress creates permalinks that include the category name (in this case, Tea) and the post name (The Origin of Tea), like this:

```
http://magicteahouse.net/tea/the-origin-
of-tea
```

This type of URL doesn't work well if you assigned some of your posts more than one category. In such a case, WordPress picks one of the categories to use in the URL, somewhat unpredictably. (Technically, WordPress uses the category that has the lower category ID, which is whatever one you created first.)

Changing a Post's Permalink

Most WordPress users prefer pretty permalinks—URLs that include the post title. If you're using WordPress.com, your posts always use pretty permalinks. If you're using a self-hosted WordPress site, you get pretty permalinks in every permalink style except Default and Numeric.

However, pretty permalinks aren't always as pretty as they should be. The problem is that a post title doesn't necessarily fit well into a URL. Often, it's overly long, or includes special characters. In this situation, you can help WordPress out by explicitly editing the *slug*—the version of the post name that WordPress uses in your permalinks.

You can change the slug when you add or edit a post. Here's how:

1. **Find the permalink line, which appears just under the post title text box.**

   WordPress creates the slug automatically, once you type in the post title and start entering the post content. After that point, the slug doesn't change, even if you edit the title, unless you edit it explicitly.

2. **Click the Edit button next to the permalink line (Figure 4-23).**

   WordPress converts the portion of the permalink that holds the slug into a text box. You can then edit to your heart's content, so long as you stay away from spaces and special characters, which aren't allowed in URLs. The best permalinks are short, specific, and unlikely to be duplicated by other posts. (Although WordPress is smart enough to refuse to use a slug you assigned to another post.)

3. **Click OK to make your change official.**

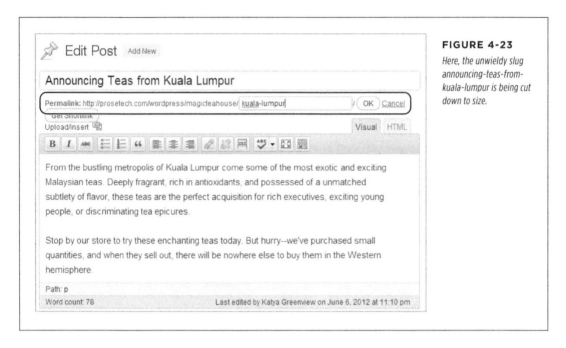

FIGURE 4-23

Here, the unwieldy slug announcing-teas-from-kuala-lumpur is being cut down to size.

> **NOTE** WordPress is very conscientious about dealing with old permalinks. If visitors try to find a post using an old permalink that has since changed, WordPress automatically forwards them to the right post and correct URL. This trick makes sure that old bookmarks and search engines that link to your site keep working.

Getting a Shorter Version of Your URL

Pretty permalinks are memorable and, if you don't include the date information, fairly simple. However, they can still be inconveniently long for certain situations. Sometimes, you might need a shorter URL that points to a post—one that's easier to jot down, or fit in the confines on a Twitter message. And although you can cut a permalink down to size when you create a post, it still might not be short enough.

WordPress is ready to help. It gives you two ways to reach every post you create: a permalink (like the ones you've been using so far), and a leaner URL called a *shortlink*. Shortlinks work just as well as permalinks, and you can use both types of link at once, depending on what you need, without confusing WordPress.

Shortlinks look different depending on whether you're using a self-hosted WordPress site or WordPress.com. In a self-hosted site, the shortlink simply uses the Default permalink style. It's your site address, with the numeric post ID:

http://magicteahouse.net/?p=13

WordPress.com takes a different approach. It uses its own URL-shortening service, called WP.me, to ensure that you get a micro URL like this:

http://wp.me/p21m89-1a

Even though it points to what seems like a completely different website, this shortlink redirects visitors to the right blog post on the right WordPress.com site. Best of all, the entire shortlink requires a mere 22 characters, which is just about as short as they come.

WordPress doesn't offer the shortlink option until you've published your post. In fact, to get it, you need to start editing your post (page 102). Once you're there, click Get Shortlink button that appears in the permalink line (or just underneath it, depending on how much room WordPress has). WordPress pops open a new window with the shortlink for your post (Figure 4-24).

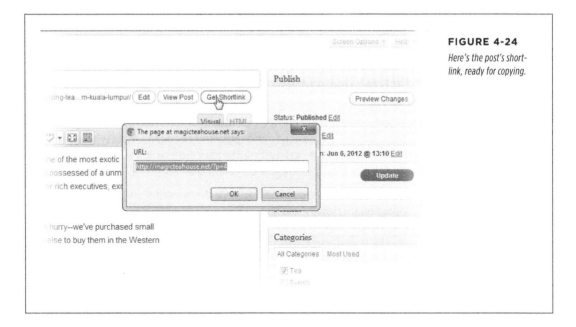

FIGURE 4-24

Here's the post's short-link, ready for copying.

Making Your Shortlinks Even Smaller

If you have a self-hosted WordPress site, the shortlink might not be as short as you want. It works great if you're using WordPress to run your entire site and you have a nice, short domain name. But if you have a long domain name with your WordPress content in a subfolder, you'll end up with a not-so-short shortlink, like this:

http://prosetech.com/wordpress/magicteahouse/?p=4

It might occur to you to use the WP.me service to get an even shorter URL, but, unfortunately, it's limited to WordPress.com sites. However, there are other UR-shortening services that will take your URL and spit out a tinier version. Popular shorteners include *http://bit.ly* (which Twitter uses for automatic URL-shrinking), *http://TinyUrl.com*, and *http://tiny.cc*.

For example, if you plug your URL into bit.ly, you'll get a new URL, like this:

http://bit.ly/LejGs9

Weighing in at a mere 20 characters, this URL is even shorter than the ones WP.me creates. If someone types that URL into a browser, they'll go first to the bit.ly web server, which will quickly redirect the browser to the original URL. The end result is that your post appears almost immediately.

Using any of these URL shortening services is easy. Just go the website, paste in your URL—either the permalink or shortlink, it doesn't matter—and then copy the new condensed URL.

■ Dashboard Tricks to Save Time and Effort

As you've learned, the dashboard is the key to unlocking your WordPress site. So far you've used it to work with posts: creating them, changing them, and deleting them. You also managed categories and tags, and tweaked a variety of WordPress settings. But you're far from exhausting the dashboard—in fact, you'll spend the better part of this book exploring its nooks and crannies.

Now, here are a few tips that can improve your dashboard skills. You'll learn to customize the dashboard display, get help, and work with lists—basics that will prepare you for the administrative tasks to come.

Being in Two Places at Once

One potential problem with the dashboard is that it lets you view only one page at a time. This limitation can become awkward in some situations. For example, imagine you're in the middle of creating a post when you decide you want to review a setting somewhere else in the dashboard. You *could* save the post as a draft, jump to the settings page, and then return to continue with your post. And for many people, this approach works just fine. But if you're the sort of power user who's comfortable with browser shortcuts, there's another approach that may appeal: opening more than one browser page at a time, with each positioned on a different part of the dashboard.

It all works through the magic of the Ctrl-click—a nifty browser trick where you hold down the Ctrl key (Control on a Mac) while clicking a link. In modern browsers, this causes the target of the link to open in a new tab. This trick doesn't work with all websites, particularly those that use JavaScript routines in the place of ordinary links. But in the WordPress dashboard, it flows without a hitch.

For example, imagine you're at the Add New Post page and you want to review your post display settings. Simply hover over Settings in the dashboard menu and Ctrl-click the Reading link. Keep in mind, however, that if you change something in one tab that affects another, you might not see the results of your change right away. For example, if you add a category in the Categories page while the Add New Post page is open, you won't see it in the Add New Post page unless you refresh the page. (But don't forget to click Save Draft first if you want to keep your post!)

Customizing a Dashboard Page

When you navigate to a dashboard page, you don't always see all the settings you can adjust. WordPress tries hard to offer you real power and flexibility without overloading your brain with features and settings.

However, sometimes you'll need to adjust one of the hidden settings that WordPress doesn't show. (Or, you'll want to hide some of settings WordPress *does* show, just to clear away the visual clutter.) Either way, the secret is the Screen Options button, which controls exactly what WordPress displays on the page.

If you haven't noticed the Screen Options button yet, that's because it's carefully tucked away in the top-left corner of the dashboard (circled in Figure 4-25). However, you'll see it on nearly every dashboard page. When you click Screen Options, a new panel pops into existence at the top of the page (Figure 4-26). To collapse the panel, click the Screen Options button again.

FIGURE 4-25

Almost every dashboard page sports the Screen Options and Help buttons shown here. They're the key to getting more options—and figuring out how they work.

FIGURE 4-26

Here are the screen options for the Add New Post page. Using them, you can manage two things: the controls WordPress displays on the page (using the checkboxes under the "Show on screen" heading), and the way WordPress presents those controls (using the settings under the "Screen Layout" section).

To understand how the Screen Options box works, you need to understand that every checkbox in it corresponds to a gray panel that WordPress can either show or hide. For example, in Figure 4-26, the Format, Categories, Tags, and Featured Image checkboxes are turned on, and so the Format, Categories, Tags, and Featured Image panels appear on the page. (So does the Publish panel, which doesn't have a corresponding checkbox, because WordPress won't let you hide it.)

But the Screen Options box in Figure 4-26 also includes several *unchecked* boxes, such as Excerpt, Send Trackbacks, Custom Fields, and so on. Many of these correspond to panels with less commonly adjusted settings. They're hidden (by default), because WordPress assumes you don't need them, and don't want to be distracted with more details. But if you turn on one (or more) of these checkboxes, the corresponding panel automatically appears on the page.

Not only can you show and hide the panels in a dashboard page, you can also move them around. Just click a title at the top of the panel (like "Categories") and drag it to a new place on the page. WordPress automatically rearranges the other panels to make room. This is a great way to make sure that the options you use most often are right at your fingertips. (Watch out, though: if you click the title of a panel and *don't* drag it somewhere else, WordPress collapses that panel so that only the title remains visible. Click the title again to expand it.)

Finally, there's one really useful dashboard-customization trick that can help when you're creating or editing a huge post. If you click the bottom-right corner of the post editor and drag down (Figure 4-27), you can make the editing box as big as you want.

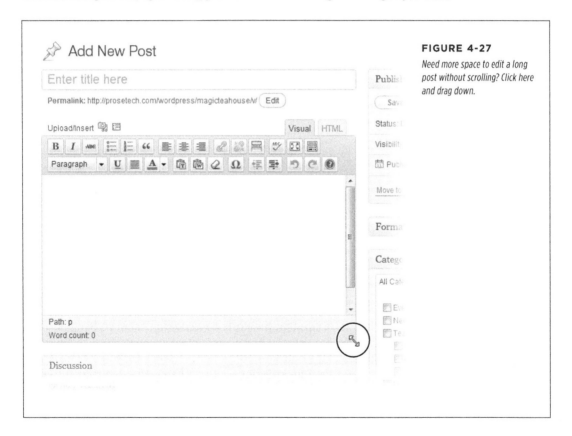

FIGURE 4-27

Need more space to edit a long post without scrolling? Click here and drag down.

Getting Help

Soon, you'll be a WordPress administration guru. But in the meantime, you'll occasionally face perplexing settings in the WordPress dashboard. The Help button isn't perfect, but it can be useful sometimes.

You'll find the Help button right next to the Screen Options button, in the top-right corner of nearly every dashboard page. When you click it, a small panel with help information drops into view. To collapse the panel, click the Help button again. Figure 4-28 shows the help for the Add New Post page.

FIGURE 4-28

WordPress's help box is packed with terse but potentially helpful information. Click a link on the left side to choose your topic. (This example shows what you see when you select "Publish Box.") On the right are additional links that can take you to WordPress's official documentation (be warned, it's sometimes out-of-date) or the forums (where you can ask friendly strangers for help).

Taking Charge of the List of Posts

You've already seen the Posts page, which lists the posts in your site. However, as your site grows larger, it becomes increasingly difficult to manage everything on one page, and in a single table. To get control of your posts, you'll need to develop your searching and filtering skills.

First, it's important to realize that the Posts page doesn't list everything at once. Instead, it shows up to 20 posts at a time—to get more, you need to click the arrow buttons that show up in the bottom-right corner of the list. Or, you can adjust the 20-post limit: just click the Screen Options button, change the number in the Posts box, and click Apply.

> **NOTE** If you allow more posts into your Posts page, you'll get a slower-to-load page and a longer list to scroll through. Of course, there's nothing wrong with bumping up the limit for certain tasks (say, to 100), and then changing it back when you finish.

Changing the number of posts is one way to fit more posts into your list, but it isn't much help if you want to home in on a specific batch of posts that might be scattered throughout your site. In this situation, WordPress has another set of tools to help you out: its filtering controls. Using the drop-down lists at the top of the table of posts (Figure 4-29), you can choose to show only posts that were made in a specific month (for example, "June 2013") or that belong to a specific category (say, "Green Tea").

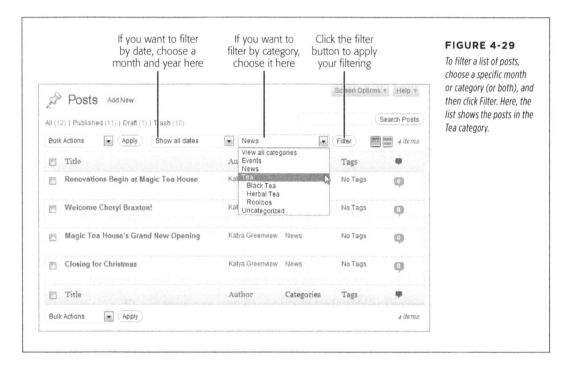

FIGURE 4-29

To filter a list of posts, choose a specific month or category (or both), and then click Filter. Here, the list shows the posts in the Tea category.

Ordinarily, WordPress displays posts in the same reverse-chronological order that they appear on your site. But you can change that by clicking one of the column headings. Click Title to sort alphabetically by headline, or Author to sort alphabetically by writer. Clicking a column more than once reverses the sort order, so if you click Date you'll reorder the list from oldest to newest.

The last trick that the Posts window offers is the search box in the top-right corner, above the posts list. You can search for all the posts that have specific keywords in their title or text. For example, to show posts that talk about veal broth, you would type in *"veal broth"* (using quotation marks if you want to turn both words into a single search term), and then click Search Posts.

Performing Bulk Actions

So far, you've dealt with one post at a time. If you're planning to change the post's title or edit its text, this approach is the only way to go. But if you want to manipulate posts in some other way—for example, change their category, add a keyword, or delete them—the Add Posts page lets you carry out your work in bulk.

The easiest bulk action is deleting. To send a batch of posts to the trash, you follow these simple steps:

1. **Choose Posts→All Posts in the dashboard.**

   That takes you to the familiar All Posts page.

2. **Find the posts you want.**

   If you don't see all the posts you want to remove, you can use the searching or filtering techniques described on page 126.

3. **Turn on the checkbox next to each post you want to remove.**

4. **In the Bulk Actions list, choose "Move to Trash."**

   The Bulk Actions list appears in two places: just above the list of posts, and just underneath it. That way, it's easily accessible no matter where you are.

5. **Click Apply.**

   WordPress moves all the posts you picked to the trash in one quick operation.

You can also use a bulk action to make certain post changes. For example, you can add tags to your post, change the author, or simultaneously publish a group of drafts. The steps are similar, but slightly more involved. Here's what to do:

1. **Choose Posts→All Posts on the dashboard.**

2. **Find the posts you want (using searching or filtering if needed).**

3. **Turn on the checkbox next to each post you want to edit.**

4. **In the Bulk Actions list, choose Edit and then click Apply.**

   A panel appears at the top of the post list with editing options (Figure 4-30).

5. **Manipulate the details you want to change.**

   Using the Bulk Edit panel, you can add tags (type them in) or apply a category. However, you can't remove tags or *change* the category. That means that if you apply a new category, your posts will actually have two categories, which probably isn't what you want. (Sadly, you'll then have to edit them individually to remove the category you don't want.)

   The Bulk Edit panel also lets you change the author (if your site has more than one), change the status (for example, turning a draft into a published post), and modify a few other settings that you'll explore in the coming chapters.

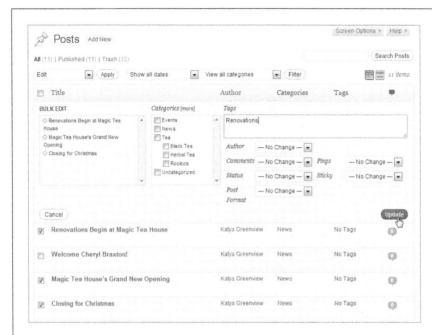

FIGURE 4-30

The Bulk Edit panel lists posts you're editing en masse (in this example, there are three), and provides a limited number of editing options. Here, you're adding a new tag.

6. **Click Update in the Bulk Edit panel.**

   Or, you can back out by clicking Cancel.

TIP Here's a dashboard double-trick that combines filtering and bulk actions. Say you decide to change all the posts in a category. First, choose the category in the filter list (above the list of posts) and then click Filter. You'll see a list that includes only the posts in that category. To select all these posts, turn on the checkbox that appears in the top-left corner of the post list, next to the word "Title." Now you can pick your action from the Bulk Actions box, and carry on.

5

Choosing and Polishing Your WordPress Theme

Using the skills you picked up in the previous chapters, you can create a WordPress site and stuff it full of posts. However, your site will still come up short in the looks department. That's because every WordPress site starts out looking a little drab, a little flat, and pretty much the same as anyone else's freshly created WordPress site. If that sounds colossally boring to you (and it does to us), keep reading, because this chapter will show how to inject some serious style into your site.

The key to a good-looking WordPress site is its *theme*. Essentially, a theme is a set of files that controls how WordPress arranges and styles your content, transforming it from raw text in a database into beautiful web pages (just before sending them to someone who's viewing your site).

Every WordPress site starts out using a standard but somewhat plain default theme called Twenty Eleven (WordPress names its themes after the year it releases them). To improve on the Twenty Eleven look—or the look of any other theme, for that matter—you have several options:

- **Tweak your theme settings.** WordPress gives you a number of useful ways to personalize your theme. Depending on the theme, you may be able to alter its color scheme, change the header picture, and shift the layout.

- **Customize your widgets.** Most WordPress themes include one or more sections you can customize, like a sidebar that you can stock with various links, for example. The sections in the sidebar are called *widgets*, and you can change them, rearrange them, and add new ones.

- **Change to a different theme.** To give your site a more dramatic facelift, you can pick a completely different theme. With that single step, you get new fonts, colors and graphics, a new layout, and—sometimes—new features. WordPress.com users have about 200 themes to pick from, while WordPress self-hosters can choose from hundreds more.

- **Edit your theme.** Advanced WordPress users can crack open their theme files, work on the code with some help from this book, and make more substantial changes. The simplest modification is to fine-tune the CSS styles that format individual sections of your pages. More ambitious theme hackers can change virtually every detail about how their site behaves.

In this chapter, you'll take your first look at how themes work. You'll learn to pick a good theme, change its layout, tweak its settings, and load up new sidebar widgets. (We'll save the hardcore theme editing for Part Four, where you'll learn how to transform an ordinary blog into virtually any type of website.) But before you pick a new theme or change the one you've got, it helps to understand a bit more about how themes work.

How Themes Work

One of WordPress's most impressive tricks is the way it generates web pages *dynamically*, by pulling your content out of a database and assembling it into just the right web page. Themes are the key to this process.

In an old-fashioned website, you format your pages before you upload them to your web server. If you want your site to look different in any respect, you need to update all your pages and re-upload the whole site. But in a WordPress site, your content and your formatting information are separate, with your theme handling the formatting. As a result, you can change the way WordPress styles your pages by editing or changing your theme, without needing to touch the content. The next time someone requests a page, WordPress grabs the usual content and quietly applies the latest formatting instructions.

So how does a theme work its content-formatting magic? Technically, a theme is a package of files. Most of them are *templates* that set out the structure for part of your pages by using a mixture of HTML markup and PHP code. For example, the template file *header.php* determines how the header at the top of every page on your site looks (see Figure 5-1). Similarly, the template file *footer.php* arranges the footer at the bottom of your pages, the template file *single.php* shows the content for a single post, and so on. You won't actually touch the template files in this chapter, but you will work with them later, in Chapter 13.

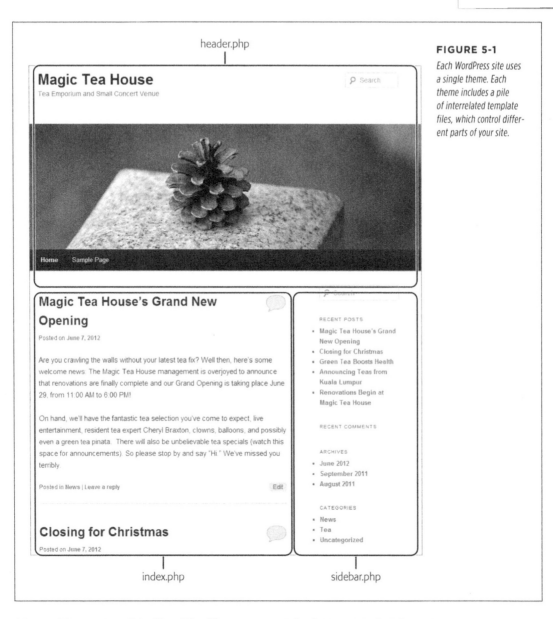

header.php

Magic Tea House

Tea Emporium and Small Concert Venue

🔍 Search

Home   Sample Page

Magic Tea House's Grand New Opening

Posted on June 7, 2012

Are you crawling the walls without your latest tea fix? Well then, here's some welcome news: The Magic Tea House management is overjoyed to announce that renovations are finally complete and our Grand Opening is taking place June 29, from 11:00 AM to 6:00 PM!

On hand, we'll have the fantastic tea selection you've come to expect, live entertainment, resident tea expert Cheryl Braxton, clowns, balloons, and possibly even a green tea pinata. There will also be unbelievable tea specials (watch this space for announcements). So please stop by and say "Hi." We've missed you terribly.

Posted in News | Leave a reply   Edit

Closing for Christmas

Posted on June 7, 2012

RECENT POSTS

- Magic Tea House's Grand New Opening
- Closing for Christmas
- Green Tea Boosts Health
- Announcing Teas from Kuala Lumpur
- Renovations Begin at Magic Tea House

RECENT COMMENTS

ARCHIVES

- June 2012
- September 2011
- August 2011

CATEGORIES

- News
- Tea
- Uncategorized

index.php   sidebar.php

FIGURE 5-1

Each WordPress site uses a single theme. Each theme includes a pile of interrelated template files, which control different parts of your site.

Along with your template files, WordPress uses a style sheet, named *style.css*, to supply formatting information for virtually every heading, paragraph, and font on your site. This style sheet uses the CSS (Cascading Style Sheets) standard, and it formats WordPress pages in the same way that a style sheet formats almost any page you come across on the Web today. There's no special WordPress magic here, but you can edit your theme's style sheet to add some special effects, like fancy fonts, as you'll see on page 448).

At the time of this writing, all new WordPress installations start out with the respectable Twenty Eleven theme. The best way to get familiar with Twenty Eleven—or any new theme—is to poke around. Try adding a post, viewing it, and browsing the list of posts on the home page, just as you did in Chapter 4. Check out the way your theme formats a home page and presents individual posts.

Next, you'll learn to tailor a theme's settings to better suit your site.

NOTE Every once in a while, WordPress changes its default theme. The rumored successor to Twenty Eleven is the long-delayed Twenty Twelve, which looks quite similar to Twenty Eleven (albeit a bit cleaner and more streamlined). Although Twenty Twelve isn't available at the time of this writing, you can take a look at a demo site that uses it at *http://twentytwelvedemo.wordpress.com*. And rest assured, when WordPress adopts Twenty Twelve in the future, or some other slightly different default theme, all the information in this chapter will still apply.

■ Tweaking Your Theme

So far, you've learned that themes control the appearance of your site, so you might assume that getting the look you want is a matter of choosing the right theme. The truth, however, isn't so simple.

Choosing a theme is the Big Choice you make about your site's visual appearance. It settles a number of important formatting issues—for example, the way WordPress uses graphics, fonts, and color across all your pages, and the overall layout of your of header, sidebar, and footer. It also determines the way WordPress presents key ingredients, like the date of a post, the post's category and tag information, and the links that let guests browse through your archives.

But even the slickest theme may not mesh perfectly with your site. To get it right, you may need to adjust a number of additional settings. Your page's header image is a perfect example—if your theme includes one, you'll almost certainly want to replace the stock image with something that better represents your site.

In this chapter, you'll start by learning how to make small changes that customize a theme. Then, once you have an understanding of exactly how flexible a theme is (and isn't), you'll go theme shopping for something with more pizzazz.

NOTE To work on a theme, you use the dashboard. As you'll soon see, WordPress groups all its theme-related commands into a single dashboard menu: Appearances.

Basic Theme Options

Every theme provides a handful of basic options (and some provide many more). To see these options, go to the dashboard and choose Appearance→Theme Options (Figure 5-2).

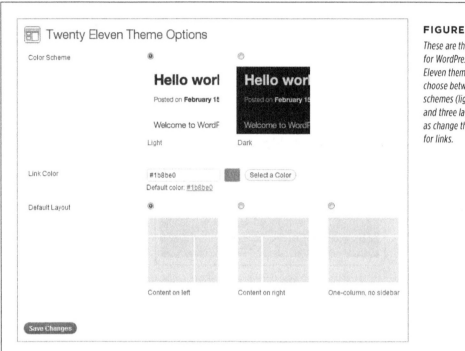

FIGURE 5-2

These are the options for WordPress's Twenty Eleven theme. You can choose between color schemes (light or dark) and three layouts, as well as change the color used for links.

Often, theme preferences let you switch between different "versions" of the same theme. For example, it's common for the same theme to offer different color schemes. Twenty Eleven has its usual light, airy color scheme as well as a white-on-black variant for darker, moodier people. Similarly, many themes offer a choice of layouts. Twenty Eleven gives you two additional layout choices: you can put the sidebar to the left of your posts (instead of keeping it in its usual spot on the right), or take it away altogether.

Finally, the Theme Options page may include a miscellaneous setting or two that has nowhere else to go. In the case of Twenty Eleven, there's an option that lets you change the standard blue hyperlink color. Other themes let you tweak font sizes, or hide some of the buttons on the home page.

NOTE Although every theme has a different version of the Theme Options page, one fact is consistent: there are rarely more than a few settings that affect its appearance. After all, a theme is meant to convey a specific design vision—if you find yourself needing to customize it too heavily, you probably need to pick a more suitable theme.

Configuring the Header

When a visitor arrives at your site, the first thing she sees is the eye-catching header that sits at the top of your home page. Right now, that's a problem, because the standard header screams "Generic WordPress Site!" It's for amateurs only.

To change the header, you need to go to the Custom Header page. From the dashboard, choose Appearance→Header (Figure 5-3).

What your header looks like, based on your current settings

Ignore the stock pictures here

Upload a more suitable picture here

FIGURE 5-3

By default, the Twenty Eleven theme displays a random stock picture every time you load a page. This trick will impress exactly no one, because these pictures have nothing to do with your site. A far better idea is to upload your own image.

As with theme layout options, every theme has slightly different header settings. However, most of them give you similar header-customizing options. You can:

- **Upload a new picture.** This is the single most important customization step for most themes.

- **Remove the header picture.** This gives your site a simple, bare-bones look.

- **Remove the header text.** This makes sense if your header image contains a graphical version of the text—for example, a stylized logo or company banner.

The header options may also let you tweak the color or size of your header text. But you can't change the text itself from the header options page because that text is part of your WordPress site settings. To modify it, choose Settings→General and edit the text in the Site Title and Tagline boxes.

Here's how to upload a new header picture for the standard WordPress theme:

1. **Prepare your picture.**

   Before you upload a new picture, look carefully at the information in the Custom Header page. It usually tells you how big your picture should be. The standard Twenty Eleven supports any header size, but recommends a picture that's 1,000 pixels wide and 288 pixels tall.

   If possible, you should resize or crop your picture to those specs, using an image-editing tool before you upload it. That way, you'll get exactly the image you want. If your image doesn't match the dimensions your theme expects, WordPress may crop or resize it, which can reduce the quality of your picture.

> **TIP** Need a good picture but lack the photographic or illustrative skills to make one? Don't do a Google image search—you're highly likely to end up stealing someone else's copyrighted work. Instead, try a free stock photography site like Stock.XCHNG (*www.sxc.hu*). It offers a vast collection of member-submitted pictures, most of which are free for other people to use. (In fact, stock.xchng was the source of the sunny yellow teapot picture that graces the Magic Tea House site; skip ahead to Figure 5-5 to see it.)

2. **In the Upload Image section, click the Browse or Choose File button (the exact wording depends on the Internet browser you're using).**

   This pops open a window where you can choose the file you want. Find the header picture on your computer, and then select it.

3. **Click Upload to upload the picture to your WordPress site.**

   If your picture doesn't fit the required dimensions, WordPress may ask you to crop it down to size. This works well if your picture is just a little too tall (see Figure 5-4) or too wide, but can cause problems in other situations. For example, if your picture isn't wide enough, WordPress enlarges the whole thing to fit and then asks you to crop off a significant portion of the top and bottom. You'll end up with the worst of both worlds: an image of lower quality (because WordPress had to scale it up) and one missing part of the picture (because you had to crop it).

FIGURE 5-4

To crop a picture, drag the highlight rectangle until you frame it the way you want it. Here, the problem is that the picture is a bit too tall—by positioning the highlight rectangle in the middle, WordPress will trim out part of the top and bottom of the picture. When you finish, click "Crop and Publish." Or, click "Skip Cropping, Publish Image as Is" if you want to ignore your theme's recommendations and use an oddly-sized header.

If you upload a perfectly sized picture, WordPress automatically puts it on your site (Figure 5-5).

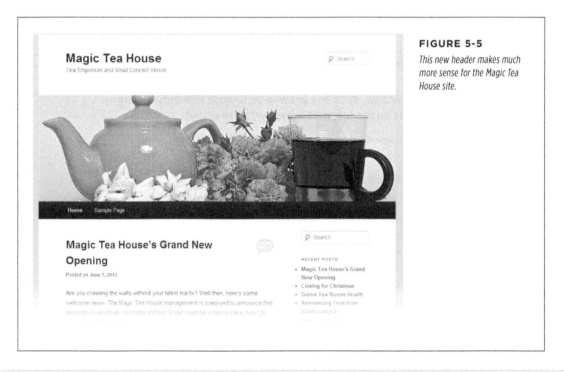

FIGURE 5-5

This new header makes much more sense for the Magic Tea House site.

4. **Optionally, return to step 1 and upload *another* picture.**

   Some themes support multiple pictures. When you upload multiple pictures with Twenty Eleven, you can choose the one you want your site to show (from the Uploaded Images section of the Custom Header page), or you can ask WordPress to randomly pick a picture for each page (choose Random).

> **NOTE** Some folks love the changing-picture trick. For example, on a food blog it's a great way to showcase a number of different and delectable dishes. However, most people prefer to pick a single header and stick with it. That gives the site a clearer identity, and helps visitors remember your site.

If you want a more streamlined look, you can take away the header picture altogether, so that only your header text appears. To do that, scroll down until you see the Remove Header Image button, and then click it. Alternately, you can keep the image but ditch the text—in this case, you need to set the Display Text setting to No. This is a great trick if your header image includes text (like the one in Figure 5-6). And if you're a truly odd duck, you can remove both the header picture and the header text, but that will make your site look just plain weird.

FIGURE 5-6

For a professional touch, remove the text from your header, and create a header image that includes the text. This example does that (and applies an out-of-focus, pointillist effect to the picture). Notice that the theme is intelligent enough to relocate the search box. It used to sit beside the header text; now it's in the menu bar.

> **NOTE** There's another part of the header that you haven't touched yet: the menu. In the Twenty Eleven theme, the menu sits just under the header picture. The menu is a great place for links to extra information (like an "About Us" page). You'll learn to customize it in Chapter 7.

Configuring the Background

The last part of a theme you can tweak is the background. To do that, choose Appearance→Background. The resulting Custom Background page usually gives you two choices:

- **Add a background image.** Most themes *tile* the background image (that means they repeat the image endlessly, from top to bottom and left to right, filling your visitor's browser window). For that reason, you need a picture that looks good when it's jammed edge-to-edge with another copy of itself. Small pictures called *textures* work well for this task, and you can find them online, but the effect is distinctly old-fashioned.

- **Change the background color.** This is the most commonly tweaked background setting. You can use it to make the page background blend in more smoothly with the background of your header image.

The background color doesn't always apply to the part of your layout that you expect. In the Twenty Eleven theme, the background color is the color that shows up on the outer edges of your site, not the color that appears directly behind your posts. To change the color behind the text in your posts, you need to tweak the theme styles, as explained on page 439. Figure 5-7 shows the difference.

The background color
(which you can change)

FIGURE 5-7

Ordinarily, the Twenty Eleven theme centers content horizontally in the browser window, and pads the edges with a nondescript gray border (see Figure 5-6). Here, the background color is set to match the yellow from the header image, giving the page a seamless effect that makes the teapot seem like it's floating. The color behind the posts remains white, ensuring easy reading.

The color behind the posts
(which you can't change)

To change the background color the standard WordPress theme uses, you can type in an HTML color code (like *#e7df84*, suitable for web nerds), or you can use the groovy built-in color picker (Figure 5-8).

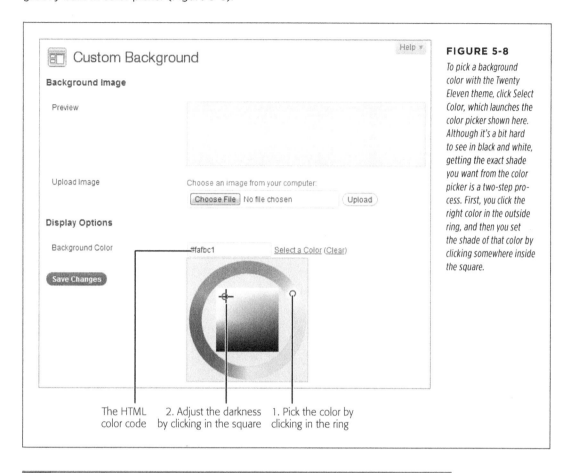

The HTML color code   2. Adjust the darkness by clicking in the square   1. Pick the color by clicking in the ring

TIP If it's getting hard to visualize the differences between the examples in the black-and-white pages of this book, check out the Magic Tea House sample site for yourself at *www.prosetech.com/wordpress*.

Customizing Your Widgets

You're not done tweaking yet. Although your theme may look a whole lot nicer, there's still one area that most WordPress site creators will want to change: the sidebar.

The sidebar is a terrifically useful place to put links, like the ones that let your visitors browse your archives. It's filled with something WordPress calls *widgets*. A widget is simply a block of useful content (like a list of links) that you can stuff into a sidebar, or put somewhere else in your site layout (Figure 5-9), Here's the neat part:

a WordPress widget works with any widget-enabled theme (which, these days, is nearly all of them).

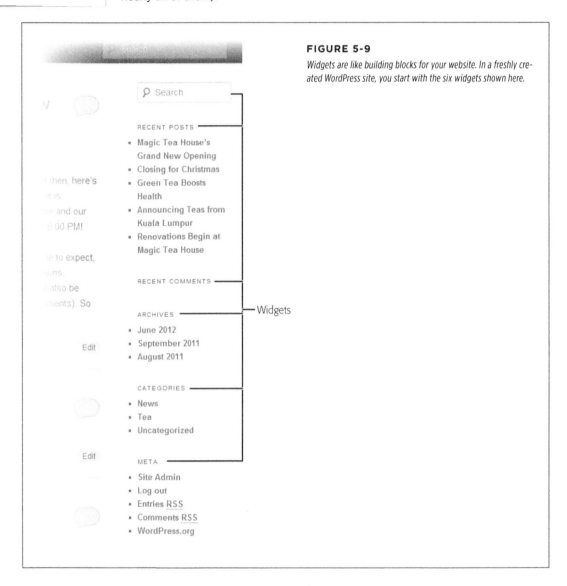

FIGURE 5-9

Widgets are like building blocks for your website. In a freshly created WordPress site, you start with the six widgets shown here.

NOTE Technically, the theme you choose provides one or more areas for widgets to go (like a sidebar and a footer). It's up to you to choose *what* widgets go in those areas, and to configure the widgets you add. The best part of this system is that you can use your favorite widgets with any theme.

Positioning Your Widgets

To see the widgets you can use, choose Appearance→Widgets. This takes you to a densely packed Widgets page, which is a bit confusing because it shows you two things at once:

- **All the widgets WordPress has to offer.** In the big box on the left, under Available Widgets, is a long list of all WordPress's widgets, including those you're using and those you aren't, in alphabetical order.

- **The widgets you're currently using.** On the right, below headings like Sidebar and Footer Area, are the widgets that are active on your site right now. WordPress arranges these widgets in individual boxes (based on what part of the site they occupy) and lists them in the order they actually appear.

Each theme dictates where you can place widgets. If you just created a new WordPress site, you'll start with a Widgets page that looks like Figure 5-10.

All the WordPress widgets   The widgets in your sidebar

FIGURE 5-10

The Twenty Eleven theme offers five locations for widgets: a sidebar, a special showcase sidebar (discussed on page 225), and three footer areas. Right now, the sidebar is the only section that actually has any widgets in it. As you can see, the six widget boxes shown here correspond to the six widgets on the site, shown in Figure 5-9.

The easiest thing you can do on the Widgets page is *move* a widget. That's as simple as dragging the widget to a new spot. Why not try relocating the Search box to the bottom of the sidebar? There's no need to click any button to save your changes—as soon as you drop the widget in its new position, WordPress makes the change and you can view your site to check out the effect.

The next-easiest widget-customization task is *deleting* a widget. Simply grab hold of your widget and drag it over to the big Available Widgets box on the left. When you drop the widget there, WordPress removes it from your site.

Next, you can try *adding* a widget by dragging it from the Available Widgets box and dropping it on your sidebar. (You'll learn what all these widgets actually do starting on page 147.)

As you get a bit more ambitious, you may want to try moving widgets to different areas. For example, you might want to move the Categories widget from the main sidebar to a footer area. Before you can do that, you need to make sure you *expand* the area where you want to put the widget. In Figure 5-10, the Main Sidebar area is expanded, but the others are collapsed. To open one (say, Footer Area One), click the down-pointing arrow on the right. Then drag the widget into the newly revealed area (Figure 5-11).

The standard WordPress theme has no fewer than *three* footer areas for widgets. Although this seems confusing, it really isn't—you simply use what you need. If you want a simple footer, use Footer Area One and ignore the others. If you want a two-column footer, which splits the footer area into columns, use Footer Area One and Footer Area Two (Figure 5-12). And if you want a pumped-up three-column footer, you know what to do: put widgets in Footer Area One, Footer Area Two, and Footer Area Three.

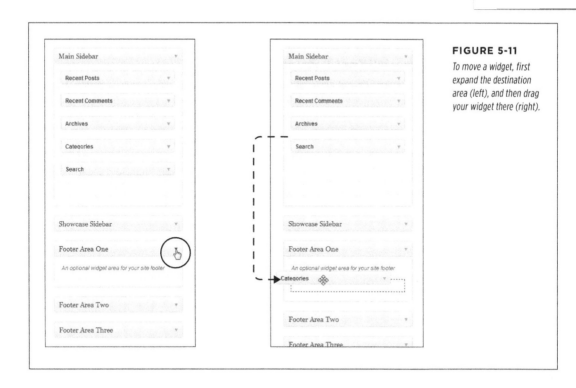

FIGURE 5-11

To move a widget, first expand the destination area (left), and then drag your widget there (right).

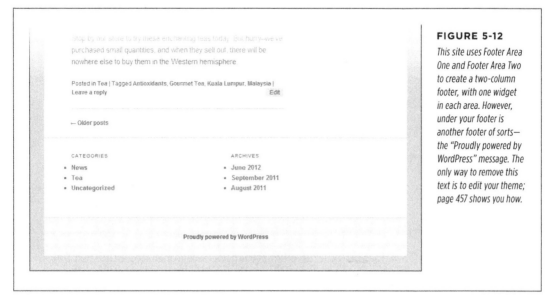

FIGURE 5-12

This site uses Footer Area One and Footer Area Two to create a two-column footer, with one widget in each area. However, under your footer is another footer of sorts— the "Proudly powered by WordPress" message. The only way to remove this text is to edit your theme; page 457 shows you how.

Changing Widget Settings

Widgets are surprisingly useful things. They let readers find recent posts, browse through your archives, and keep track of recent comments. As you refine your site, you won't be happy just shuffling them around. You'll also want to configure the way they work.

Every widget provides a few settings you can adjust. To see them, expand the widget by clicking the down-pointing arrow in its right corner. Change the settings you want, and then click the Save button to make the changes permanent. Figure 5-13 shows the settings for the Recent Posts and Categories widgets.

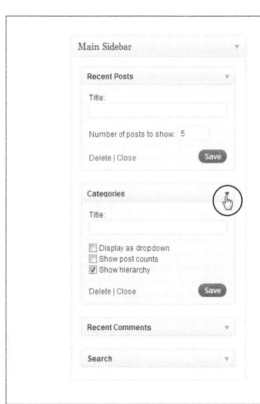

FIGURE 5-13

You can change the Recent Posts widget to show as many posts as you want (not just the latest five). The Categories box gives you three special options. "Display as dropdown" compresses the category into a drop-down list box, which saves space but forces people to click the box open. "Show posts counts" shows the number of posts in a category in parentheses after the category name. And "Show hierarchy" displays the category tree, which is especially handy if you use subcategories, as described on page 109.

Even if a widget provides no other settings, it always includes a Title text box, which you can use to give the widget its caption—for example "Hot News!" instead of "Recent Posts" or "What People Are Saying" instead of "Recent Comments." If you leave the Title box blank, the widget uses its default name.

When you add a new widget, it starts out with its default settings. In some cases, you might want to remove a widget from your site without throwing away its settings—for example you may be planning to add it back later on. WordPress has a special Inactive Widgets box designed for exactly this situation. To remove a widget but keep its settings, simply pull the widget in the Inactive Widgets box instead of the Available Widgets box. (If you don't see the Inactive Widgets box, scroll down—it's right underneath the Available Widgets box.)

The Basic Widgets

You are now the master of your widgets. Before you go any further, take a closer look at exactly what WordPress's widgets can do for you.

Table 5-1 describes the essential WordPress widgets you'll see in a freshly installed, self-hosted WordPress site. In Chapter 9, you'll learn how to expand your widget collection with plug-ins.

TABLE 5-1 *WordPress widgets*

WIDGET NAME	DESCRIPTION	FOR MORE INFORMATION...
Archives	Shows links that let readers browse a month of posts at a time. You can convert it to a drop-down box, and display the number of posts in each month.	-
Calendar	Shows a miniature calendar that lets guests find posts on specific dates.	See page 149.
Categories	Shows links that let readers browse all the posts in a category. You can convert it to a drop-down box, and display the number of posts in each category.	Categories are explained on page 105.
Custom Menu	Shows a menu of pages or other links that you create, using WordPress's menu feature.	Menus are explained in Chapter 7.
Links	Shows a batch of links that you specify. Usually these links point to other websites. Bloggers use them to point out other blogs they follow.	See page 150.

WIDGET NAME	DESCRIPTION	FOR MORE INFORMATION...
Meta	Shows administrative links (for example, a "Log in" link that takes you to the dashboard). Once you're ready to go live with your site, you should delete the Meta widget.	-
Pages	Shows links to the static pages you pick. (Static pages act like ordinary web pages, not posts. You can add them to your website to provide extra information or resources.)	Static pages are explained in Chapter 7.
Recent Comments	Shows the most recent comments left on any of your posts. You can choose how many comments WordPress displays (the default is 5).	Comments are explained in Chapter 8.
Recent Posts	Shows links that let readers jump to one of your most recent posts. You can choose how many posts WordPress displays (the default is 5).	-
RSS	Shows links extracted from an RSS feed (for example, the posts from another person's blog).	See page 408.
Search	Shows a box that lets visitors search your posts. You might want to remove this from the sidebar if your theme includes it somewhere else on the home page (as the home page in Figure 5-1 does).	-
Tag Cloud	Shows the tags that your blogs use most often, sized according to their popularity. Readers can click a tag to see the posts that use it.	See page 154.

WIDGET NAME	DESCRIPTION	FOR MORE INFORMATION...
Text	Shows a block of text or HTML. You can put whatever content you want here, which makes it an all-purpose display tool for small bits of information.	See page 155.
Twenty Eleven Ephemera	Shows the titles of posts that use the Aside, Link, Status, or Quote format. Unlike all the other widgets, this widget is designed exclusively for the Twenty Eleven theme.	Post formats are explained in Chapter 6.

You're already well acquainted with the basic set of widgets that every blog begins with: Search, Archives, Recent Posts, Categories, Recent Comments, and Meta. In the following sections, you'll tour a few more widgets you might consider adding to your site.

> **TIP** You can add the same widget more than once. For example, you can add two Links widgets to your page, give each one a different title, and use each one to show a separate set of links.

The Calendar Widget

The Calendar widget gives readers a different way to browse your site—by finding the posts published on a specific day (Figure 5-14). It's most commonly used in blogs.

FIGURE 5-14

JUNE 2012

M	T	W	T	F	S	S
				1	2	3
4	5	6	7	8	9	10
11	12	13	14	15	16	17
18	19	20	21	22	23	24
25	26	27	28	29	30	

« Sep

FIGURE 5-14

In the month of June, two days have at least one post—the 6th and the 7th. Click the day to see them.

The Calendar widget used to be a staple of every blog. These days, it's less popular. The problem is that unless you blog several times a week, the calendar looks sparse and makes your blog feel half-empty. Also, it emphasizes the current month of posts while neglecting other months. Most readers won't bother clicking their way through month after month to hunt for posts.

You probably won't use the Calendar unless your posts are particularly time-sensitive, and you want to emphasize their dates. (For example, the Calendar widget might make sense if you're chronicling a 30-day weight-loss marathon.) If you use the Calendar widget, you probably won't use the similarly date-focused Archives widget, or you'll at least place it far away, at the other end of your sidebar or in another widget area.

The Links Widget

The Links widget does what its name says—lets you show a group of links (Figure 5-15). These links can point to anything. For example, you could use the Links widget to point to sites you like or to highlight some extra-special posts on your site.

> **NOTE**   In the old ays, blogs would provide a list of related blogs called a *blogroll*. For example, bloggers writing about cooking would have a blogroll with other food-related blogs in it, bloggers writing about their personal lives would have a blogroll with their friends' blogs in it, and so on. Many blogs still use blogrolls, although they're less likely to call them that.

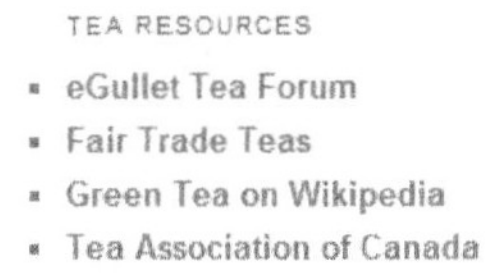

TEA RESOURCES

- eGullet Tea Forum
- Fair Trade Teas
- Green Tea on Wikipedia
- Tea Association of Canada

FIGURE 5-15

This Link widget shows four links from the "Tea Resources" category.

There's a trick to using the Links widget. To make it work, you need to define the links in a separate section of the dashboard. Interestingly enough, every WordPress site starts out with some sample WordPress links. To seem them in a nifty table view that looks suspiciously like the Posts page, choose Links→All Links.

More usefully, you can define your own links. Here's how:

1. **First, consider deleting the sample links.**

    Before you get started, you may want to delete the stock links, so they don't distract you. To do that, turn on the checkbox in the header row, at the very top-left of the table, next to the word "Name." This selects every link at once. Then, choose Delete from the Bulk Actions list, and click the Apply button.

NOTE You don't *need* to delete the sample links. WordPress organizes links into categories, and it keeps the sample WordPress links in a category called "Blogroll." So long as you use a different category name for your links, WordPress can keep them separate, and the sample links won't end up in your Links widget. However, if you wipe them out you can avoid any possibility of confusing yourself.

---

2. **Choose Links→Add New.**

    This brings you to the Add New Link page (Figure 5-16).

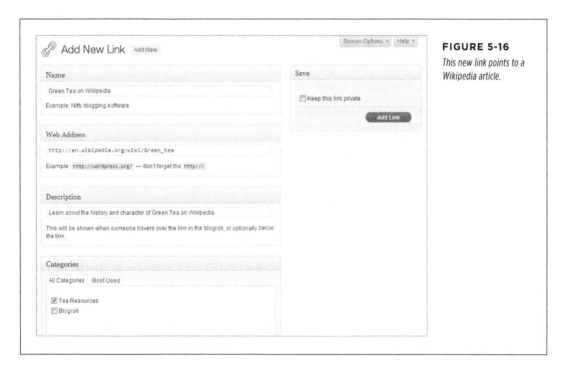

FIGURE 5-16

This new link points to a Wikipedia article.

3. **Fill in the name, address, and description of your link.**

   The *name* is the text that appears in the link—the reader clicks this text to fol-low the link.

   The *web address* is the URL a browser navigates to when a guest clicks the link.

   You can use the *description* to add information about the link. Ordinarily, it pops up in a tooltip when a visitor hovers over the link, but you can choose to have WordPress display the description in the Links widget, next to the link name.

4. **Create a new category for your link.**

   The category you specify groups your links together. The Links widget shows just a single category of links at a time. However, you can add several copies of the Links widget to your site, and use each one to display a different group of links.

   To add a category, click the Add New Category link. Fill in a good name, and then click Add. WordPress uses the category name as the title of the link box (it's "Tea Resources" in Figure 5-15), so make sure you pick a good name.

   If you already created the category you want, simply turn on the checkbox next to it, just as you do when you add a post. (And remember, post categories and link categories are separate, even though they're conceptually similar.)

   TIP If you need to change the name of a link category later on, go to Links→Link Categories, and edit your category there.

5. **Optionally, fill in any other link settings you wish to use.**

   The Add New Link page includes some less commonly used settings. Look for these boxes:

   - **Target.** This box tells browsers what to do when a guest clicks a link. Ordinarily, the browser opens the new page in the same browser window, leaving your blog behind. If this isn't the behavior you want, choose "_blank" to launch a new window or tab.

   - **Link Relationship.** This box lets you describe how the link destination relates to you—is it a site run by a friend, acquaintance, or lover? WordPress doesn't display this information anywhere on your site—it keeps it hidden in a comment in the HTML of your page. Someday, some cool web tool may use this informa-tion, but right now mostly everyone ignores it.

   - **Advanced.** This box includes several miscellaneous settings. You can add a tiny thumbnail picture (which will appear next to the link), an RSS feed (page 408), some notes (which aren't shown to visitors, but may help you remember why you chose this link), and a rating from 0 to 10 (which you can choose to show, but is typically used for your own personal record-keeping).

6. **Click Add Link.**

If you want to add a link that won't appear in the Links widget, turn on the checkbox next to "Keep this link private" before you click Add Link. Typically, you'll use this technique if you have a link that you don't want to use right now, but want to consider including in the future. You can edit the link later and remove the privacy setting to make it visible.

Once you click Add Link, WordPress adds the link, clears the text boxes, and lets you add another link. To do that, return to step 3.

Once you add all the links you want, carry on to the next step.

7. **Choose Appearance→Widgets.**

   This brings you to the familiar Widgets page.

8. **Drag the Links widget from the Available Widgets box (on the left) to an area in your theme (on the right).**

   When you add a new widget, it expands itself, so you can easily change its settings.

9. **Choose the link category from the list in the Links widget.**

   In Figure 5-15, the category is Tea Resources.

   Optionally, you can choose to show the link description, the image, or the rating next to your links. If you want to use one of these less-common settings, just turn on the corresponding checkbox.

10. **Click Save.**

    You can now try out your new box of links.

How to Show Links in a Different Order

Ordinarily, WordPress arranges links in alphabetical order. This isn't necessarily what you want. For example, you may prefer to put more important links first. Accomplishing this is surprisingly tricky.

If your site is on WordPress.com, there's a reasonable solution. That's because the WordPress.com version of the Links widget lets you sort by one of the pieces of information attached to the link. For example, you could use the otherwise unimportant link rating (a number from 0 to 10) to sort a handful of links. Assign a rating of 0 to the link you want to show first, a rating of 1 to the link you want to show second, and so on. Then, in the Links widget, in the "Sort by" list, pick "Link rating." (This approach assumes that you don't actually want to use the link rating to rate the quality of each site.)

Oddly enough, the self-hosted version of WordPress doesn't include this feature. Still, there are three possible workarounds. The first, and best, option is to create a custom menu instead of a set of links (page 210). You can order its items however you want—the only disadvantage is that you give up the conveniences of the Links section in the dashboard.

Another option is to put your links in the Text widget (page 155), which allows any content. The problem here is that the Text widget needs you to supply your links with real HTML markup, which takes a bit more work (although you can cut and paste what you need from an HTML editing program).

The last choice is to use a plug-in that gives you a more powerful version of the Links widget (see, for example, My Link Order at *http://tinyurl.com/7ds4o4*).

The Tag Cloud Widget

You've already seen how the Categories widget lets visitors browse through the posts in any category. The Tag Cloud widget is similar in that it lets readers see posts that use a specific tag.

There's a difference, however. While categories are well-defined and neatly organized, the typical WordPress site uses a jumble of overlapping keywords. Also, the total number of categories you use will probably be small, while the number of tags could be quite large. For these reasons, it makes sense to display tags differently than categories. Categories make sense in a list or tree. Tags work better in a *cloud*, which shows the most popular tags sorted alphabetically and sized proportionately. That means that tags attached to a lot of posts show up in bigger text, while less-frequently used tags use smaller text (Figure 5-17).

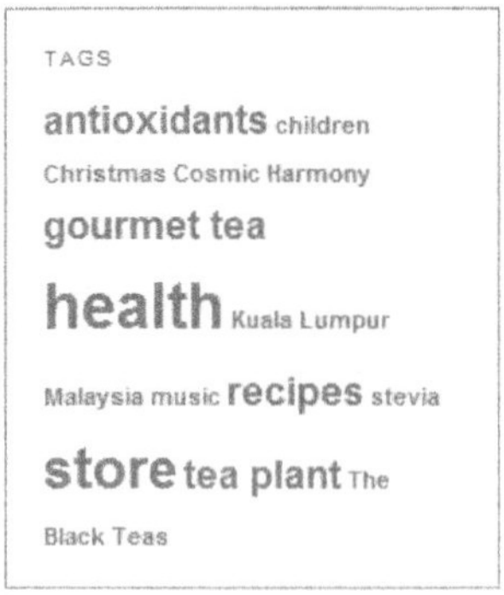

TAGS

antioxidants children

Christmas Cosmic Harmony

gourmet tea

health Kuala Lumpur

Malaysia music recipes stevia

store tea plant The

Black Teas

FIGURE 5-17

This tag cloud shows that "health" is the most frequently used tag, with "store" close behind. As with categories, clicking a tag link shows all the posts that use that tag.

There's no secret to using the Tag Cloud widget. Just drag it into an area of your theme, and see what tags it highlights. The tag cloud might also tell *you* something about your site—for example, what topics keep coming up across all your posts.

NOTE   If clouds work so well for tags, it might occur to you that they could also suit categories, especially in sites that have a large number of categories, loosely arranged, and with no subcategories. Happily, a category cloud is easy to create. If you're using WordPress.com, the handy Category Cloud widget does the job. If you're using the self-hosted version of WordPress, you'll notice an extra setting in the Tag Cloud widget: a list called Taxonomy. Simply change the setting there from Tags to Categories to create your category cloud.

Taming the Tag Cloud

What do I do if my tag cloud shows too many tags? Or not enough? Or makes the text too big?

The Tag Cloud widget is surprisingly uncustomizable. If you use fewer than 45 tags, it shows every one of them (although it ignores any tags you added to the Posts®Tags list but haven't yet used in a post.) If you use more than 45 tags, the Tag Cloud widget shows the 45 most popular.

Occasionally, people want a tag cloud with more tags. But usually they have the opposite concern, and want a smaller tag cloud that's slim enough to fit into a sidebar without crowd-ing out other widgets. If you want to tweak a tag cloud on a WordPress.com site, you're out of luck. But if you're running a self-hosted site, there is a solution, provided you're willing to crack open your template files. That's because the behind-the-scenes code (the PHP function that creates the cloud) is actually very flexible. It lets you set upper and lower tag limits, and set upper and lower boundaries for the text size. You can get the full details from WordPress's function reference at *http://tinyurl.com/wptagcloud*. However, this information won't be much help until you learn how to dig into your WordPress theme files to change your code, a topic explored in Chapter 13.

The Text Widget

The Text widget is simple but surprisingly flexible. You can use it anywhere you want to wedge in a bit of fixed content. For example, you can use it in a sidebar, to add a paragraph about yourself or your site. Or you can put it in your footer with some copyright information or a legal disclaimer.

However, the Text widget becomes much more interesting if you stick some markup in it. That's because it supports HTML programming, so you can stuff in lists, links, pictures, and more. (In, fact, WordPress self-hosters often use the Text widget to stuff in a video or image, as explained on page 191.)

Figure 5-18 shows two uses of the Text widget.

ABOUT THE STORE

The Magic Tea House is a quirky mash-up: it's a fine tea importer with the rarest gourmet teas, and a music venue for small-venue jazz, chamber, and coffeehouse bands.

Customers tell us The Magic Tea House is a truly special spot: relaxing, inspiring, and engaging. Come stop by to sample our teas, and don't miss our next concert!

ABOUT THE STORE

The **Magic Tea House** is a quirky mash-up: it's a fine tea importer with the rarest gourmet teas, and a music venue for small-venue jazz, chamber, and coffeehouse bands like:

- The Black Teas
- Cosmic Harmony
- U.V.Q.
- Samantha Told Me So

See our location.

FIGURE 5-18

At its simplest, the Text widget shows a display that looks like this: a title (formatted according to the theme you're using) with one or more paragraphs of text underneath (left). Add some HTML, and the Text widget can do a whole lot more (right).

Using the Text widget is easy. First, drag it onto your page (as with any other widget). When you expand it, you get a nice big, multiple-line box to type into. If all you want is ordinary text, just fill in a title and type your text underneath. Make sure you also turn on the "Automatically add paragraphs" checkbox. That way, wherever you separate the text (by pressing the Enter key), WordPress adds an HTML line break element (that's <br>) to give you the space you need.

It's almost as easy for you to put HTML in the Text widget. First, turn off the "Automatically add paragraphs" settings. Then, just type in your HTML exactly the way it looks, like this:

```
The following word will be <b>bold</b> on the page.
```

And here's the formatted text from Figure 5-18 (right):

```
The <b>Magic Tea House</b> is a quirky mash-up: it's a fine tea importer with
the rarest gourmet teas, and a music venue for small-venue jazz, chamber,
and coffeehouse bands like:

<ul>
<li>The Black Teas</li>
<li>Cosmic Harmony</li>
<li>U.V.Q.</li>
<li>Samantha Told Me So</li>
</ul>
See our <a href="http://tinyurl.com/cyboj83">location</a>.
```

If you're HTML skills are a bit sketchy, you can copy markup from an HTML editor into the Text widget. Before you do, make sure you look over the markup and strip out any unnecessary details, like inline styles. That gives it a better chance of blending into your site without disrupting the rest of your WordPress page.

▓ Choosing a New Theme

As you've seen throughout this chapter, there's a lot you can do by customizing the standard Twenty Eleven WordPress theme. In fact, it's a reasonable starting point for a wide range of polished, professional blogs. But if you're interested in a dramatic change, these tweaks won't be enough. Instead, you'll want to give your site a radical new style by changing its theme.

At this point, you may be wondering when it's worth abandoning the standard theme and using something more exotic. Here are some reasons why you would:

- **You want something completely different.** Changing background colors and header pictures is one thing, but a new WordPress theme can rework almost every visual detail of your site (Figure 5-19).

- **You want your theme to reflect the subject of your site.** For example, there are custom themes for travel blogs, photo blogs, magazine-style news blogs, and so on (see Figure 5-20). There's even a theme for coordinating and celebrating a wedding (called Forever). Although your site still works the same way, picking a specialized theme changes the way other people see your site.

- **You want your site to work differently.** Themes also control the way your site works, in ways subtle and profound. For example, some themes let you tile your posts instead of putting them in a top-to-bottom list (which is great if you want your site to show a portfolio of work rather than a list of articles, as demonstrated on page 333). Or, your theme may include a fancy frill, like a slideshow of featured posts (page 186).

FIGURE 5-19

The Greyzed theme creates a grungy effect with lined paper on stone. Every detail—from the menu to the widget titles—is different from a plain-vanilla WordPress site.

Even if you're happy with the standard WordPress theme, it's worth trying out a few different ones, just to open your mind to new possibilities. As you'll see, although changing a theme has a profound effect on the way your site looks, doing it is almost effortless. And most themes are free, so there's no harm in exploring.

NOTE The only limitation with WordPress themes is that somewhere in cyberspace, there are sure to be plenty of other websites using the same theme that you pick. This isn't a huge problem, provided you're willing to customize your site in little ways—for example, by choosing a suitable header picture, as described in this chapter. (And it's also true that no matter what your site looks like, its content makes it unique.) However, if you're a style-conscious site designer and you're using a very distinctive, graphical style, it's worth your while to customize it further. The simplest approach is to change the formatting in the theme's *style.css* file, but more ambitious WordPress self-hosters can create completely unique, one-of-a-kind sites by editing their template files by hand. You'll learn to do both in Chapter 13.

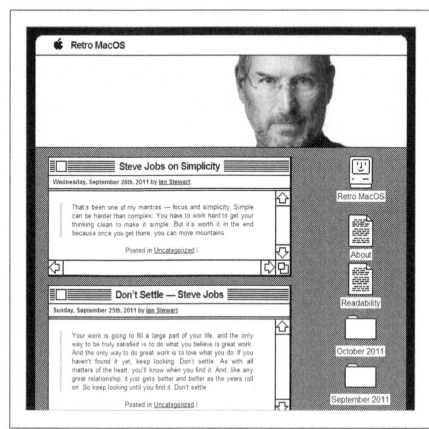

FIGURE 5-20

A theme for old-school Mac aficionados (called Retro MacOS) may be stretching it, but just a bit. Here, the theme is put to good effect on a Mac-centric sample site.

To change your theme, you choose Appearance→Themes. This takes you to the Manage Themes page (Figure 5-21).

The theme gallery looks slightly different in a WordPress.com site than it does in a self-hosted WordPress site.

If you're using WordPress.com, the gallery includes every supported theme. At the time of this writing, that gives you 190 distinct theme choices. Some themes come with a price tag, in which case you'll see a Purchase link with a dollar figure—usually between $50 and $100.

If you're running a self-hosted WordPress site, you'll find that the theme gallery is empty (except for the standard Twenty Eleven theme that comes with WordPress), and you'll need to install any other theme you want to use. Fortunately, there's no reason to fear this process—new themes take up very little space, installing them takes mere seconds, and you can do it all without leaving the dashboard.

FIGURE 5-21

At the top of the Manage Themes page, WordPress describes the theme you're currently using, and provides some links or buttons that launch the various theme-customization tasks you learned about in this chapter (tweaking the header, changing the widgets, and so on). Ignore this section and look underneath, where WordPress lets you browse through a gallery of available themes.

The following sections explain the exact theme-changing steps you need to follow, depending on how you host your site.

NOTE A few web hosts preinstall extra WordPress themes. If you're using one of these hosts, your theme gallery won't start out quite as empty as we describe. However, you'll probably still need to install new themes to find the one you *really* want.

Activating a Theme in WordPress.com

Ordinarily, WordPress.com lists all its themes on a single page, in random order. You can use the links above the theme gallery to change the order, making it alphabetical (click "A-Z"), showing the most popular themes first, or putting the newest first. You can also focus on just those themes that cost money (click Premium) or those select few developed by official WordPress.com partners (click "Friends of WP.com").

Because the list isn't long, the most effective way to find a theme you want to try is usually to sort it in the order you think is most promising, and then start scrolling through the gallery. But if you remember a theme you browsed before, or you have a theme characteristic in mind (say, "minimalistic" or "dark"), you can type that into the search box that appears just above the list of themes.

When you find a promising theme, click one of three links underneath (see Figure 5-22):

- **Details** displays a short paragraph describing the theme.

- **Live Preview** opens a preview window that shows your site dressed in this theme. It's called a *live* preview because you can treat it exactly as you would a real site—clicking links, browsing content, and feeling your way around. Usually, the live preview is enough for you to decide whether you really do want the theme you're checking out.

- **Activate** reconfigures your existing site to use this theme. The changeover happens instantaneously.

FIGURE 5-22

Each theme in the theme gallery has its own thumbnail, with three important links underneath.

Don't be shy—you can activate one theme, and then another, and then another, until you find the right candidate for your website. Once you settle into a new theme, you need to go through the customization steps described earlier in this chapter to get the perfect fit.

Installing a Theme on a Self-Hosted Site

Before you can switch to a new theme with a self-hosted WordPress site, you need to install the theme itself. To see the themes you can install, click the Install Themes tab, which appears at the top of the Manage Themes page (Appearance→Themes).

At the top of the page, you'll see a small set of links. Your choices are:

- **Search** lets you search for a theme by keyword or feature (Figure 5-23). This is the most common approach (and where you'll start when you first visit the Install Themes page).

- **Upload** lets you install a theme you already have on your computer. You won't use this option unless you find a theme on another site, you buy a premium theme from a third-party company, or you build the theme yourself. (You'll see an example that requires a custom theme upload on page 477.)

- **Featured** lets you browse a small selection of WordPress-selected themes.

- **Newest and Recently Updated** lets you browse just recently added or recently changed themes.

If you decide to perform a search, you have two choices. If you want to search by keyword (for example, "magazine" or "industrial" or "professional"), simply type that in the search box and then click the Search button. If you want to search for themes that have a specific feature, turn on the appropriate checkboxes in the Feature Filter section (for example, you could choose Green for the color, and Three Columns). Then, click the Find Themes button underneath. You can't search by name and filter by feature at the same time.

> **TIP** Here's a trick to see even more themes. Leave the search box empty, and then click the Search button. You'll see a list with hundreds of themes.

When you find a potential theme, you'll see two links underneath it (Figure 5-24, left). Click Preview to take a closer look. This opens a new browser window that shows a sample site using the theme you picked. Click Install to copy the theme to your site. From that point on, the theme will be available in your theme gallery, but you still need to activate it to actually start using it.

> **TIP** Don't be afraid to install a theme that you might not want to use—all WordPress themes are guaranteed to be safe and spyware-free. And don't worry about downloading too many themes—not only are they tiny, but you can easily delete those you don't need.

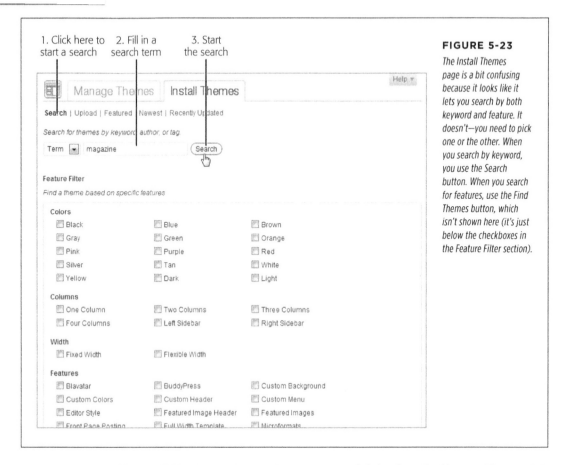

1. Click here to start a search 2. Fill in a search term 3. Start the search

Manage Themes | **Install Themes**

Search | Upload | Featured | Newest | Recently Updated

Search for themes by keyword, author, or tag.

Term ▼ magazine (Search)

Feature Filter

Find a theme based on specific features

Colors
- Black
- Gray
- Pink
- Silver
- Yellow
- Blue
- Green
- Purple
- Tan
- Dark
- Brown
- Orange
- Red
- White
- Light

Columns
- One Column
- Four Columns
- Two Columns
- Left Sidebar
- Three Columns
- Right Sidebar

Width
- Fixed Width
- Flexible Width

Features
- Blavatar
- Custom Colors
- Editor Style
- Front Page Posting
- BuddyPress
- Custom Header
- Featured Image Header
- Full Width Template
- Custom Background
- Custom Menu
- Featured Images
- Microformats

Help ▼

FIGURE 5-23

The Install Themes page is a bit confusing because it looks like it lets you search by both keyword and feature. It doesn't—you need to pick one or the other. When you search by keyword, you use the Search button. When you search for features, use the Find Themes button, which isn't shown here (it's just below the checkboxes in the Feature Filter section).

To see all the themes installed on your site, click back to the Manage Themes tab and scroll down. Under each of the themes in your gallery, you'll see three links (Figure 5-24, right):

- **Activate.** Click this to start using the theme.

- **Preview.** This launches a window that shows you what your site would look like if WordPress applied the chosen theme. Think of it as a test drive for a prospective theme. You can read posts, perform searches, and click your away around your content, secure in the knowledge that you haven't changed the real, live version of your site.

- **Delete.** Use this link to clear away themes you don't plan to use. That said, there's nothing wrong with keeping old, unused themes, perhaps for future reference. The only disadvantage is that WordPress will prompt you to update them when new versions are available, even if you're not using them.

 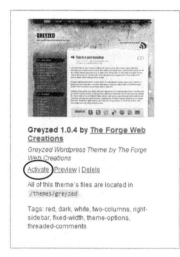

FIGURE 5-24

Getting a new theme takes several steps. First, you need to find it in the Install Themes tab (left) and click Install to put it on your site. Then, you need to find it in the Manage Themes tab (right), and click Activate to start using it.

The Theme Customizer

Once you activate a new theme, you'll want to check out its options and consider tweaking it. Some themes provide their own page of custom options, which appear in the dashboard, somewhere under the Appearance menu. For example, if you install the Absolum theme, you'll get a new page of options that you can review by choosing Appearance→Absolum Settings.

Even if your theme doesn't have extra options, you still need to take care of the basics—changing your header, shuffling around your widgets, setting up your menus (page 210), and so on—before your site looks polished. You can take care of these tasks separately, using the appropriate part of the dashboard menu, or you can click the Customize link that appears under the current theme on the Appearance→Themes page. This loads up a tool WordPress calls the *theme customizer*. It doesn't offer you any settings you can't access through the dashboard menu, but it does put them all together in one useful, multi-tabbed page (Figure 5-25).

FIGURE 5-25

To customize your theme with WordPress's theme customizer, click the tab on the left that has the settings you want to change (like Colors, shown here). Then, make your changes and watch the preview unfold on the right. If you like the result, click the Save & Publish button at the top of the panel on the left. If you don't, pick something else, or click Cancel to back out of all your changes.

NOTE Themes are complex creations, and it will take a bit of fiddling before you have a good idea of which theme suits your site best. You'll see plenty of examples in the following chapters that show you how to capitalize on the features found in different themes.

Mobile Themes

The themes that work well for a browser on a desktop or laptop computer aren't so swell on a tablet or smartphone. Figure 5-26 shows the difference. In a properly designed mobile page, the content is rearranged in a streamlined, readable way that fits the small screen. In the case of WordPress, that means the page is compressed into a single column. At the top is the header, followed by the menu (if you're using one). After that is the lists of posts, each one sized to neat, easily readable dimensions. Only after that do the sidebar widgets appear, with their post-browsing links and ancillary content.

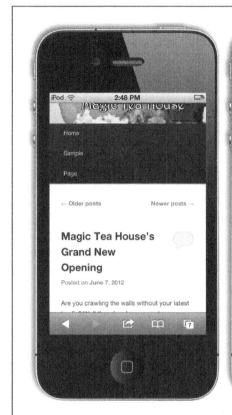

FIGURE 5-26

Left: This mobile-optimized display shows your blog postings in a friendly, readable page. Right: Without it, you get the familiar bird's-eye-view of the page. Navigating this view will require plenty of zooming in and zooming out.

So how do you make sure your WordPress site adjusts itself for mobile devices? The trick is *theme substitution*. That means that when someone browses to your site using a smartphone, WordPress uses a different layout—one that's both simpler and carefully rearranged.

WordPress substitutes themes two ways. Some themes have built-in support for mobile displays. When they detect a visitor using a mobile device, they automatically send back a mobile version of the theme. The standard WordPress theme (Twenty Eleven) has built-in mobile support, which creates the optimized display shown in Figure 5-26 (on the left). The previous WordPress theme (Twenty Ten) does not have mobile support, and the same is true for many other themes. Unfortunately, there's no easy way to search for themes with mobile support—it isn't even an option in the Feature Filter. Instead, you need to look for newer themes and then carefully review the theme description. (Look for the words "responsive" and "mobile.")

The other option is to ask WordPress to take control of the theme substitution job itself, instead of your theme. If your site is on WordPress.com, this feature is on by default. You can turn it off, which you might choose to do if you're using a very specialized theme and the mobile view doesn't reflect it faithfully, or if your theme has mobile support built-in and you'd rather use that. To turn off WordPress.com's mobile support, choose Appearance→Mobile. Next to "Enable mobile theme," click No.

If you're using a self-hosted WordPress site and your theme doesn't have built-in mobile support, you'll need a plug-in to do the theme substitution. One example is WPtouch (*http://tinyurl.com/wptouch*), which correctly identifies smartphones and other mobile devices, and makes sure they get a simplified theme that better suits their capabilities (and looks pretty slick, too). You haven't yet learned how to use plug-ins, but you'll consider WPtouch when you do, on page 294.

If you use WordPress.com, you can also turn on a related feature called Onswipe, which optimized your site for iPad viewing by adding swiping and other cool touch-navigation features. To turn on Onswipe, choose Appearance→iPad, and then click the setting "Display a special theme for iPad users." At present, there are no other settings, and no way to tailor how Onswipe does its magic. The best way to see if you like it is to try it out and visit your site on an iPad. To get similar features on a self-hosted site, you can try out the Onswipe plug-in at *http://tinyurl.com/onswipe*.

6

Jazzing Up Your Posts

You know what an ordinary WordPress post looks like—it starts with a title, followed by one or more paragraphs of text. And there's nothing wrong with that. Providing you pick the right theme, your WordPress site can look surprisingly hip, even if it holds nothing more than plain text.

However, there are plenty of types of sites that need more from a post. For example, if you're posting news articles, you certainly want to add pictures. And if you're writing long posts (on anything from business analytics to relationship advice), you'll make the reading experience much better if you use subheadings to structure your thoughts. To add details like these, along with lists, links, and the other accoutrements of a web page, you need to take charge of WordPress's post editor, which you'll do in this chapter.

Fancy posts aren't just about formatting—they're also about *features*. For example, you can use specialized tags to show just a portion of a post on your home page (rather than the whole thing), giving you a ridiculously useful way to promote many posts in a small space. Or, you can use images from your posts to create a slide-show that, say, promotes your top posts on the home page. (WordPress calls these presentations *sliders*.)

In this chapter, you'll use all these techniques to expand the possibilities for your site.

■ Making Fancier Posts

You've seen plenty of WordPress posts so far, but none are likely to impress your web designer friends. Fortunately, you don't need to stick with the plain and ordinary. WordPress is packed full of tools for creating epically formatted posts.

The easiest way to start styling your posts is to start with a new one (to do that, choose Posts→Add New, as usual). Then look at the toolbar that sits at the top of the editing box. It's stocked with useful formatting commands (Figure 6-1).

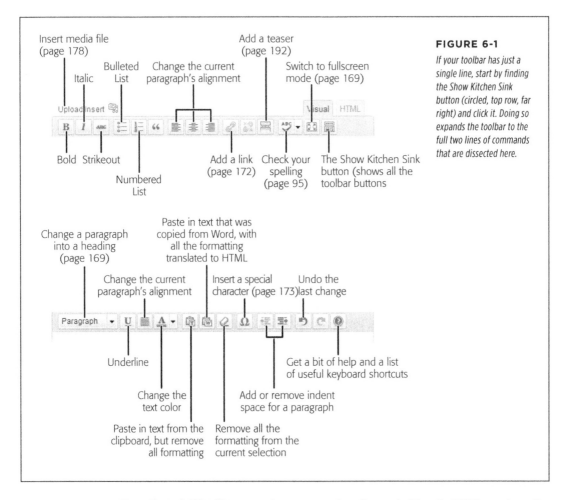

FIGURE 6-1

If your toolbar has just a single line, start by finding the Show Kitchen Sink button (circled, top row, far right) and click it. Doing so expands the toolbar to the full two lines of commands that are dissected here.

Even though WordPress creates your posts using web-friendly HTML markup, the toolbar buttons work in almost the same way they do in a word processor, complete with a basic Undo feature. It's like having a miniature Microsoft Word in your browser.

You can format your posts two ways. One is to select the bit of text that needs formatting and then click the corresponding toolbar button. For example, you can select a single word and add bold formatting by clicking the B button. Another approach is to use the toolbar buttons to turn a feature on or off (which computer nerds call *toggling*) as you write. For example, you could click the *I* button to turn on italic formatting, type something, and then click the *I* button again to turn off italics. The same on-off strategy works if you, say, convert a paragraph of text to a blockquote or a numbered list to a bulleted list.

TIP If you want to start a new line of text without starting a whole new paragraph, press Shift+Enter at the end of the preceding line (instead of hitting just the Enter key). Why? If you click just Enter, WordPress thinks you want to start a new paragraph, and adds space just before the beginning of the paragraph. When you use the Shift+Enter key combination, WordPress doesn't add the extra space.

The following sections explain a few of the finer points of post formatting. You'll see the proper way to work with headings, add links and special characters, and unlock even more capabilities by editing your post's HTML.

GEM IN THE ROUGH

Get More Space to Work

Need more space to write and review your content? You can make the post box a bit bigger by tweaking WordPress's settings. Choose Settings→Writing, look for the "Size of the post box" setting, and increase the number of lines (the default is 20). Or, you can expand the content box by clicking the bottom-right corner and dragging it down, as shown on page 125.

If you're craving even more screen real estate, check out the toolbar's Toggle Fullscreen Mode button (Figure 6-1). Click it, and WordPress resizes the editing boxes (those are the post title and post content boxes) to fill a larger portion of the web page, temporarily hiding the other parts of the Add New Post page and the dashboard menu. This mode is also called *distraction-free writing*, because the toolbar disappears while you type. (If you need a button, hover your mouse near the top of the page and the toolbar reappears.) When you finish writing, you can get back to the normal Add New Post page easily

enough: hover at the top of the page to show the WordPress editing toolbar, and then click the "Exit fullscreen" link.

Technically, WordPress's full-screen view doesn't occupy the full screen—it's more like full *browser* view. But you can go beyond that limit by switching your browser to *its* fullscreen view, too. On most browsers, you do that by pressing F11 (press it again to return the browser window to its normal state). When your browser is in full-screen mode, its window fills the entire screen (sans toolbars), and WordPress can claim virtually all of it to display your post.

There's one quirk, however: No matter how big you make your browser window, WordPress limits the width of the editing box, for two reasons. First, it's awkward to read and edit long lines of text. Second, most WordPress templates limit the width of posts to ensure readability. As a result, an unnaturally wide editing window would give you a false sense of the post's layout.

Using Subheadings

Every blog post starts with a heading—it's the title of your post, and it sits above the post content. But if you're writing a long post, it's often a good idea to subdivide your writing into smaller units, using subheadings inside your post.

To create a heading, you use the Format menu, on the far left of the second row of the toolbar (Figure 6-2). Usually, it displays the word "Paragraph," which tells you that WordPress is styling the current text as an ordinary paragraph.

FIGURE 6-2

The Format drop-down menu offers six levels of headings. Choose one, and you'll be rewarded with bigger, bolder text. If you know even a little about HTML, you won't be surprised to learn that a level-1 heading uses the <h1> element, a level-2 heading uses <h2>, and so on.

The heading level you use depends, at least partly, on your theme. Usually, you'll use a level-2 heading or level-3 heading to create subsections inside your post. (The box on page 171 has some more background information that can help you make your choice.) Whatever you do, don't add level-1 headings to your post sections. They can confuse search engines and assistive devices like screen readers.

NOTE The size, typeface, and exact appearance of a heading depends on your theme. You won't see exactly what your heading looks until you publish or preview your page.

Picking the Proper Heading Level

In the past, most WordPress themes displayed your site's name with a level-1 heading on the home page, and used a level-2 heading for each post title. WordPress aficionados would then use level-3 headings to divide their posts, and everything fit neatly together.

However, this system wasn't perfect. Most themes formatted the standalone post pages differently from the home page. In the single-post page, the post title became a level-1 heading. That makes sense, because search engines pay special attention to level-1 headings when they try to figure out what a page is all about. But it also causes a structural problem with subheadings, because a post could end up with a level-1 heading in the title and level-3 headings in the content, with no level-2 heading in between.

Then HTML5 hit the scene and changed all the rules. All of sudden, it was considered acceptable to have multiple level-1 headings on the same page, skip heading levels, and even put headings in the wrong order. In fact, those rules were in large part an attempt to simplify exactly the sort of situation that WordPress faces—how to put the same content (like a post) into different pages without confusing everyone.

The truth is, there's no single answer right now. But the best advice is this:

- If you're using the Twenty Eleven theme, use level-2 headings to subdivide a post. That's because the Twenty Eleven theme tries to straighten things out by making sure post titles *always* use level-1 headings, even when they're on the home page.

- If you're using an older theme, either level-2 or level-3 headings may work. But try level-3 headings first, and see how they look, because that's the safest and most common approach.

- If the size of your heading is too small, think twice before you switch the heading level. Instead, use the level that makes logical sense, and adjust the formatting by using styles (page 439).

Showing a Code Listing

You may notice that the Format list has more than just headings in it. It also includes the Paragraph, Address, and Preformatted formats, which map to the HTML elements <p>, <address>, and <pre>, respectively.

You use <p> for ordinary paragraphs, and you've already seen plenty of those. The <address> element is meant for contact information about who wrote the page, but it's rarely used. But the <pre> element is more useful—it displays text in a fixed-width font, which is ideal for listing programming code or simulating computer output (Figure 6-3).

FIGURE 6-3

In some themes, the <pre> element adds a gray background (as shown here in the Twenty Eleven theme). That separates the <pre> text from the rest of the page. Remember to use Shift+Enter to add line breaks between each line of code, rather than just Enter, which would add extra spacing and start a new paragraph.

Adding Links

The Web wouldn't amount to much without links, those blue underlined bits of text that bind one page to another. You can easily add links to a post. For example, imagine you have this sentence:

> This story was reported in the *New York Times*.

To turn "*New York Times*" into a link, select the text, and then click the Insert Link toolbar button. A window appears where you can either supply a full website address or link to one of the posts on your own site (Figure 6-4).

NOTE If you want to link to a file—for example, a document that your guest can download or a picture that they can view—you need to store that file in WordPress's media library. You'll get the full details on page 188.

To remove a link, click anywhere inside the link text and then click the Unlink button.

FIGURE 6-4

To add a link, you need to supply the URL (the website address) and a Title (the text that appears in a tooltip when a visitor hovers over the link). Alternatively, you can search for a post on your site, select it, and add a link to it. Either way, clicking Add Link seals the deal.

Inserting Special Characters

Special characters are usually defined as characters you don't see on your everyday keyboard. For example, if you use a standard U.S. keyboard, special characters include things like accented letters and typographic symbols.

WordPress lets you drop in one of a small set of special characters by using the Insert Custom Character command. Click it, and a window appears with a grid of unusual characters. Hover over one to get a closer look at it, and then click it to close the window and insert the character into your post (see Figure 6-5).

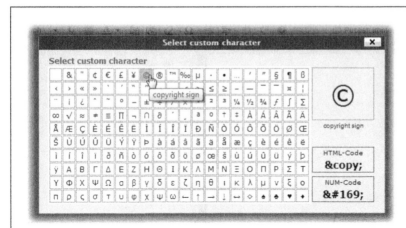

FIGURE 6-5

Here, you're about to insert the copyright symbol into a post.

You may not need all the special characters you think you do. WordPress automatically substitutes special characters for some character combinations. For example, if you type two dashes (--) between words, WordPress turns them into a seamless *en dash* (–) when you publish the post. Three dashes in a row creates a slightly longer *em dash* (—). Similarly, WordPress turns ordinary straight quotes ("") into typographically correct quotation marks (""). It works the same magic with apostrophes.

NOTE The oddest special characters WordPress supports are smilies, character combinations like :) that turn into emoticons like ☺. WordPress performs this substitution automatically, and you can learn about the smilies it supports (and what characters you need to enter them) at *http://codex.wordpress.org/Using_Smilies*. On the other hand, if the smilies feature is running amok and changing character sequences when you don't want it to, choose Settings→Writing and turn off the checkbox next to "Convert emoticons like :-) and :-P to graphics on display."

Formatting Your Text

How can I adjust typefaces and font sizes?

WordPress's post editor lets you structure your content (for example, put it into lists and headings), add more content (like pictures), and apply certain types of formatting (like boldface and *italics*). However, there are plenty of formatting details that aren't under your control. The size and typeface of your fonts is one of them.

This might seem like an awkward limitation, but it's actually a wise design decision on the part of the people who created WordPress. If WordPress gave you free reign to change fonts, you could easily end up with messy markup and posts that didn't match each other. Even worse, if you switched to a new theme, you'd be stuck with your old fonts, even though they might no longer suit your new look.

Fortunately, there's a more structured way to change the appearance of your text. Once you're certain you have the right theme for your website, you can modify its styles. For example, by changing the style rules, you can apply new font, color, and size settings to your text, and you can either make these changes to all your content, or to just specific elements (like all level-3 headings inside a post).

Modifying styles is a great way to personalize a theme, and you'll learn how to do that in Chapter 13. However, one caveat applies—if you're using WordPress.com to host your site, you need to buy the Custom Design upgrade to edit your styles (page 439). Self-hosted WordPress sites face no such restriction.

Using the HTML View

All the toolbar buttons you studied so far work by inserting the right HTML into your posts, behind the scenes. But if you've got a bit of web design experience, you don't need to rely on these conveniences. Using WordPress's HTML view, you can directly edit your post's HTML markup. You won't be limited by the buttons in the toolbar—instead, you can enter any HTML element you want.

To switch to HTML view, click the HTML tab that sits just above the post content box, on the right (Figure 6-6). To go back to the visual editor, click the Visual tab. In fact, there's no reason you can't spend time in both places. For example, you might write your post in the visual editor, and then switch to HTML view to inspect the markup.

In HTML view, you have a slightly different toolbar. It still has the useful "fullscreen" button, but most of the other shortcuts, which insert various HTML formatting tags, aren't much help. If you're savvy enough to prefer the HTML view, you probably want to type your markup in by hand.

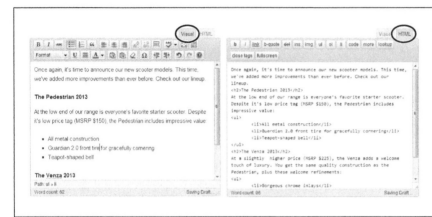

FIGURE 6-6

Here's the same document—with a heading and a list—shown in both the visual editor (left) and the HTML editor.

If you're a seasoned web designer, you might feel that WordPress's HTML editor isn't up to snuff. Full HTML editing programs like Dreamweaver and Expression Web are packed with little frills that can make editing easier—for example, they automatically add closing tags and suggest possible tag names as you type. (HTML editors also have more powerful layout and styling features, but those features make more sense when you're designing the look and layout of an entire site, not just adding a bit of content to a post.)

Most WordPress developers don't need the full features of a program like Dreamweaver. But there are exceptions. If you write long, complex posts—for example, the articles in the Internet Encyclopedia of Philosophy (page 20)—you probably don't want to do all your editing in a web page window. Hardcore HTML lovers who find themselves in this situation can write posts in an HTML editor like Dreamweaver, copy the markup, and then paste it into the HTML editor box in the Add New Post page. But don't try this trick unless you really understand your markup. That's because you need to make sure you don't end up transferring a whack of formatting details with your content—things like <span> elements with hardcoded font settings. If you do, you'll introduce some serious issues, including inconsistencies between posts and problems changing themes.

Getting a Better Post Editor

Most WordPress fans will do their work directly in their web browsers, using the WordPress editor. But if you're working with long documents and you're missing your favorite conveniences, here are some possible solutions:

- **Upgrade the WordPress editor.** If you're happy creating your posts in the familiar Add New Post web page but you just don't feel like you're getting enough help from the WordPress editor, you can replace it with something that has a bit more muscle. For example, advanced editors often add a search-and-replace feature, support for creating tables, and the ability to directly pick and choose the styles you want to apply from the current theme. To change the WordPress editor, you need to use a plug-in (Chapter 9), so it's a possibility for self-hosted WordPress sites only. You can search for a pumped-up post editor on the WordPress plug-in page (*http://wordpress.org/extend/plugins*). Although you'll find many free choices, TinyMCE is one the most popular. Check it out at *http://tinyurl.com/tinyeditor* and learn about installing plug-ins on page 275.

- **Use your tablet or phone.** It's impossible to beat the convenience of posting far from your computer, wherever you are, using a few swipes and taps on your favorite mobile device. In the past, developers created plug-ins that made mobile posting possible. Today, WordPress itself has taken over that role, and it offers an impressive range of free mobile apps at *http://wordpress.org/extend/mobile*. You'll find apps that work with iPads, iPhones, Android devices, BlackBerries, Windows phones, and more. All the apps are polished, professional, and free.

- **Use your word processor.** Usually, it's a bad idea to try to take formatted word processor text and stick in on the Web, unless you want a markup mess. However, some software—like Microsoft Word and the free Windows Live Writer (*http://tinyurl.com/24h2x65*)—has built-in WordPress support. That means you can compose a properly formatted post in these desktop programs— even if you don't have an Internet connection—and send your post to WordPress when you're ready to publish it. If you have a self-hosted WordPress site, you need to make a small change to your settings. In the dashboard, choose Settings→Writing, find the Remote Publishing section, and then turn on the XML-RPC checkbox. Sites on WordPress.com work automatically, and need no changes.

Using Post Formats

Some themes support *post formats*, a feature that styles different types of posts in slightly different ways. If your theme supports post formats, you'll see a Format box in the Add New Post and Edit Post pages. There, you'll find a list of all the formats the theme supports. You can pick any one of them to use for the current post, but if you don't make a choice, your post sticks with Standard. For example, a theme might include a post format named Highlighted, which makes the post stand out in the main home page by giving it a bigger title or a different background color.

Twenty Eleven supports post formats and includes six extra styles. However, few people use these formats, because they add minor formatting changes that aren't useful to most sites. For example, if you pick the Aside post format (intended for short posts of a paragraph or less), WordPress shows the post content on the home page, but hides the post title. The only reason you're likely to use the Twenty Eleven post formats is if you're creating a microblog (see the box on page 178).

Creating a Microblog

Microblogging is a blogging trend that focuses on small bits of content: news headlines, interesting links, personal status updates, random thoughts, and stream-of-consciousness chatter. Microblogs tend to be less formal, more personal, and more conversational than posts—almost like a cross between traditional blogs and old-school messaging systems like email and chat. The kings of microblogging are Twitter and Tumblr, but WordPress fans can join in, too.

Along with Aside, Twenty Eleven supports several other post formats tailored for microblogging: Link (a post that includes a link to another website, with little or no extra text), Quote (a block of text excerpted from a source indicated in the title), Status (a brief update about your status), Chat (the transcript of an online chat between two people), Image (a post that contains single picture, on its own), and Gallery (a post that contains a picture gallery, like the kind you'll learn to create on page 316). To see what the formatting looks like for different post formats, create a sample post and look at it on the home page. You can also add the Twenty Eleven Ephemera widget to your site, which shows the most recent Aside and Link posts.

One potential problem with the Twenty Eleven theme is that it allows microblogging *and* traditional posts. Although this scores points for flexibility, it can also encourage people to create slightly confused blogs, where the smaller microposts are drowned out by longer entries. If you're creating a personal blog that mixes long ruminations with microposts, think carefully about what the result will look like. One good idea is to use teasers for long posts (page 192), so that they don't dominate the homepage.

■ Using Pictures

You've now toured many of the post-enhancing features the Add New Post page offers. But there are several frills you haven't yet touched. The most obvious is adding graphics.

Virtually every good WordPress site can be made better with pictures. WordPress gives you several ways to display them, from the obvious (plopping them in your posts, alongside your text) to the more interesting (using them to build photoblogs, create slideshows, and advertise new posts on your home page). In the following sections, you'll learn how to take advantage of these slick picture tricks.

Putting Pictures in a Post

The most obvious place for a picture is in a post, right along with your content. WordPress makes it easy to insert pictures—in fact, you can put as many as you want into any post.

Here's how to add a picture as you create a post (in the Add New Post page) or edit one (in the Edit Post page):

1. **Click in the edit box, in the position where you want to add the picture.**

It doesn't matter whether you use the visual editor or the HTML editor. If you use the visual editor, you'll see every picture you insert right inside the editing box, along with your text. If you use the HTML editor, you'll see the markup: an <img> element for the picture, wrapped in an <a> anchor element (to turn the picture into a link), and possibly some other elements if you add a title or caption.

2. **Just above the box where you type in your content, you'll see a set of buttons labeled "Upload/Insert." Click the first button, Add Media, which is represented by a camera/music note icon (see Figure 6-3).**

   The Add Media window appears (Figure 6-7).

   The Add Media window includes three tabs, each of which gives you a different way to find a picture. You can upload a file from your computer (the From Computer tab), use a file that's somewhere else online (From URL), or grab a file you already uploaded to WordPress's media library (Media Library).

   In this example, you want to stick to the From Computer tab. Grabbing pictures from other website addresses (using From URL) might be worthwhile if you store graphics on another part of your site. But if it's someone else's site, don't chance it—the risk that the picture is copyrighted, or that it could be changed or moved after you link to it, is too great. The Media Library tab is also useful, but only after you build up a collection of pictures. You'll take a look at it on page 188.

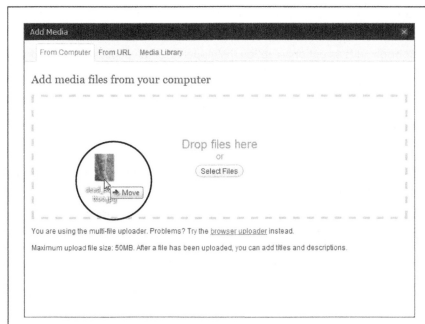

FIGURE 6-7

Using the From Computer tab, you can upload one or more pictures from your computer. First, you drop a picture into the "Drop files here" box. Once you release the image, WordPress begins uploading it.

3. **Pick the files you want to upload.**

WordPress gives you two options. The quickest approach is to drag files from an open file browser window (like Windows Explorer or the Mac's Finder) and drop them in the "Drop files here" box. You can drag as many files as you want, either all at once or one at a time, and it doesn't matter if you keep dropping in new files before WordPress finishes uploading the old ones.

Your other option is to pick your files from a standard dialog box—to do that, click Select Files, browse to the right folder, and pick what you want. If you hold down the Ctrl key (or Command key on a Mac), you can select multiple files at once, although they all need to be in the same folder.

No matter which approach you use, WordPress begins uploading your files as soon as you drop them into the "Drop files here" box. WordPress shows a progress bar for each file underneath the box.

When WordPress finishes an upload, it replaces the progress bar with a large box that includes a thumbnail of your image and a pile of text boxes asking you for all kinds of information (see Figure 6-8). You need to scroll down to see everything.

4. **Scroll down and fill in the information for your picture.** WordPress asks for the following:

Title is the text that appears in a tooltip when someone hovers over a picture.

Alternate Text is the text that's sent to assistive devices (like screen readers) to help users with disabilities interpret pictures they can't see.

Caption adds an optional caption that appears on the page near your picture. Different themes handle captions differently, but they usually place them under your picture, as in Figure 6-9. Captions can include HTML tags (for example, <b> for bold formatting), but you need to type them in yourself.

Description is a longer, more detailed explanation of the picture. You can use it for your records, or you might decide to display it on your page—but you need to find a theme that shows image descriptions (most don't) or edit your theme by hand (Chapter 13). If you don't plan to use the description, you can leave this box empty.

Link URL is the web address where WordPress sends visitors if they click your pic. Usually, when someone clicks your picture, the browser loads up the full-size picture file without any headers, sidebars, captions, or extra content. Alternatively, you can tell WordPress to take readers to something called an *attachment page*, which features the full-sized version of your picture and a section for reader comments (select Attachment Post URL) or to go to another web address that you specify. Or, you can tell WordPress not to make the picture clickable at all (select None).

Alignment determines where a picture appears relative to its text. If you choose None, the picture stands on its own, wherever you inserted it. Paragraphs may appear before it or after it, but the post content won't flow on either side of the picture. If you choose Left or Right, WordPress puts the picture on one side of the page, and the text flows around the other side in the most convenient way possible (see Figure 6-9).

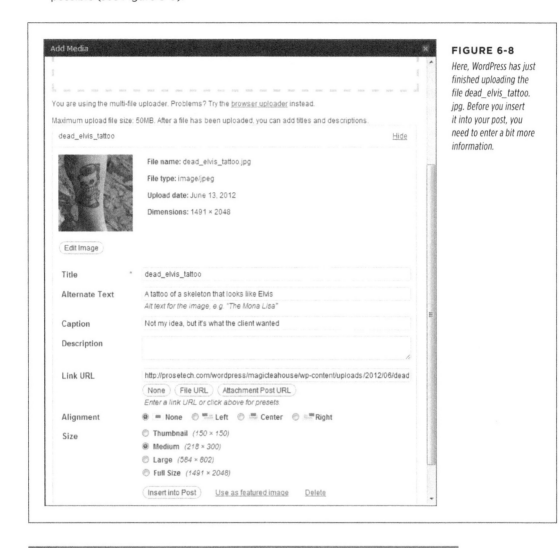

FIGURE 6-8

Here, WordPress has just finished uploading the file dead_elvis_tattoo. jpg. Before you insert it into your post, you need to enter a bit more information.

TIP If your text narrates your pictures, you'll probably choose None so that you have the pictures exactly where you want them. Examples include food blogs with pictures of meals, travelogues with pictures of tourist sites, and home renovation stories with a photo journal of the step-by-step process. On the other hand, if you have a rich layout that's more like a glossy magazine, you might decide to use Left or Right for your picture alignment.

Size tells WordPress how big the picture should be in your post. You can choose Full Size to use the original dimensions of uploaded file. Or, you can use one of the scaled-down versions of your picture, which WordPress creates automatically when you upload a file. You'll notice that WordPress maintains the relative proportions of your picture—it never squashes a picture more width-wise than it does height-wise. If you use the picture's address for the Link URL box, readers can click a scaled-down picture to see the full-size image on a new page.

NOTE Normally, WordPress creates three extra versions of every picture: a 150 x 150 pixel thumbnail, a 300 x 300 medium size, and a 1024 x 1024 large size. You can change these defaults in the Settings→Media section of the dashboard, under the "Image sizes" heading. However, the changes will affect only new pictures, not the ones you've already uploaded.

Dead Elvis

Here's my latest work. I call it the "Dead Elvis" tattoo, for obvious reasons.

What do you think—ridiculously cool, or completely creepy?

— Not my idea, but it's what the client wanted

This entry was posted in Uncategorized by Katya Greenview. Bookmark the permalink.

FIGURE 6-9

This theme aligns images on the left, which means the text in the post flows down the right side of the image. Notice that the Twenty Eleven theme keeps the picture and the caption together using a light gray background.

5. **Optionally, you can edit your picture by clicking Edit Image (Figure 6-10). Click Save when you finish.**

You can *crop* your picture by clicking and dragging a rectangle around the region you want to keep. Then click the Crop button.

You can *scale* your picture, reducing it in size until it matches the size you want in your post. This is a good idea if you have a very large image (like one taken with a digital camera), because there's no point in forcing your visitors to download a huge file when you're not displaying it full-size. To scale a picture, click the Scale Image link and enter in either a new width or a new height, in pixels. WordPress adjusts the other dimension proportionally, ensuring you don't distort the picture. Then click Scale to make the change.

Less usefully, you can flip or rotate your picture.

To perform these tasks, just click the corresponding button, which appear in a small strip above the picture. The most common reason to edit a picture is to cut it down to size. Smaller pictures download faster, which means visitors with a slow Internet connection endure less waiting. But if you have lots of big pictures to scale, you can probably resize them more quickly on your computer, using basic image-editing software.

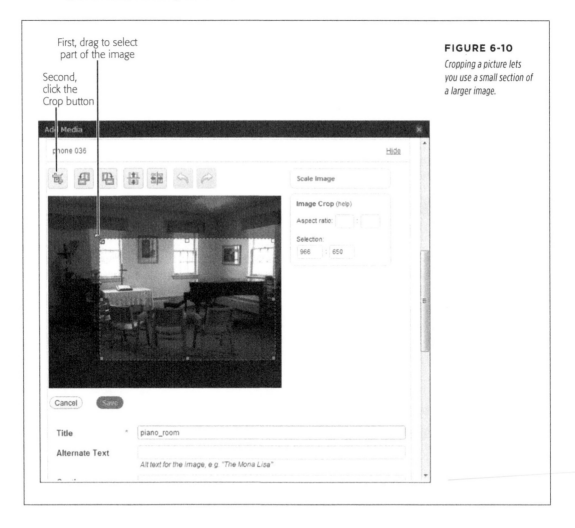

First, drag to select part of the image

Second, click the Crop button

FIGURE 6-10

Cropping a picture lets you use a small section of a larger image.

When you edit a picture, WordPress actually creates a new file. If you look at the URL, you'll notice that WordPress appends a number to the end of the file name, so *dead_elvis_tattoo.jpg* becomes *dead_elvis_tattoo-e1339626522667.jpg*, for example. There are two reasons for this sleight-of-hand. First, it prevents problems if one of your posts needs to use the original version of the picture. Second, it lets you get your original picture back later if you ever need it. To do that, just edit the image in the media library (page 188), and then click Restore Original Image.

6. **Click the "Insert into post" link to add the picture to your post.**

   When you insert a picture, you'll see it in the visual editor. If you chose left or right alignment, you can type your text around the side of the picture. If you chose None for the alignment, you can only type text above and below the image.

   If you decide you want to tweak your picture, just click inside it once. Doing so selects the picture, and calls up two small buttons in the picture's top-left corner. Use the Edit Image button to open the same editing window you used earlier. Use the Delete Image button to remove the picture from your post.

If you delete a picture from your post, it still exists on your WordPress site. This might be what you want (for example, it lets you add the picture to another post later), or it might be a problem (if you're worrying about someone stumbling across an embarrassing incident you made the mistake of photographing). To wipe a picture off your site, you need to use the media library, as described in the next section.

You can add as many pictures as you want to a post. To add a new picture, just follow the preceding steps all over again.

GEM IN THE ROUGH

Attaching Other Files to Your Post

Pictures aren't the only file you can put in a post. WordPress. com allows a number of document formats, including PDFs, Word documents, Excel spreadsheets, and PowerPoint presentations. In a self-hosted site, you face no restrictions, so you can upload any file you want.

The difference is what happens *after* you upload the file. There's no way to embed the types of content mentioned above along-

side the text of a post. Instead, WordPress displays an ordinary link that leads to the uploaded file. If a reader clicks the link, the browser may display the document or offer to download it. It all depends on whether the browser has an add-in that's able to display that type of file. For example, many browsers have add-ins that can display PDF documents.

Featured Images

Instead of simply including a picture in a post, you can designate it as a featured image. A featured image represents a post, but it doesn't actually show up as part of the post content. Instead, its role varies depending on the theme you use. Some themes ignore featured images altogether, while others have devised ingenious ways to exploit them. For example, in the standard Twenty Eleven theme, featured images replace the site header on your home screen. Figure 6-11 shows how this works.

FIGURE 6-11

When you read this post in single-post view, the featured image (some green tea leaves) temporarily replaces the site header. This works even though the picture doesn't actually appear anywhere in the post.

NOTE The header-replacement trick works only if the featured image is at least as big as the header image. If your featured image isn't as wide, WordPress won't display it at all on the single-post page, nor will it explain the image's perplexing absence.

The changing-header trick is interesting, but the real magic is the way that different themes can use featured images in completely different ways. Many themes use them to promote posts—for example, to highlight them in some sort of scrolling banner or gallery. Depending on the theme, this detail might be a built-in part of the home page, or it might rely on a theme-specific widget.

Figure 6-12 shows the free Brightpage theme, which is available to self-hosted WordPress sites. It uses a featured image slideshow on the home page. This slider automatically grabs all the posts in the category named Featured (which you must create). It then shows the featured image for each of the posts, one after the other.

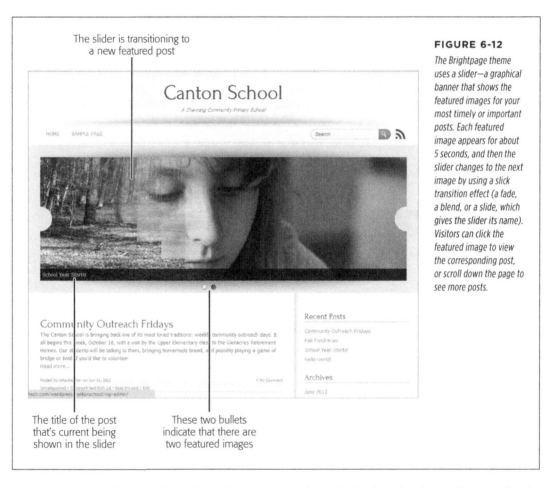

The slider is transitioning to a new featured post

FIGURE 6-12

The Brightpage theme uses a slider—a graphical banner that shows the featured images for your most timely or important posts. Each featured image appears for about 5 seconds, and then the slider changes to the next image by using a slick transition effect (a fade, a blend, or a slide, which gives the slider its name). Visitors can click the featured image to view the corresponding post, or scroll down the page to see more posts.

The title of the post that's current being shown in the slider

These two bullets indicate that there are two featured images

The nice thing about the Brightpage theme is that it makes it easy for you, the site designer, to choose what posts appear in the slider. When you create a new post that you want to appear in the slider, simply assign it to the Featured category (in addition to whatever more meaningful category you're already using to classify your post). After some time passes and you decide that the post is no longer as important, go to the Edit Post page and remove it from the Featured category.

You can assign just one featured image to a post. To do so, you need to be in the Add New Post or Edit Post page. Then follow these steps:

1. **Find the Featured Image box in the bottom-right corner of the page. Click the "Set featured image" link.**

This opens a window that looks exactly like the Add Media window you saw earlier (Figure 6-7).

2. **Upload the picture you want to use.**

   You can upload your featured image by dragging it into the "Drop files here" area, or by clicking Select Files and browsing for it.

3. **Add the image information.**

   Once you upload a pic, the Set Featured Image window expands so you can add details about the image (title, alternate text for screen readers, caption, and so on). How much of this information WordPress uses in your post depends on the theme you chose, but it's worth supplying the info just in case.

4. **Click Edit Image, take a moment to scale and crop your picture, and then click Save to make your changes permanent.**

   When you insert a standard image into a post, you get the chance to size it. But if you use a theme that automatically displays featured images, you don't have this control. If you upload a big picture, it's possible that your theme will automatically crop out a large part of it. (The Brightpage theme does this, for example.) To prevent this, you need to scale the picture down before you upload it, using an image editor like Photoshop Elements, Windows Photo Gallery, Picasa, or the Mac's Preview program. To find the right dimensions, you need to experiment or scour the documentation for your theme. (Self-hosters: search for your theme at *http://wordpress.org/extend/themes*, and then click your way through to the "Theme Homepage" link. WordPress.com users: search for your theme at *http://theme.wordpress.com*.)

5. **Click the "Use as featured image" link that appears underneath the picture information, and then close the Set Featured Image window by clicking the X in the top-right corner.**

   If you decide at some future point that you don't want this picture as your post's featured image, just click the "Remove featured image" link in the Featured Image box.

6. **Publish your post (or update it, if you had already published it).**

   Remember, some themes don't use featured images at all. If you use such a theme, you may not even know that your post has a featured image, because your theme never displays it.

NOTE Featured posts are interesting because they rely on the interplay between WordPress features and theme features. WordPress simply defines the concept of the feature (in this case, featured images), and the theme decides how to exploit that concept, opening a wide, uncharted territory of possibilities. The same idea underpins many other WordPress features. For example, later in this chapter you'll see how WordPress defines the concepts of post excerpts (page 196) and post formats (page 177), but allows themes to use them in a variety of clever ways.

■ The Media Library

When you upload a picture to your site, WordPress stores it in the *wp-content/uploads* folder of your site. For example, if you upload a picture named *face_photo.jpg* to the Magic Tea House site on January 2013, WordPress will store it at *http://magicteahouse .net/wp-content/uploads/2013/01/face_photo.jpg*. Behind the scenes, WordPress also creates large, medium, and thumbnail-sized copies of your picture with names like *face_photo_300x200.jpg*, and it stores them in the same folder. (You can choose one of these resized copies when you insert the picture into a post, as described on page 181.)

WordPress might store more files than you think. In addition to all the pictures you insert into posts, all the featured images you use, and any custom header or background images you add to your theme, WordPress stores files that you attach to your posts here, too, like PDFs, Word documents, and spreadsheets (page 184). Furthermore, if you change a picture (using the basic cropping, resizing, and rotating tools described on page 182), WordPress stores a new, separate version of the picture as well.

WordPress calls this repository, which holds your pictures and files, the *media library*. To see the current contents of your site's media library, choose Media→Library (Figure 6-13).

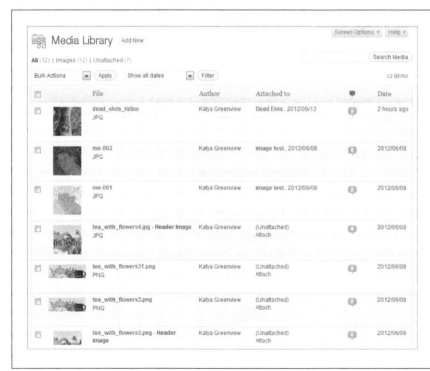

FIGURE 6-13

WordPress's media library lists all the files you've uploaded. The "Attached to" column indicates whether you've used a file in a post (and, if you have, which post features it). For example, the owner of this site used the first picture in this list (me.jpg) in the post "Green Tea for Health Seminar."

There are two reasons that you might want to use the media library: to remove files you don't need anymore, and to upload files you want to use in the future.

Deleting Pictures from the Library

You might choose to delete a media file as part of your basic website housekeeping. After all, why keep around a file that you aren't using, especially if it's distracting you from the files you really *do* want?

To delete a media file, simply hover over a file name and then click the Delete Permanently link that appears underneath. It's much the same way that you remove a post.

If you delete a picture that other posts are using, you have a small problem. When someone reads the post, they'll see the broken-picture-link icon, the universal browser sign that something's missing. Correcting this problem is easy (just edit the post and delete the picture box), but it's up to you to find the post.

NOTE WordPress doesn't let you *replace* a picture. If you upload a new picture that has the same name as one already in your library, WordPress gives it a slightly different web address. The same thing happens if you change a picture that's already in the media library. This system prevents a number of seriously frustrating problems, but it also means that there's no way to update the picture in a post without editing the post.

Adding Pictures to the Library

You might choose to add a media file to your library to prepare for future posts. Maybe you have a batch of pictures that detail a home renovation project, and you plan to write about the process on your blog, "Home Sweet Home." However, you don't want to start writing those posts yet. To make sure the pictures are ready when you need them, you can upload them straight to the media library, and then use them later. Here's what to do:

1. **Choose Media→Add New.**

   You'll see an Upload New Media page that looks almost identical to the From Computer tab of the Add Media window (Figure 6-7).

2. **Add your files.**

   You upload media files just as you did in the Add Media window: by dragging them onto the "Drop files here" box or by clicking the Select Files button.

3. **Optionally, fill in the information for each picture.**

   You can fill in the picture details (like the title and caption) and edit the image (say, cropping it or flipping it). When you actually insert the image into a post, you'll still have the chance to enter new information or reedit the picture. But if you get some of the preliminary details down when you upload the picture, you'll save some time when you insert it.

To insert a picture from the media library into a post, use the same Upload/Insert button you learned about earlier. Here's what to do as you create or edit a post:

1. **Move to the place in the post where you want to insert the picture and then click the Upload/Insert button.**

   The Add Media window appears.

2. **Click the Media Library tab.**

   You'll see a list of all the files in your library (Figure 6-14).

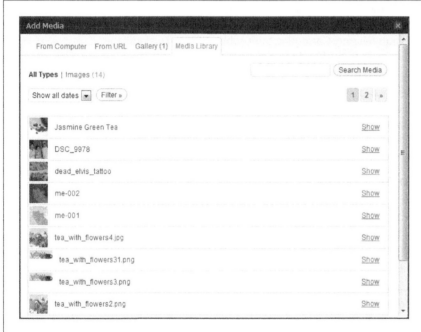

FIGURE 6-14

You'll see a Show link next to each file in your media library. Click it, and the familiar Add Media box appears with a thumbnail of the picture and the picture details (alternate text, caption, and so on).

3. **Find the picture you want, and then click the Show link next to it.**

   You'll see the familiar picture thumbnail and picture details.

4. **Change the text and edit the image, if necessary.**

5. **When you're ready to add the picture, click "Insert into Post."**

   Or, if you want to use this picture for the post's featured image, click the "Use as featured image" link.

Using the Media Library to Put a Picture in Your Sidebar

As you already know, the media library stores all the pictures you use in your posts. You can also use it to store files you want to use in some other way. For example, you can link to one of your media files from an ordinary web page on a traditional, non-WordPress website. All you need to do is take note of the file URL. (To get that, choose Media→Library to visit the media library, and then click the file you're interested in. You'll see the file's location in the File URL text box.)

You can use the same trick to inject an image into the Text widget (page 155), that all-purpose tool for showing scraps of content outside your posts. As you learned in Chapter 5, the Text widget accepts almost any HTML you can throw at it. So if you know you have a picture in the media file with the URL *http://magicteahouse.net/wp-content/uploads/2012/06/dead_elvis_tattoo.jpg*, you can stick in an <img> tag like this:

```
<p>I'm a <b>hotshot tattoo artist</b>
living in the Bay Area. My work pushes the
bounds of taste and decency, just like you
know you want.</p>
```

```
<img src="http://magicteahouse.net/wp-
content/uploads/2012/06/dead_elvis_tattoo.
jpg">
```

If you've been around the web block, you probably know that it's better to trim the picture link down to just */wp-content/ uploads/2012/06/dead_elvis_tattoo.jpg*. It's on the same site as the rest of your WordPress content, so there's no need to include the domain name.

Either way, Figure 6-15 shows the result.

FIGURE 6-15

With the help of the media library, you can mix text and pictures in WordPress's Text widget.

◼ Showing Part of a Post

At the heart of every WordPress blog is a home page, and the heart of the home page is a reverse-chronological list of recent posts, called the *post stream*. This list serves a vital purpose, showing a snapshot of current content so readers can tell, at a glance, what's going down on your site.

However, the home pages you've seen so far have had one potential problem—they're long, sometimes awkwardly so. Having multiple posts fused together into one long page is a great convenience for new visitors who want to read your content from end-to-end, but it's not so helpful for return visitors who want to survey your new content and decide where to dive in.

Fortunately, WordPress has a handy solution. You can decide to show only the first part of each post, called a *teaser,* on your home page, and then your visitor can click a link to read the standalone post.

One advantage to this approach is that you can pack quite a few teasers into your home page and keep them close together, no matter how long the posts really are. You can also put posts into tighter layouts—for example, creating a site that looks more like the front page of a newspaper. Another advantage is that it encourages readers to click through to the post, where they'll also see the post comments and get the opportunity to join in the discussion.

However, trimming down posts introduces two possible disadvantages. First, there's the extra link readers need to follow to read a full post. If someone wants to read several posts in a row, this extra step can add up to a lot more clicking. Second, you need to explicitly tell WordPress what part of a post belongs on the home page. It's an easy job, but you need to do it for *each post* you create. If you've already written a few posts, you'll need to update them.

> **NOTE** As a general rule of thumb, informal, conversational blogs work well with the standard one-post-after-another stream that WordPress puts on the home page. But WordPress sites that have more detailed article-like posts, use multiple sections, or feature multiple authors, often work better with a tighter, leaner style that uses teasers.

In the following section, you'll learn how to use teasers instead of full posts. You'll also consider two related features: breaking posts into multiple pages and using post excerpts.

Displaying Teasers Using the "More" Quicktag

The best way to cut a post down to size is with a special WordPress code called the *More quicktag.* You place the More quicktag at the spot where you want to divide a post. The content that falls before the tag becomes the teaser, and Word-Press displays it on the home page (Figure 6-16, left). If a reader clicks through to the single-post page, he sees the entire post, with no trace of the More quicktag (Figure 6-16, right).

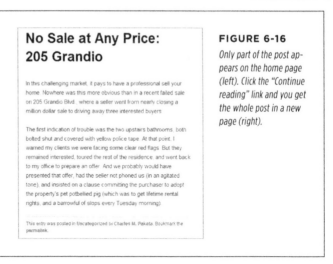

FIGURE 6-16

Only part of the post appears on the home page (left). Click the "Continue reading" link and you get the whole post in a new page (right).

To insert the More quicktag in the visual editor, move to the position where you want to put the tag, and then click the Insert More Tag button. You'll see a light gray dividing line (Figure 6-17).

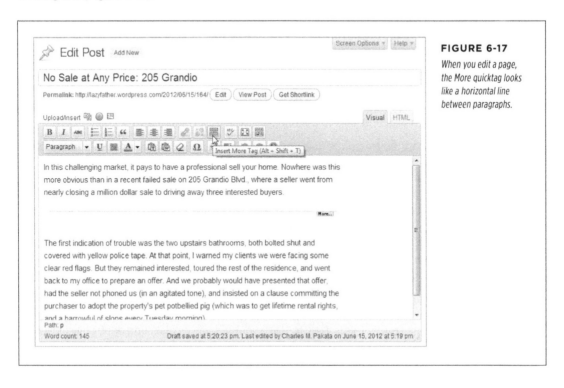

FIGURE 6-17

When you edit a page, the More quicktag looks like a horizontal line between paragraphs.

You can also add the More quicktag in the HTML editor. You could click the button labeled "more," but it's just as easy to type in yourself, wherever you want it:

```
<!--more-->
```

HTML nerds will recognize that the More quicktag looks exactly like an HTML comment—the sort of thing you might put in your markup to leave notes to yourself. Browsers ignore HTML comments, and WordPress borrows this system to sneak in some of its own special codes.

NOTE WordPress uses the More quicktag whenever your site displays more than one post at a time. The home page is the most obvious example, but you'll also see multiple posts when you browse by category, date, or keyword. In these situations, the More quicktag serves the same purpose—it trims long posts down to more manageable teasers.

There's one more trick you can do with the More tag. In the previous example, a "Continue reading" link led from the teaser to the full post. The theme determines this detail, but if you want, you can override the text with something else. To do that, you need to edit your post in HTML view, and stick the link text in the middle of the More tag, exactly as shown here:

```
<!--more Tell me more-->
```

It's best to use this trick sparingly, to customize posts that need to stand out in some way. If you want to change the link text for every teaser, editing your theme is far more efficient (see Part Four).

Dividing a Post into Multiple Pages

The More quicktag lets you split a post into two pieces: the teaser, and the rest of the content. There's another choice—you can use the lesser-known *Nextpage quicktag* to split a page into as many sections as you want. When you do, WordPress adds a set of navigation links to the bottom of the post (Figure 6-18).

To insert the Nextpage quicktag, switch to the HTML view and then add this code where you want to start a new page:

```
<!--nextpage-->
```

The Nextpage quicktag still shows up in the visual editor, as a gray line with the words "Next Page" above it. The Nextpage quicktag isn't customizable, although you can create custom page links if you're willing to edit your theme files, as described in Part Four. The trick is to master WordPress's *wp_link_pages()* function, which is described at *http://tinyurl.com/wplinkpages*.

You can use the More quicktag and the Nextpage quicktag in the same post. However, it's generally a bad idea, because the page links will appear under the post teaser on the home page. This is likely to strike your readers as plain odd or utterly confusing.

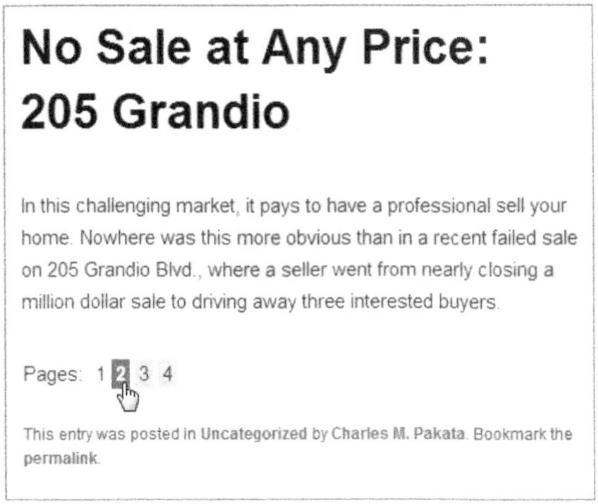

No Sale at Any Price: 205 Grandio

In this challenging market, it pays to have a professional sell your home. Nowhere was this more obvious than in a recent failed sale on 205 Grandio Blvd., where a seller went from nearly closing a million dollar sale to driving away three interested buyers.

Pages: 1 **2** 3 4

This entry was posted in Uncategorized by Charles M. Pakata. Bookmark the permalink.

FIGURE 6-18

These page navigation links are a great way to split a long article into more manageable pieces. But use it sparingly—readers will resent being forced to click without a very good reason.

Summarizing Posts with Excerpts

There's another way that WordPress shortens posts: by using a feature it calls *excerpts*. Ordinarily, an excerpt is the first 50-or-so words in a post (the exact number depends on the theme).

Before you can understand how excerpts work, you need to know when WordPress uses them. But the answer isn't straightforward, because it depends on your theme. In many WordPress themes, including the standard Twenty Eleven theme, WordPress uses excerpts when a visitor performs a search. To see what excerpts look like, try typing something into the Search box, and then press Enter (Figure 6-19).

So far, excerpts seem straightforward and automatic (and they are). However, the first few sentences of a post isn't always a good reflection of its content. For that reason, you may want to write your own excerpt—in other words, explicitly provide a brief summary of the content in a post. You can do that from the Add New Post or Edit Post pages. First, choose Screen Options in the upper-right corner, and then turn on the checkbox next to Excerpt. A new box appears where you can write a better description of your post.

NOTE Things can get a bit confusing if you use excerpts *and* teasers. In that case, WordPress uses an excerpt if the post has one, a teaser if the post uses the More quicktag, or the first 55 words in the post if it has neither an excerpt or a teaser.

FIGURE 6-19

When you search posts, WordPress doesn't display full posts on the results screen. Instead, the Twenty Eleven theme automatically strips out the first 55 words, and uses that. That way, you can see a page of search results without needing to scroll all day.

Using Excerpts on Your Home Page

At this point, you might think that it's not worth the trouble of writing excerpts for all your posts. And you could well be right, if you're using the standard theme and you don't expect your visitors to be launching many searches. However, there's another wrinkle. Some themes use excerpts for other purposes.

For example, many themes use excerpts as the display text for posts on the home page. This way, the excerpt acts a bit like a teaser. The difference is that the standard WordPress teaser comes from the first part of a post, whereas an excerpt can include any text you want.

The Brightpage theme described earlier (page 186) uses this system. If you provide an excerpt for a post, that's what shows up on your home page, not the post content. The Oxygen theme, available for both WordPress.com and self-hosted sites, does the same thing, as you can see in Figure 6-20.

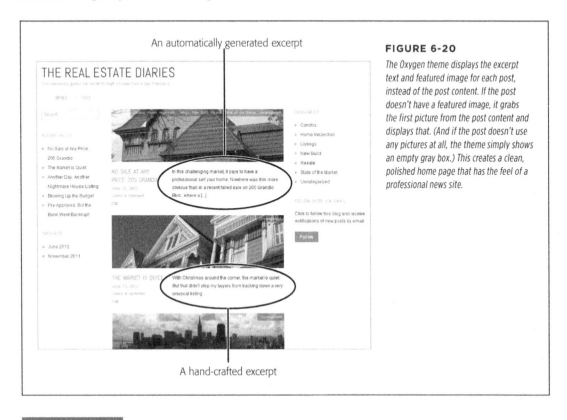

An automatically generated excerpt

A hand-crafted excerpt

FIGURE 6-20

The Oxygen theme displays the excerpt text and featured image for each post, instead of the post content. If the post doesn't have a featured image, it grabs the first picture from the post content and displays that. (And if the post doesn't use any pictures at all, the theme simply shows an empty gray box.) This creates a clean, polished home page that has the feel of a professional news site.

Writing Good Excerpts

The best thing about excerpts is that they don't need to be directly linked to the text in your post. But don't abuse your freedom—to write a good, genuinely useful excerpt, you need to follow a few rules:

- **Keep it brief.** Usually, when a visitor searches your site, WordPress finds several matching posts. By keeping your excerpts short (around the 55-word mark, just like WordPress does), you keep the search results short, which makes them easier to read.

- **Summarize the content of the page.** The goal of an excerpt is to give someone enough information to decide if they want to click a link to read the full post. An excerpt isn't a place to promote yourself or make flowery comments. Instead, try to clearly and honestly describe what's in the post.

- **Don't repeat the post title.** If you want to make sure every word counts, don't waste time repeating what's clearly visible in the title.

If you switch to a theme that makes heavy use of excerpts, you might find that the summary is so valuable you want all your posts to use them, even the ones you already created. WordPress has some plug-ins that can help. For example, you can use the Excerpt Editor (*http://tinyurl.com/csudedx*) to add summaries to existing posts without needing to edit each post individually.

Changing from Full-Posts Display to Summaries

If you create a self-hosted site, you can make any theme display excerpts or full posts. But first, you need to learn the basics about WordPress theme files and the WordPress loop, topics that are covered in Chapters 13 and 14.

Once you know your way around a WordPress theme and the PHP code inside, you're ready to make this relatively straightforward edit. Usually, you need to make the change in your *index.php* file, which creates the post listing on the home page of your site.

To get the display style you want, your code needs to use the right WordPress function. If you use a function named *the_content()*, your page will show the full content for each post (or the teaser, if you're using the More quicktag described on page 192). But if you use a function named *the_excerpt()*, your page will display your post summary only. Usually, you can switch between the two display modes by modifying the line of code that has the function in it.

If you want a bit more technical information, check out what the WordPress function reference has to say on the topic at *http://tinyurl.com/the-excerpt*.

7

Adding Pages
and Menus

In previous chapters, you focused most of your attention on WordPress *posts*—the blocks of dated, categorized WordPress content at the heart of most WordPress blogs. But WordPress has another, complementary way to showcase content, called *pages*. Unlike posts, pages aren't dated, categorized, or tagged. They exist independently of posts. The easiest way to understand the role of WordPress pages is to think of them as ordinary web pages, like the kind you might compose in an HTML editor.

You're likely to use pages for two reasons. First, even in a traditional blog, there will be some content you want to keep around permanently, rather than throw into your ever-advancing sequence of posts. For example, personal blogs often include a page named About Me, where you provide biographical information. You don't want to tie this page to a specific date—you want it easily accessible all the time. Similarly, businesses might use pages to provide contact information, a map, or a list of frequently asked questions.

The other reason to use pages is to build simple sites that don't feel like blogs. Some people call these sites "brochure sites," and the description isn't entirely complimentary. That's because brochure sites present a collection of fixed information, while blogs feel live and interactive. However, there's a wide range of possibility between these two extremes. For example, if you create a site for your small business, you might use pages to display the core content of your site (filling them with information about your company, your policies, the brands you carry, and so on), while adding a blog-powered section of posts for news and promotions. Is this a blog, a brochure-site, or something in between? No matter what the answer, it's a great solution for plenty of people.

In this chapter, you'll learn to use pages in your site, either to supplement your blog or to create a brochure-style site. You'll also learn to manage page navigation with menus, so your visitors can find the content they want. Lastly, you'll consider some of the innovative ways that themes exploit pages. For example, you'll see how you can use pages to build a showcase of posts.

■ Creating Pages

Although pages behave differently from posts, the process of creating and managing them is similar. In the dashboard, you use the Pages submenu.

1. **Choose Pages→Add New.**

   This takes you to a screen named Add New Page (Figure 7-1), which resembles a slightly simpler version of the Add New Post page.

   If your site is on WordPress.com, you can take advantage of another path to page creation—the Copy Page shortcut, which creates a new page based on an old one. Choose Pages→Copy a Page (instead of Pages→Add New), find the page you want to duplicate in the resulting list of pages, and then click the Copy button next to it. You'll still end up at the Add New Page screen, but you'll start out with an exact duplicate of the page you picked, which you can then modify to suit your needs.

FIGURE 7-1

Pages are similar to posts. Both let you include pictures, fancy HTML markup, and featured images. But pages don't let you add the classification details that posts do, like category and tag information, which is why you don't see those options here.

2. **Give the page a title and some content.**

    You'll see the same content-editing box you use to create posts, with its choice between the visual editor and the HTML view.

    For now, don't worry about the Page Attributes box—you'll learn about the options there a bit later.

3. **Finally, click Publish to make the page live on your site.**

    Or, choose one of the other options in the Publish box. Just as with posts, you can save a page as a draft (page 96) or schedule it for future publication (page 99).

    When you publish your page, a familiar yellow message box appears at the top of the page, confirming that it's up and open to the public. Now's a good time to click the "View page" link to take a look (Figure 7-2).

Understanding Pages

Why do some people call pages "static pages"?

Although WordPress calls this feature *pages*, many webheads find that confusing. After all, isn't a page anything that you view on the Web with a browser? And don't posts appear in web pages?

For these reasons, WordPress experts—and WordPress itself, sometimes—often use a different term. They call WordPress pages *static pages*. Sadly, this term is almost as confusing. It stems from the old days of the Web, when designers distinguished between dynamic pages that could do incredible feats with the help of code, and static pages that showed fixed, unchanging content. That fits with the way that most people use WordPress pages—they create them, fill them with content, and then publish them.

However, WordPress pages aren't really static—they *do* change. Flip your blog over to a different theme, and all your posts

and pages update seamlessly to match the new style. That's because WordPress stores all the content for your pages—as well as the content for the rest of your site, including posts—in its database. And, finally, a static page changes when you decide to open one up and update its information.

If you're still confused, here's the bottom line: A WordPress site can hold both pages and posts, which you create, format, and manage in much the same way. The key difference is that WordPress automatically dates, orders, and groups posts. WordPress also puts them on the home page, and assumes that people will want to read them from newest to oldest. From WordPress's point of view, posts are the lead actors on your site, while pages are supporting characters. But you're not bound by that narrow definition of a site, as you'll see on page 220.

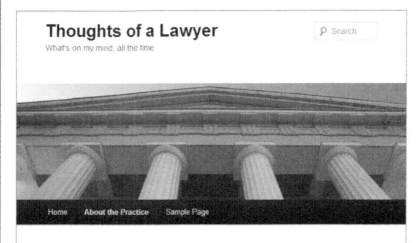

FIGURE 7-2

A page looks suspiciously like a post. If you keep WordPress's default settings, your page even has room for comments, which you'll learn to use in Chapter 8. (You can also turn comments off for your pages, as explained on page 230.)

To review a list of all the pages on your site, choose Pages→All Pages. You'll see a familiar table of pages, which works the same way as WordPress's list of posts and media files. Hover over a page, and you have the choice to view it, edit it, or delete it (see Figure 7-3). And if you're working with piles of pages, you can use the same bulk actions you use with posts to delete or change a whole group of pages in one step—but you already guessed that.

FIGURE 7-3

Every WordPress site starts with a sample page called, rather unimaginatively, Sample Page. Now's a good time to delete it. Just hover over the page and then click Trash.

Viewing Pages

You can probably think of a couple of pages that would improve your site. If nothing else, you could add an About Me page with your biographical information in it. But a key question remains: How do your guests visit your published pages?

Like posts, every page gets a unique web address (URL), called a permalink. The permalink appears under the page's title box as soon as you start entering the page content. WordPress uses the same rules to create post permalinks as it does when it creates page permalinks (as explained on page 115) and you can edit the permalink for any page (page 119). But the important detail here is that each page gets its own unique address, and you can find the page by typing that address into your browser.

Of course, your readers aren't likely to type in any URLs other than the address for your home page, so you need to provide links so visitors can get to your pages. One way to do this is by putting individual links in posts and pages so you can connect them together. For example, you could add a link to the page shown in Figure 7-2 that takes readers to a new page when they click "Family Law" (Figure 7-4).

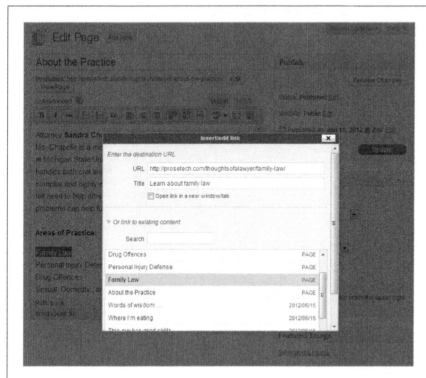

Links are a decent way to join related posts and pages, but they aren't much help if a guest wants to *browse* the pages on your site. This isn't a problem with posts—if your visitors want to read your posts, they can browse them easily on the home page, starting with the most recent one and moving back in time. But WordPress doesn't put pages in chronological order, as it does with posts, which means people can't browse pages that way. Similarly, pages don't get tag or category information, which means visitors obviously won't find them when browsing by category or tag. However, visitors *can* find them through a keyword search (by typing something into the Search box and pressing the Enter key), because searches scan both posts and pages. But searching is a clumsy way to find a page, and it's no substitute for a more convenient navigation system.

Fortunately, WordPress has several better, ready-made solutions to help visitors find your pages:

- **The Pages widget.** Add this to your page, and visitors will always be able to see a list of all your pages, in the order you want. This widget works best if you want to show all (or almost all) of your pages.

- **An automatic menu.** Many themes automatically put all your pages in a menu on the home page. The only problem is that this auto-generated menu includes *every* page in your site. If that results in an overly cluttered menu, you'll prefer the next option.

- **A custom menu.** You pick the pages you want to showcase and arrange them just so. You then display the menu somewhere prominent on your home page (often where the automatic menu used to go). Most WordPress gurus go this route.

You'll explore all these options in the following sections.

Showing Pages in the Pages Widget

The Pages widget displays a simple list of links (Figure 7-5). Like any other widget, you can place it anywhere on your home page, such as in a sidebar. Just choose Appearance→Widgets and drag it to the right spot.

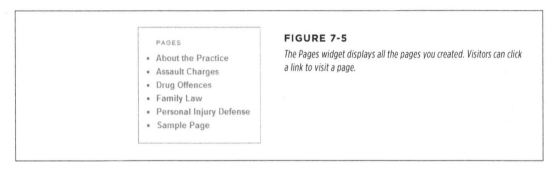

FIGURE 7-5

The Pages widget displays all the pages you created. Visitors can click a link to visit a page.

You may want to use the Pages widget to show just some of your pages. To do that, you need to explicitly indicate what pages you *don't* want to show. Each page has a unique ID number, and you indicate the pages you want to exclude by adding a comma-separated list of ID numbers in the Exclude box (Figure 7-6).

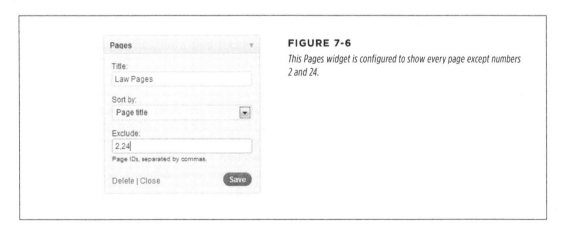

FIGURE 7-6

This Pages widget is configured to show every page except numbers 2 and 24.

The slightly tricky part is figuring out the page's ID number. If you run a self-hosted blog and you haven't changed WordPress's permalink style (page 117), the ID appears right in the URL. But if you use WordPress.com or you switched to more readable title-based permalinks, you need to take a different tack. First, go to Pages→All Pages to see all the pages in your site. Then hover over the title of the page you want to exclude. The page's full link appears in your browser's toolbar, in this format:

```
http://prosetech.com/thoughtsofalawyer/wp-admin/post.php?post=24&action=edit
```

In this example, the page ID is 24. (Don't be confused that the URL actually calls the page a post—it's an old but harmless WordPress quirk.)

> **TIP** If you have trouble seeing a page's permalink in your browser, try copying the address. Right-click the page title and choose a command with a name like Copy Shortcut or Copy Link Address (the exact wording depends on your browser). You can paste the link into a text editor like Notepad, and find the page ID there.

WORD TO THE WISE

Use the Exclude Box Sparingly

It might occur to you that you could add several Pages widgets to different parts of your home page, each of which shows a different subset of pages. This is an interesting idea, but a bad one, because of the way the exclusion list works.

If you use the Pages widget to create three page lists, for example, every time you add a new page, you need to edit each widget to add the new page to the exclusion list of each one. That extra work can cause a serious headache. To avoid this, use the Pages widget only when you want to show most or all of your pages. If you want to show a smaller group of just a few pages, create a custom menu with the Custom Menu widget instead; see page 219.

The Pages widget also lets you sort your list of pages. You set the sort order using the drop-down menu in the "Sort by" box. Ordinarily, the order is "Page title," which means that WordPress compiles your posts alphabetically by name. Alternatively, you can choose "Page ID," and WordPress will list pages from oldest to newest (because newer pages always get higher ID numbers). Lastly, you can choose "Page order," which lets *you* pick the order, as you'll see on page 207.

Showing Pages in a Menu

A WordPress menu is a set of links arranged hierarchically. Unlike desktop programs, which typically have strict, consistent rules about where menus go and what they look like, menus on the Web take many forms. In fact, the way your menu looks is completely in the hands of your theme. (That's why WordPress puts the menu management command in the dashboard's Appearances menu, alongside the controls for other theme features.)

If you're still experimenting with the standard WordPress theme, your menu looks like a traditional menu bar, arranged horizontally. It sits between the header image at the top of your site and the posts that follow (Figure 7-7). By default, this theme uses an automatic menu, which means that it grabs all the pages in your site and displays a separate clickable button for each one.

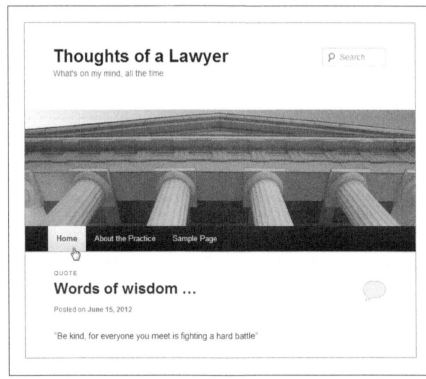

FIGURE 7-7

If you use WordPress's Twenty Eleven theme, you start with this menu bar. At first, it holds just two menu commands: a Home button that goes to your home page, and a Sample Page button that loads up the WordPress sample page (unless you took our earlier advice and deleted it). But every time you add a new page, like "About the Practice" here, Twenty Eleven adds a matching button in the menu.

> **TIP** If the Twenty Eleven theme runs out of horizontal space for all your menu buttons, it creates a new row and wraps the additional commands onto the next line. In fact, there's no limit to how many lines Twenty Eleven adds. (That said, this design gets messy, so you'll want to group related links or use a custom menu if your site has more than a handful of pages.)

If you want to exert more control over how your theme arranges pages in a menu, you have two choices: You can use the ordering and grouping features described next, or you can create a custom menu (page 210). Custom menus take slightly more work, but pay off with more flexibility and features.

Ordering and Grouping Pages

Often, when you display a list of pages, you want to dictate which ones show up first and which ones are last. You can do this by filling in the "Page order" box when you create (or edit) each page.

The page order setting affects the order of your pages in two situations: when you display pages in an automatic menu, and when you display them in the Pages widget with the "Sort by" box set to "Page order."

Ordinarily, WordPress sets the order of every page to 0. Technically, that means that each page is tied for first position, and the page order setting has no effect. But if you want to set the order (say you want "Our Story" followed by "Our Location" followed by "Contact Us"), you'd assign these pages steadily increasing page-order numbers (say, 0, 1, and 2). The actual numbers don't really matter—the important thing is how they *compare*. WordPress always displays larger-numbered pages toward the bottom of the list or on the right end of a horizontal menu, while smaller-numbered pages appear closer to the top of a list or the left of a menu bar. When two or more pages have the same page-order value, WordPress orders them alphabetically.

TIP If you rearrange a bunch of pages, you need to change their page-order values. The easiest way to do this is to go to the Pages list (choose Pages→All Pages) and use the Quick Edit link. This lets you quickly modify some page information, including the order, without opening the whole page for editing.

There's another way to group pages: you can designate some pages as *child* pages that belong to a specific *parent* page. (You may have used this type of organization before, to create subcategories for your posts, as described on page 109.) For example, you could edit the Family Law page and change the Parent list box from "(no parent)" to "About the Practice." Now, Family Law is a subpage in the "About the Practice" group.

To better understand the effect of ordering and grouping, imagine you created these pages:

PAGE TITLE	ORDER	PARENT
About the Practice	0	-
Assault Charges	3	About the Practice
Drug Offenses	2	About the Practice
Family Law	0	About the Practice
Personal Injury Defense	1	About the Practice
Legal Disclaimers	1	-
Referrals	0	-

These settings create the nicely nested list shown in Figure 7-8. The Pages widget slightly indents nested pages, while in a menu, nested pages show up in a submenu.

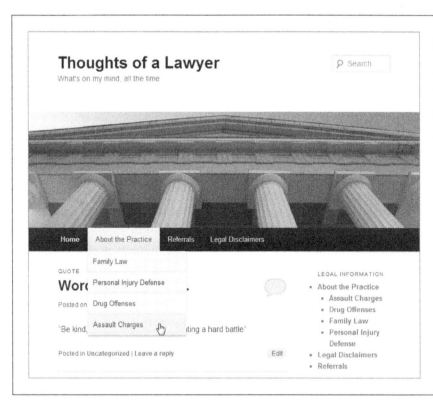

FIGURE 7-8

This site displays its pages in two places. At the top is the familiar menu bar, now with a submenu. On the right side, the Pages widget shows an identical collection of pages.

Life can get a bit confusing when you order and group pages. Just remember that when WordPress orders pages, it compares only the pages at the same level. For example, you can use the page order to adjust the position of the Assault Charges, Drug Offenses, Family Law, and Personal Injury Defense pages with respect to one another. However, WordPress won't compare the order values of the Family Law and Legal Disclaimers pages, because they don't appear at the same level and won't ever be shown next to each other.

NOTE If you use post names in your permalinks (page 117), child pages get their own permalink. It includes two posts titles: the name of the child page itself and the name of the parent page. For example, if the child page Family Law has the parent "About the Practice," the full permalink might be something like *http://thoughtsof alawyer.net/about-the-practice/family-law*.

▓ Custom Menus

WordPress's ordering and grouping features give you enough flexibility to create a good-looking, well-ordered menu. However, there are a few good reasons that most WordPress developers eventually decide to build a custom menu:

- **To get more types of menu items.** An automatic menu includes links to your pages, and that's it. But if you create a custom menu, you can stock it with other types of links—for example, ones that lead to a particular post, a whole category of posts, or even another website.

- **To hide pages.** An automatic menu always includes *all* your pages. This might not be a problem for a relatively new WordPress site, but as your site grows, you'll probably add more and more pages and start using them for different types of information. Eventually, you'll create pages that you don't want to include in your main menu (for example, maybe you want to add a page that readers can visit by clicking a link in a post). The only way to hide a page from a menu is to abandon the automatic menu and build your own custom menu.

- **To have multiple menus.** Some themes support more than one home page menu. However, a site can only have one automatic menu. To take advantage of the multiple-menu feature, you need to create your additional menus as custom menus.

- **Because sometimes automatic menus are hard.** To get an automatic menu to look the way you want it to, you need to think very carefully about the order and parent settings. If you have dozens of pages, this sort of planning can twist your brain into a pretzel. If you build a custom menu, you can drag-and-drop your way to a good-looking menu. It still takes time and work, but it requires a lot less planning and a lot less thinking.

Building a Custom Menu

When you're ready to replace your theme's automatic menu with a menu of your own creation, here are the steps to follow:

1. **Choose Appearance→Menus.**

   This brings you to the sophisticated Menus page (Figure 7-9), which takes care of three tasks. You'll use it to:

   - **Create and delete menus.** You can't edit the automatic menu your WordPress site starts out with. Instead, you need to create an entirely new menu of your own.

   - **Edit menus.** In other words, you need to fill your new, blank menu with some useful commands. You also arrange the menu items, choosing which ones go first and which ones go in submenus.

- **Assign menus to your themes.** For example, you need to tell the Twenty Eleven theme which menu to use for the menu bar under the header. Some themes have more than one menu area, and so support more than one menu.

In the following steps, you'll take care of each of these tasks.

FIGURE 7-9

If you haven't yet created a menu, WordPress disables most of the Menus page. The exception is the box on the right side, which holds a single text box (Menu Name) and a single button (Create Menu).

2. **Give your menu a name.**

The name is simply so you can recognize a menu in case you create more than one. Normally, you name the menu after its function (Main Menu, Navigation Menu, Page Menu, and so on). You shouldn't name it based on its position (as in Top Menu Bar), because that detail may change if you switch themes.

3. **Click Create Menu to build the menu you just named.**

Now the Menus page gets more interesting. You'll see three boxes for adding menu items, each with a button in it named Add to Menu (Figure 7-10).

The newly created menu

FIGURE 7-10

Once you create a menu, the column of boxes on the left side of the page becomes active. You use the topmost box (Theme Locations) to attach your menu to the right place in your theme. The other boxes let you add different items to your menu.

Add a link to the menu

Add a page to the menu

Add a category to the menu

4. **Add a custom link, page link, or category link to your menu.**

   A *custom link* goes to some location on the Web, either on your site or another site. For example, you could create a custom link that points to a specific post (using its permalink), a Wikipedia page, a friend's blog, or something else. Use the Label box to specify the text you want for this link.

   A *page* is, obviously, a link to one of the pages you created. This box provides more than one tab—use Most Recent to zero in on the newest pages you created,

View All to browse through all your pages, and Search to find a page by name (useful if your site has dozens or more pages).

A *category* is a link to the category archive page, which displays all the posts in a given category in reverse chronological order. It has the same effect as the links in the Categories widget.

TIP It makes sense to add a custom link named "Home" or "Posts" to most new menus. That way, your guests always have a way to get back to your home page. To create a home page link, choose the View All tab in the Pages box, turn on the checkbox next to Home, and continue with the next step.

GEM IN THE ROUGH

Getting Even More Menu Links

The Menus page makes it easy to add a link to another page on your site, to a category of posts, or to another website entirely. But you can get even more menu-creating options if you click the Screen Options button (found in the top-right corner of the page) and turn on the Posts and Tags checkboxes.

If you do, you'll get two more boxes for adding menu items. The Posts box shows a list of all your posts, letting you add a link to a specific post without needing to remember the permalink. The Tags box is similar to the Category box—it lets your visitors browse all the posts that have a specific tag.

5. **Once you make a choice, click the "Add to Menu" button.**

   You'll see your new item appear in the menu section on the right (Figure 7-11).

TIP The Page and Category sections let you add more than one page and more than one category to a menu at once. For example, if you want to add three pages in one fell swoop, put a checkmark next to each one and then click "Add to Menu." (Don't worry about the order; you can rearrange all your menu items once you add them.)

6. **Optionally, customize the label and pop-up text (the title) of your menu item.**

   When you first add an item, it shows up as a collapsed gray box. To change the options for that item, you must first click the down-pointing arrow on the right side of the box. This expands the box so you can see (and edit) all the settings for that item.

   The settings you can change include:

   Navigation Label, which is the text that appears in the menu. If you add a page or a category, the navigation label is the name of that page or category, which keeps things simple. But sometimes you might want to edit the text, particularly if it's too long to fit comfortably in your menu.

   Title Attribute, which is the text that pops up when someone hovers over a menu item. Usually, the title attribute is blank, and the pop-up text is the same as the menu text. But you could get fancy and use the Title attribute to supply a more detailed description.

Remove does the obvious, deleting a menu item you don't want anymore.

FIGURE 7-11

Once you start creating a menu, the Menus page works a lot like the Widgets page. WordPress represents each menu item with a separate gray box, and you can see the settings for an item by expanding its box. In this example, the menu holds three items.

7. **Return to step 4 to add another item to your menu, and repeat these steps until you stock your menu with all the items you want.**

   WordPress adds items to the menu in the order *you* add them. So the items you add first are on the left of a horizontal menu. However, don't worry about the order yet, because you'll learn how to move everything around in the next step.

8. **Now it's time to arrange your menu item. Drag them around to position them and group them into submenus.**

   Unlike automatic menus, custom menus don't pay attention to the Order or Parent settings of your pages. This is good for flexibility (because it means you arrange some of the same commands in different ways, using different menus), but it also means you need to do a little bit more work when you create the menu.

Fortunately, arranging menu items is easy. To move an item from one place to another, you simply drag it, just as you move widgets in the Widgets page. WordPress displays items in top-to-bottom order, so if you use a horizontal menu (as the WordPress standard theme does), the topmost item is on the left, followed by the next menu item, and so on.

Creating submenus is just as convenient, once you know the trick. First, arrange your menu items so that the child items (the items you want to appear in the submenu) appear immediately after the parent menu item. Then, drag the child menu item slightly to the right, so that it looks like it's indented one level. Figure 7-12 shows what the result should look like, and Figure 7-13 shows the formatted WordPress page.

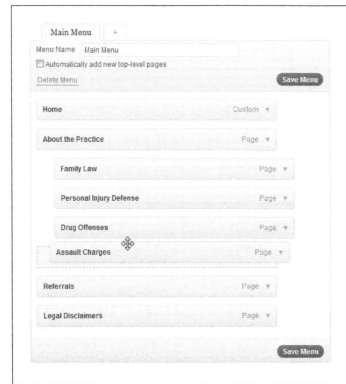

FIGURE 7-12

By dragging the Assault Charges page slightly to the right, it becomes a submenu item under the "About the Practice" page, along with several other pages. Figure 7-13 shows the result.

FIGURE 7-13

Now the "About the Practice" page has a submenu.

NOTE You can easily create multilayered menus (menus with submenus inside of submenus). All you do is keep dragging items a bit more to the right. However, most well-designed WordPress sites stop at one level of submenus. Otherwise, guests may find it awkward to dig down through all the layers in a pull-down style menu (like the one in Twenty Eleven) without accidentally moving the mouse off the menu.

FREQUENTLY ASKED QUESTION

Creating a Menu Item that Does Nothing

Can I make a submenu heading that visitors can't click?

WordPress menus work a little differently from the menus in traditional desktop computer programs. When you have a submenu in a desktop program, you click the parent menu item to open the submenu, and then you click one of the items inside the submenu. But in WordPress, you hover over the parent menu item to open it. The parent item is still a real menu item that leads somewhere—if you click it, you'll go to a new page, category, or custom URL. For example, in Figure 7-13 you can hover over "About the Practice" to open its submenu, or you can click it to go to the About the Practice page.

But perhaps this isn't the behavior you want. For example, you might want the "About the Practice" menu item to be a non-clickable heading, which exists solely to identify and give you access to the submenu underneath. To create an unlinked heading, you need to add a custom link. Set the label to "About the Practice" and then set the URL to # (the number sign character—that's all). To browsers, the # symbol represents the current page, so when you click the menu item ("About the Practice" in this example), you won't go anywhere. In fact, you won't even see the page flicker, which is exactly what you want.

9. **Optionally, you can turn on the "Automatically add new top-level pages" setting.**

If you do, every time you create a new page, WordPress automatically tacks it onto the end of your custom menu. This is similar to the way that an automatic menu works, although you can edit your custom menu any time to move newly added items to a better place. Most WordPress experts avoid this setting, because they prefer to have complete control over what gets into their menu and where it goes.

10. **Click the Save Menu button.**

WordPress stores your menu. However, you won't see it anywhere until you tell your theme when to use it, in the next step.

11. **In the Theme Locations box, choose your custom menu and then click Save.**

Some themes have several choices in the Theme Locations box. The WordPress Twenty Eleven theme has just one, named Primary Menu (Figure 7-14).

Once you assign your new custom menu to your theme, you can try it out on your site's home page.

FIGURE 7-14

This site has one custom theme, named Main Menu. The blank box above the highlight bar represents an automatic menu; choose that and WordPress automatically creates a menu that lists all your pages.

Multiple Menus

Many themes support more than one menu. Consider, for example, the Oxygen theme you tried out in Chapter 6 (Figure 7-15). It allows no fewer than three menus. The primary menu appears under the header, the secondary one shows up in the left-hand sidebar, and the tertiary menu appears below that, in the footer section. You can imagine using these menus for distinctly different tasks—using the top menu to navigate the whole site, for example, the side menu to drill into specific posts or categories, and the bottom menu to link to other sites with related content.

FIGURE 7-15

One page, three different menus. All of them support pop-up submenus (not shown).

NOTE You don't *need* to use all the menus a theme provides. Initially, WordPress creates an automatic menu and uses it as the theme's primary menu. Any additional menus start off hidden, and appear only if you attach custom menus to them.

To use the Oxygen theme's three menus, you need to create at least two custom menus, and probably three (because, although you can use an automatic menu for the primary menu, you'll probably want more control). You create all three menus in the familiar Menus page. Just look for the plus (+) button that lets you add a menu (Figure 7-16).

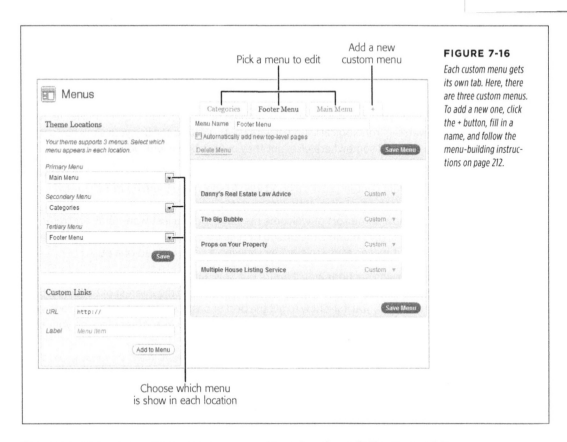

Pick a menu to edit

Add a new custom menu

Choose which menu is show in each location

FIGURE 7-16

Each custom menu gets its own tab. Here, there are three custom menus. To add a new one, click the + button, fill in a name, and follow the menu-building instructions on page 212.

Once you create your custom menus, you need to put each one in the appropriate location in your theme. You do that in the Theme Locations box on the left side of the Menus page. Simply choose your menu in the appropriate list, and then click Save when you're ready to put your menus into action.

The Custom Menu Widget

There's one more way to display a custom menu: in the Custom Menu widget.

Now that you've played with menus in depth, the Custom Menu widget won't impress you much. To use it, simply drag it onto your page (say, in a sidebar), give it a title (optional), and pick the menu it should show. The Custom Menu widget shows a bulleted list of links, using nested bullets for the items in a submenu. In fact, the Custom Menu widget looks a lot like the Pages widget, as shown back in Figure 7-8.

The advantage of the Custom Menu widget is that it's more flexible than the Pages widget. The Pages widget shows all (or almost all) of your pages, but the Custom Menu widget shows just the ones you want, and can optionally include other category links and links to other websites, provided you've added them to your custom menu.

Changing Your Home Page

Right now, your WordPress site has a home page dominated by a familiar feature: the reverse-chronological listing of your posts. Visitors can use your site's navigation menu to travel somewhere else, but they always begin with your posts.

This setup is perfectly reasonable—after all, your posts typically contain the newest, most relevant content, so it's a good idea to showcase them up front. However, this design doesn't fit all sites. If the list of posts is less important on your site, or you want to show some sort of welcome message, or you just want to direct traffic (in other words, give readers the option of reading posts or going somewhere else on your site), it makes sense to start by showing a page instead of a post.

In the following sections, you'll figure out how. First, you'll learn to use one of your custom-created pages as your site's home page, all in the interest of building a bro-chure site. Next, you'll see how to get the best of posts worlds: a fixed home page with the content you want *and* a list of posts, tucked away in another place on your site.

Creating a Brochure Site

The simplest way to change your home page is to ditch the post system altogether, using pages instead of posts throughout your site. The resulting type of all-pages site is sometimes called a *brochure site*, because it resembles the sort of informational pamphlet you might pick up in a store (Figure 7-17).

To create a brochure site, you follow some simple principles:

- You build a site that consists entirely of pages, each one hand-crafted by you.

- You add these pages to a custom menu, and arrange the pages the way you want.

- When visitors arrive at your site, the first thing they see is one of your pages (and a navigation menu).

You already know how to perform each of these tasks, except the last one (changing the home page). That's what you'll learn next.

Should You Build a Brochure Site?

A brochure site may make sense if you're building a small site with very simple content. The restaurant site in Figure 7-17 is one example.

If you're trying to decide between a brochure site and a post-based site, consider two questions. First, would your site be more attractive to readers if you included posts? Even the barebones restaurant site might be more interesting with posts that chronicle restaurant news, menu experiments, and special events. Not only that, but the fact that posts are frequent, dated, and personal makes the site more vibrant. In addition, if you want to get people talking on your site—for example, posting comments about recent meals or sending in requests and off-the-wall recipe ideas—you'll have more luck

if you include posts. Think of it this way: A brochure site feels like a statement, while a blog feels like a constantly unfolding conversation.

Then again, you may decide that a brochure site is exactly what you want. Maybe you really don't have time to spend updating and maintaining a site, so you simply want a place to publish some basic information on the Web and leave it at that. You can still take advantage of several of WordPress's best features, like themes, which ensure that your pages look consistent. You'll also get WordPress's help if you want to track visitors (page 419), add sharing buttons (page 392), or add any one of a number of different features described in this book.

FIGURE 7-17

This restaurant website is a collection of WordPress pages, including those labeled Location, Philosophy, and Menu. Unlike posts, pages aren't related in any obvious way, and they aren't dated, categorized, or tagged.

The key step in building a brochure site is changing your home page, replacing the traditional list of posts with a page of your own devising. So your first step is to create a substitute home page, using the familiar dashboard command Pages→Add New.

You might want to make a few changes to the home page, since it serves as the welcome mat to your site. For example, you may want to include navigation links in the home-page text that take visitors straight to important content. However, this isn't necessary. As long as your theme includes a menu, visitors can use that to click through to more content.

You may also want to tweak the comment settings for your custom home page. By default, all pages, just like all posts, allow comments. However, it seems a bit unstructured to allow people to comment directly on the home page of your website. Fortunately, it's easy enough to turn comments off for any page. First, use the Screen Options button (page 123) to show the Discussion box. Then, turn off the "Allow comments" checkbox.

Once you create your new, replacement home page, you can follow these steps:

1. **Choose Settings→Reading.**

2. **In the "Front page displays" setting, choose "A static page" (rather than "Your latest posts").**

3. **In the "Front page" list underneath, pick the page you want as your new home page.**

4. **Click Save Changes at the bottom of the page.**

Now, when you surf to your site's home page, WordPress automatically serves up the page you picked (although the URL won't change in the browser's address bar—it's still the home page of your site). Similarly, when you click Home in the menu, you'll return to your custom home page.

TIP If you use a custom page for your home page, you may want to jazz it up with a few more navigational features. Many themes provide page templates that can help you out by adding a widget-stocked sidebar alongside your page content, for example. You'll learn more on page 224.

Creating a Custom Entry Page

Even if you want to change your home page, you might not want to ditch the post system. In such a case, use a static home page (called a welcome page), and include a full complement of posts on another page.

The trick to doing this is that once you replace the default home page, you need to pick a new URL for the page that displays all your posts. Here's where things get slightly bizarre. To pick the URL for your posts, you create yet another page. This page is just a placeholder—its sole purpose is to tell WordPress what address to go to to launch your posts page. You won't actually put any content on this page, because if you do, WordPress ignores it.

Here's the whole process:

1. **Decide on a URL for the posts section of your site.**

   For example, if you're home page is at *http://magicteahouse.net*, you might want to put the posts at *http://magicteahouse.net/posts* or *http://magictea house.net/blog*.

NOTE If you use a self-hosted version of WordPress, you need to make sure you've changed your site's permalink setting to use post titles rather than post IDs (page 117). Otherwise, the link to your placeholder page will use the post's ID, not its name. This is terribly confusing—it means you'll end up with a permalink with a name like *http://magicteahouse.net/?p=583* that actually shows your list of posts.

---

2. **Create a page with a name that matches the URL you want.**

   For example, you can create a page named Posts or Blog. Don't put any content in this page—think of it as a placeholder for your old home page.

3. **Publish your page.**

   Your placeholder page is ready. Now all you need to do is change your site settings.

4. **Choose Settings→Reading.**

   This brings you to the Settings page, where you set your custom home page and your new posts page.

5. **If you haven't already set a custom home page, do that now.**

   In the "Front page displays" setting, choose "A static page" (rather than "Your latest posts"). In the "Front page" list underneath, pick the page you want to use for your new home page.

6. **In the "Posts page" list, pick the page you created in step 2.**

   This activates the placeholder page.

7. **Click Save Changes at the bottom of the page.**

   Now, visitors can see your old home page—the list of posts—by using the URL for the placeholder page you created in step 2. So if you created a page named Posts, when you request that page (say, *http://magicteahouse.net/posts*), you'll see your list of posts. But if someone requests the home page (*http://magicteahouse.net*), they'll see the custom home page picked in step 5 instead of the list of posts.

8. **Optionally, edit your menu and add a new menu item for your new posts page.**

Even though you created a posts page, that doesn't mean your visitors know about it. They need a way to get there, and the best option is a link in your menu. Creating that is easy—you simply need to add a new menu item that points to your placeholder page (Figure 7-18).

FIGURE 7-18

Here's the new home page for the Magic Tea House. You can continue on to the site by using the text-based links on this page, or by using the menu below the header image. The Posts link takes you to the posts page, which looks the same as the old Tea House home page.

In some cases, you may decide not to lump all your posts together in a single reverse-chronological stream. In that case, you don't need to create the placeholder page. Instead, you can add category links to your menu, so that visitors browse all the posts that fall into a particular category.

This is a great approach, but it may become less practical if you have a lot of categories, because you don't want to burden your site with a crowded, clumsy menu. One solution—provided you have a self-hosted site—is to customize your home page with the theme-editing tricks described in Chapter 14. For example, page 486 shows a site that uses custom themes to create a hand-tailored home page with category browsing links.

Pages with Sidebars

If you start relying on pages for more of the content in your site, or you start using them instead of the standard home page, you may want your pages to get a few more features. Many themes include specialized *page templates*. When you create a page by using a different page template, your page may acquire a few new frills.

For example, the standard Twenty Eleven theme includes a template named Sidebar Template. Use that, and your page gets a widget-filled sidebar (Figure 7-19). In fact, this sidebar is exactly the same as the sidebar that appears on the posts page, and you can configure it in the Appearances→Widgets section of the dashboard.

FIGURE 7-19

The Sidebar Template is a great choice for a custom home page. It lets you combine your page content with the handy navigation features you love about widgets (like links to recent posts, recent comments, or post categories).

To give your page a sidebar, you simply need to choose Sidebar Template instead of Default Template in the Template list. You specify the template when you create a page, when you perform a full edit, or when you perform a quick edit (which is the easiest way to retrofit old pages).

NOTE If you start adding sidebars to your pages, be consistent. You might choose to add sidebars to all your pages, none of your pages, or just the custom home page. But be wary of mixing and matching your sidebar choice, because it can make your visitors feel that your site is unpredictable or poorly organized.

Showcase Pages

Altogether, the Twenty Eleven theme includes three page templates: the standard (the Default Template), a page template with a sidebar (Sidebar Template), and a souped-up page template with a number of extra frills (Showcase Template). Now that you've seen the first two, you're ready to see what a showcase page can do.

A showcase page fuses the static content you supply with the more dynamic information from your posts. Many themes include their own version of a showcase-style template, but most include a few common elements, like a featured post section. Figure 7-20 shows a showcase page in the Twenty Eleven theme.

You'll probably find that the best use of a showcase page is as a more customizable version of the WordPress home page. It gives you the best of both worlds: the page content you want to highlight (which appears at the top), along with a group of featured posts (underneath) and a list of recent posts (at the bottom).

There's no magic to creating a showcase page. You simply create a page, add the content you want, and then choose Showcase Template from the Template list. Finally, you publish your page. When someone requests a page that uses the showcase template, WordPress goes to work.

Here's how WordPress assembles a showcase page for the Twenty Eleven theme:

- First, it takes your sticky posts (page 104), and adds them to the Featured Post gallery. To get a picture to appear alongside a featured post, make sure you set a featured image (page 184).

- Underneath the Featured Post gallery, WordPress shows the content for the most recent non-sticky post. If you want WordPress to show only a portion of the most recent post, you need to use the More quicktag (page 192).

- Underneath that, WordPress lists the titles of next four most recent posts (not including sticky posts). To view one of these posts, your guest must click the title.

- WordPress adds a sidebar to the left side of the page, next to the list of your most recent posts. However, this isn't the standard sidebar you see on your normal home page (and all the pages that use the sidebar template). Instead, it's called the showcase sidebar, and you can fill it with widgets by choosing Appearance→Widgets and directing your attention to the Showcase Sidebar area. By default, it starts out empty.

It might occur to you that you like the showcase page, but you want to take the idea further. For example, maybe you want to control what posts appear in the list of recent posts, or you want to create several showcase pages that highlight different categories of posts, like the sections of a newspaper. Unfortunately, showcase pages don't give you this flexibility. However, you can begin building a system like this if you're running a self-hosted WordPress site and you're not afraid to get your hands dirty. You'll start exploring that option in Chapter 14.

NOTE Showcase pages are best suited to the role of fancied-up home pages. There's rarely a reason to have more than one showcase page on your site.

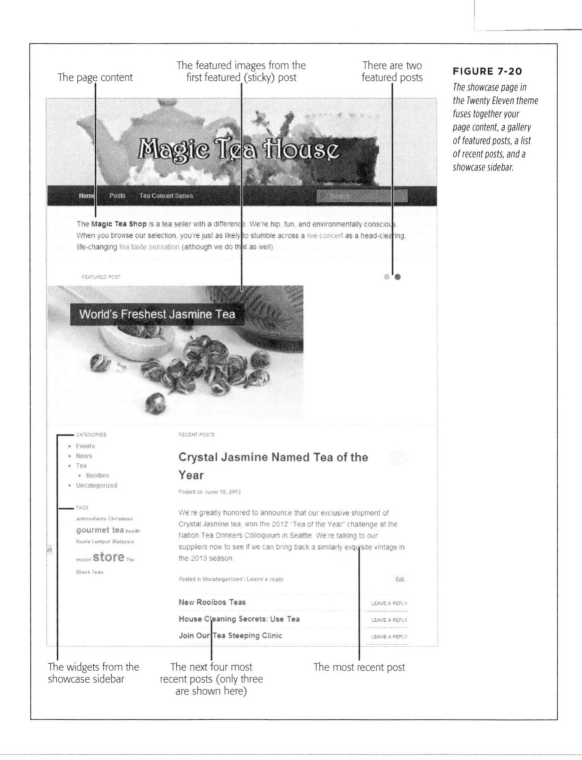

The page content — The featured images from the first featured (sticky) post — There are two featured posts

The widgets from the showcase sidebar — The next four most recent posts (only three are shown here) — The most recent post

FIGURE 7-20

The showcase page in the Twenty Eleven theme fuses together your page content, a gallery of featured posts, a list of recent posts, and a showcase sidebar.

Comments: Letting Your Readers Talk Back

In the chapters you've read up to this point, you've learned to create the two most essential ingredients of any WordPress site, posts and pages. They're the *vehicles* for your content—the way you'll reach friends, potential customers, or hordes of devoted readers.

Still left to explore is the WordPress commenting system, which is a keenly important part of almost every WordPress site, whether it's a chatty blog or a buttoned-up business website. Used properly, comments can change your site from a one-way lecture to a back-and-forth conversation with your readers or customers. Commenting isn't just a fun way to make friends—it's also a serious tool for promoting your work, getting more traffic, turning casual browsers into repeat visitors, and even making money.

In this chapter, you'll learn how to manage comments on your site. You can banish offensive ones, insert yourself into the discussion, and even tweak the way WordPress displays comments by adding author pictures and formatting them to make them more readable. Once you understand the basics of comment management, you'll be ready to confront one the single biggest hassles that every WordPress site faces: *comment spam*—the messages that dubious marketers and scammers slap across every site they can find. You'll learn strategies for preventing spam without aggravating your readers, and you'll take a side trip to explore the spam-crushing Akismet plug-in.

NOTE This chapter points out a few optional plug-ins that self-hosting WordPressers can use to fill in the gaps in WordPress's commenting features. However, you'll probably want to wait until you read Chapter 9, which explains how to manage plug-ins, before you try any of them out on your site.

Why Your WordPress Site Needs a Community

Once upon a time, people thought comments belonged only in personal blogs and discussion forums. Serious-minded web publishers ignored them. Small business avoided them—after all, if people really needed to get help or make their opinions known—well, that's what email's for, right?

Today, the website landscape has changed dramatically. Web commenting is an essential ingredient for sites small and large, fun and serious, casual and moneymaking. Here's what a comments section can do for you:

- **Attract new visitors.** New visitors immediately notice whether a website has a thriving conversation or just a single lonely comment. They use that to evaluate how popular a website is. It's crowd mentality, working for you—if new visitors see that other people find a topic interesting, they're more likely to dive in to check out your content for themselves.

- **Build buzz.** If you've taken to the Web to promote something—whether it's a new restaurant, a book, a community service, or whatever—you can only do so

much to persuade people. But if you get your fans talking to other people, the effect is exponential. Comments help you spread the good feelings, getting your readers to talk up your products or services. And once they're talking on your blog, it's just a short hop away for other bloggers to post about you on *their* blogs.

- **Build loyalty.** A good discussion helps make a site *sticky*—in other words, it encourages people to return. Put another way, people may come to your site for the content, but they stay for the comments.

- **Encourage readers to help other readers.** Often, readers will want to respond to your content with their own comments or questions. If you ask them to do that by email and your site is popular, you readers will easily overwhelm you. But with comments, your audience can discuss among themselves, with you tossing in the occasional follow-up comment for all to see. The end result is that your site still has that personal touch, even when it's big and massively popular.

Allowing or Forbidding Comments

If you haven't changed WordPress's default settings, all your posts and pages already support comments. You've probably already noticed that when you view an individual post or page, there's a large "Leave a Reply" section just below your content.

But it doesn't always make sense to allow comments on everything you publish. Many static pages don't lend themselves to discussion. You probably won't get a great conversation going on an About Us or Our Location page, for example, so it makes sense to disable comments for these pages and let people have their say somewhere else on your site.

Posts usually allow comments. However, you might want to disable commenting if you're writing on a contentious subject that's likely to attract an avalanche of inflammatory, insulting, aggressive, or racially charged feedback. News sites sometimes disable comments to avoid legal liability (for a libelous comment someone posted, for example, or for a trade secret someone revealed). Allowing comments on posts or pages isn't an all-or-nothing decision—you can pick and choose what content allows comments.

NOTE Comments apply equally to posts and pages. For convenience, most of the discussion in this chapter refers to posts, but everything you'll learn applies equally to pages.

Changing Comment Settings for a Post

You can turn off comments for an individual post or page by changing the comment settings when you create or edit that post or page. However, WordPress usually hides the settings. To see them, you need to click the Screen Options button in the top-right corner of the Add New Post or Edit Post page, and then turn on the checkmark next to Discussion. This adds a Discussion box to your post-in-progress, which offers just two settings (Figure 8-1).

Use this button to show the Discussion box

Switch off this setting to remove comments

FIGURE 8-1

You can opt out of comments for a single post or page by turning off the "Allow comments" checkbox. You can also disable trackbacks and pingbacks, which you'll consider on page 248.

If you have a pile of posts that allow comments and you want to remove the comment feature from all of them, WordPress makes it easy by letting you edit posts in bulk. To do that:

1. **Choose Posts→All Posts.**

   WordPress lists all your posts.

2. **Turn on the checkbox next to each post you want to change.**

3. **Choose Edit from the Bulk Actions drop-down menu, and then click the Apply button.**

   The editing panel appears at the top of the post list, with a number of settings you can change (see page 128).

4. **In the Comments drop-down menu, pick "Do not allow," and then click Update.**

   You can use the same trick to turn commenting back on and to change the comment settings on your pages.

Changing the Default Comment Settings Site-Wide

To create a site that's mostly or entirely comment-free, you probably don't want to fiddle with the Discussion settings for every post. Instead, set a default that applies to all new posts and pages. To do that, choose Settings→Discussion on the dashboard, and then turn off the checkmarks next to "Allow link notifications from other blogs (pingbacks and trackbacks)" and "Allow people to post comments on new articles." Then, scroll down to the bottom of the page and click Save Changes.

Now, all new posts and pages will be comment-free. However, you can add the comment feature back to specific posts or pages by turning on the "Allow comments" setting in the Discussion box, as shown back in Figure 8-1.

There are many more options in the Settings→Discussion page that change the way comments work. You'll learn to use them in the rest of this chapter.

The Life Cycle of a Comment

The easiest way to understand how WordPress comments work is to follow one from its creation to the moment it appears on your site and starts a conversation.

Depending on how you configure your site, comments travel one of two routes:

- **The slow lane.** In this scenario, anyone can leave a comment, but you need to approve it before it appears on the site. There's an exemption for repeat commenters, but most people will find that the conversation slows down significantly, no matter how quickly you review new comments.

- **The fast lane.** Here, each comment appears on your site as soon as someone leaves it. However, unless you want your website drowned in hundreds or thousands of spam messages, you need to use some sort of spam-fighting tool when you use this option—usually, it's an automated program that detects and quarantines suspicious-looking messages.

For most sites, the second choice is the best approach, because it allows discussions to unfold quickly, spontaneously, and with the least possible extra work on your part. However, this solution introduces more risk, because even the best spam-catcher will miss some junk, or allow messages that aren't spam but are just plain offensive. For that reason, WordPress starts your site out on the safer slow lane instead.

In this chapter, you'll consider both routes. First, you'll learn the slow-lane approach that WordPress starts you out with. Then, when you're ready to step up your game with more powerful spam-fighting tools, you'll consider the fast-lane approach.

Leaving a Comment

Leaving a comment is easy, which is the point—the more convenient it is to join the conversation, the more likely your visitors are to weigh in.

Assuming you haven't tweaked any of WordPress's comment settings, visitors need to supply two pieces of information before they can make their thoughts known: their name and their email address. They can optionally include a website address, too (Figure 8-2).

NOTE If you're logged into your website as the administrator, you won't see the commenting interface shown in Figure 8-2. Instead, you'll see just the box for comment text, because WordPress already knows who you are. This won't help you understand what life is like for ordinary readers, however, so before you go any further, log out (click the "Log out" link above the comment box) or try accessing the page from another computer or browser.

Here's what WordPress does with the information it requests from a potential commenter:

- **Name.** It displays the commenter's name prominently above her comment, thereby identifying her to other readers.

- **Email address.** WordPress doesn't display this publicly, so commenters don't need to worry about spam. In fact, WordPress won't stop visitors from inventing imaginary email addresses (although it will prevent them from typing in gibberish that obviously doesn't make sense). WordPress won't even send would-be commenters one of those pesky "Confirm that this is your address" email messages. However, email addresses are important if you want to display a tiny picture of each commenter next to each comment (see page 251 for details).

- **Comment text.** This is the meat of the comment (Figure 8-2).

- **Website.** If your commenter includes this detail, WordPress turns the commenter's name, which appears above posts, into a link. Other readers can click this link to travel to the commenter's site.

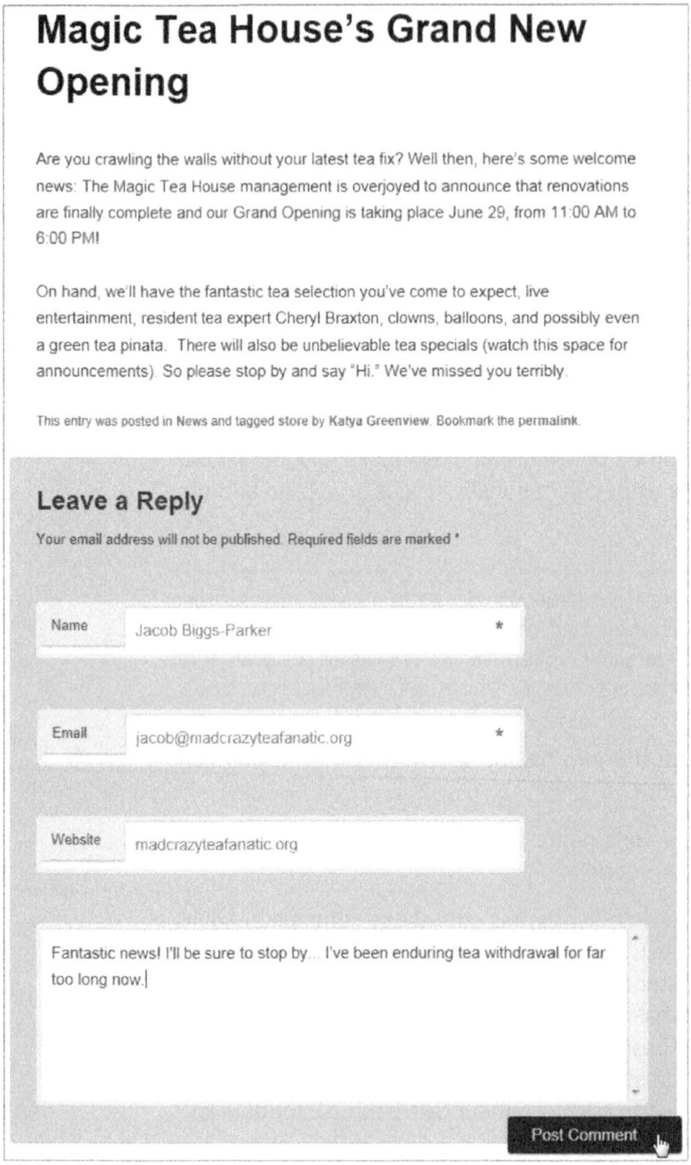

Magic Tea House's Grand New Opening

Are you crawling the walls without your latest tea fix? Well then, here's some welcome news: The Magic Tea House management is overjoyed to announce that renovations are finally complete and our Grand Opening is taking place June 29, from 11:00 AM to 6:00 PM!

On hand, we'll have the fantastic tea selection you've come to expect, live entertainment, resident tea expert Cheryl Braxton, clowns, balloons, and possibly even a green tea pinata. There will also be unbelievable tea specials (watch this space for announcements). So please stop by and say "Hi." We've missed you terribly.

This entry was posted in News and tagged store by Katya Greenview. Bookmark the permalink.

Leave a Reply

Your email address will not be published. Required fields are marked *

| Name | Jacob Biggs-Parker | * |

| Email | jacob@madcrazyteafanatic.org | * |

| Website | madcrazyteafanatic.org |

Fantastic news! I'll be sure to stop by... I've been enduring tea withdrawal for far too long now.

Post Comment

FIGURE 8-2

Ordinarily, a commenter needs to include their name and email address (although WordPress doesn't verify either). Optionally, a commenter can supply a website address (if he has one), or leave this box blank.

To see how comments work, try typing in one of your own. First, make sure you aren't logged in as the administrator (if you are, you'll bypass the moderation process described below, because WordPress figures you'll always allow your own comments). Assuming you're logged out and you see the text boxes shown in Figure 8-2, type in a comment and then click Post Comment.

Now, WordPress plays a slight trick on you. When you submit a comment, WordPress immediately adds it below your post (Figure 8-3), making it look as though your comment has been published. But in reality, when you use the slow-lane commenting route, no one can see the comment until the site owner (that's you) reviews it and formally approves it. This process is called *moderation*.

Here's the truth: there are no formally accepted comments yet

FIGURE 8-3

Here's what your upcoming comment will look like, when it's published. Right now, no one can see it but you.

Magic Tea House's Grand New Opening

Are you crawling the walls without your latest tea fix? Well then, here's some welcome news: The Magic Tea House management is overjoyed to announce that renovations are finally complete and our Grand Opening is taking place June 29, from 11:00 AM to 6:00 PM!

On hand, we'll have the fantastic tea selection you've come to expect, live entertainment, resident tea expert Cheryl Braxton, clowns, balloons, and possibly even a green tea pinata. There will also be unbelievable tea specials (watch this space for announcements). So please stop by and say "Hi." We've missed you terribly.

This entry was posted in News and tagged store by Katya Greenview. Bookmark the permalink.

0 THOUGHTS ON "MAGIC TEA HOUSE'S GRAND NEW OPENING"

Jacob Biggs-Parker on June 25, 2012 at 5:42 pm said:

Your comment is awaiting moderation.

Fantastic news! I'll be sure to stop by... I've been enduring tea withdrawal for far too long now.

Reply ↓

Leave a Reply

The fine print: your comment is in moderation

This is the comment you just added, visible to your eyes only

Comments that Use HTML

Most people who comment on a post or page will type in one or more paragraphs of ordinary text. However, craftier commenters may include a few HTML tags to format their comments.

For example, you can use the <b> and <i> elements to bold and italicize text. Type this:

I'm <i>really</i> annoyed.

and your comment will look like this:

I'm *really* annoyed.

You can also add headlines, line breaks, bulleted and numbered lists, and even tables. You could use the <a> element to create a link, but that's not necessary—if you type in text that starts with *www.* or *http://*, WordPress automatically converts it to a clickable link.

Now that you know you can use HTML in a comment, the next question is, *should* you? Most site owners don't mind the odd bit of bold or italic formatting, but they may trash messages that include shamelessly self-promotional links or one that attempt

to steal focus from the conversation with wild formatting—it's like an attention-starved kid throwing a grocery-store tantrum.

As a safeguard, some site owners disallow certain HTML elements, turn links into non-clickable text, or even erase links altogether. You can do all of this by hand-editing the comments that have HTML in them, but that's clearly a lot of work. A better approach is to use a plug-in that handles the job. For example, Comments Cleaner (*http://tinyurl.com/cleancomments*) automatically strips out all links and comment HTML, with no questions asked. (Remember, plug-ins work only on self-hosted WordPress sites. You'll learn how to install and activate the ones you want in Chapter 9.)

Finally, it's worth noting that some site owners don't just tolerate HTML in comments, they *promote* it, replacing the ordinary comment text box with a toolbar-driven visual editor, like the one you see in the dashboard when you create a new post or page. To do that, you need a plug-in like Rich Text Editor For Comments (*http://tinyurl.com/richcomments*).

Moderating Comments Through Email

When a comment awaits moderation, the discussion on your site stalls. WordPress takes two steps to notify you of waiting comments:

- It sends you an email message, with information about the new comment (and the links you need to manage it).

- It adds an eye-catching number-in-a-circle icon to the Comments button on your dashboard menu, where you can manage all your comments.

These two actions underlie the two ways you moderate WordPress comments: either by email or through your site's dashboard. First, you'll consider the email approach.

Email moderation is, for practical purposes, only an option for a small site that receives a relatively small number of comments. If you're the sort of person who carries around a web-connected device (like a smartphone) everywhere you go, email moderation gives you a convenient way to approve or discard comments mere minutes after they're made (Figure 8-4).

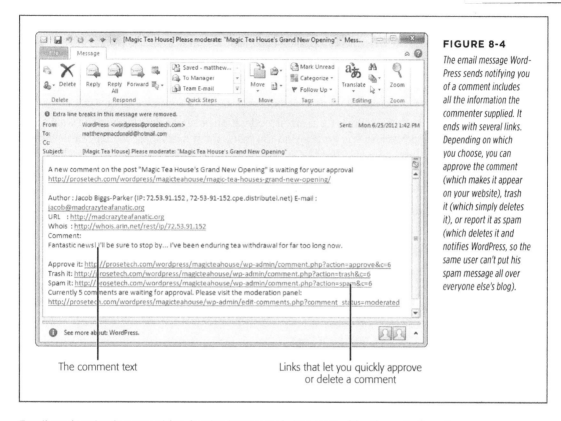

FIGURE 8-4

The email message WordPress sends notifying you of a comment includes all the information the commenter supplied. It ends with several links. Depending on which you choose, you can approve the comment (which makes it appear on your website), trash it (which simply deletes it), or report it as spam (which deletes it and notifies WordPress, so the same user can't put his spam message all over everyone else's blog).

The comment text

Links that let you quickly approve or delete a comment

Email moderation is a great idea, but it's increasingly impractical for the websites of today. The problem is comment spam—advertisements for Viagra and Cialis, porn, shady discount deals, and so on—attempts to sneak its way onto virtually every blog on the Web.

If you use email moderation, you'll receive an ever-increasing load of notifications as a host of black-hat characters try to insert their junk onto your pages. Not only is it difficult to manage the sheer number of messages you get, it's often difficult to quickly verify that a message is legitimate, because spammers try to make their comments sound real. Often, the only way to confirm that a comment is bogus is to visit the commenter's site, where you usually find ads unrelated to anything in the comment. If you plan to review comments on a mobile device, this extra step is neither quick nor convenient.

For these reasons, few people use email moderation to manage spam. You can try it, and it may work wonderfully at first, but you'll probably need to abandon it as more and more spammers discover your site, or you'll need to supplement it with one of the antispam plug-ins you'll learn about on page 263. That way, your plug-in can take care of the massive amounts of obvious spam, while you concentrate on moderating the comments that make it past the spam filter.

By default, WordPress turns email moderation on. If you decide you don't want to be notified because you're receiving too many spam messages, you can easily switch it off. Just choose Settings→Discussion, find the "Email me whenever" section, and clear the checkmarks next to "Anyone posts a comment" and "A comment is held for moderation."

FREQUENTLY ASKED QUESTION

Where Are My Emails?

I have the comment notification settings switched on, but I'm not getting any emails.

Ironically, email programs often misinterpret the notifications that WordPress sends as junk mail. The problem is that the messages contain quite a few links, which is a red flag suggesting spam. To find your missing messages, check your junk mail folder.

To avoid having your comment notifications identified as junk mail, tell your email program to always trust the address that sends them. The sending address is *wordpress* followed by your website domain, as in *wordpress@magicteahouse.net*.

Moderating Comments from the Dashboard

The other way to moderate comments is through the dashboard. The disadvantage here is that you need to open a browser, visit your site, and log in. The advantage is that you'll see all your messages in one place, and you can accept or discard them en masse.

If you have comments awaiting moderation, you'll see a black circle-with-a-number icon in the dashboard menu. This circle looks the same as the one that points out WordPress and plug-in updates (page 76), except that this one appears over the Comments menu and indicates the number of unreviewed comments (Figure 8-5). If you go to the dashboard's home page (Dashboard→Home), you'll also see the most recent comments in the Recent Comments box.

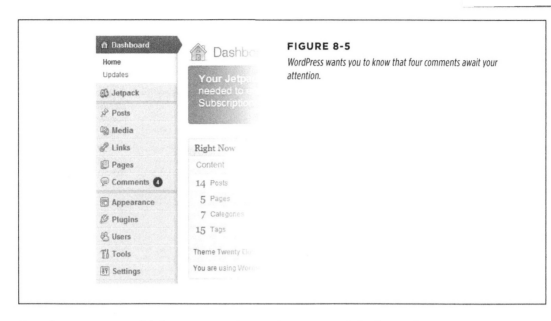

FIGURE 8-5

WordPress wants you to know that four comments await your attention.

To review comments, click Comments in the dashboard menu. Initially, you'll see a list of all the comments left on all the posts and pages of your site, ordered from newest to oldest. Click the Pending link above the comment list to focus on just the comments you need to review (Figure 8-6).

UP TO SPEED

Evaluating Comments

When you review comments, your goal is to separate the well-meaning ones from the offensive ones (which you may not want to allow) and to delete spam (which you definitely don't want). Be careful, because spammers are often crafty enough to add a seemingly appropriate comment that actually links to a spam site. Often, they'll identify keywords in your posts, cobble them together, and throw in some flattery in a desperate attempt to get approved.

For example, in Figure 8-6, the last three comments are spam. Some sort of automated spam-generating program picked up on the text "Kuala Lumpur" in the "Announcing Teas from Kuala Lumpur" post and generated a series of fake comments. They range from slightly perplexing nonsense (the second and fourth comments) to innocent-seeming but vague praise (the third comment).

The acid test for spam is to view the commenter's website. To do that, click the corresponding link (to the left of the comment in the comment list). If you do that for any of the three spam comments shown in Figure 8-6, you'll end up at a blog selling hotel rooms.

Once you identify one spam message, you may be able to detect others sent from the same spammer by using the message's IP address (a numeric code that uniquely identifies web-connected computers). For example, in Figure 8-6 two spam messages come from the same IP address (175.142.212.18). WordPress even gives you a shortcut—click the IP address and it shows you only the comments that originated from that address. You can then flag them all as spam in a single bulk action (see page 127).

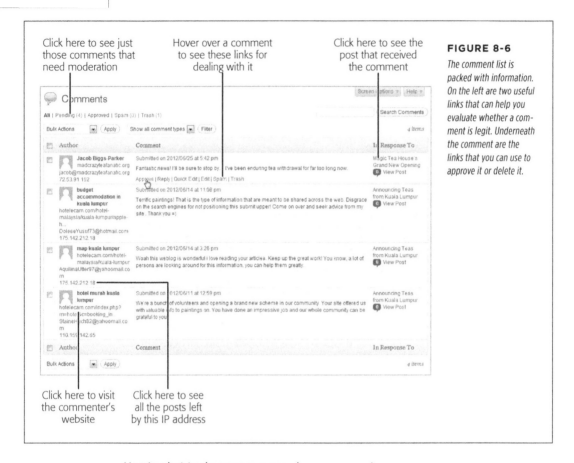

Click here to see just those comments that need moderation

Hover over a comment to see these links for dealing with it

Click here to see the post that received the comment

FIGURE 8-6

The comment list is packed with information. On the left are two useful links that can help you evaluate whether a comment is legit. Underneath the comment are the links that you can use to approve it or delete it.

Click here to visit the commenter's website

Click here to see all the posts left by this IP address

Here's what to do once you examine a comment:

- If it's spam, click the Spam link. Do *not* click Trash. Yes, both links remove the comment from your list, but only Spam reports the spammer to WordPress, which can help intercept the spam before it hits other sites.

- If it's a valid comment, click Approve to publish it on your site. If the same person returns and posts another comment using the same email address, WordPress lets it through automatically, no moderation required. (This works because the "Comment author must have a previously approved comment" is turned on.)

- If it's a valid comment that you don't want to allow, click Trash. For example, if someone actually read your posting but is replying to it in an abusive manner, you don't need to publish their comment on your site—it's entirely up to you.

You don't need to deal with comments one at a time. You can use a handy bulk action to deal with multiple comments at once. This is particularly useful if you need to clear out a batch of suspicious-looking junk.

To deal with a group of comments, start by adding a checkmark to each one you want to process. Then, pick a comment-handling action from the Bulk Actions dropdown list. Your options include Approve, Unapprove, Move to Trash, and Mark as Spam. Finally, click Apply to carry out your action.

TIP Remember, if you accidentally put a comment you want in the Spam or Trash bin, you can get it out if you act fast. Just click the Spam or Trash link above the comments list to show the list of removed comments, which you can then restore to your site.

Sanitizing Comments

By now, you're well-acquainted with your role as supreme comment commander. Only you can decide which comments live to see the light of day, and which ones are banished to the trash or spam folder.

WordPress gives you one more power over comments that may surprise you. You can crack open any comment and edit it, exactly as though it were your own content. That means you can delete text, insert new bits, change the formatting, and even add HTML tags. You can do this by clicking the Edit link under the comment, which switches to a new page named Edit Comment, or you can edit it more efficiently by clicking the Quick Edit link, which opens a comment-editing text box right inside the list of comments.

You might use this ability to remove something objectionable, such as profanity or site links from a comment before you allow it. However, few site administrators have the time to personally review their readers' comments. Instead, they get WordPress to do the dirty work.

One way to do that is to use the Comment Moderation box. Choose Settings→Discussion and fill the box with words you don't want to allow (one per line). If a comment uses a restricted word, WordPress adds it to the list of comments that need your review, even if you approved an earlier comment from the same person, and even if you disabled moderation (page 263). However, mind the fact that WordPress checks *inside* words, so if you disallow *ass*, WordPress won't allow jack*ass* or *Ass*yria. If you want to be even stricter, you can use the Comment Blacklist box instead of the Comment Moderation box. You again provide a list of offensive words, but this time WordPress sends offending comments straight to your spam folder.

If you run a self-hosted site, you can use a gentler approach, one that *replaces* objectionable words, but still allows the comment. For example, the WP Content Filter plug-in (*http://tinyurl.com/wpcontentfilter*) changes words you don't want (like jackass) with an appropriately blanked-out substitution (like j******, j*****s or *******). Of course, crafty commenters will get around these limitations by adding spaces and dashes (jack a s s), replacing letters with similar-looking numbers or special characters (jacka55), or just using creative misspellings (jackahss). So if you have a real problem with inappropriate comments and you can't tolerate them even temporarily (in other words, before you have the chance to find and remove them), you need to keep using strict moderation on your site so you get the chance to review every comment before it's published.

◼ The Ongoing Conversation

You've now seen how a single, lonely comment finds its way onto a WordPress post or page. On a healthy site, this small step is just the start of a long conversation. As readers stop by, more and more of them will add their own thoughts. And before long, some people will stop replying to your content and start replying to each other.

WordPress keeps track of all this in its *comment stream*, which is similar to the stream of posts that occupies your site's home page. The comment stream is sandwiched between your content (the text of your post or page), which sits at the top, and the "Leave a Reply" box, which sits at the bottom. Unlike the post stream, the comment stream starts with the older comments, followed by the newer ones. This arrangement makes it easy to follow an unfolding conversation, where new comments refer to earlier ones.

> **TIP** If you have lots of comments and want to emphasize the newest ones, you can flip the order, so that the newest comments appear first. Choose Settings→Discussion, find the setting that says "Comments should be displayed with the older comments at the top of each page," and pick "newer" instead of "older."

Threaded Comments

The most interesting part of the comment stream is the way it *threads* comments—the way it orders comments that visitors post in reply to other comments. When new readers stop by your post and join the conversation, they have two options. They can reply directly to your post by scrolling to the "Leave a Reply" section at the bottom of the page, or they can reply to one of the existing comments by clicking the Reply button (or link) next to the comment.

When a guest comments on another comment, WordPress puts the reply underneath the original note, indented slightly to show the relationship. Figure 8-7 shows how the standard WordPress theme handles threaded comments.

> **TIP** WordPress has a handy shortcut that lets you, the site owner, join a conversation straight from the dashboard. When reviewing a comment on the Dashboard→Comments page, click the Reply link, fill in some text, and then click the Reply button (or "Reply and Approve" if you're responding to a comment you haven't approved yet).

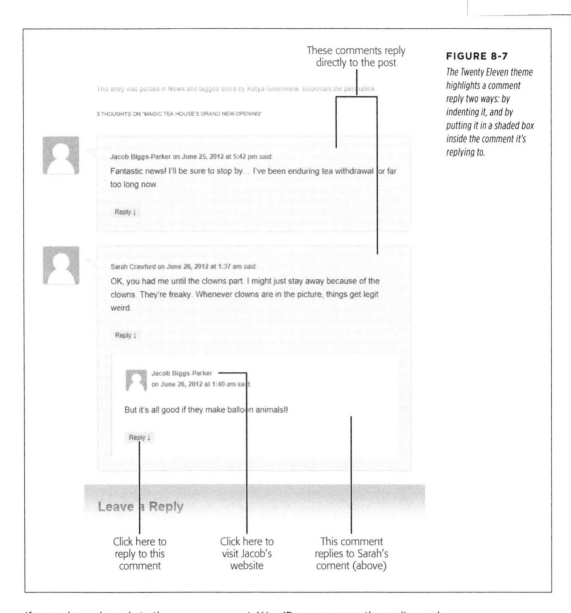

These comments reply
directly to the post

FIGURE 8-7

*The Twenty Eleven theme
highlights a comment
reply two ways: by
indenting it, and by
putting it in a shaded box
inside the comment it's
replying to.*

This entry was posted in News and tagged store by Katya Greenview. Bookmark the permalink.

3 THOUGHTS ON "MAGIC TEA HOUSE'S GRAND NEW OPENING"

Jacob Biggs-Parker on June 25, 2012 at 5:42 pm said:

Fantastic news! I'll be sure to stop by... I've been enduring tea withdrawal for far
too long now.

Reply ↓

Sarah Crawford on June 26, 2012 at 1:37 am said:

OK, you had me until the clowns part. I might just stay away because of the
clowns. They're freaky. Whenever clowns are in the picture, things get legit
weird.

Reply ↓

Jacob Biggs-Parker
on June 26, 2012 at 1:40 am said:

But it's all good if they make balloon animals!!

Reply ↓

Leave a Reply

Click here to
reply to this
comment

Click here to
visit Jacob's
website

This comment
replies to Sarah's
coment (above)

If several people reply to the same comment, WordPress arranges the replies underneath the comment and indents them, either from oldest to newest (the default) or
newest to oldest (if you changed the discussion settings as described on page 242).

Comment replies can go several layers deep. For example, if Sarah replies to your post, Jacob can reply to Sarah's comment, Sergio can reply to Jacob's comment, and then Sarah can reply to Sergio's reply, creating four layers of stacked comments (Figure 8-8).

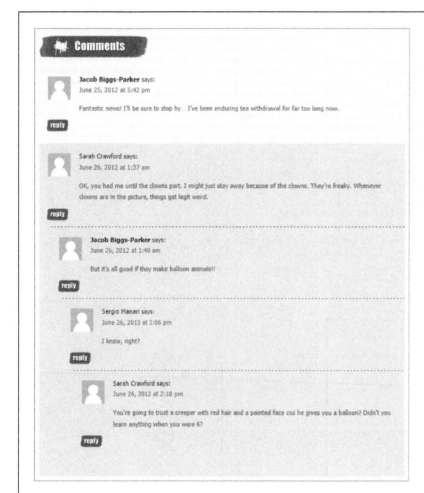

FIGURE 8-8

If you expect to get piles of comments, the standard WordPress Twenty Eleven theme might not be the best choice for you. It tends to spread comments out with plenty of whitespace in between, which makes for more visitor scrolling. Many other themes pack comments tightly together, like the Greyzed theme shown here.

WordPress allows this replying-to-replies madness to continue only so far; once you get five levels of comments, it no longer displays the Reply button. This prevents the conversation from becoming dizzyingly self-referential, and it stops the ever-increasing indenting from messing with your site's layout. However, you can reduce or increase this cap (the maximum is 10 levels). To do so, choose Settings→Discussion, find the setting "Enable threaded (nested) comments 5 levels deep," and pick a different number. Or, turn off the checkmark for this setting to switch threaded comments off altogether, which keeps your conversations super-simple, but looks more than a bit old-fashioned.

Author Comments

Don't forget to add your voice to the discussion. Authors who never take the time to directly engage their readers lose their readers' interest—quickly.

Of course, it's also possible to have too much of a good thing, and authors who reply to every comment will seem desperate (at best) or intrusive (at worst). They'll suffocate a conversation like a micro-managing boss. The best guideline is to step in periodically, answering obvious questions and giving credit to good feedback (while ignoring or deleting the obvious junk). Do that, and your readers will see that your comments section is well cared-for. They'll know that you read your feedback, and they'll be more likely to join in.

WordPress makes site owners' comments stick out from those of the riffraff so your readers can easily spot your contributions. The way it does this depends on the theme, but most themes change the background color behind your comment. If you run a self-hosted blog, or if you bought the Custom CSS upgrade for your WordPress.com site, you can make your replies even more obvious. The trick is to tweak the formatting the *bypostauthor* style applies. Page 446 explains how.

Paged Comments

WordPress also provides a feature called *paging* that organizes masses of comments by dividing them into separate pages. The disadvantage here is that readers need to click more often to follow a discussion. The advantage is that you split awkwardly long discussions into more manageable (and readable) chunks.

To use pages, choose Settings→Discussion and turn on the checkbox next to "Break comments into pages." You can type in the number of comments you want included on each page (the default is 50).

You can also choose the page that readers begin on—the default setting is "last," which means that new readers will start on the last page of comments first, seeing the most recent chunk of the conversation before they see older exchanges. But the overall effect is a bit weird, because the very latest comment appears at the *bottom* of this page. What you probably want is the latest comment to appear at the *top* of the first page. To get this effect—paged comments, with the most recent comment at the top of the list on the first page—change "last" to "first" (so the setting says "and the first page displayed by default") and change "older" to "newer" (so the setting says "Comments should be displayed with the newer comments at the top of each page").

Advertising a Post's Comments

As you've seen, comments appear right underneath the post they refer to. They don't appear at all in the post stream—that reverse-chronological list of posts that acts as the home page for most WordPress sites. You can think of it this way: Each post is like a separate room at a party, with its own conversation. The same guests can wander between rooms and join different conversations, but the conversation from one room doesn't intrude onto the next.

However, WordPress does attempt to alert readers to the *presence* of comments in the post stream, if not their content. If a post has at least one comment, WordPress shows the comment *count* next to that post. If a post doesn't have any comments, WordPress displays a "Leave a comment" link. Technically, your site theme controls this detail, but most are fairly consistent in this practice (Figure 8-9).

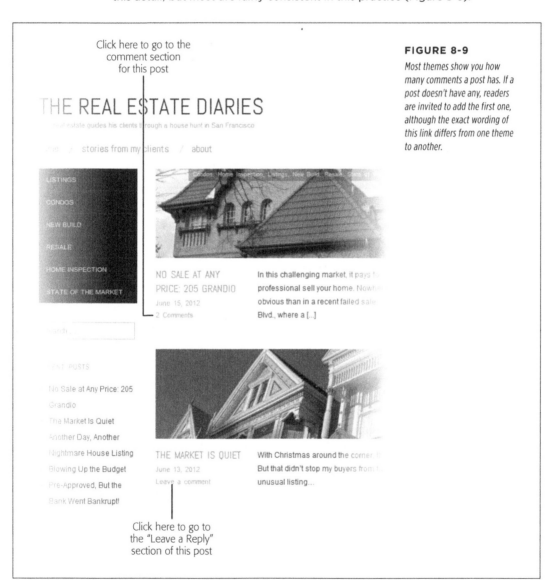

Click here to go to the comment section for this post

FIGURE 8-9

Most themes show you how many comments a post has. If a post doesn't have any, readers are invited to add the first one, although the exact wording of this link differs from one theme to another.

Click here to go to the "Leave a Reply" section of this post

Here's another way to highlight comments on your home page: Use the Recent Comments widget, which highlights the most recent comments made on *any* post or page (Figure 8-10). When you add this widget (in the Appearance→Widgets section of the dashboard), you can choose the number of recent comments it lists. The standard setting is 5.

RECENT COMMENTS

- Katya Greenview on **Magic Tea House's Grand New Opening**
- Katya Greenview on **Magic Tea House's Grand New Opening**
- Katya Greenview on **Magic Tea House's Grand New Opening**
- Jacob Biggs-Parker on **Magic Tea House's Grand New Opening**
- Sarah Crawford on **Magic Tea House's Grand New Opening**

FIGURE 8-10

The Recent Comments widget tells you who's commenting and on what post. However, it doesn't show you any of the comment content, which is a shame. Readers can click a comment link to see both the comment and the corresponding post.

TIP If you want a better Recent Comments widget, there are plenty of plug-ins that attempt to fill the gap. Most excerpt the first part of the comment and display it right inside the widget to give readers a taste of the conversation (and to encourage them to join in). See, for example, the Better WordPress Recent Comments plug-in (*http://tinyurl.com/wprecentcomments*).

Comment Ratings

You've no doubt seen sites that allow readers to rate each other's comments, often by clicking a tiny thumbs-up or thumbs-down icon (Figure 8-11). It's one more form of audience participation.

Bloggers and other web authors are divided over the value of comment ratings. On the upside, comment ratings encourage readers to get involved, and allow people to feel like they're taking part in a discussion even if they don't write a comment. On the downside, comment ratings have a nasty habit of turning discussions into arguments. If you're dealing with a contentious subject, readers may simply scan the list of comments to vote up the ones they agree with and vote down ones they don't. (Some sites try to reduce the negativity by replacing comment voting with a Like button that allows readers to vote for comments but not against them. But even this type of rating encourages readers to gang up with the people who share their opinions.)

Philosophical questions aside, it's fairly easy to add comment ratings to your site if it's running on WordPress.com. In the dashboard, choose Settings→Ratings, click the Comments tab, and then turn on the "Enable for comments" checkbox. You can position the voting icons above the comments (as in Figure 8-11) or below them. When you finish, click Save Changes.

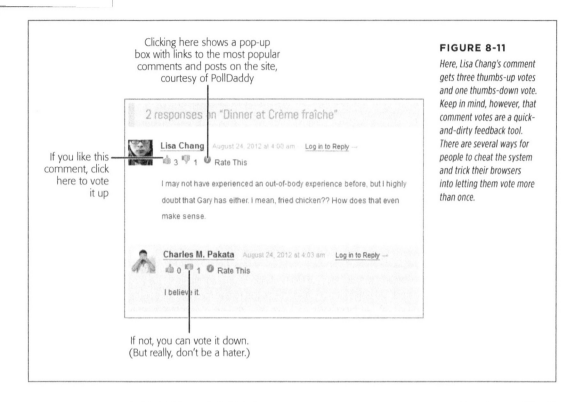

Clicking here shows a pop-up box with links to the most popular comments and posts on the site, courtesy of PollDaddy

FIGURE 8-11

Here, Lisa Chang's comment gets three thumbs-up votes and one thumbs-down vote. Keep in mind, however, that comment votes are a quick-and-dirty feedback tool. There are several ways for people to cheat the system and trick their browsers into letting them vote more than once.

2 responses on "Dinner at Crème fraîche"

Lisa Chang August 24, 2012 at 4:00 am   Log in to Reply →
👍 3 👎 1 ⓘ Rate This

I may not have experienced an out-of-body experience before, but I highly doubt that Gary has either. I mean, fried chicken?? How does that even make sense.

If you like this comment, click here to vote it up

Charles M. Pakata August 24, 2012 at 4:03 am   Log in to Reply →
👍 0 👎 1 ⓘ Rate This

I believe it.

If not, you can vote it down. (But really, don't be a hater.)

> **NOTE** You can also use a similar WordPress.com feature to add star ratings to posts. You'll learn abut it on page 400.

Unfortunately, self-hosted WordPress sites don't get the comment rating feature. The solution is to install a comment voting plug-in, like GD Star Rating (*http://tinyurl.com/gd-star-rating*). But first, you need to learn a bit more about plug-ins, as detailed in Chapter 9,

Linkbacks

There's one type of comment you haven't yet seen: the *linkback*, a short, automatically generated comment that lets you know when somebody's talking about your post. Figure 8-12 shows what a linkback looks like—but be warned, it's not particularly pretty.

FIGURE 8-12

The original post

Community Outreach Fridays

The Canton School is bringing back one of its most loved traditions: weekly community outreach days. It all begins this week, October 18, with a visit by the Upper Elementary class to the Glenacres Retirement Homes. Our students will be talking to them, bringing homemade bread, and possibly playing a game of bridge or two!

If you'd like to volunteer to help or assist with the pre-visit baking, you can still volunteer to be one of two parent coordinators. Contact Susan Credmore at the office (344) 424-1291.

Posted by smackerdon on Jun 15, 2012 • 1 Comment

Uncategorized • Comment feed RSS 2.0 • Read this post | Edit

One Response to "Community Outreach Fridays"

Some Fun at Glenacres Retirement | Time for Diane says:

June 26, 2012 at 8:34 pm (Edit)

[...] more at http://prosetech.com/wordpress/cantonschool/?p=18 Share this:TwitterFacebookLike this:LikeBe the first to like [...]

Reply

If you allow linkbacks on your site, this is the potential result. You write a post (in this example, that's "Community Outreach Fridays"). Someone else writes a post that links to your post (that's "Some Fun at Glenacres Retirement)," and WordPress adds the comment shown here as a way of letting the whole world know that someone is talking about you.

Depending on the theme, a linkback comment may show up as a clickable link, or it may show up as an excerpt from the original post, like this

The link that leads back to the referring site

NOTE Linkbacks *are* comments. They appear in the comment list, and need your approval just as any other comment does before WordPress publishes them on your site.

The neat thing about linkback comments is that WordPress creates them *automatically*. Here's how it happened in the example shown in Figure 8-12:

1. First, the "Community Outreach Fridays" post is published on the Canton School site.

2. Then, the "Fun at Glenacres Retirement" post is created for the Time for Diane site. Although it isn't shown in Figure 8-12, that post has a link that points to the "Community Outreach Fridays" post.

3. When the "Fun at Glenacres Retirement" post is published, the Time for Diane website sends a notification to the Canton School site, saying "Hey, I linked to you" in computer language. (The person who wrote the "Fun at Glenacres Retirement" post doesn't need to take any action, and probably doesn't even know that a notification is being sent.)

4. On the Canton School site, WordPress springs into action, and adds the linkback comment shown in Figure 8-12.

NOTE Linkbacks aren't a WordPress-only feature. Many web publishing platforms support them, and virtually all blogs can send linkback notifications and add linkback comments.

The purpose of linkbacks is two-fold. First, they show that people are reading and discussing your content, which makes it seem more popular and more relevant. Second, it provides a link to the person who's referring to you. That means readers on your site (say, Canton School) can click a linkback comment to head to the referring post on the other site (Time for Diane). In an ideal world, this is a great way to network with like-minded sites.

In the not-so-distant past, a certain faction of bloggers cared dearly about linkbacks and saw them as an important community-building tool. Nowadays, popular opinion has shifted. Here are some reasons why you might not want to allow linkbacks:

- **Clutter.** Extra comments, no matter how brief, can end up crowding out real conversation. Some themes (like Bueno) separate linkbacks from the main comment stream, but most mix them together. If you have a popular topic that gets plenty of mention on other sites, your linkbacks can split up the more interesting human feedback and push it out of sight.

- **Why risk spam?** More comments equals more spam, and shady advertisers can send linkbacks to your site just as often as they send other types of comment spam.

- **Links are a good way to reward your commenters.** If someone writes a good comment, they can include a link in their comment text ("I was also frustrated with the stains my kids left, everywhere and on everything. I even wrote a post with my favorite stain tips. Check it out at http://helpfatheroftwelve.com."). And if a commenter fills in the website box (page 233), WordPress automatically turns the name at the top of the comment into a clickable link. With all this linking goodness, why reward someone who hasn't even bothered to comment on your site?

In short, most people find that linkbacks aren't worth the trouble. To disable them, choose Settings→Discussion and remove the checkmark next to the setting "Allow link notifications from other blogs (pingbacks and trackbacks)." Technically, WordPress supports two linkback mechanisms: pingbacks and trackbacks. The technical details about how pingbacks and trackbacks send their messages aren't terribly interesting. The important thing is that if you allow linkbacks (and, by default, your site does), you may start getting comments like the ones shown in Figure 8-12.

Optionally, you can clear the checkmark next to the setting "Attempt to notify any blogs linked to from the article." When this setting is on and you write a post that links to another post on someone else's site, WordPress automatically sends a notification to that site, and they can choose whether to display a linkback comment.

Oddly enough, if you have the "Attempt to notify any blogs linked to from the article" setting switched on, WordPress notifies even *your* site if you create a post that links to another one of your own posts. In this situation, it creates a linkback comment in the target post that points to the referring post, just as though the posts were on two different sites. (Of course, you're free to delete this comment if it bothers you.)

■ Making Comments More Personal

On a really good website, you won't feel like you're debating current affairs with anonymous_guy_65. Instead, you'll have the sense that you're talking to an actual person, someone who exists in the real world, beyond the pixels on your computer screen.

Often, all you need to do to personalize comments is include a few small details in the right places. One key enhancement is including a user-supplied profile picture with comments. WordPress gives you two ways to do that—you can get pictures from its excellent Gravatar service, or you can take them from a person's Facebook or Twitter account. The following sections show you how to do both.

The Gravatar Service

To give comments a personal touch, you can display a tiny picture next to each person's thoughts. This picture, called an *avatar*, could be an actual photograph of the person or something quirkier, like a mythical creature or cartoon character. The idea is that the avatar helps your guests see, at a glance, which comments belong to the same person, and it just might give them a taste of the author's personality (Figure 8-13). Avatars also add a visual complement to web discussions, making a page of comments seem just a bit more like a real conversation.

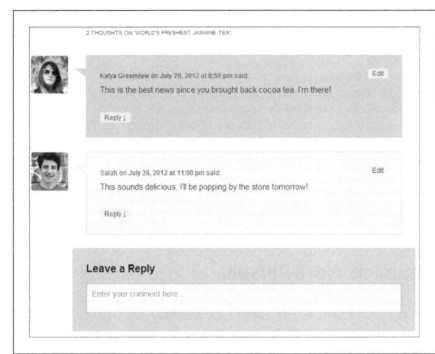

2 THOUGHTS ON "WORLD'S FRESHEST JASMINE TEA"

Katya Greenview on July 26, 2012 at 8:50 pm said: Edit

This is the best news since you brought back cocoa tea. I'm there!

Reply ↓

Salah on July 26, 2012 at 11:00 pm said: Edit

This sounds delicious. I'll be popping by the store tomorrow!

Reply ↓

Leave a Reply

Enter your comment here ..

WordPress uses an avatar service called Gravatar, which is short for "globally recognized avatar." The idea is that ordinary people can use Gravatar to set up an avatar and include some basic personal information. They can then use that image and profile info on sites throughout the Web. Originally, Gravatar was a small service cooked up by a single person, but these days Automattic runs the service, making it freely available to virtually any blogging platform or website-building framework. (A Gravatar-supplied avatar goes by the name *gravatar.*)

You don't need to take any special steps to enable avatars. WordPress uses them automatically, As you already know, every would-be commenter has to enter an email address. When a reader enters this email address, WordPress contacts the Gravatar service and asks if it has a picture that's affiliated with that address. If it does, WordPress displays the picture next to the comment. If it doesn't, WordPress shows a featureless gray silhouette instead.

Why Gravatars Make Good Sense

The obvious limitation to gravatars is that you won't see personalized images unless your readers sign up with the Gravatar service. And unless your visitors are web nerds, they probably haven't signed up yet—in fact, they probably haven't even heard of Gravatar.

However, this dilemma isn't as bad as it seems, for the following reasons:

- **Gravatars are optional.** Some people use them, other people don't. There's no downside to allowing gravatars on your site. And if someone notices that another commenter gets a personalized picture, that person just might ask about how to get the same feature.

- **Gravatars can be auto-generated.** As the box on page 255 explains, you can replace the boring gray silhouettes for non-Gravatar users with an auto-generated gravatar. The neat thing about auto-generated gravatars is that they're unique *and* consistent, which means they can help people

identify comments left by the same person.

- **Gravatar can co-exist with Facebook and Twitter pictures.** As you'll learn on page 259, you can get comment pictures from Facebook and Twitter accounts. In this case, Gravatar is just one more picture-gathering option that works in harmony with the others.

- **Gravatars have WordPress.com support.** WordPress.com users are more likely to have gravatars than other people, because the Gravatar service is integrated with the WordPress.com profile feature. If you're a WordPress.com user, choose Users→My Profile from the dashboard to set your gravatar quickly and painlessly.

- **You can remind your readers to get a gravatar.** If you run a self-hosted site, you can edit the *comments.php* file in your theme (page 456) to add a reminder, like a link that says "Sign up for a Gravatar and get a personalized picture next to your comment." Just don't expect that many people will follow your recommendation.

Signing Up with Gravatar

If *you* aren't a Gravatar fan yet, here's how you sign up:

1. **Go to *http://gravatar.com* and click the "Get your Gravatar" button.**

2. **Type in your email address and click the Signup button.**

   Gravatar dispatches a confirmation message to your email address.

3. **When you get the confirmation email, click the activation link inside.**

   This opens a new browser tab so you can complete the sign-up process.

4. **Enter a user name and password, and then click Signup (again).**

   You arrive at the Manage Gravatars page, which informs you that you don't yet have any images associated with your account.

5. **Click the "Add one" link.**

   Gravatar gives you a number of ways to find an image. You can upload it from your computer's hard drive (the first, and most common, option), snag it from a website, or snap a new one with a webcam (assuming you have one).

6. **Click the appropriate button for your image (for example, "My computer's hard drive") and follow the instructions to find and crop your picture.**

   Gravatars are square. You can use an image as big as 512 x 512 pixels, and Gravatar will shrink it down to a thumbnail-size tile and displays it next to each comment you leave.

7. **Choose a rating for your Gravatar (see Figure 8-14).**

   Ordinarily, WordPress sites show only gravatars that have a G rating. If you want to tolerate more friskiness on your site, go to the Settings→Discussion page. Scroll to the Avatars section and ratchet up the "Maximum Rating" setting to PG, R, or X.

Choose a rating for your Gravatar

By clicking on one of these ratings

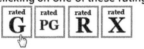

FIGURE 8-14

Some sites may not display gravatars that are mildly naughty (PG), violent or sexually explicitly (R), or way-over-the-top disturbing (X). It's up to you to pick the rating that represents your image best, but if you're using an ordinary head shot, G is the right choice.

G A G rated gravatar is suitable for display on all websites with any audience type.

PG PG rated gravatars may contain rude gestures, provocatively dressed individuals, the lesser swear words, or mild violence.

R R rated gravatars may contain such things as harsh profanity, intense violence, nudity, or hard drug use.

X X rated gravatars may contain hardcore sexual imagery or extremely disturbing violence.

8. **Now Gravatar associates your avatar with your email address.** All new comments you leave will include your new picture, and comments you already made will get it, too (assuming you haven't changed your email address since you posted the comment). If, in the future, you decide you want a different picture, log back into Gravatar and upload a new one.

Changing the "Mystery Man" Gravatar

Ordinarily, if a commenter doesn't have a gravatar, WordPress displays the infamous gray silhouette that it calls Mystery Man. You can replace Mystery Man with one of several other pictures from the Settings→Discussion page. Just scroll down to the Avatars section and change the Default Avatar option.

Other possibilities for avatars include a completely blank image or a stock Gravatar logo. More interestingly, you can give mystery commenters a tailor-made, completely unique gravatar (for your site only) that an algorithm generates. To create this gravatar, WordPress takes your guest's email address, uses it to generate some semi-random computer gibberish, and then translates that into a specific type of picture (according to the algorithm's strict but secret rules).

WordPress offers four algorithm-spawned gravatar types, including Identicon (geometric patterns), Wavatar (cartoon-like faces), MonsterID (whimsical monster drawings), and Retro (video-game-style pixelated icons). Figure 8-15 shows two examples.

FIGURE 8-15

Algorithmically generated gravatars add some fun to your site, even if your readers don't have real profile pictures. Here are two examples: Wavatar (left) and Retro (right). Notice that Sarah Crawford's gravatar remains consistent for both her comments.

Gravatar Hovercards

The tiny comment pictures that Gravatar provides give a personal touch to your comments section. But the Gravatar service doesn't limit itself to pictures. It can also smuggle in a bit of extra personal information about each commenter. This information shows up as a *hovercard*—a small box that pops up when someone hovers over another person's avatar (Figure 8-16).

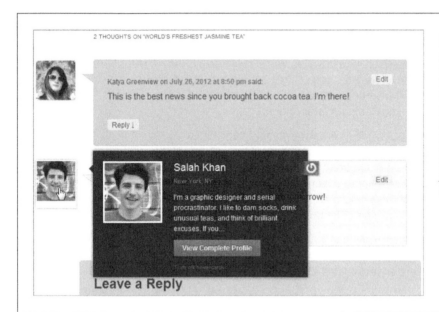

FIGURE 8-16

A hovercard is like a virtual business card. It carries your personal information around, no matter what Gravatar-enabled site you visit. (If you're curious about what happens when you click View Complete Profile, jump ahead to Figure 8-18.)

But here's the catch: Hovercards appear only if your site runs on WordPress.com, or if you're a self-hoster using Jetpack (the ridiculously useful free plug-in you'll learn to install on page 284). If you meet one of these requirements, your comments probably have hovercard support already. To check, choose Settings→Discussion, scroll down to the Avatars section, and make sure the checkbox next to "View people's profiles when you mouse over their Gravatars" is turned on. (If you run a self-hosted site but don't have Jetpack installed, you won't see this setting and you won't be able to use hovercards.)

Hovercards are a small feature, but a nice one. They help your readers feel like they can learn a little bit about your commenters. But to make sure your hovercards have the right information, you need to understand where that information comes from.

You might assume that the hovercard details are part of your visitor's WordPress profile, but they're not. (In fact, hovercards work even if guests don't have a WordPress account.) Instead, hovercards get their information from the profile that

Gravatar users optionally set up. This design is both good and bad. The advantage is that it makes hovercard information portable—it travels with the avatar, no matter what Gravatar-enabled site you go to (even if the site *doesn't* run WordPress). The disadvantage is that if your readers don't bother to fill out the profile information, it won't appear at all (Figure 8-17).

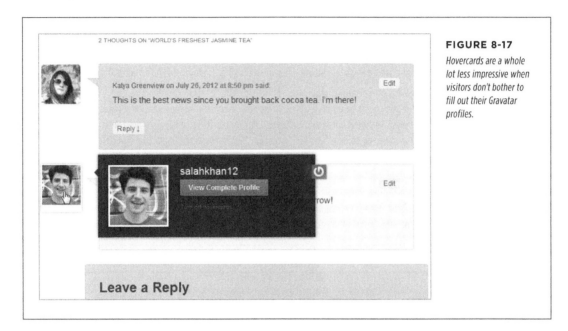

To make sure *your* hovercard looks good, you need to fill in that information, too. Visit the Gravatar site (*http://gravatar.com*), click the My Account button, and then choose Edit My Profile. There's plenty of information you can fill in, but the details that appear on the hovercard are your full name (Display Name), where you live (Location), and a short blurb that describes yourself (About Me), which the hovercard truncates after the first couple of sentences. When you finish, click Save Profile to store your information with your Gravatar, allowing it to appear on hovercard-supporting sites everywhere.

Gravatar Verified Services

As you've now seen, the Gravatar service is more than just a way to display your picture on different websites. It's also a way for you to store a mini-profile with a bio, some basic personal details, and links to all the Gravatar-enabled websites you use .

This last part is one of Gravatar's niftier features. It lets you add links in your Gravatar profile that point to other social websites or blogging services where you have an account. For example, you can add links to your Facebook or Twitter accounts. Or, you can include a link to your photos on Flickr, your videos on YouTube or Vimeo, your blog on WordPress (or Blogger, or Tumblr), and many other social sites.

When you first sign up with Gravatar, it doesn't include any of these links, You need to add the ones you want by editing your Gravatar profile and clicking the Verified Services section. Choose a service from the list (for example, Facebook), and then click Add. Gravatar asks you to sign in to set up the link. (This is why Gravatar calls them *verified* services—it doesn't actually add the link unless it can verify that it truly belongs to you.)

In the past, if a person added a verified service, Gravatar would add a tiny icon for it in that person's hovercard (which was quite cool and very convenient). Sadly, Gravatar no longer takes this step, possibly to prevent spammers from abusing hovercards. However, verified service links still appear in a clearly visible place at the top of the Gravatar profile page (Figure 8-18). To see them, simply click the View Complete Profile button that appears in every hovercard (Figure 8-16).

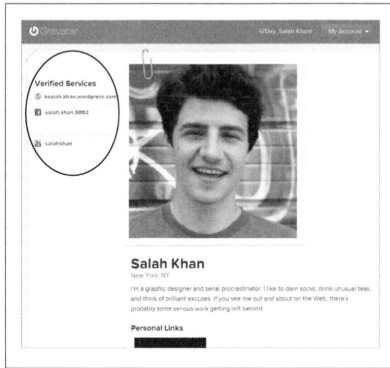

FIGURE 8-18

Salah Khan has three verified services with Gravatar: a WordPress. com blog, a Facebook account, and a YouTube account.

Facebook and Twitter Comments

Gravatars are a great idea, but they might not be practical for your site because people might not bother to use them (or they might not even realize *how* to use them). No matter—you can give visitors other comment options. For example, you can let them log into your site using their Facebook or Twitter credentials, and then post a comment. In such a case, WordPress grabs your guest's Facebook or Twitter profile picture and displays it next to that person's comments (Figure 8-19).

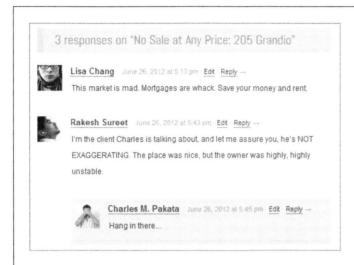

FIGURE 8-19

In this example, Charles Pakata is a WordPress. com user who has signed up with the Gravatar service. But Lisa and Rakesh are Facebook users. As long as they log into Facebook, WordPress uses their Facebook profile picture, without forcing them to sign up with Gravatar or take any extra steps.

If your site runs on WordPress.com, you already have the Facebook and Twitter sign-in feature, and there's no way to switch it off.

If you run a self-hosted blog, the best way to get Facebook and Twitter comments is with the Jetpack plug-in (page 284). However, you won't be able to see the comments until you explicitly enable them. To do that, click Jetpack in the dashboard menu. Look for the box named "Jetpack Comments," and click the Activate button inside (Figure 8-20). Incidentally, this setting isn't just for Facebook and Twitter users—it also lets people with WordPress.com accounts join in.

TIP You might find that once you enable Jetpack comments, your comment section gets a new background that doesn't blend in with the rest of your page. To fix this, choose Settings→Discussion, scroll down to the "Jetpack Comments" section, and try a different "Color Scheme" options. You can pick Light, Dark, or Transparent, and it's a trial-and-error process to find out what looks best.

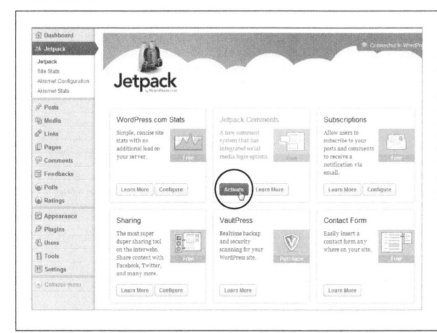

Some WordPress sites use Facebook and Twitter comments in conjunction with the "Users must be registered and logged in to comment" setting (in the Settings→Discussion page). Their thinking goes something like this:

> "I've been flexible, and now I want something in return. I've given my readers three good options for establishing their identity (Facebook, Twitter, and Word Press.com). By making them use one, I can lock out spammers and force people to bring their virtual identities to my site."

Think carefully before you take this step. It will protect your site against spam, but only partly, because many spambots have fake Facebook identities. It's also guaranteed to scare away at least some potential commenters, including those who don't have a social media account, those who can't be bothered to log in, and those who don't want to reveal their identity to you.

▣ Stamping Out Comment Spam

So far, you've focused on the comments that are *supposed* to be on your site—the ones your visitors leave in response to your posts. Up to now, this discussion has skirted a disquieting fact: on the average WordPress site, spam comments outweigh legit comments by a factor of 10 to 1. And spammers don't discriminate—they don't attempt to chase the most popular blogs or the ones that cover their favorite topics. Instead, they spew their dreck everywhere.

Understanding Spam

You're no doubt familiar with the idea of email spam—trashy chain letters and hoaxes that try to get you to download malware or send your banking information to a Nigerian gentleman with a cash flow problem. However, blog spam is a different creature altogether. While email spam tries to lure you in, blog spam tries to slip right past you. That's because blog spammers aren't after you—they're targeting your *readers*. The goal is for them to sneak their advertisements onto your site, where they can attract the attention of people who already trust your blog. Every bit of blog spam is trying to lure a reader to travel to the spammer's site, either by clicking the commenter's name or a link in the comment text.

In the past, spammers were crude and their messages easy to identify. Today, they're trickier than ever. They attempt to disguise themselves as actual readers to fool you into allowing their comment (with its link to their site). Or they pretend to sell real products (which they never deliver). And spammers hire low-paid workers to hand-write spam messages and circumvent the safeguards that spot automated spam bots, like Captchas (page 268).

Some WordPressers tell horror stories of receiving hundreds or thousands of spam messages a day. The problem is severe enough that, if you're not careful, you can wind up spending more time dealing with spam than managing the rest of your site. Fortunately, you can use the tools and strategies discussed below to fight back.

UP TO SPEED

Caught in the Wild

Spammers take great care to make their messages look as natural as possible. The spammer's payload is a link, which is submitted with the comment and hidden behind the commenter's name.

Here are some of the spam messages that we caught on this book's example sites. Would any have fooled you?

"Glad to know about something like this."

"Perhaps this is one of the most interesting blogs that i have ever seen. interesting article, funny comment. keep it up!"

"i was exactly talking about this with a friend yesterday, and now i found about it in your blog. this is awesome."

"Could you tell me when you're going to update your posts?"

"I've also been thinking the identical thing myself lately. Grateful to see another person on the same wavelength! Nice article."

"We're a bunch of volunteers and opening a brand new scheme in our community. Your site offered us with valuable info to paintings on. You have done an impressive job and our whole community can be grateful to you."

Spam-Fighting Strategies

You can choose from several approaches to defend against spam. They include:

- **Forbidding all comments.** This is obviously a drastic, ironclad approach. To disable comments, you turn off the "Allow people to post comments on new articles" checkbox on the Settings→Discussion page. But be warned that if you do, you'll sacrifice the lively conversation that your visitors expect.

  Verdict: An extreme solution. The cure is worse than the disease.

- **Using moderation.** This is the default WordPress approach, and it's the one you've learned about in this chapter. The problem is that you just can't keep moderating a site that's growing in size and popularity—it becomes too labor-intensive. It also has a distinct drawback: it forces commenters to wait before their comment appears on your site, by which point they may have lost interest in the conversation.

  Verdict: Not practical in the long term, unless you combine it with a spam-catching tool (like Akismet, which you'll meet in a moment).

- **Forcing commenters to log in (for self-hosted sites only).** To use this approach, you need to add each visitor's ID to your WordPress site, or create some way for them to register on your site themselves. This approach definitely isn't suitable for the average public blog. However, it may work if you have a small, captive audience—for example, if you're building a site for family members only, or for a team of co-workers.

  Verdict: For special cases only. You'll learn about multiuser blogs in Chapter 11.

- **Making commenters log in, but allowing third-party log-ins.** A third-party login verifies your guests through an authentication service—typically one provided by WordPress.com, Facebook, or Twitter. This requirement may work, because many people already have a Facebook or Twitter account that they don't mind using (whereas they definitely won't bother creating a new account just to leave a single comment). Still, forcing logins may drive away as many as half of your would-be commenters. And it's still not truly spam-proof, because clever spam-bots can create Facebook accounts, just like real people can.

  Verdict: A good idea, but not a complete spam-fighting solution.

- **Using Akismet or another spam-catching plug-in.** Many WordPress administrators swear that their lives would not be livable without the automatic spam-detecting feature of Akismet. It isn't perfect—some site owners complain that legitimate comments get trashed, and they need to spend serious time fishing them out of the spam bucket—but it usually gives the best spam protection with the minimum amount of disruption to the commenting process.

  Verdict: The best compromise. It's also essential if you turn off moderation.

The pros and cons of managing comments by moderation versus spam-fighting are a lot to digest, even for seasoned webheads. However, the verdict is clear: most

WordPress pros eventually start using a spam-catching tool. They may use it in addition to moderation, or—more likely—instead of it.

NOTE If you don't have a spam filter, *you* are the spam filter. And given that an ordinary WordPress site can attract dozens of spam messages a day, you don't want to play that role.

If you're ready to ditch comment moderation in favor of a livelier, more responsive, and less controlled discussion, choose Settings→Discussion and turn off the checkboxes next to these settings: "An administrator must always approve the comment" and "Comment author must have a previously approved comment." Then click Save Changes at the bottom of the page.

Now, continue to the next section to make sure you have a proper spam-blocker to intercept bad comments.

WordPress's Other Spam-Catching Options

WordPress has a few built-in spam-fighting options on the Settings→Discussion page. In the past, they were a practical line of defense that could intercept and stop a lot of junk comments. Unfortunately, spamming evolved in the intervening years, and now these settings are only occasionally useful. They include:

- **"Hold a comment in the queue if it contains 2 or more links."** Use this setting to catch posts that have a huge number of links. The problem is that spammers are on to this restriction, so they've toned down their links to make their spam look more like real comments.

- **The Comment Moderation and Comment Blacklist boxes.** Try these boxes, described earlier (page 241), as a way to keep out offensive text. They also double as a way

to catch spam. However, don't rush to put in obvious spammy keywords, because you'll just end up doing a clumsier version of what Akismet already does. Instead, consider using these boxes if you have a spam problem that's specific to your site—for example, a certain keyword that keeps coming up when spammers target your posts.

- **"Automatically close comments on articles older than 14 days."** By default, this option isn't switched on. However, it's a potentially useful way to stop spammers from targeting old posts, where the conversation has long since died down. And you don't need to stick to the suggested 14 days. You can type in any number, even making the lockout period start a year after you publish a post.

Understanding Akismet

Akismet is one of many spam-fighting plug-ins developers created for WordPress. However, it has a special distinction: Automattic, the same folks who built WordPress, makes it. It's also the only spam-blocking tool that's allowed on WordPress.com blogs.

Akismet works by intercepting each new comment. It sends the details of that comment (including its text and the commenter's website, email, and IP addresses) to one of Akismet's web servers. There, the server analyzes it, using some crafty algorithms and a secret spam-fighting database, to attempt to determine whether it's legitimate. Any one of a number of details can betray a spam message, including links to known spam sites, a known spammer IP address, keywords that are commonly found together in spam messages ("free Viagra" for instance), and so on. Akismet quickly makes its decision and reports back to your website. Your site then either publishes the comment or puts it in the Spam folder, depending on Akismet's judgment.

WordPress experts report that Akismet's success rate hovers at around 97 percent. Usually, when Akismet errs, it does so by flagging a safe comment as spam (rather than allowing real spam through). However, Akismet's success depends on the site and the timing. When spammers adjust their tactics, it may take Akismet a little time to catch up, during which its accuracy will drop.

Akismet is free, mostly. Personal sites pay nothing (unless you volunteer a small donation). However, small businesses and money-making blogs are expected to contribute $5 per month. Large publishers that want to spam-proof multiple sites are asked for $50 per month.

NOTE Akismet uses an honor system, and there are plenty of sites that earn a bit of money but don't pay the Akismet fee. But if you want a totally free business-friendly solution for a self-hosted site, you need to find a different plug-in. Several good alternatives are described in the box below.

FREQUENTLY ASKED QUESTION

Akismet Alternatives

I need a spam-catching tool, but I don't want Akismet. Are there other options?

If you're running a self-hosted WordPress site, there's no shortage of spam-fighting plug-ins. Unlike Akismet, many are free for almost everyone. (Some plug-in developers collect donations, charge for only the highest-traffic sites, or make extra money charging support fees to big companies. Others do it simply for the prestige.)

One caveat applies. Anti-spam developers and spammers are locked in an ever-escalating arms race. The spam blocker that works perfectly this week might falter next week when clever spammers work around its detection rules. For that

reason, it's impossible to know which anti-spam tools are the best—you simply need to try them out on your own site. Four good Akismet alternatives include:

- Antispam Bee (*http://tinyurl.com/spambee*)
- AVH First Defense Against Spam (*http://tinyurl.com/avhspam*)
- Defensio Anti-Spam (*http://tinyurl.com/defensio*)
- FV Antispam (*http://tinyurl.com/fvantispam*)

If you want to try one of these out, you need to install it by using WordPress's plug-in feature. Before you try, review the basics of plug-in management described in Chapter 9.

Installing Akismet

If your site is on WordPress.com, you're already using Akismet, and there's no way to turn it off. As soon as you turn off comment moderation, you leave the entire process in Akismet's hands. (Skip ahead to the next section to learn more about that.)

If you have a self-hosted site, there's a little more to Akismet's set-up. The plug-in is so valuable that Automattic bundles a copy with every WordPress site. However, it isn't activated, which means it's simply a file sitting on your web server, idle. To actually make Akismet spring to life, you need to sign up for an Akismet key and activate the plug-in. Here's how:

1. **First, you need an *Akismet key*. To get that, head to *http://akismet.com/ wordpress*.**

   You can think of the Akismet key as a license to use Akismet on your site.

2. **Click the "Get an Akismet API key" button.**

   Before Akismet will give you a key, it checks to see if you're willing to pay for the privilege. First it shows three sign-up options (Figure 8-21), depending on the type of site you're using.

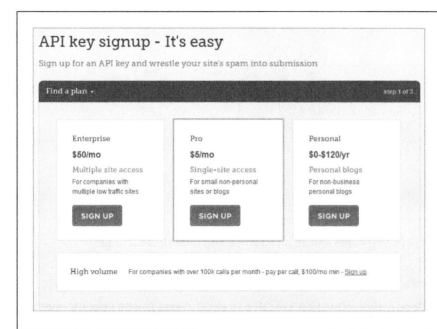

FIGURE 8-21

If you run a small, not-for-profit site or a personal blog, you can click the Sign Up button in the Personal box without guilt. If you have a more serious site, your conscience compels you to click the Sign Up button in the Pro box.

3. **Click the appropriate Sign Up button.**

   If you picked the personal plan, Akismet still asks for a donation (Figure 8-22). You choose an amount using a slider with the title "What is Akismet worth to you?" (Although in fairness to freeloaders everywhere, it's difficult to answer this question *before* you actually start using Akismet.)

FIGURE 8-22

Akismet asks for a donation of $36 a year. Drag the slider either way to change the amount you're willing to pay. Go all the way to the left and your voluntary contribution declines to nothing, and the credit card options disappear.

4. **Fill in your name and email address, and then click Continue.**

   If you elected to pay for Akismet, you need to enter your credit card or PayPal information, and then click Continue again.

5. **Shortly thereafter, you'll receive an email message with your Akismet key in it.**

   It's a funny-looking code like 0286f4c389b2. Make a note of it, because you'll need it for the next step.

6. **Return to the dashboard for your site, and then choose Plugins→Installed Plugins.**

   You'll see a list of plug-ins, with Akismet at the top.

NOTE You'll learn far more about plug-ins, including how to manage them and how to find more, in the next chapter. But for now, these steps walk you through the very simple process of activating the Akismet plug-in you already have.

---

7. **Hover over Akismet so that the Activate link appears, and then click it.**

   At this point, WordPress informs you, in a polite yellow message box, that you need an Akismet key.

8. **Click the "Enter your Akismet API key" link.**

   This brings you to a page with a few Akismet settings, including one for the key.

9. **Copy the key from your email message and then paste it into the text box (Figure 8-23).**

   Optionally, you can set two Akismet settings:

   "Auto-delete spam submitted on posts more than a month old" tells Akismet to periodically delete old messages in your spam folder, whether you've reviewed them or not.

   "Show the number of comments you've approved beside each comment author" tells Akismet to add an extra piece of information to the comments list in the dashboard. This is a count with the number of comments you've previously approved from each would-be commenter. Presumably, if you've approved plenty of messages from the same person, you can trust their newest contributions.

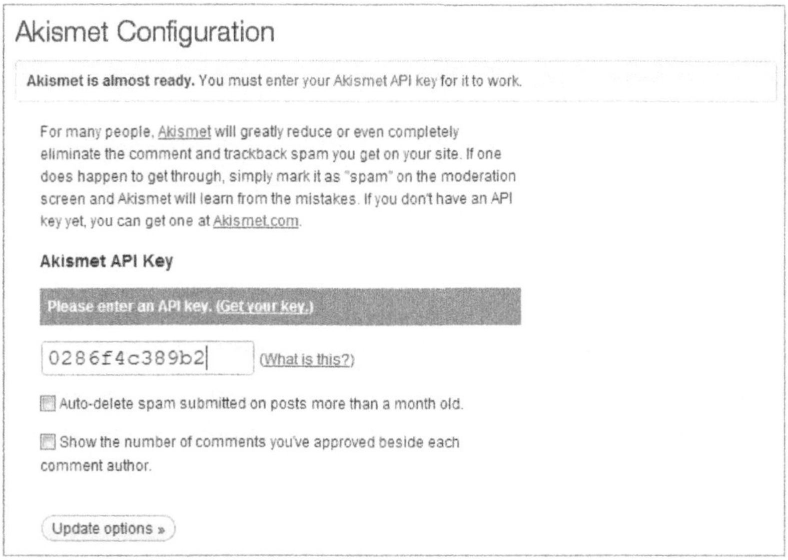

Akismet Configuration

Akismet is almost ready. You must enter your Akismet API key for it to work.

For many people, Akismet will greatly reduce or even completely eliminate the comment and trackback spam you get on your site. If one does happen to get through, simply mark it as "spam" on the moderation screen and Akismet will learn from the mistakes. If you don't have an API key yet, you can get one at Akismet.com.

Akismet API Key

Please enter an API key. (Get your key.)

`0286f4c389b2` (What is this?)

☐ Auto-delete spam submitted on posts more than a month old.

☐ Show the number of comments you've approved beside each comment author.

(Update options »)

FIGURE 8-23

Before Akismet can start catching spam, it needs your API key, which looks like the series of letters and numbers shown here.

10. **Click the "Update options" button.**

    Akismet adds a message to the options page that says "Your key has been verified. Happy blogging!" This confirms that everything worked out and your setup is complete.

Using Akismet

Akismet integrates so seamlessly into WordPress's comment system that you might not even realize it's there. It simply takes over the comments list, automatically moving suspicious comments to the spam folder and publishing everything else.

To give Akismet a very simple test, sign out of your site, and then try adding a few comments. If you enter ordinary text, the comment should sail through without a hiccup. But type in something like "Viagra! Cialis!!" and Akismet will quietly dispose of your comment.

Just because you disabled moderation and started using Akismet doesn't mean your comment-reviewing days are over. Once your site is up and running with Akismet, you should start making regular trips to the Comments section of the dashboard. Only now, instead of reviewing pending comments that haven't been published, you should click the Spam link and check for any valid comments that have been accidentally removed. If you find one, hover over it and click the Not Spam link. If you find several, you can restore them all with a bulk action—first, turn on the checkboxes next to the comments, pick Not Spam from the Bulk Actions list, and then click Apply. You'll soon get a feeling for how often you need to check for stray messages.

Fighting Spam with Captcha

Some WordPress administrators find that a traditional spam-analysis tool like Akismet isn't enough to stop the inevitable avalanche of spam. Others find that Akismet consistently flags good comments as spam, creating a different sort of comment-moderation headache. If you're in the first camp, you might want to supplement Akismet with something else. If you're in the second camp, you might want to try switching Akismet off and plugging the hole with a different sort of tool.

Either way, one good candidate is a Captcha (which computer nerds can translate into the phrase "Completely Automated Public Turing test to tell Computers and Humans Apart"). The idea behind Captcha technology is to force commenters to do something that automated spam-bots can't, at least not easily. If you've ever registered with a site that asks you to re-type a set of fuzzy letters or distorted words, you've seen Captcha in action. Facebook, Hotmail, and Gmail all use it, for example.

The problem with Captchas is twofold. First, there's no Captcha that's too hard for some spam-bot to crack. Second, there's no Captcha that's so easy that it won't annoy your readers, at least a little. But if you use an easy, unobtrusive Captcha, you just might be able to reduce spam to more manageable proportions, without annoying any of your visitors too much. (Hint: You don't want to use the fuzzy letter system.)

To add a Captcha, you need to be running a self-hosted WordPress site, and you need to add a plug-in. If you search the WordPress plug-in repository, you'll find dozens. Here are three worth considering:

- **Growmap Anti-Spambot** (*http://tinyurl.com/growmapspam*). This is almost the simplest Captcha you can have. It simply asks the commenter to check a checkbox. Thus, it annoys almost no one, but it still trips up the majority of automated spam-bots.

- **Captcha** (*http://tinyurl.com/wp-captcha*). This generically named plug-in lets you use simple math questions, like "seven + 1." Yes, shockingly enough, some would-be commenters will still manage to get these questions wrong. However, it won't drive visitors away as quickly as a fuzzy-word-reading test.

- **Anti-Captcha** (*http://tinyurl.com/wp-anticaptcha*). This plug-in performs an invisible test. Essentially, it asks a guest's web browser to run a snippet of JavaScript. That snippet then sets a hidden value in the web page. Automated spam-bots usually ignore JavaScript code, so they won't be able to set the hidden value that Anti-Captcha looks for, and thus they'll fail the test. Overall, this plug-in catches the least amount of spam, but presents no inconvenience to your readers.

Remember, Captcha isn't fool-proof. It won't stop human spammers (which typically account for less than 10 percent of spam), and it won't stop the sneakiest spam bots. However, it can reduce the total amount of spam enough to improve your life.

Supercharging
Your Blog

9

Getting New Features with Plug-Ins

WordPress offers an impressive set of built-in features. In the previous chapters, you used them to write posts and pages, and to glam up your site. But serious WordPress fans have a way to get even more from WordPress—or technically, about 20,000 ways to get more, because that's the number of free WordPress *plug-ins* you can use to supercharge your site.

Before you go any further, be aware of one critical point: WordPress plug-ins work on self-hosted WordPress sites *only*. If you're using WordPress.com, you won't be allowed to install even a single plug-in. This restriction isn't quite as bad as it seems, however, because WordPress.com already has a few extra features and preinstalled plug-ins, as chosen by the fine people at Automattic. For example, WordPress.com sites come with social media sharing buttons for Facebook and Twitter, while self-hosted WordPress sites need a plug-in to do the same thing. So even though WordPress.com users can't pack on new features, they do start off slightly ahead.

If you're a WordPress.com site-builder, you don't need to go any further in this chapter. Skip ahead to Chapter 10 to keep using what you've got. But if you're running a self-hosted WordPress site, you need to know how to add plug-ins to make your site truly great. This chapter shows you how to find, evaluate, and install plug-ins on your website, and then tweak their settings. You'll also explore several of WordPress's most popular and practical plug-ins, including:

- **Jetpack.** Automattic created this plug-in to give WordPress self-hosters most of the features available to WordPress.com sites, all in one easy step.

- **WPtouch.** This plug-in gives your site sophisticated support for mobile devices, like iPhones and iPads.

- **Online Backup for WordPress.** Use this plug-in as part of your backup routine to help you crash-proof your site.

- **WP Super Cache.** This popular plug-in uses clever caching tricks to boost the speed of heavily trafficked pages.

You'll see plenty more plug-ins in the following chapters, where you'll use them to solve problems, fill gaps, and add all sorts of frills.

▓ Managing Plug-Ins

WordPress reserves a section of the dashboard for plug-ins. It's the predictably named Plugins menu, and you get started by choosing Plugins→Installed Plugins. This shows you a list of all the plug-ins installed on your website (Figure 9-1).

FIGURE 9-1

WordPress installations usually include these two plug-ins. The Akismet tool helps you catch comment spam (page 263). The Hello Dolly sample doesn't do much, other than let you test the plug-in system (page 282).

Usually, a WordPress site starts with two plug-ins that are installed but not active. That means the plug-ins are sitting on your website, ready to be called into service, but they're not actually doing anything yet. (It's the same as when you install a theme but don't activate it.)

How Plug-Ins Work

Technically, a plug-in is a small program written in the same programming language (PHP) that runs the entire WordPress system.

Plug-ins work by inserting themselves into various WordPress operations. For example, before WordPress displays a post, it checks to see if you installed any plug-ins related to displaying posts. If you did, WordPress calls them into action. This sort of check is called a *hook*, and WordPress has a long list of hooks that launch plug-ins. A WordPress page can also use a special code, called a *template tag*, to ask a plug-in to insert something in a specific place on a page. Either way, the interaction between a WordPress site and its plug-ins happens behind the scenes, without your intervention.

Building plug-ins is a fairly ambitious task, because it requires programming skills and an intimate knowledge of the way WordPress works. Fortunately, there are plenty of good plug-ins you can use without writing a stitch of code. Most WordPress developers spend a good deal of time picking the right plug-ins for their sites, and tweaking them just so. Very few write their own.

NOTE If you want to learn more about creating plug-ins, you probably want to finish this book first, paying particular attention to Part Four, where you'll take a peek at the PHP infrastructure that holds WordPress together. Then, you can continue with the somewhat terse WordPress plug-in documentation at *http://codex.wordpress .org/Writing_a_Plugin.*

Searching for a Plug-In

The process of installing plug-ins is simply the process of copying the plug-in files to your site's plug-in directory, which WordPress names */wp-content/plugins*. For example, if you put WordPress on your site at *http://pancakesforever.com/news*, the plug-in folder is *http://pancakesforever.com/news/wp-content/plugins*. Of course, you don't need to worry about the exact location of the plug-in directory, because WordPress always puts your plug-ins in the right place.

To install a plug-in, choose Plugins→Add New, which takes you to the Install Plugins page. You'll see five links at the top of the page that let you decide how to find the plug-in you want. Your options are:

- **Search.** If you can put a name to the sort of WordPress plug-in you want (for example, "mobile" or "Twitter"), you can probably find it through a search. Type one or more keywords in the Search box, and then click the Search Plugins button (as shown in Figure 9-2). Or, you can click one of the links in the "Popular tags" section underneath, which displays the most common search keywords. Either way, WordPress scans its massive plug-in directory for matches.

Don't get confused by the fact that WordPress uses "plug-in directory" to refer to two things. First, there's your website's plug-in directory, which is the folder on your web server where you store the plug-in files for your website. Second, there's the official WordPress plug-in directory, which is the giant catalog of thousands of plug-ins you can download and install on your site.

- **Upload.** If you already downloaded the plug-in you want to your computer, all you need to do is transfer it to your website. To do that, click the Upload link, browse to your plug-in ZIP file, and choose Install Now. You'll use this technique if you create your own plug-in, or if you acquire a plug-in from somewhere other than WordPress's plug-in directory (for example, if you bought a commercial plug-in from a third party).

- **Featured, Popular, or Newest.** All these links let you *browse* the WordPress plug-in directory, which can help you discover plug-ins you might not know about. "Featured" shows useful plug-ins that WordPress has chosen to highlight, "Popular" shows the most downloaded plug-ins (ones that other people are using), and "Newest" focuses on plug-ins that have been available for just a few days.

FIGURE 9-2

The Install Plugins page has five links to help you find plug-ins. In this example, you're about to search for plug-ins that have the keyword "jetpack" in their name or description.

The WordPress plug-in directory, with its staggering collection of more than 20,000 mini-programs, is the place most WordPress experts look for plug-ins first. If you search for plug-ins, WordPress shows you a list of programs that match your keywords (Figure 9-3). If you browse by category, like Featured or Newest, WordPress lists plug-ins that fall into that category).

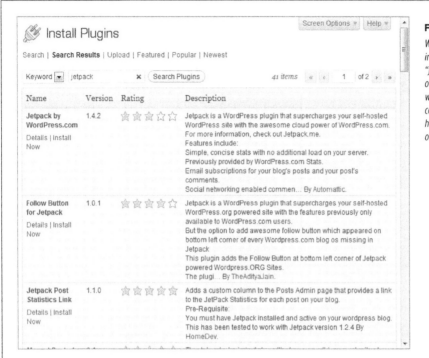

FIGURE 9-3

WordPress found 41 plug-ins that use the word "jetpack." The first is the official Jetpack plug-in, which adds WordPress.com features to self-hosted sites (as described on page 284).

The next step is to decide if you actually want to install the plug-in you found. Before you do, it's worth clicking the Details link that appears under the plug-in name. That pops open a window with extra information about the plug-in, including a more detailed list of its features, the current version number, the person who created it, the compatibility with different versions of WordPress, and the plug-in's rating (Figure 9-4).

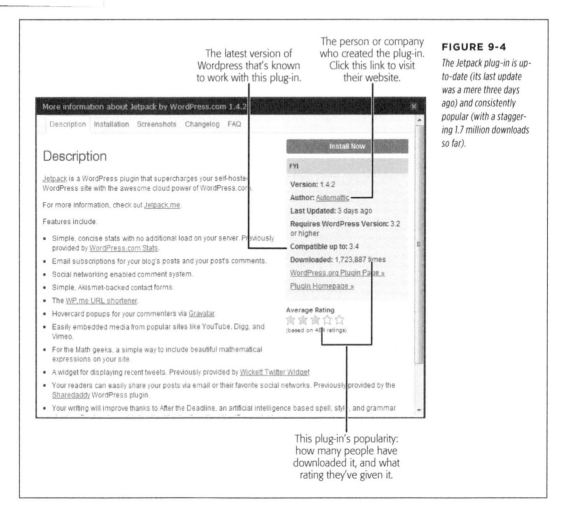

FIGURE 9-4

The Jetpack plug-in is up-to-date (its last update was a mere three days ago) and consistently popular (with a staggering 1.7 million downloads so far).

The latest version of Wordpress that's known to work with this plug-in.

The person or company who created the plug-in. Click this link to visit their website.

This plug-in's popularity: how many people have downloaded it, and what rating they've given it.

The most important information about a plug-in is its WordPress compatibility, which you determine by looking at three of the plug-in's characteristics:

- **Requires WordPress Version.** This tells you the minimum version of WordPress that your site needs to use this plug-in. Because you're a security-conscious webmaster who always makes sure your site runs the latest WordPress updates, this part isn't so important.

- **Compatible up to.** This detail tells you the *latest* supported WordPress version. Sometimes, people create plug-ins, maintain them for a while, and then abandon them. The result is that the old plug-ins keep kicking around the WordPress plug-in directory, even though they're of no use to sites that use newer editions of WordPress. By checking the "Compatible up to" information, you can avoid these clunkers.

- **Last Updated.** You may want to check this date as you try to avoid old and out-of-date plug-ins. Although old plug-ins sometimes keep working, your best bet is to stick with plug-ins that have been updated within the last year (at least). Regular maintenance also increases the chances that a plug-in is getting new features and fixes, which are two more attributes that make it a good candidate for your site.

If you're still not satisfied, you can click one of the other tabs in the "More information" window to get still more information about your plug-in. Initially, you start at the Description tab (Figure 9-4), but you may also want to check out Screenshots (to get a feel for what the plug-in looks like), Changelog (to see what changes or fixes have recently been made), and FAQ (to read the answers to common webmaster questions).

You may also want to look for information about the plug-in on the author's page or website. You'll often find the author's blog, other plug-ins the author maintains, and some additional support information. To go looking, make sure you're on the Description tab and then click the author's name (which appears as a link in the information box, as shown in Figure 9-4).

WordPress Isn't the Last Word on Plug-Ins

The WordPress plug-in directory is the first and best place to look for plug-ins. It gives you thousands to choose from, and you can be reasonably certain that they're safe and stable. And they'll always be free. (The most obvious disadvantage is that the WordPress plug-in repository is crowded with a number of old and slightly out-of-date plug-ins, and so you need to get good at sniffing out and avoiding these dead ends.)

However, there are also a number of companies that *sell* plug-ins. These mini-programs are sometimes called *premium plug-ins*, and they don't appear in the WordPress plug-in directory. Instead, you might find them though a Google search, a friend who's in the know, a premium plug-in repository, or one of the many "Top WordPress Plug-In" articles. The problem with premium plug-ins (besides the fact that they cost money) is that you need to carefully scope out the company that makes it to make sure you aren't paying for a mediocre

product or, even worse, a bit of malicious spamware that will compromise your site.

In this book, you'll stick to using free plug-ins from the WordPress directory. However, if you need something more (for example, if you're a professional WordPress site designer who's creating sites for other companies), you'll eventually want to check out the high-end plug-in market. You can get more information by reading an advanced WordPress and web design site like Smashing Magazine (*http://wp.smashingmagazine .com*) or by browsing a premium plug-in site like WP Plugins (*http://wpplugins.com*) or CodeCanyon (*http://codecanyon .net*). But remember, even though premium plug-ins cost more, they aren't necessarily better. Some of the best plug-ins in the industry are built by open-source developers and companies with WordPress-related businesses, and they don't ask for anything more than an optional donation.

Installing a Plug-In

If you decide to go ahead with a particular plug-in, installing it is simple. Just click the Install Now link. It's easy to find—it appears next to each plug-in in your search results (Figure 9-3), and in the "More information" window (Figure 9-4). When WordPress prompts you to confirm your installation, click OK.

Typically, the plug-in installation whizzes by in a matter of seconds. WordPress gives you minimal feedback as it grabs the plug-in's ZIP file, pulls all the plug-in files out of it, and transfers them to an ad hoc folder it creates on your website (Figure 9-5). For example, if you install Jetpack on the WordPress site *http://magicteahouse. net*, WordPress creates the folder *http://magicteahouse.net/wp-content/plugins/ jetpack* for the plug-in files.

 Installing Plugin: Jetpack by WordPress.com 1.4.2

Downloading install package from
http://downloads.wordpress.org/plugin/jetpack.1.4.2.zip...

Unpacking the package...

Installing the plugin...

Successfully installed the plugin **Jetpack by WordPress.com 1.4.2**.

Activate Plugin | Return to Plugin Installer

FIGURE 9-5

This is what you see if you install Jetpack. To start using it, click Activate Plugin. If you want to search for another plug-in, choose Return to Plugin Installer.

Using the Plug-In Links in This Book

In this chapter (and throughout this book), you'll frequently come across links to useful WordPress plug-ins. These links take you to WordPress's plug-in directory, at *http://wordpress. org/extend/plugins*. There, you'll get extensive information about the plug-in, including how it works, the number of times it's been downloaded, its star rating, and its compatibility information (just as you can in the plug-in details window shown in Figure 9-4).

You can also download the plug-in from WordPress's plug-in directory—presumably so you can upload it to your site later, from the Plugins→Add New page. However, there's no need to go to the trouble of downloading and uploading a plug-in. Instead, if you want to install one of the plug-ins discussed in this book, the easiest approach is to log in to your site's dashboard, search for the plug-in by name, and then click the Install button to transfer it in one step.

Activating a Plug-In

A plug-in doesn't do anything until you activate it. In this way, plug-ins are like themes—you can install as many as you want, but they have no effect on your website until you turn them on.

One way to activate a plug-in is to click the Activate Plugin link that appears when you first install the mini-program (Figure 9-5). But if you want to activate a plug-in you already installed, go to Plugins→Installed Plugins to see a list of available programs. Then, click the Activate link that appears under the name of the plug-in you want to use. (If the plug-in is already active, you'll see a Deactivate link instead—click that to switch off the plug-in.)

WordPress doesn't give you any feedback when you successfully activate a plug-in. Often, there'll be evidence that a plug-in is active somewhere else in the dashboard, but every plug-in works differently. Some provide new a page of options in the dashboard menu, others add new widgets, some change the Add New Post or Edit Post pages, and some simply start doing their work quietly in the background.

In a newly created WordPress website, you start with two inactive plug-ins, as you saw back in Figure 9-1. To practice plug-in activation without risking anything on your site, you can activate the harmless (but also useless) Hello Dolly sample plug-in. When you switch it on, it adds a random lyric from Louis Armstrong's song "Hello, Dolly" at the top of every dashboard page (Figure 9-6).

FIGURE 9-6

The Hello Dolly plug-in adds song lyrics to every dashboard page. This is just enough to let you know that the plug-in is active. However, it's safe to assume that no one uses Hello Dolly for long on a real website.

The Hello Dolly plug-in needs no configuration. However, many plug-ins add their own Settings link in the Plugins page (Figure 9-7). Click that, and WordPress takes you to a new part of the dashboard that your plug-in has created.

Unfortunately, plug-ins aren't consistent about where you go to change their settings. For example, a plug-in like WPtouch adds an option to the Settings menu (so you pick Settings→WPtouch to review and tweak your options). But the Jetpack plug-in takes a different approach. It creates a new top-level menu button called Jetpack, which appears just under the dashboard's menu button, as shown in Figure 9-7. Other plug-ins, like Online Backup for WordPress (page 301), use the Tools menu to stash their options.

As you can see, different plug-ins often work in ways that are *similar*, but not the same. For that reason, you need to learn the way each plug-in works individually. In the remainder of this chapter, you'll take a close look at several prime plug-in examples.

FIGURE 9-7

This site has three active plug-ins. The Hello Dolly plug-in has no additional settings, but both the Jetpack and WPtouch plug-ins do (hence the inconsistently placed Settings link that both display). You'll also notice that the Jetpack plug-in adds a blue-boxed message to the top of the Plugins page, warning you that your plug-in won't work until you set up a WordPress.com account (page 285).

TIP You don't need to keep plug-ins you don't use. If you decide to trash a particular plug-in, choose Plugins→Installed Plugins to call up the plug-in list, click Deactivate to switch a plug-in off (if it's currently active), and then click Delete to remove it entirely.

Why You Don't Want Too Many Plug-Ins

When new WordPress users discover plug-ins, their first instinct is to load as much free goodness as they can onto their sites. After all, if one plug-in is great, two dozen must be mind-blowingly fantastic.

But before you get carried away, it's worth pointing out the many reasons that you *don't* want to install every plug-in you can find:

- **Performance.** As you already learned, plug-ins use PHP code to carry out their tasks. The more plug-ins you have, the more work you're asking WordPress to do. Eventually, this work might add up to enough of an overhead that it begins to slow down your site.

- **Maintenance.** The more plug-ins you have, the more plug-ins you need to configure and update (when new versions become available). It's a relatively small job, but pile on the plug-ins and you might find yourself with some extra work.

- **Security.** Plug-ins can have security holes, especially if they're poorly designed or out-of-date. So more plug-ins

means more risk.

- **Compatibility.** Sometimes, one plug-in can mess up another. If your site uses a huge thicket of plug-ins, it's difficult to track down which one's at fault. You need to resort to disabling all your plug-ins and then reenabling them one at a time, until the problem reappears.

- **Obsolescence.** Often, plug-ins are developed by helpful people in the WordPress community who need a given feature and are ready to share their work. But there's a downside to this development model—it makes it more likely for an author to stop developing a plug-in (for example, when they don't need it anymore or when they just don't have the time). Eventually, a new version of WordPress may break an old plug-in you depend on, and you'll need to scramble to find something else that's suitable.

The best way to avoid problems like these is to use popular, regularly updated plug-ins, make sure they're always up-to-date, and keep the number of plug-ins you use small.

■ The Jetpack Plug-In

As you already know, user-picked plug-ins are forbidden on WordPress.com sites. But to keep people happy, Automattic adds extra frills with its own, carefully tested plug-ins. Every WordPress.com site gets these extras, and as a result, a stock Word-Press.com site actually has *more* features than a newly installed self-hosted site. (But now that you know how to browse the plug-in directory, with its thousands of site enhancements, you can get your revenge pretty easily.)

If you don't want to do the work of tracking down dozens of plug-ins, but you want a simple way to give your site the same features that its WordPress.com cousins have, there's a simple, all-in-one solution. It's Jetpack, a plug-in developed by the folks who built WordPress.com, and equipped with almost all the same great features.

To learn about Jetpack's features, visit the Jetpack site at *http://jetpack.me*. Highlights include a picture carousel (covered on page 318), contact forms (page 288), enhanced comments (Chapter 8), Twitter and Facebook sharing (Chapter 12), and statistics about the people who visit your site (Chapter 12).

NOTE The Jetpack plug-in is a useful way to get a pile of handy features in one package. You'll use it on and off throughout this book. However, many WordPress experts avoid Jetpack's cornucopia of plug-ins, preferring to pick and choose plug-ins that provide just the features they need. For example, they may use separate plug-ins for Facebook buttons, website statistics, and contact forms, rather than try to get them all through Jetpack. This is a bit more work, but it's really a matter of preference—it's up to you to decide what works best for your site.

Signing Up with WordPress.com

You already know how to install the Jetpack plug-in—just search the plug-in directory for "jetpack" and click the Install Now link.

However, Jetpack has one additional (and slightly irritating) setup requirement. To use it, you need a WordPress.com account. Even though you don't plan to host any sites on WordPress.com, you still need a WordPress.com user ID and password to access Jetpack's features.

After you activate Jetpack, the plug-in notifies you about this extra requirement with a large banner above the plug-in list (Figure 9-7). Here's how to get Jetpack to recognize your single-purpose WordPress.com account and get the plug-in working on your hosted site:

1. **Click the "Connect to WordPress.com" button to set up the connection.**

   The Jetpack plug-in takes you to the *http://jetpack.wordpress.com* site and invites you to fill in your WordPress.com user name and password.

   If you've ever created a site with WordPress.com, you already have these details—you don't need to create a new account, because you can use the same one for as many Jetpack-enabled websites as you want. To finish the setup process, enter your information and click Authorize Jetpack.

   If you've never used WordPress.com before, now's the time to create a WordPress.com account. Continue on to the next step.

2. **Click the "Need an account" link.**

   This takes you to the standard WordPress.com sign-up page. The difference is that now WordPress.com assumes you want an account only, not a WordPress.com site. (If for some reason you *do* want a WordPress.com site, you could create it later, or you can click the "Sign up for a blog, too" link to get it right now, as part of the sign-up process.)

3. **Type in a user name, password, and email address.**

   Your user name can be any combination of letters and numbers, so long as there isn't another WordPress.com member already using it.

Your password can be anything, but it definitely should not be the same as the password you use for your WordPress installation or for your web host's administrative interface.

Your email address is an essential detail, because WordPress.com sends you an activation email. If you don't get it, you can't activate your account.

4. **Click the "Sign up" button.**

   Now you need to wait for the activation email message.

5. **When the email arrives, click the activation link inside.**

   This brings you back to the site where you started, and logs you into your WordPress.com account automatically (Figure 9-8).

6. **Click Authorize Jetpack.**

   WordPress brings you back to your self-hosted site, where Jetpack is now running.

FIGURE 9-8

Before WordPress activates Jetpack, it asks a clear question: Do you want to use this Word-Press.com user account (charles_p) to activate Jetpack on this site (Magic Tea House)?

You'll see many of Jetpack's features in later chapters. In the following sections, you'll try out three of them to get a taste of what the plug-in can do.

Using the Image Widget

You may remember from Chapter 6 that you can use the Text widget to display a picture in your site's sidebar, using a tiny bit of HTML. The trick is to put an <img> element that points to your picture inside the Text widget (page 191).

However, WordPress.com users have an easier (albeit less flexible) tool: the Image widget. And now that you signed up with Jetpack, you've got the same advantage. Here's how to put the Image widget to use:

1. **Choose Appearance→Widgets.**

   This takes you to the familiar Widgets page in the dashboard. There you'll see a few new widgets that have Jetpack in the name, including one called "Image (Jetpack)."

2. **Drag the Image widget to one of the widget areas on the right.**

   When you drop the widget into place, it expands to show a number of text boxes where you can fill in important details (Figure 9-9).

FIGURE 9-9

You can add the Jetpack Image widget to the sidebar of your site, just as you can with WordPress's standard widgets.

3. **Fill in the information for your widget.**

Obviously, the most important detail is the image URL—the location of the image you want to show. Usually, this is a file that you uploaded to your site's media library. If you don't remember the address, you need to browse the Media→Library section of the dashboard, as explained on page 188.

Along with the image URL, you can choose a title for the widget, give the picture a caption and alternate text, and turn it into a link that takes viewers to a web address you specify. You can also set a display size. If you don't, WordPress displays the image as close as possible to its full, natural size, without exceeding the space available in the sidebar (or other widget area where you've placed it).

4. **Click Save.**

Now the widget appears on your site, showing the image you picked.

Adding a Contact Form

The Image widget is far from being an essential tool. But it *is* a real convenience, as are many of Jetpack's features. However, Jetpack also includes some features that would be significantly more work to duplicate on your own. One is its contact form feature, which lets you solicit readers for any sort of information you want (Figure 9-10).

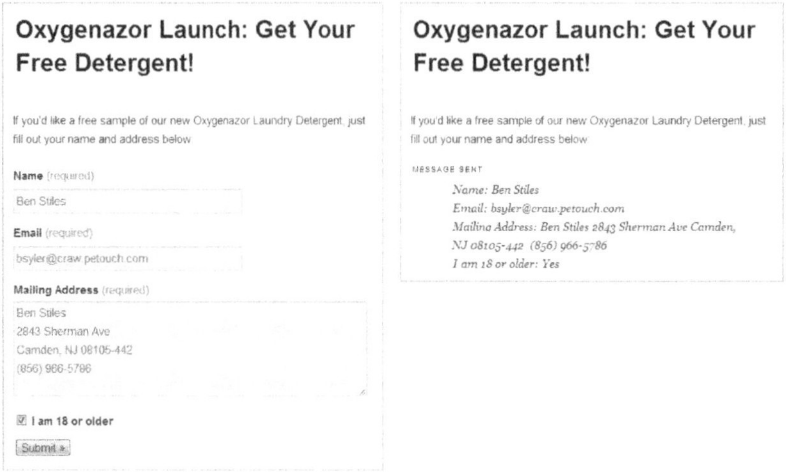

FIGURE 9-10

The basic idea behind a contact form is this: your post includes blank text boxes. A reader fills these boxes up with info (left), and then submits the data (right). WordPress collects the information, and passes it along to you in an email.

Often, you use contact forms to collect names, email addresses, postal addresses, or support questions. However, Jetpack is clever enough to let you build your own, completely customized contact form, which you can edit to collect whatever information you want. To get started, you create a new post, and then click the "Add a custom form" button, which looks like a tiny picture of a form (Figure 9-11). It appears above the content box, right next to the "Add media" icon you used in Chapter 8.

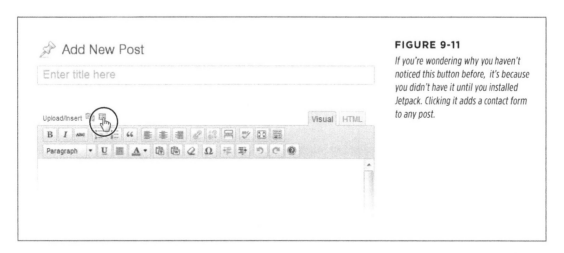

When you click the "Add a custom form" button, the "Add a custom form" window appears (Figure 9-12). This is the place where you can design the exact contact form you want.

Here's what you can do in the form builder:

- **Remove a field.** Click the minus sign (-) on the right side of the text box and it's gone.

- **Add a new field.** Click "Add a new field" and enter your field information. Every field needs a Label (the text above the text box) and a "Field type" (that's the kind of information the text box collects). Use Text for an ordinary single-line text box and Textarea for a big, multiline text box (or pick one of the more specialized field types described in the box on page 291). Optionally, turn on the Required checkbox if you want to force readers to fill in this text box before they can submit the form. When you finish, click "Save this field."

- **Rearrange your fields.** Hover over the field you want to move until the "move" link appears in the top-right corner. Then, click the link and drag the field up or down to a new position. (You can't put fields side-by-side.)

- **Change your email settings.** Ordinarily, WordPress sends the data from every form a visitor submits to your administrator email. If you want to use a different email account, click the "Email notifications" tab and fill in the new address.

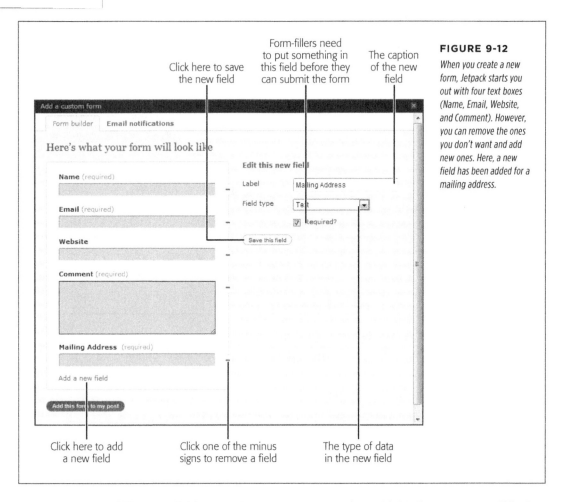

Click here to save
the new field

Form-fillers need
to put something in
this field before they
can submit the form

The caption
of the new
field

FIGURE 9-12

*When you create a new
form, Jetpack starts you
out with four text boxes
(Name, Email, Website,
and Comment). However,
you can remove the ones
you don't want and add
new ones. Here, a new
field has been added for a
mailing address.*

Click here to add
a new field

Click one of the minus
signs to remove a field

The type of data
in the new field

When you finish perfecting your form, click the "Add this form to my post" button
at the bottom of the window. Jetpack inserts a series of strange-looking codes into
your post, wrapped in square brackets (Figure 9-13).

Using Different Field Types

Wordpress's contact forms support a small set of *field types*—types of data that your text box can collect. Here are your choices:

- **Text.** This is your standard-issue single-line text box.

- **Textarea.** This is a bigger text box that can fit whole paragraphs of information. Once you add a field that uses this type, you can drag the bottom-right corner of the text box to make it as big as you want.

- **Checkbox.** This is a way to let guests turn options on or off.

- **Drop down.** This is a list of possible values (that you specify), which are stuffed into a drop-down list. The person filling out the form picks just one of these options.

- **Radio.** This is a list of possible values, just like the "Drop down" field type. The difference is that you can see all

your choices at once (they're listed on the page), and person filling out the form clicks a small circle next to the option they want. Usually, you use this field type if you have just a few choices, and use "Drop down" for a long list of options.

- **Email, Name, and Website.** All these field types look like ordinary text boxes. However, WordPress is smart enough to pre-fill the boxes with the current guest's email and name, if it knows those details (for example, if the person recently left a comment on your site). WordPress also performs some basic error-checking to catch bad email addresses.

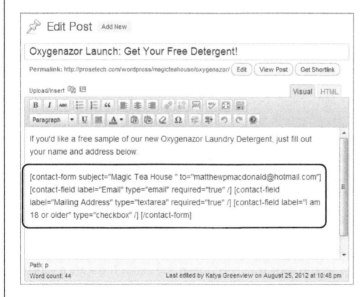

FIGURE 9-13

To create a contact form, Jetpack uses shortcodes, a WordPress feature you'll learn about on page 315. However, you don't need to pay them any attention—as long as you leave them alone, your form will appear in the published post just the way you want it. (Adding content above or below the form code, however, is perfectly acceptable.)

Every time someone views your post, fills out the contact form, and submits it, you'll get an email. The same person can even fill out the same form more than once (in which case WordPress sends you multiple messages). If you're tired of juggling the emails, WordPress also lets you review all the responses you've received in the dashboard. Just click Feedbacks in the dashboard menu, and you'll see a list of contact form submissions, arranged just like the dashboard's comment list.

Adding a Mathematical Equation

The creators of WordPress aren't preoccupied with Serious Business Features. They also find time to throw in some more specialized, quirkier frills. One intriguing example is the mathematic equation feature demonstrated in Figure 9-14, which is the last Jetpack feature you'll look at in this chapter.

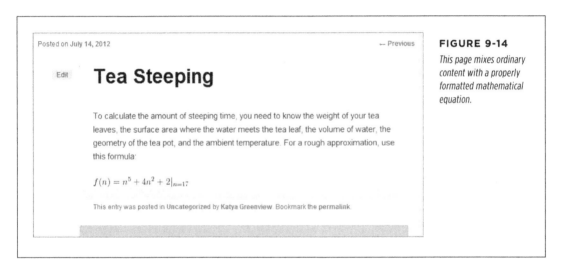

Posted on July 14, 2012   ← Previous

Edit   **Tea Steeping**

To calculate the amount of steeping time, you need to know the weight of your tea leaves, the surface area where the water meets the tea leaf, the volume of water, the geometry of the tea pot, and the ambient temperature. For a rough approximation, use this formula:

$$f(n) = n^5 + 4n^2 + 2|_{n=17}$$

This entry was posted in Uncategorized by Katya Greenview. Bookmark the permalink.

FIGURE 9-14
This page mixes ordinary content with a properly formatted mathematical equation.

To create an equation with Jetpack, you must first write an instruction, using the LaTex typesetting language. For example, the equation shown in Figure 9-14 is written like this in LaTex:

```
f(n) = n^5 + 4n^2 + 2 |_{n=17}
```

LaTex is a staple of the technical publishing industry, but it's not part of HTML, and browsers don't know anything about it. To translate a LaTex expression into a formatted equation for your web page, you need something extra. There are a variety of JavaScript libraries that do the job, with varying degrees of success. But if your site uses Jetpack, you don't need to worry about another plug-in. Instead, you simply need to slip your LaTex expression between two special codes: [latex] and [/latex].

For example, if you're creating the post shown in Figure 9-14, you can type the equation right into the post editor, as shown here:

```
To calculate the amount of steeping time, you need to know the weight of your
tea leaves, the surface area where the water meets the tea leaf, the volume
of water, the geometry of the tea pot, and the ambient temperature. For a
rough approximation, use this formula:
[latex]f(n) = n^5 + 4n^2 + 2 |_{n=17}[/latex]
```

Now, when WordPress processes this page, the Jetpack plug-in notices the [latex] code, and interprets the content inside as a LaTex expression. It then replaces the ordinary text of the expression with a series of stitched-together image files. The result is a properly formatted equation that any mathematician can understand and any browser can display.

> **NOTE** Technically, the [latex] and [/latex] syntax is part of a WordPress *shortcode*—a way of getting WordPress to insert special content using an instruction in square brackets. WordPress has a few shortcodes that it recognizes automatically, and plug-ins can add their own. You'll learn more about this handy feature in Chapter 10.

Of course, you can't take advantage of Jetpack's LaTex wizardry unless you know a bit about the LaTex standard (or you have a prewritten equation in LaTex format). To learn more, start with the general tutorial at *http://tinyurl.com/latexmath*. If you find that writing your own LaTex expression daunting, you can get some help from the LaTex equation generator at *http://tinyurl.com/latexequation*. It lets you build a LaTex expression by clicking your way through a mess of buttons. Finally, you can review WordPress's documentation for the LaTex feature at *http://support.word press.com/latex*, which covers a few extra, WordPress-specific details (for example, it explains how to change the size of the generated equation, and how to adjust its background color if you want it to stand out on your page).

The next time you'll use Jetpack is in Chapter 10, to give your site a photo carousel or slideshow. But now it's time to review some other useful plug-ins.

■ Adding Mobile Support

In Chapter 5, you considered a thorny question—what does your carefully crafted WordPress site look like if someone views it on a mobile device, like a smartphone or tablet computer?

For self-hosted sites, the answer all depends on the theme you choose. If you use a mobile-aware theme (sometimes called a *responsive* theme), it automatically adapts itself to the mobile device, substituting a simpler, streamlined layout that fits on small displays. The standard Twenty Eleven theme is an example of a mobile-aware theme.

If your theme doesn't have these built-in smarts, you'll get a result that's much less ideal. When people visit your site with a mobile device, they'll see the normal, full-size layout of your pages, which means they'll need to zoom-and-scroll around it awkwardly. The effect is a minor inconvenience on a mid-sized device like an iPad, but a serious aggravation on a small-sized device like an iPhone. Most readers will find that reading your site isn't worth the finger cramps.

So what's the solution if your favorite theme doesn't have mobile support, and you don't want to leave mobile users out in the cold? You can patch the gap with a plug-in that adds mobile support without disrupting your chosen theme. There are several popular plug-ins, and they all work the same way, by swapping in a different theme when they detect a mobile device. The best mobile plug-ins are smart enough to tailor the substitute theme for the destination device. That means that iPad users see something a bit different from iPhone users, for example.

WPtouch, a wildly popular WordPress plug-in with millions of downloads to its name, works just this way. You can find it at *http://tinyurl.com/wptouch*.

The WPtouch Mobile Theme

WPtouch recognizes a range of smartphones and touch devices, including Apple products (that's the iPhone, iPad, and iPod Touch), devices running the Google Android operating system or Blackberry OS6, most Samsung touch devices, and even old-school Palm gadgets. WPtouch uses its own slick mobile theme on these devices.

Once you install and activate WPtouch, you're ready to try it out. Figure 9-15 shows what happens when a visitor hits up a WPtouch-enabled site with an iPhone.

The WPtouch mobile theme departs from the average WordPress theme in several important ways:

- **WPtouch ignores widgets completely when it renders a mobile version of your site.** This is quite different from the mobile version of the Twenty Eleven theme (shown on page 165). Twenty Eleven keeps the widgets, but arranges them before and after the main content. This ensures that the mobile view doesn't sacrifice anything important, but it also creates a long and somewhat unwieldy page.

- **WPtouch doesn't show a site's header.** To further streamline the viewing experience, WPtouch's mobile theme leaves out the customary banner image. In its place, WPtouch simply shows the site title, along with the handy drop-down menu shown in Figure 9-15, right.

- **WPtouch doesn't display any content in post listings.** Instead, it simply shows the title, author, category, and tags for each post (Figure 9-16). Mobile surfers need to tap a post to read it. Once again, this differs from the Twenty Eleven standard, which lists all the content and forces mobile readers to scroll the day away. (Incidentally, you can tweak the way WPtouch shows posts by using post excerpts, as described on page 195.)

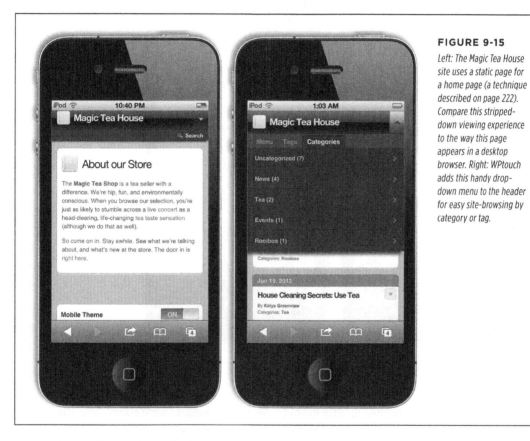

FIGURE 9-15

Left: The Magic Tea House site uses a static page for a home page (a technique described on page 222). Compare this stripped-down viewing experience to the way this page appears in a desktop browser. Right: WPtouch adds this handy drop-down menu to the header for easy site-browsing by category or tag.

- **WPtouch doesn't load all your posts at once.** Instead, the page ends with a "Load more entries..." link. Click that, and the page fetches a new batch of posts and adds them to the bottom of the page. Best of all, the page uses clever JavaScript code to stuff in just the new content without refreshing the whole page.

FIGURE 9-16

Left: WPtouch's mobile theme keeps the list of posts simple, highlighting the date and number of comments, but leaving the content itself out. Right: Scroll to the bottom of the screen and you'll see a link to load more posts, along with a switch that lets you turn the WPtouch mobile theme off. If you do the latter, WordPress redirects visitors to the desktop version of the website.

Configuring WPtouch

The WPtouch mobile theme overrides your standard theme completely. That means that even if your current theme has its own mobile-specific version, WPtouch replaces it. (If you *do* want to use the mobile support that may be built into your theme, disable the WPtouch plug-in.)

That said, WPtouch does give you some leeway to customize the way it looks. To review your options, choose Settings→WPtouch. You'll see a page of settings that include some truly useful gems (Figure 9-17). They include:

- **WPtouch Home Page.** Ordinarily, WPtouch respects your WordPress settings, meaning that visitors start at the list of posts on your home page or on a static page, depending on your "Front page displays" setting (page 222). However, you might decide that mobile viewers should start somewhere other than that. Maybe you want them to bypass the ordinary home page because it's too long and bloated with graphics. Or maybe you want them to start with a page that provides links to specific posts.

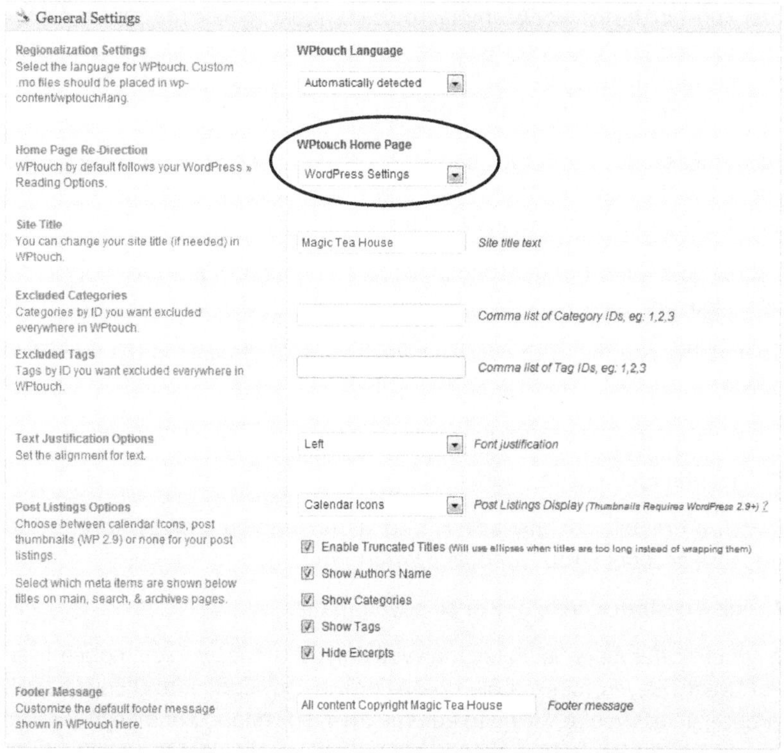

FIGURE 9-17

Right now, the WPtouch home page is set to "WordPress Settings." This means WPtouch uses WordPress's "Front page displays" setting to decide what to put on the main page of your mobile site. If this isn't what you want, you can pick a different page from the drop-down list.

- **Site Title.** Remember, WPtouch displays the title of your site, but no header picture. If you want to change the site title that appears in the mobile theme without changing the site title for everyone else, you do that here. This is handy if you need to shorten a long site title so it fits comfortably on smaller screens.

- **Excluded Categories and Excluded Tags.** Perhaps there are some posts on your site that aren't appropriate for mobile viewing or aren't likely to interest mobile users. As long as these posts belong to a specific category or have a specific tag, you can tuck them out of sight. Excluded posts won't appear in the mobile site's post stream, in search results, or in category-browsing or tag-browsing pages. To exclude a category or tag, you need to enter its ID, which you can find in the Posts→Categories or Posts→Tags section of the dashboard. (To exclude several categories or tags, write the whole list in the text box, separating each ID with a comma.)

- **Post Listings Display.** This option sets the icon that appears next to every post. Usually, it's a calendar, but you can choose to show the post's featured image instead.

- **Post Listings Option.** In this section, you can set what information appears on every post in the list. For example, you can choose to hide the author, category, or tags, and you can choose to show the post's excerpt (page 195). You can also decide whether WPtouch wraps long post titles over more than one line or chops them off at the end of the first line with an ellipsis (...).

- **Footer Message.** This is the text that appears at the bottom of every page, just above the "Powered by WordPress + WPtouch" notation. Ordinarily, WPtouch uses a copyright notification like "All content copyright Magic Tea House."

If you scroll past these basic settings, you find a number of advanced options. Using them, you can:

- Change the content of the drop-down menu that appears in the mobile site's header.

- Set whether mobile users can leave comments on posts and pages.

- Change the font and site colors.

- Switch on mobile-friendly advertising, assuming you already have a Google AdSense account (*http://google.com/adsense*).

- Assign a custom icon to any or all of your pages.

These options offer more flexibility than you'd get with the average mobile-friendly theme. (Twenty Eleven, for example, doesn't provide any options to change its mobile appearance, unless you're willing to edit the theme by hand.) For many WordPressers, this level of control is more than enough. They simply want to give their mobile visitors an attractive, comfortable viewing experience. They don't need to customize the fine details of formatting or add extra pomp.

Other WordPress developers are more ambitious. They like the basic WPtouch theme, but feel it's a bit generic. They want to add touches of style, and distinguish their site from competitors'. If you fall into this camp, WPtouch won't satisfy you. However, the creators of WPtouch sell an enhanced version of the plug-in named WPtouch Pro. It offers much more powerful theme customization options, along with a pile of extra features (see *http://tinyurl.com/wptouchpro*). Currently, WPtouch Pro is available for $49 for a single website (or $99 for five). Although you certainly don't need the pro version, it's money well spent if you expect that a large portion of your audience will visit your site, using a mobile device.

WordPress Sites on the iPad

WPtouch seems geared to smartphones. Are there any plug-ins that take advantage of the iPad's fancy features?

WPtouch treats the iPad more or less the same way it treats any other mobile device, switching to its streamlined mobile theme. But as iPad fanatics know, Apple's miraculous little device is capable of so much more.

WPtouch doesn't include any extra iPad frills. But WPtouch Pro—the $49 upgrade—provides an enhanced iPad support feature, which aims to make your site behave more like an iPad app. Switch it on, and WPtouch piles on the iPad frills, with pages that respond to iPad touch gestures, little details like popovers and fly-in forms, and the ability for iPad viewers

to load your site in standalone mode, without the Safari web browser wrapped around it. All these features are optional. If you're unsure about whether they suit your site, try switching them on and then browsing your content with an iPad.

WPtouch isn't the only game in town when it comes to iPad support. Another popular plug-in is Onswipe (*http://tinyurl. com/onswipe*), which promises to turn your site into a rich, magazine-style app for any tablet. Once you activate Onswipe, you can pick from a variety of slick layouts that let iPad fans swipe their way through your posts. Incidentally, Onswipe isn't limited to WordPress. The same technology is at work in big, non-WordPress media sites like Slate and Wired.

◼ Backing Up a WordPress Site

It's easy to be casual about the safety of the files on your website. After all, even small web hosting companies take reliability seriously. They use systems that have a high level of *redundancy*—web servers with multiple hard drives, for example, and groups of computers that work together so that a hardware failure in one won't sideline an entire website. Many web hosts also perform some sort of data *backup*, copying the files they host to a storage location so they can recover them after catastrophes, like floods and fires.

But these measures, no matter how well-intentioned, aren't enough to protect your WordPress site. Unless you do your own backups, your site is exposed to serious risks that your web hosting company can't prevent. For example, an attacker could break into your administrator account and sneak some advertising or malware into your site. In some cases, these attacks are stealthy enough that you won't notice any effect for weeks. By that point, the only backup your web host still has may be a copy of the infected site, making it useless and forcing you to rebuild from scratch. Other problems can occur, too. The Web has plenty of backup horror stories, including cases where a host's backups go mysteriously missing, or an unexpected event puts a web host out of business, taking its websites with it.

To give your site a better chance of weathering crises like these, you need a separate backup solution. You have two choices:

- You can use an automated backup service that visits your site every day and transfers its content to another set of servers elsewhere in the world.

- You can do the work yourself, periodically downloading your content to your own personal computer for safe-keeping.

In the following sections, you'll consider both approaches.

Using an Automated Backup Service

This approach is the most convenient. Once you sign up with the right company, the process happens automatically, without another thought from you. The premiere example for WordPress is VaultPress (*http://vaultpress.com*), a backup service run by Automattic that stores every post, page, comment, and setting change from the moment you sign up. VaultPress gives you the ability to roll back to any point in the past if disaster strikes.

Automated backup services have a significant drawback—they aren't free, and what you pay for backups can easily outweigh your hosting fee. The basic VaultPress package costs $15 per month, and its no-frills competitor blogValue, which stores just 30 days' worth of backups, charges $10 per month.

If you have the money to sign up with an automated service, and you're willing to pay to save a little time and a few headaches, check out VaultPress. It comes as part of Jetpack, although it's not activated. To get started, you need to sign up at *http://vaultpress.com/jetpack*.

If you're willing to take a slightly more hands-on approach, consider BackupBuddy (*http://ithemes.com/purchase/backupbuddy*). You can buy the plug-in for a steal— a one-time cost of $75 gets you a license for up to two sites, and $100 buys you a license for up to 10 business sites. However, BackupBuddy isn't in the storage business. To use it, you need an account with a web storage service, so BackupBuddy has somewhere to store the backups it creates. BackupBuddy supports several such services, including DropBox (*www.dropbox.com*), which is free for the first 2 GB; Google Drive (*http://drive.google.com*), which is free for the first 5 GB; and Amazon S3 (*http://aws.amazon.com/s3*), which costs pennies per Gigabyte. So if you have a modestly sized site (one that doesn't include a library of 5,000 pictures or massive video files) and you don't mind juggling a storage account, BackupBuddy is a reasonable compromise.

Backing Up with a Plug-In

If VaultPress is too pricey, and you don't want to fiddle with BackupBuddy, you need to take charge of backups on your own. Fortunately, plenty of free plug-ins can help you out. But before you get started with any of them, you need to understand one key fact. Every WordPress site needs *two* types of backup:

- **A backup of your database.** As you learned in Chapter 1, WordPress stores every post, page, comment, and stitch of content in a database on your web server. This is the most important part of your site, because without content all you have is an empty shell.

- **A backup of your files.** These files include the contents of your media library, including every picture and resource you've uploaded (page 188), the theme files that tell WordPress how to lay out your content, and any plug-ins you installed.

NOTE You back up theme files for two reasons. First, as you become a more advanced WordPress designer, you may begin customizing the themes (as explained in Part Four). Second, it's always possible that the particular version of a theme you're using will disappear from the Web, making it difficult to restore an old copy of a backed-up site.

If you're handy with an FTP program, you can back up your files any time. All you need to do is browse to your web hosting account and copy the contents of your WordPress folder to your computer. If you're using Windows, this is as simple as firing up Windows Explorer, pointing it to your web host's FTP site, logging in, and dragging the folder you want (the one with your WordPress site in it) onto your desktop.

However, even if you copy every file you see, you still won't get the contents of your WordPress database, which is the heart of your WordPress site. To get that, you need a tool that can access the database, extract its contents, and put it in a file. (This tool also needs to be able to do the reverse, copying the data from a backup file into a new database, in case you need to re-create your site.) Unless you're a MySQL guru, your best bet is to use a WordPress plug-in to help you out.

Many WordPress plug-ins concentrate on backing up a site's database. They leave you to figure out an approach to copy the actual files on your site. Plug-ins that work this way include the popular WP-DB-Backup (*http://tinyurl.com/wp-db-backup*) and WP-DBManager (*http://tinyurl.com/wp-dbmanager*).

However, there are a few plug-ins that back up your site's database *and* its files. Two good examples are BackWPup (*http://tinyurl.com/backwpup*) and Online Backup for WordPress (*http://tinyurl.com/wponlinebackup*), the plug-in described in the next section.

WARNING There's no perfect backup tool for everyone. (That's why this book provides links to so many different backup plug-ins.) Every plug-in provides a different set of options, and some of backup tools have strange quirks or don't work well with certain web hosts. For example, your web host may restrict the PHP emailing features to fight spammers. If your backup tool works by automatically sending backed-up data to an email account, it might not be able to finish its work. Backup tools also differ in their ability to deal with unexpected errors, like corrupted data or databases that appear to be locked. For all these reasons, you need to test whatever backup plug-in you pick, and regularly check to make sure it's backing up your site.

The Online Backup for WordPress Plug-In

Online Backup for WordPress gives you two ways to back up your site:

- **Manually.** You can perform a complete backup by using the dashboard, whenever you want. You can then download the backed-up data in one big ZIP file.

- **Scheduled.** You can schedule a backup to run at certain times (for example, every night at midnight) and then email the backed-up ZIP file to an account you specify. If you choose this route, you may as well create a dedicated Gmail account (at *www.gmail.com*) for your back-up emails. With 7 GB of free storage, Gmail lets you stash quite a few backups without paying a penny.

The first thing you should do once you install Online Backup for WordPress is to try a manual backup. That way, you'll know if the plug-in is working properly, and you'll have at least one complete backup of your website to start you off. Here's how:

1. **Choose Tools→Online Backup.**

   This brings you to the control panel for Online Backup for WordPress. Here, you can start a manual backup, schedule a backup, or change back-up settings.

2. **Click the Backup link at the top.**

   Choose what you want to back up (Figure 9-18).

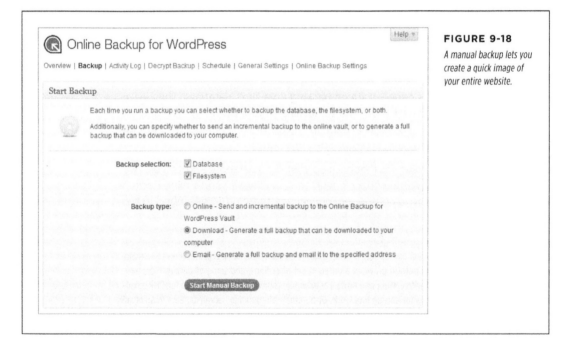

3. **Make sure you turn on both the Database and Filesystem checkboxes.**

   That way, you'll back up the contents of your database and all the files on your website, packaged up in a single ZIP file.

4. **Choose Download for the backup type.**

   Your other options are to send backups to the WordPress Vault or to an email address.

   The WordPress Vault is a service offered by BackupTechnology, the creators of the Online Backup for WordPress plug-in. The catch is that the Vault grants you just 100 MB of space—to get more, you need to pay.

NOTE   If you want to use the WordPress Vault, you first need to sign up. You can get the process started by clicking the Online Backup Settings link.

   The email option tells WordPress to send the backed-up data to the email address you supply. This option is more useful when you use scheduled backups, but you might use it with a manual backup if you're backing up a huge site and you don't want to stick around, waiting for the process to finish.

5. **Click Start Manual Backup.**

   The Online Backup for WordPress plug-in starts gathering your website data and archiving it into a single compressed file, which it puts in a temporary location on your web server. While it works, you see a progress bar ticking away. You don't need to stay and supervise the backup—even if you navigate to a different part of the dashboard or log out of the dashboard altogether, the backup process continues. However, if you leave, you need to return eventually (by choosing Tools→Online Backup) to download the final result—the file with your backup.

   When the backup is finished, a new button appears, named Download Full Backup (Figure 9-19).

6. **Click Download Full Backup.**

   Depending on your browser, it may start downloading the file immediately or it may first ask you where you want to store it and what you want to name it. The download process may take some time, depending on your Internet connection and the size of your site. Once you have the backup file safe and sound on your computer, your work is done.

   If you need to reclaim space on your web server, you can delete the backup (once you copy it to a safe place) by clicking Delete. However, unless your site is gargantuan, there's no reason to worry. The next time you perform a full backup, the Online Backup for WordPress plug-in overwrites your old backup with the new one.

FIGURE 9-19

This website has a recent backup, which is stored on the web server in a single file that's roughly 27 MB big. You can download this file, or start a new backup, which will overwrite the older one.

TIP It's a good idea to peek inside the backup file to make sure it has everything it should. (Remember, it's just an ordinary ZIP file that you can view on your computer.) Inside, you'll find two folders. The *Database* folder has a database script file with the SQL instructions needed to rebuild your database and fill it with your data. The *FileSystem* folder holds all the folders and files from your website, exactly as if you'd downloaded them from your web host over FTP.

Scheduling Regular Backups

You can do a perfectly good job disaster-proofing your site with manual backups. The problem is that it's up to you to start every backup, download the final product, and keep your backed-up files somewhere smart. As time passes, you might find yourself forgetting to make backups, leaving your website at risk.

The solution is to stop relying on yourself. Instead, tell your plug-in to do the backup work for you, at regularly scheduled intervals. In Online Backup for WordPress, you do this by choosing Tools→Online Backup from the dashboard menu and then clicking the Schedule link (at the top, just under the "Online Backup for WordPress" title). You can ask it to perform weekly, daily, twice-a-day, four-times-a-day, or hourly backups (which is probably excessive, and may earn the ire of your web hosting company). You can then choose the type of backup—either an incremental backup that grabs the changed files only and stores them in the WordPress Online Vault, or a full backup that sends the results to an email address you supply. When you finish, click Apply Schedule.

You can keep an eye on your scheduled backups by clicking the Overview link (at the top). There you'll see basic information about when the last backup took place, whether it succeeded, how big the backup file was, and when the next backup will occur. You can get a more detailed summary of recent backup activity by clicking the Activity Log link, which is handy if you need to track down a mysterious error that's interrupted one of your scheduled backups.

Finally, if you decide to send regular backups through email or store them on the WordPress Online Vault, it's a good idea to encrypt them to make sure that Internet eavesdroppers can't peek at your data. To do that, click the General Settings link, pick a type of encryption (the recommended AES128 algorithm is fine), and then type in an *encryption key*. This is a password used to encrypt your data, and without which you can't decrypt it. Writing this password down on paper is a very good idea, because it's rather frustrating to have a crashed WordPress website and a full backup that you can't open.

Restoring Your Site

Creating regular backups is important. But just as crucial is knowing how to use one to restore your site in the event of an electronic catastrophe. Fortunately, the process is fairly straightforward. Here's a basic overview, using Online Backup for WordPress:

1. **You create your new WordPress site from scratch, by installing the WordPress software.**

2. **Install your backup plug-in.**

   In this case, that's Online Backup for WordPress. You don't need to pick your theme, tweak your settings, or make any other changes.

3. **Choose Tools→Online Backup from the dashboard, and then click the Decrypt Backup link.**

4. **Now, you need to upload the backup file.**

   If you used compression to scramble your data to protect it from prying eyes, you'll also need to enter your encryption key.

5. **Finally, click "Decrypt backup" to rehydrate your site.**

If all goes well, your site will come back to life in the same state it was in the last time you made your backup. Of course, life isn't always this simple. Sometimes minor configuration issues can thwart the restore process, and you may need to enlist the help of your web host, a MySQL expert, or the folks at BackupTechnology.

Better Performance with Caching

As you learned at the very beginning of this book, WordPress websites are powered by code. When a visitor arrives at one of your pages, the WordPress code grabs the necessary information out of your database, assembles it into a page, and sends the final HTML back to your guest's browser. This process is so fast that ordinary people will be blissfully unaware of all the work that takes place behind the scenes.

However, even the fastest web server can't do all that work (run code, call the database, and build a web page) instantaneously. When someone requests a WordPress page, it takes a few fractions of second longer to create it than it would to send on ordinary HTML file. Normally, this difference isn't noticeable. But if a huge crowd of visitors hits your site at the same time, the WordPress engine will slow down slightly, making your entire website feel just a bit laggy.

However, there's a trick called *caching* that will satisfy even the most performance-obsessed WordPresser. The basic idea is this: the first time someone requests a page on your site, WordPress goes to work, running its code and generating the page dynamically. But once it delivers the page, the plug-in stores the result as an ordinary HTML file on your web server. Now here's the ingenious part: the next time a visitor asks for a page, the caching plug-in sends back the previously generated HTML, side-stepping the usual page-generating process and saving valuable microseconds (Figure 9-20). This shortcut works no matter how many people visit your site—as long as the plug-in has an ordinary HTML copy of the finished page, it uses that instead of creating a new copy all over again.

NOTE Caching takes extra space on your website, because it stores extra HTML files. However, these files are rarely big enough to worry about. Bigger files, like pictures and other resources in the media library, don't need specialized caching, because they aren't dynamically generated and they don't use code.

Caching plug-ins are smart enough to know when they need to regenerate the cached copy of a page. For example, if you update a post or a visitor leaves a new comment, the plug-in regenerates the page. Caching plug-ins can use other tactics, too, such as caching just part of the content, compressing the stored files, and discarding cached copies after a certain amount of time.

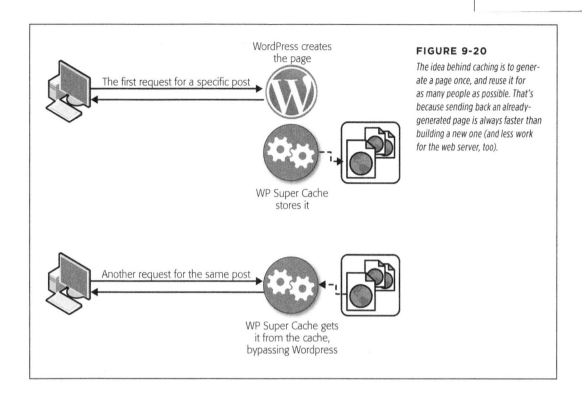

FIGURE 9-20

The idea behind caching is to generate a page once, and reuse it for as many people as possible. That's because sending back an already-generated page is always faster than building a new one (and less work for the web server, too).

NOTE A cached page can still use JavaScript code. That's because the code gets embedded as part of the final HTML file that WordPress sends to your visitors, and this code runs in their browsers. For that reason, caching shouldn't interfere with web statistics (like Google Analytics), ad services (like Google AdSense), fancy music and video players, and other JavaScript-powered widgets.

There are several caching plug-ins in the WordPress directory, but by far the most popular is WP Super Cache (*http://tinyurl.com/wpsupercache*). To start using it, install the plug-in, activate it in the usual way, and *then* turn on caching. To perform this last step, choose Settings→WP Super Cache, click the Caching On option at the top of the page, and then click the Update Status button (Figure 9-21).

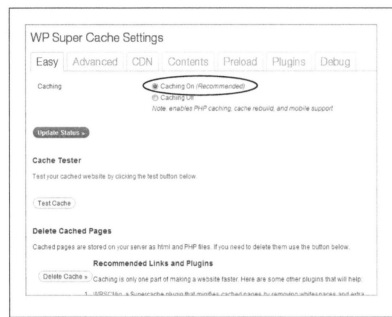

FIGURE 9-21

WP Super Cache packs in a pile of settings. But the most important is the Caching On option shown here—without that, WP Super Cache sits idle.

WP Super Cache and Other Plug-ins

Caching changes the way your website works, and it can have unexpected side effects on other plug-ins. Here are some tips to help you steer clear of plug-in conflicts:

- **Check the documentation for your plug-ins.** WP Super Cache is popular enough that other plug-in creators often test their plug-ins with it. To see if the plug-ins you use need special settings to get along with WP Super Cache, look up the plug-in in WordPress's plug-in directory (*http://wordpress.org/extend/plugins*) and check the FAQ tab.

- **Visit the Plugins tab in the WP Super Cache Settings.** There are a few plug-ins that get special attention from WP Super Cache. If you have one of them, you can tell WP Super Cache to change the way it works to avoid disrupting the other plug-in. To do that, you need to go to Settings→WP Super Cache, click the Plugins tab, find your plug-in, and then click the Enabled option next to

it. (The WPtouch plug-in you used earlier in this chapter is in this list, for instance.)

- **Delay caching until you're ready to go live.** Switching on caching is the very last thing you should do with your WordPress site, after you polish your theme, tweak your layout, and start using your site for real.

- **Learn to troubleshoot.** If something goes wrong, you need to be ready to track it down. Usually, the most recently activated plug-in is the culprit—try disabling it and seeing if your site returns to normal. If that doesn't work, you need to deactivate every plug-in, and then activate them one at a time, testing after each step. Also be on the lookout for theme vs. plug-in conflicts, which are less common but occasionally occur. If you change your theme and part of your site stops working, switch off all of your plug-ins and activate them one at a time.

To confirm that WP Super Cache is working, open a new browser window and look at a couple of posts. Then, return to the WP Super Cache settings and click the Contents tab. Finally, click the "Regenerate cache stats" link. WP Super Cache will report how many cached files it's created (Figure 9-22). Even though these pages don't look any different in a browser, WordPress sends them to your visitors more quickly, bypassing most of the processing the WordPress engine ordinarily does.

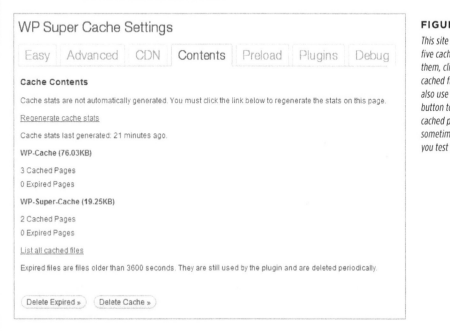

FIGURE 9-22

This site currently has five cached pages. To see them, click the "List all cached files" link. You can also use the Delete Cache button to discard every cached page, which is sometimes useful while you test WP Super Cache.

NOTE You'll notice that the cached pages appear in two lists, representing two slightly different types of caching. WP Super Cache automatically chooses the type of caching that makes sense for your page. For example, if you visit your site as a logged-in user, the plug-in uses less powerful WP Cache caching instead of WP Super Cache caching. But you don't need to worry about these technical details, because WP Super Cache makes sure your pages are as fast as possible—which is always faster than they would be without caching.

Once you verify that your site still works properly, you're ready to adjust a few WP Super Cache settings. Click the Advanced tab and look for settings that have "(Recommended)" next to them, in *italics*. This indicates a setting that improves the way WP Super Cache works for most people, but may cause problems in rare situations (and, for that reason, may be initially switched off). One example is the "Compress pages so they're served more quickly to visitors" setting, which improves performance for most people but causes trouble with some web hosts that don't support compression properly. You can try turning this setting on, but leave the more advanced options alone, unless you really think you know what you're doing.

Even More WordPress Plug-Ins

In this chapter, you considered several of the most useful Word-Press plug-ins. However, in a directory of thousands, it's no surprise that there are many more plug-ins worth considering.

You'll learn about some of them in the following chapters (and some you'll need to discover on your own). Here's a list of some of the most popular:

- **Akismet.** This spam-fighting tool is the only plug-in that ships preinstalled with WordPress (but not activated). You learned about it in Chapter 8.

- **WordPress SEO by Yoast.** Search-engine optimization (SEO) is the art of attracting the attention of web search engines like Google, so you can lure new visitors to your site. SEO plug-ins are among the most popular in the WordPress plug-in directory, and WordPress SEO by Yoast is an all-in-one package by one of the most renown developers in the WordPress community. You'll take a closer look at it on page 416.

- **WordPress Importer.** Moving your WordPress site from one web host to another? The WordPress Importer handles the job with relatively few speed bumps. (In Appendix A, you'll learn how to use the WordPress Importer to migrate from WordPress.com to a self-hosted site.) The WordPress Importer was built by the same folks who develop WordPress. They also provide importers for other blog sites, like Blogger, Movable Type, and LiveJournal.

- **TinyMCE Advanced.** You learned about the existence of this slick editor, suitable for beefing up your post-writing powers, on page 177.

- **WP e-Commerce.** If you want to sell products on your site, complete with a professional shopping cart and checkout process, this could be the plug-in for you. Although you won't use it in this book, you'll try out a simpler shopping cart plug-in on page 505.

- **BuddyPress.** If your website is bringing together a tightly knit community—for example, the students of a school, the employees of a business, or the members of a sports team, you can use BuddyPress to add instant social networking features to your site. Users get profiles, the ability to message each other, add photos, create content, and talk together in groups. To learn more, visit *http://buddypress.org*.

10

Adding Picture Galleries, Video, and Music

By now, you know that the simplest way to enhance any WordPress post is to toss in a picture or two. The Web is a visual medium, and a bit of eye candy is essential for capturing (and keeping) your readers' attention.

But modern websites rarely stop with ordinary pictures. Today's Web is splattered with rich media, including slideshows, video clips, webcasts, podcasts, and song players. In traditional websites, adding these sorts of ingredients is a chore that often requires copying hefty chunks of HTML and JavaScript code—the programming magic that powers many of these goodies. But WordPress makes adding media a lot easier with a small family of useful features, including specialized themes and plug-ins, along with the arcanely named "automatic embeds" and "shortcode" features. Using these tools, you can enrich your posts or pages with rich media almost as easily as you do with ordinary pictures.

In this chapter, you'll explore all the ways to add rich media to your site. First, you'll supercharge your pictures by replacing ordinary images with slideshows and galleries, and you'll learn how to transform your entire site into a photoblog or portfolio. Next, you'll see how to embed a video window in a post, and how to host your video files on YouTube or your own web server. Finally, you'll get readers jammin' with audio tracks and podcasts.

■ Understanding Embeds and Shortcodes

Before you go any further, you need to know about two WordPress features you'll rely on throughout this chapter. They're called embeds and shortcodes. Both serve the same purpose: They let you slip special types of content (like slideshows and videos) into your posts and pages without forcing you to type in a bunch of JavaScript or HTML markup. Instead, when you use embeds and shortcodes, you ask WordPress to fill in the necessary details for you.

Automatic Embeds

One of the shortcuts, called *automatic embed*, takes web addresses that point to certain media files and replaces the URL with the media file itself—in other words, it automatically embeds the real media instead of displaying just a link pointing to it.

For example, imagine you type in this URL of a photo in someone's Flickr stream:

```
http://www.flickr.com/photos/82337026@N02/7544952876/in/photostream
```

In the WordPress post editor, this web address looks ordinary enough (Figure 10-1). But WordPress works a bit of magic when you publish the page. At that point, it realizes that your URL points to a Flickr picture. Instead of showing a boring link, WordPress grabs the corresponding picture from the Flickr site and embeds it in your post, without you even needing to ask (Figure 10-2).

> **NOTE** Flickr, for those who haven't come across it yet, is a website for storing and sharing photos. With tens of millions of users (and billions of pictures), Flickr is the world's most popular picture-hosting service. It's also a thriving online community, with groups that attract professional photographers, hobbyists, and ordinary people who just want to show off their snapshots. You can learn more at *www.flickr.com*.

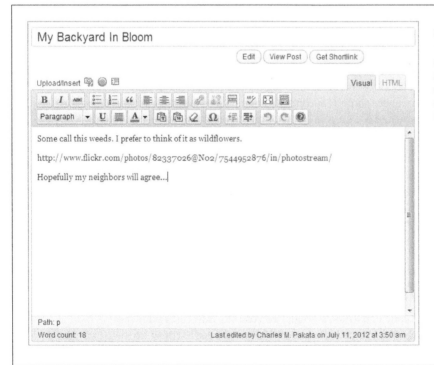

FIGURE 10-1

When you create a post (or page), there's no sign that WordPress will auto-embed any content. All you see is an ordinary URL.

MY BACKYARD IN BLOOM

July 10, 2012 · by Charles M. Pakata · in Uncategorized

Some call this weeds. I prefer to think of it as wildflowers.

Hopefully my neighbors will agree...

FIGURE 10-2

When you view the published page (or preview a draft of it), WordPress pulls a clever sleight of hand: It turns an address that points to a Flickr picture into a small preview of the picture itself. Even better, WordPress makes the picture preview a link. Click it, and you'll end up on the corresponding Flickr page, where you can see the full-size picture, along with a description of it, additional details, and comments.

For automatic embeds to work, you need to meet several criteria:

- **The URL must be on a separate line.** Don't crowd it up next to your text. As you can see in Figure 10-1, the URL stands alone, with paragraphs of text above and below it.

- **The URL can't be formatted as a link.** When you paste a website address into the WordPress editor, WordPress may format that address as a real, clickable link (that's an <a> anchor element for you HTML mavens). Here's the problem: Links show up in the final post as, well, links. WordPress doesn't swap in rich content in their place.

TIP If your URL is colored blue in the post editor (and the address becomes underlined when you move your mouse over it), the URL is a link. To turn it into plain text, select it and then click the Unlink button in the toolbar. Now the address turns into ordinary black text, which lets WordPress perform the URL-to-embedded-content switcheroo when it generates the page.

- **You must have auto-embeds switched on.** This is WordPress's default setting. To verify it (or to turn auto-embedding off if you don't want WordPress to do anything for you automatically), choose Settings→Media in the dashboard, and adjust the "Enable auto-embeds" checkbox. Click Save Changes when you finish.

- **WordPress must recognize the site.** WordPress performs auto-embedding for only a select group of sites. Most are picture or video services, but WordPress supports a few additional sites, like Twitter and PollDaddy. For the full list, which is currently fewer than 20 sites, see *http://codex.wordpress.org/Embeds*.

Some WordPress aficionados write auto-embed URLs differently from the earlier example, in this form:

```
[embed]http://www.flickr.com/photos/...[/embed]
```

Here, the web address is the same, but it has an [embed] code at the beginning of it and a similar [/embed] code at the end. This line of code produces the same effect as in the previous example—WordPress replaces the URL with the appropriate embedded content (provided you've satisfied the four conditions described previously).

There are two reasons you might write your URLs by using the [embed] code. First, you may have disabled WordPress's "Enable auto-embeds" setting; in that case, you need to *explicitly* tell WordPress when you want to embed something, and the [embed] code is the only way to do that.

Second, you can add *height* and *width* attributes to the [embed] code to set the maximum size of the embedded content. For example, here's how you might tell WordPress you don't want your embedded picture preview to be any bigger than 200 pixels wide and 300 pixels tall:

```
[embed width="200" height="300"]http://www.flickr.com/photos/...[/embed]
```

If you don't restrict the size of your embedded content, WordPress lets it grow until it hits the maximum sizes listed in your media settings. To check or change these settings, choose Settings→Media in the dashboard, look for the "Maximum embed size" label, adjust the numbers in the Width and Height boxes, and then click Save Changes. Ordinarily, WordPress imposes no width restriction, but limits embedded content to no more than 600 pixels tall.

TIP You can remove the height and width restrictions completely by leaving both the Width and Height boxes blank. In this case, WordPress lets your embedded content grow as big as the theme layout allows (see the box on page 315).

Avoiding Gigantic Pictures

Most themes have a layout that restricts width but not height. For example, in WordPress's standard theme, Twenty Eleven, the width of your content is constrained by the width of the column you place it in. However, the height of your content isn't constrained by anything.

This is a potential problem if you embed something like a tall and skinny picture, because the picture can easily expand to fill the better part of the browser window (or more) before it hits the top of the column and stops growing. To prevent this from happening, the default WordPress settings use a maximum height of 600 pixels. That way, pictures can't grow out of control. Note, however, that the default WordPress settings don't bother to limit the width, because the theme layout takes care of that.

Shortcodes

Shortcodes are special instructions you put in your post or page. Like an auto-embed URL, a shortcode tells WordPress to insert something extra in the current location. But auto-embeds are limited to a relatively small set of known websites, while shortcodes offer a much broader range.

To use a shortcode, you put a predetermined code inside square brackets. For example, the following shortcode takes all the pictures attached to a post and combines them into a picture gallery:

```
An image gallery will show up here:
```

[gallery]

You'll take a much closer look at galleries in the next section. For now, the important thing to understand is that a shortcode is a code that, when you put it in a page or post, tells WordPress to insert something out of the ordinary.

Shortcodes always have the same syntax—each one consists of a bit of text wrapped in square brackets. In fact, the [embed] instruction you learned about in the previous section is actually a shortcode that tells WordPress to examine a web address and embed the appropriate content.

NOTE You can type shortcodes into the visual editor or the HTML editor; it really doesn't matter. Either way, WordPress recognizes the code by its square brackets.

The truly neat part about shortcodes is that they're *extensible*. If you're ambitious and you're running a self-hosted WordPress site, you can create your own shortcodes (technically, it's all about editing the *functions.php* file, as described on page 467). Even better, a clever plug-in developer can create useful shortcodes that you can then use in your posts and pages to get additional features. Examples include fancy buttons, contact forms, documents, maps, charts, ads, a view counter, and a PayPal donation link.

If you use WordPress.com, you don't have these options, but you'll be happy to know that WordPress.com already stuffs in a number of shortcodes (including one for a picture gallery) that self-hosted sites don't have. For the full list, visit *http://support.wordpress.com/shortcodes*.

> **NOTE** If you run a self-hosted WordPress site, you start with just two shortcodes: [embed] and [gallery]. Fortunately, there are plenty of plug-ins that give you more. And if you want to add the dozen-or-so shortcodes that WordPress.com sites get, you can use the handy Jetpack plug-in (page 284).

FREQUENTLY ASKED QUESTION

Shortcodes and Sidebars

Can I use a shortcode or an auto-embed URL in a sidebar widget?

Ordinarily, WordPress doesn't check sidebar text for auto-embed URLs and shortcodes. For example, if you add a Text widget (page 155) and put a Flickr URL in it, that URL will appear in your sidebar as ordinary text, not as an image preview.

If you use WordPress.com, you need to live with this restriction. If you're on a self-hosted site, there's a fairly easy workaround, but you need to be familiar with theme editing, an advanced topic that's explored in Part Four.

The solution is to add two commands (shown on page 469) to a special code file called functions.php. These commands tell WordPress to process widget text in the same way that it processes the text in a post or page—in other words, to check for auto-embed URLs and shortcodes. Using this technique, you can put tiny videos, slideshows, galleries, and more in your sidebar without relying on a specialized widget.

◼ Showing Groups of Pictures

Individual images are an important part of most posts and pages. As you already know, there's no limit to the number of pictures you can include in a single post—you simply need to arrange your text around them in the best way possible.

But this approach isn't ideal for posts where you want the pictures as the focal point (for example, a travelogue of your trip through Nepal) or where pictures are the *whole* point (for example, an amateur photographer's snaps on a photoblog). In both of these cases, you need to tame your piles of pictures and present them in a way that lets visitors browse them at their leisure. In the following sections, you'll consider a range of options for posts like these, starting with WordPress's basic gallery feature.

Creating a Gallery

A gallery displays a series of thumbnail images, arranged together on a page so it's easy for visitors to scan them at a glance (Figure 10-3). And if your guests want to take a closer look at a pic, all they need to do is click a thumbnail.

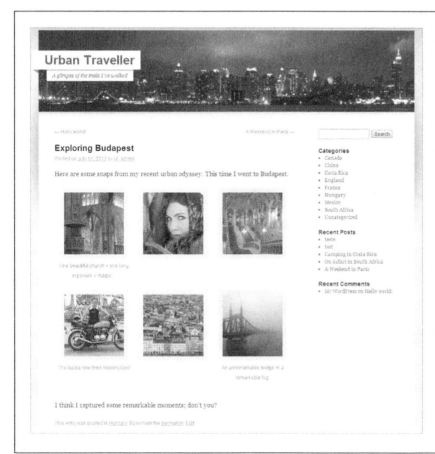

FIGURE 10-3

By default, WordPress crops a square tile out of each picture, and arranges them into a series of rows to create a gallery. If you wrote captions for your pictures, they appear underneath the corresponding tile.

When someone clicks a picture in a gallery, you'd expect to see a larger version of the image. But WordPress does something a little different, and its exact behavior depends on how you host your site.

If you run a self-hosted site and one of your visitors clicks a thumbnail, WordPress launches what it calls an *attachment page*, which displays the larger-size picture along with its description (if you included it), and offers a place for comments (Figure 10-4).

FIGURE 10-4

 WordPress's attachment page, which looks like a simple version of a single-post page, comes complete with an area for comments.

WordPress.com is a bit fancier—it loads the picture up in a photo carousel, and viewers can step from one picture to the next (or former) by clicking the arrows on either side of the image (Figure 10-5).

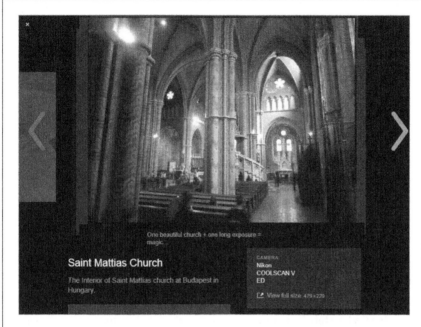

FIGURE 10-5

When a visitor clicks a thumbnail image. instead of a simple attachment page, WordPress.com launches a photo carousel It includes most of the same information as an attachment page does, including a comment section (not shown). It also displays each picture's EXIF data if the file includes it. (EXIF data is information that digital cameras and photo-editing software add to a photo file. For example, it may record the type of camera that took the picture, the global coordinates where the picture was taken, the time it was taken, and the camera settings that were used.)

You can turn off the WordPress.com photo carousel, in which case viewers will see the attachment page when they click a picture. To do that, head to the dashboard, choose Settings→Media, turn off the "Display images in full-size carousel slideshow" checkbox, and then click Save Changes.

> **TIP** The photo carousel dramatically showcases your pictures without taking the reader away from your post. Self-hosted sites can get the same feature by installing the Jetpack plug-in (page 284). However, some WordPress-ers have found that the photo carousel doesn't work with certain theme-browser-plug-in combinations. So if you install Jetpack but you still see ordinary attachment pages instead of the photo carousel, you've probably run into one of these conflicts.

Now that you know what a gallery looks like, you're ready to add one of your own. Follow these steps:

1. **Create a new post or edit an existing one.**

   Or, create or edit a page; either way, the gallery-adding process is the same.

2. **Click the Upload/Insert link just above the edit box.**

   This is the same link you use to add single pictures (page 178). When you click it, the Add Media window opens.

3. **Using the From Computer tab, add the files you want in your slideshow.**

   As you already know, you can upload files from your computer two ways: drag them into the "Drop files here" area, or click the Select Files button and pick them from there. Either way, WordPress starts uploading the files immediately.

NOTE Here's where things start to get a little wonky. WordPress expects you to upload all the pictures you want to use in a slideshow from your computer. Oddly enough, you can't grab slideshow pictures from your site's media library. There's a reasonably effective workaround (see page 323), but for now it's best to stick to the official procedure and upload some new picture files for your slideshow.

---

4. **Once you upload the files, go to the Gallery tab to confirm your uploads, and then click the "Save all changes" button underneath.**

   WordPress adds a new Gallery tab to the Add Media window, and then takes you there (Figure 10-6).

5. **Drag your pictures into the order you want.**

   The WordPress gallery displays pictures in the top-to-bottom order they were in in the Gallery tab. To rearrange them, simply drag the one you want to move to a new place in the list. If you prefer to order your pictures by title, date, or randomly, you can skip this step, and use the ordering options in step 8.

6. **Enter a description for each picture.**

   This is the same process you follow when you insert a single picture. Start by clicking the Show button, and then fill in the boxes underneath:

   • **Title.** This is the text that pops up when someone mouses over the picture.

   • **Alternate Text.** Use this box to describe the picture so accessibility tools like screen readers can "speak" the text. Alternate text also helps search engines understand what a picture shows.

   • **Caption.** This is a bit of optional text that, if provided, shows up under the picture.

   • **Description.** This box contains additional text that appears on the picture's attachment page, along with the image's title and caption (Figure 10-4).

   Don't worry about the alignment and size settings, because you're not inserting the picture into your post. And don't click the "Insert into Post" button, either. Instead, click Show beside the next picture to edit its details.

7. **Once you add descriptive information for all your pictures, click the "Save all changes" button under the picture list.**

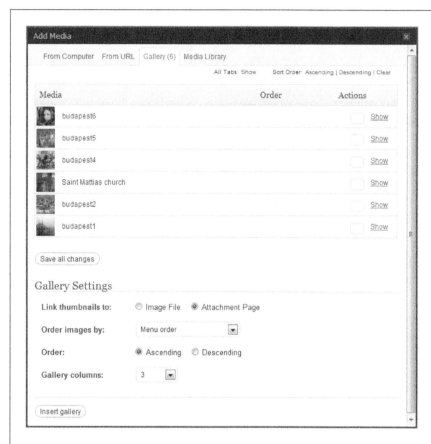

FIGURE 10-6

Here, the Gallery tab lists the six pictures you just uploaded. The pictures are now attached to the current post, but there isn't a gallery where you can showcase them yet.

8. **Tweak your gallery settings.**

   Under the list of pictures is a section called "Gallery Settings" with a few gallery-specific settings. They include:

   • **Link thumbnails to.** This determines what page appears when someone clicks a thumbnail in the gallery. Ordinarily, this is the attachment page (choose Attachment Page to make it so), but you can keep things simple by showing the full-size image on its own, with no extra information (choose Image File).

   NOTE If you're using the photo carousel feature (page 318), WordPress ignores the "Link thumbnails to" setting. Instead, it shows a photo carousel when a visitor clicks a picture.

- **Order images by.** Use the default value, Menu order, to insert pictures in the order they're listed. Or use the drop-down list to order your pictures another way: alphabetically by title (Title), chronologically by date (Date/Time), or in a completely different way each time someone views the page (Random). If you use the Title or Date/Time option, you get another choice: You can use the Order setting underneath to reverse the picture sequence (choose Descending instead of Ascending). Alternatively, if you display pictures by date, Ascending puts the oldest pictures first, while Descending shows recent pics first.

- **Gallery columns.** Ordinarily, a gallery row displays three thumbnails (see Figure 10-3). But some themes have more space to spare, and they can accommodate more mini-pics. If that's the case for you, choose a different number here. But be warned, if your layout column isn't wide enough for your pictures, WordPress breaks up the pics in the gallery rows unevenly. For example, if you pick five gallery columns but your layout only has space for three pictures, WordPress splits each row of five into a row of three, followed by a row of two, creating a distracting zig-zag effect.

9. **Click the "Insert gallery" button at the bottom of the Gallery tab.**

   This adds the gallery to your post (Figure 10-7). You can now publish your post and take a look.

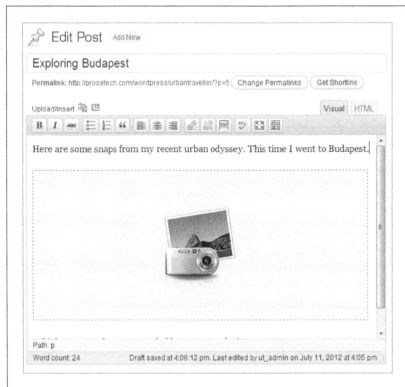

FIGURE 10-7

In the visual preview, the gallery looks like a rather unusual blue box. But when you view the published page, you'll see the gallery with your thumbnails in it.

Editing a Gallery

If you need to edit a gallery later on, simply edit your post and, in the visual editor, select the blue box that represents the gallery. Two icons appear in the top-left corner of the gallery: Edit Gallery and Delete Gallery.

Click Edit Gallery and you'll wind up on the Gallery tab of the Add Media window. You can then do any of the following:

- **Edit picture information or rearrange the order of your pictures.** Just remember to click the "Save all changes" button when you finish.

- **Edit gallery settings.** These settings appear under the list of pictures. When you finish, click "Update gallery settings."

- **Delete pictures.** This is a three-step operation. First, click the Show link next to the picture you want to remove. Then, click the Delete link that appears below all the picture details. Finally, click Continue to make it official. However, be aware that removing a picture from the gallery also deletes it from your post, which means there's no way to add it *back* to the gallery without re-uploading it.

- **Add new pictures.** Click the From Computer tab and drag one or more new pictures into the upload area, and then click the "Save all changes" button. WordPress adds the pictures to the gallery and switches you to the Gallery tab. You can then edit the picture's descriptive details and rearrange the order of the images.

Creating a Gallery with Pictures from Your Media Library

As you learned in Chapter 6, WordPress stores all the pictures you use in your site in a place called the media library. One of the advantages of this design is that you can easily find pictures you've used before, and you can use the same image in more than one post or page.

Unfortunately, WordPress galleries don't work that way. The Add Media window lets you create a slideshow from *newly uploaded* pictures, not existing ones. However, if you understand the shortcode system, you can work around this problem. Here's how:

1. **If you haven't already uploaded your pictures, do so now.**

   To add pictures, visit the media library (choose Media→Add New) and then upload your pictures one at a time. (If you don't remember how, page 189 has step-by-step instructions.)

2. **Choose Media→Library.**

   This brings you to a list of all the pictures in your media library, including the ones you just uploaded.

3. **Now you need to get the attachment ID of each picture you want in your gallery.**

   When you upload a picture to your media library, WordPress stores it in your website's database and gives it a unique number. Although WordPress doesn't advertise this number, you need it to show your picture in a gallery.

   To get a picture's ID, find the image in the media library list, and then click it. The picture's URL will appear in your browser's address bar, and it will look something like this:

   `http://urbantraveller/wp-admin/media.php?`**`attachment_id=70`**`&action=edit`

   The detail you want is *attachment_id*—that's 70 in this example. As you find each picture you want in your gallery, record its ID on a scrap of paper.

   Now you're ready to create your gallery.

4. **Create a new post or start editing an old one. Then switch to HTML view.**

   HTML view is the easiest place to enter a complex gallery shortcode. That's because you don't need to worry about WordPress replacing it with a blue box (which makes the gallery impossible to edit).

5. **Add the [gallery] shortcode.**

   You need to add an attribute called *include* to the [gallery] shortcode. The value of that attribute is a comma-separated list of the attachment IDs of the pictures you want in the gallery. Here's an example that shows five pictures—numbers 12, 70, 72, 73, and 89:

   `[gallery include="12,70,72,73,89"]`

NOTE The *include* attribute isn't the only detail you can add to the gallery shortcode in HTML view. You can set the same gallery options you saw in the Gallery tab in the Add Media window, too. These details include the number of columns in your gallery ("columns"), the ordering method ("orderby"), the type of page that's shown when the picture is clicked ("link"), and so on. WordPress has the full details in its documentation at *http://tinyurl. com/cfc29n*.

---

6. **Publish your post.**

   Now you can take a look at your gallery.

Changing the Thumbnails that Appear in a Gallery

Is there any way to change the way WordPress displays my thumbnails?

You're bound to encounter this at some point: Your thumbnails are too small. Or too big. Or you don't want them square-shaped. What to do?

Ordinarily, WordPress creates square thumbnails, measuring 150 pixels wide by 150 pixels tall. If your picture isn't a perfect square, WordPress simply crops off the edges to *make* it a square.

There are two ways to change the size and shape of your thumbnails. The first is to edit the [gallery] shortcode in HTML view, and add the *size* attribute, which can take one of several values. The default is *thumbnail*, but your other choices are *medium* or *large*, which tells WordPress to get medium-sized or large-sized versions of your picture and display them instead. In both cases, WordPress sizes the picture proportionally, rather than cropping it into a square.

This raises an excellent question: How does WordPress decide how big to make your thumbnails in the first place, not to mention the medium- and large-sized versions of your pictures? The answer leads to the second way to change your gallery thumbnails—by changing the settings in the Settings→Media section of the dashboard. There you'll see settings that let you tweak the standard thumbnail size (150 x 150), as well as the maximum dimensions for medium-size pictures (300 x 300) and large ones (1024 x 1024). On a self-hosted site, you'll also find a setting named "Crop thumbnail to exact dimensions." Turn off its checkbox and WordPress proportionally sizes your thumbnails to match the dimensions of the actual picture, rather than cropping it into a square (see Figure 10-8).

One caveat applies when you change these settings: WordPress creates the thumbnails when you upload your pictures. Even if you change the thumbnail settings, the galleries you created so far will continue using the old thumbnails (unless you re-upload the pictures and re-create the gallery). If you run a self-hosted WordPress site, you can fix the problem using the Regenerate Thumbnails plug-in (*http://tinyurl.com/rthumb*). Once you install and activate it, you can create new thumbnails by vising the media library (choose Media→Library). Turn on the checkbox next to all the pictures you want to change, and then choose Regenerate Thumbnails in the Bulk Action list. Finally, click Apply to re-create the thumbnails for those pictures.

Creating a Slideshow

A slideshow is similar to a gallery in that it gives you an elegant way to deal with a group of related pictures. But where a gallery shows a group of photos all at once, a slideshow displays your pictures one at a time, typically framed by a small box (Figure 10-9).

Exploring Budapest

Posted on July 11, 2012 by ut_admin

Here are some snaps from my recent urban odyssey. This time I went to Budapest.

One beautiful church + one long
exposure = magic...

The locals love their motorcycles!

An unremarkable bridge in a
remarkable fog.

FIGURE 10-8

Here, WordPress has proportionally sized the thumbnails. If a picture is tall and skinny, WordPress makes it 150 pixels tall and as wide as necessary. If a picture is short and wide, WordPress makes it 150 pixels wide and as tall as necessary. (Of course, you can adjust these size maximums on the Media Settings page.)

FIGURE 10-9

Left: A slideshow starts with an unremarkable shortcode. Right: When you publish a page that contains a slideshow, you'll see a box with a black background that moves through your images, spending about 4 seconds on each. Although you can't change the speed of the slideshow, viewers can use the pause button to halt it, and the arrow buttons to move through the pictures at their own pace.

If you use WordPress.com, it's easy to add a basic slideshow. In fact, you follow the same process you followed to create a gallery, with one exception: In the very last step (that's step 9, on page 322), you click the "Insert slideshow" button instead of "Insert gallery." That adds a slideshow shortcode to your HTML, which looks, unsurprisingly, like this:

```
[slideshow]
```

Self-hosted WordPress sites don't have slideshow support. That means you won't see an "Insert slideshow" button, and WordPress will ignore the [slideshow] shortcode if you attempt to use it.

Surprisingly, slideshows aren't part of the Jetpack plug-in either (at least not yet). To create slideshows on a self-hosted site, you need a different plug-in. There are plenty of candidates if you search "slideshow" in the WordPress plug-in directory. However, many suffer from awkward quirks, and may crop or rescale your pictures in ways you don't want.

One reliable plug-in is the Portfolio Slideshow (*http://tinyurl.com/port-show*). Once you install and activate it, you can present a slideshow with minimum fuss. First, add an ordinary WordPress gallery with the images you want to show (page 319). Then, select the big blue box and press Delete (or delete the [gallery] shortcode, if you're in HTML view). In its place, write this:

```
[portfolio_slideshow]
```

When you publish the page, you'll get a slideshow like the one in Figure 10-10.

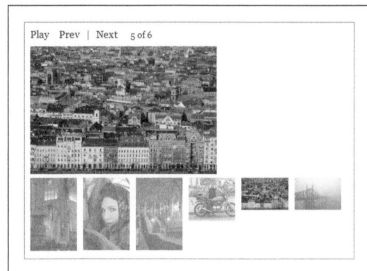

FIGURE 10-10

If you don't do any extra customization, the Portfolio Slideshow plug-in gives you a set of links so you can browse the pictures (on top) and a group of picture thumbnails (below). You can adjust these options and change the slideshow timing by choosing Settings→Portfolio Slideshow in the dashboard.

To create an even better slideshow, you need to go beyond WordPress and its plug-ins. Flickr offers the gold standard for slideshows, and if you have a Flickr account you can drop a Flickr slideshow into any WordPress post or page. All you need is the right URL.

The easiest way to create a Flickr slideshow is to get a link for your entire photo stream (all the pictures you've uploaded to Flickr, in other words). To do that, click on your photo stream, and then click the tiny Slideshow button near the top-right corner of the page (see Figure 10-11). Your browser will direct itself to a URL that ends in *show*, like this:

```
http://www.flickr.com/photos/82337026@N02/show/
```

Using this web address, you'll see a slideshow that steps through all your Flickr pictures.

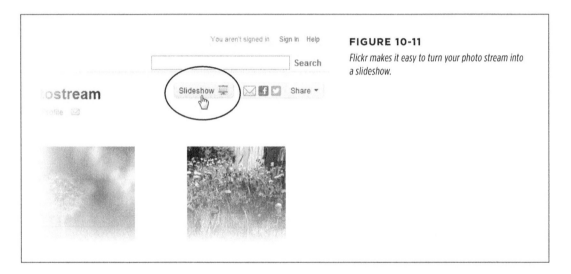

FIGURE 10-11

Flickr makes it easy to turn your photo stream into a slideshow.

Now you need to copy this URL into a post or page. Make sure WordPress doesn't turn it into a link. (If it does, select the URL and then click the Unlink button.)

Finally, publish your page. Through the magic of auto-embedding, WordPress recognizes your slideshow URL and embeds a small version of the slideshow in your post (Figure 10-12).

Summer Bloom

Here are some pictures I snapped walking through Regency Park. It seems they've let things go a bit.

What do you think. Raw beauty or weed disaster?

This entry was posted in **Uncategorized** by **Katya Greenview**. Bookmark the **permalink**.

FIGURE 10-12

This post includes a Flickr slideshow. Readers can browse through the pictures by clicking a thumbnail, using the arrow buttons, or just letting the show unfold.

TIP If you're a Flickr expert, you know that you can make a *photo set* that includes just some of your pictures. Conceptually, a photo set is like an album of shots you select and arrange in any order, which makes it more suitable for a slideshow. Once you create a photo set (which takes just a few drag and drops, using Flickr's Organizr tool), you can view it and click the familiar Slideshow button to get a URL for it.

Using a Slideshow from Another Site

Some websites have perfectly good slideshows, but they don't offer the super-cool convenience of WordPress auto-embedding. Examples include Picasa, Photobucket, and SmugMug. In the future, WordPress may offer better integration with these services. In the meantime, self-hosters have two good options.

The first is to use a plug-in that supports your favorite photo site. One good example is Photonic (*http://tinyurl.com/wp-photonic*), which supports galleries and slideshows from Flickr, SmugMug, Picasa, and 500px.

The second option is to add your slideshow the old-fashioned way, with HTML. The basic idea is this: you ask your picture-sharing service to give you the HTML markup you need for an embedded slideshow. Usually, this is a block of cryptic code that starts with an <object> or <iframe> element. But the details don't matter, because you don't need to actually understand this markup. You simply need to copy and paste it.

The exact steps depend on the photo site you use. Usually, the first step is to click a button named "Share" or "Embed." You may need to specify a few details, like the size of your slideshow window, before the site generates the HTML you need. Once you finish, select and then copy the HTML, switch your WordPress to HTML view, and then paste the markup in. But be warned—if you switch back to the visual editor, it may disrupt your new code.

Themes that Make the Most of Pictures

Some sites are all about pictures and little else. For example, you might create a photoblog to showcase your nature photography. You could use the techniques you learned above to add galleries and slideshows, but the results won't be ideal. Standard WordPress themes split up your pictures, making it impossible for visitors to browse your portfolio from beginning to end. And worse, ordinary WordPress themes deemphasize pictures, hiding them deep in your site, behind a wall of posts.

The solution is to find a picture-centric theme, one that puts the focus on your pictures, without letting text, menus, and needless clicking get in the way. Happily, you can build specialized, picture-heavy sites like this in WordPress. All you need is a *photoblog* or *portfolio* theme.

There are several good options in the WordPress.com theme gallery, and many more in the much larger theme collection for self-hosted sites. Either way, you can dig up good candidates by searching for words like "photo," "photoblog," "picture," and "portfolio."

NOTE There's no clear dividing line between photoblogs and portfolio sites. Usually, photoblogs show off your photography skills and the snapshots you've taken, while portfolio sites go beyond images. They include sites that display items you've hand-made or products you sell. However, there's a considerable overlap between photoblogs and portfolio sites, and it's worth checking out both options if you want to build a site that emphasizes images.

Every photoblog and portfolio theme works a bit differently, but most share some key features. First, the home page likely displays the *pictures* in your posts rather than the posts themselves. Figure 10-13 shows an example from Foto, a photography theme for self-hosted sites.

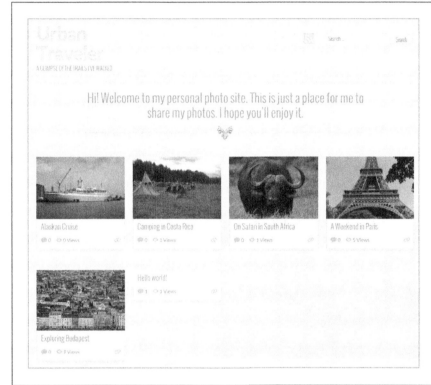

FIGURE 10-13

Instead of an ordinary list of posts for its home page, Foto creates a tiled display of images. It also adds a neat animated effect: When you move your mouse over a picture, it expands slightly. You can then click the tile to read the full post.

The Foto theme requires that you set a featured image for each of your posts (page 184). If you haven't, that post's home-page tile will be blank. Many photoblog and portfolio themes work this way, so if you don't see the pictures you expect to after you switch themes, you most likely haven't assigned featured images to your posts.

Other themes aren't as picky, and grab the first picture in a post, no matter what it is. One example is the self-hosted theme PinBlack. Like Foto, PinBlack creates a home page of tiled pictures. Unlike Foto, PinBlack uses any post picture it can get. If you try out PinBlack, you'll notice other, more subtle differences as well. For example, its home page feels a bit more serious and businesslike, with a sleek gray-and-black color scheme with lime accents. (PinBlack is the starting point for the custom theme that powers the furniture store example developed in Chapter 14.)

Often, photoblog and portfolio themes assume that, for each of your posts, you'll include just a single picture. They give special attention to this picture (which may be the featured image or just the first image in the post) by making it larger than normal and placing it at the top of the post.

Photoblog and portfolio themes often include back and forward buttons that let readers move from one post to another, without making an interim stop at the home page and forcing you to select from the full list of posts. This way, readers can browse through your pictures and posts just as though they were scanning an image gallery, even if the pics appear in separate posts. Figure 10-14 shows how the back and forward buttons work with the Foto theme.

FIGURE 10-14

The Foto theme is designed for picture browsing. You use the arrow buttons to move from one post to another. If you click the featured image, it expands into a lightbox, dimming the content behind it.

NOTE When a picture appears in a lightbox, it floats over the web page, with the content behind it dimmed. This is the same effect you get when you view one of the pictures in a photo carousel, as described earlier. To douse the lightbox, you click the X in the top-right corner of the picture box.

WordPress.com also includes attractive photoblog and portfolio themes. One notable example is the Duotone theme, which is designed to be a simple but beautiful way to showcase your photography.

Duotone doesn't include a picture-tile home page. Instead, it takes viewers straight into picture-browsing mode. Guests begin with a picture from your most recent post, and use the arrow buttons to step from one post to the next, just as visitors do with the Foto theme (Figure 10-15). The Duotone theme also has an unusual frill—every time a visitor moves to a new post, the theme picks a color from that post's picture and uses it to set a complementary background color.

FIGURE 10-15

The Duotone theme takes the first picture from a post, moves it above the post title, and enlarges it as much as possible. If a post has more than one picture, the other pictures remain in their original location in the post.

WordPress.com also includes portfolio themes. One is the professionally polished Imbalance 2. Much like Foto, Imbalance 2 creates a tiled picture display of featured images, but it also includes an excerpt from each post, as you can see in Figure 10-16.

Imbalance 2   Home   Contact us   About   Search

FIGURE 10-16

This demo site for the Imbalance 2 theme demonstrates its remarkable layout. It accepts and neatly arranges irregularly sized tiles made up of featured images (page 184) and text excerpts (page 195) into a seamless grid. If you move your mouse over a tile, the theme highlights it with an arresting orange background.

Finally, it's worth noting that some themes, while not all-out photoblogs or portfolio sites, offer some enhanced picture features. For example, many themes place a strip of pictures from recent posts across the home page. Sometimes they animate the strip, so that the pictures slide by or blend into each other, one after the other, as you saw with the Canton School example on page 186.

■ Embedding a Video Window

Now that you've jazzed up your site with pictures, it's time for something even more ambitious: video.

There are two reasons you might put a video window in a post (or page). First, the video may actually *be* your content. For example, you might use video to show your band's latest live performance, a bike-repair tutorial you filmed in your garage, or a blistering web rant about the ever-dwindling size of a Pringles can. In all these cases, you create the video and then use your WordPress site to share it with a larger audience.

The other possibility is that you're using someone else's video to add a little something extra to your content (which is the ordinary text in your post). For example, if you comment on a local protest concert, your post will be more interesting if it includes a clip of the event. Similarly, if you review a new movie, you might include its trailer; if you're talking about a trip to Egypt, you might want to take visitors inside the pyramids. In all these examples, the video adds a bit of context to your post.

If you want to present someone else's video on your site, you simply find the movie on a video-sharing site and copy the link. Most of the time, that video-sharing site will be YouTube, the wildly popular video sharing hub that rarely drops out of the top three world's most visited websites.

And if you want to show your *own* videos, you'll probably *still* turn to a video-hosting service like YouTube because the alternative—uploading your video files straight to your web server—has some significant drawbacks. Here are some of the reasons you should strongly consider a video-hosting service:

- **Bandwidth.** Video files are large—vastly bigger than any other sort of content you can put on a site, even truckloads of pictures. And although you'll probably have room for your video files on your web server, you might not have the bandwidth allotment you need to play back the videos for all your visitors, especially if your website picks up some buzz and has a hot month. The result could be extra charges or even a crashed website that refuses to respond to anyone.

- **Encoding.** Usually, the format you use to record a video differs from the one you use to distribute it. When recording, you need a high-quality format that stands up well to editing. But when viewing a video over the Web, you need a heavily compressed, streamlined format that ensures smooth, stutter-free playback. Sadly, the process of converting your video files to web-friendly format is time-consuming, and it often requires some technical knowledge.

- **Compatibility.** In today's world, there's no single web-friendly video format that accommodates the variety of web browsers, devices (computers, tablets, and mobile phones), and web connections (fast and slow) out there. Video services like YouTube solve this problem by encoding the same video file multiple times, so that there's a version that works well for everyone. You can do the same on your own, but without a pricey professional tool, you're in for hours of tedium.

For all these reasons, it rarely makes sense to go it alone with video files, even if you're producing them yourself. Instead, pick a good video service and park your files there. In the following section, you'll start with YouTube.

The Dangers of Using Other People's Video

The risk of embedding other people's videos is that the video hosting service may take the videos down, often because of copyright issues, and so they'll disappear from your site, too. This is a particularly acute danger for videos that include content owned by someone other than the uploader. Examples include scenes from television shows and fan-made music videos.

Usually, WordPress authors don't worry about this problem—if a video goes dead, they simply edit their posts after the fact. To avoid potential problems from the get-go, stay away from clips that are obviously cribbed from someone else's content, especially if they're recent. For example, a video that shows a segment from last night's Saturday Night Live broadcast is clearly at risk of being taken down. A decades-old bootleg recording of a Grateful Dead concert is probably safe.

Showing a YouTube Video

Hosting a YouTube video in WordPress is ridiculously easy. All you need is the video's web address.

To get it, start by visiting the video page on YouTube. You may need to search around to get exactly the video you want. (If you're one of the six people who hasn't yet visited YouTube, start at *www.youtube.com*.)

When you find the right video, click the Share button under the video window. A panel of information pops open, including a text box with the URL you need (Figure 10-17).

The URL will look something like this:

```
http://youtu.be/OxKKroQrcjg
```

The first part, *youtu.be*, is a more compact form of the video's full web address (which starts with *www.youtube.com/watch?v=*). The string of letters and numbers after it uniquely identifies the video you picked.

The next step is even easier. Paste the video URL into your WordPress post, on a separate line, in the location where you want the video to appear, like this:

If you consider yourself a fan of popping and locking (and I do), the World Classic is an event you cannot miss.

http://youtu.be/OxKKr0Qrcjg

Here, Jutsu breaks out some sick moves against the battle-master Salah ...

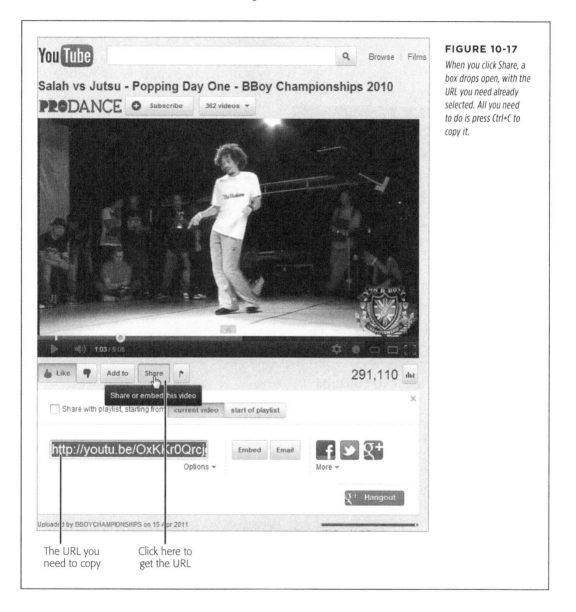

FIGURE 10-17

When you click Share, a box drops open, with the URL you need already selected. All you need to do is press Ctrl+C to copy it.

The URL you need to copy

Click here to get the URL

Make sure WordPress doesn't turn the URL into a link. If it does, select it and click the Unlink button. Then publish your post. You'll be rewarded with another transformation, courtesy of WordPress's auto-embed feature. This time the URL turns into an embedded video window (Figure 10-18).

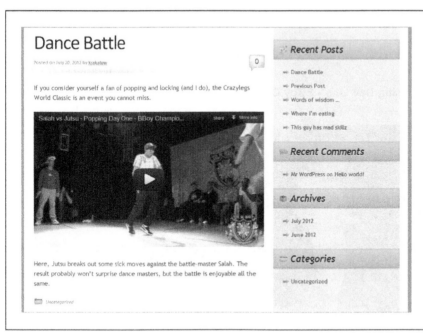

FIGURE 10-18

The main difference between visiting a video on YouTube and seeing it in a post is that videos in posts don't start playing automatically. The reader needs to click the video window to get things started. Also, the ancillary information that appears on the YouTube video page, such as the description of the video and the viewer comments, doesn't appear in the embedded video window.

Uploading Your Videos to YouTube

The process of playing your videos through YouTube is essentially the same as the one for showcasing someone else's. The only difference is that you begin by signing up with YouTube (if you don't already have an account) and then uploading your video. The steps are fairly straightforward—click the Upload link at the top of the home page, next to the YouTube search box, and follow the instructions YouTube gives you from there. Make sure you designate your video as *public*, which means that it appears in YouTube's search results. If you don't use this setting, you won't be able to embed your video in a WordPress post. Other settings (for example, whether you allow comments and ratings) have no effect on how the video shows up in your pages.

For best results, YouTube recommends that you upload the highest quality video file you have, even if that file is ridiculously big. YouTube will encode it in a more compressed, web-friendly format, while preserving as much of the quality as possible. And if the quality of your video is good enough, YouTube will offer high-speed viewers the option to watch it in high-definition format, using the H.264 standard.

Uploading videos takes a while, because the files are huge and transferring all that data takes time, even on the fastest network connection. YouTube also needs to process your video, although its industrial-strength servers can do most of that as you upload your video. When you get the video live on YouTube, click the Share button to get the URL you need for your WordPress post, exactly as you did before.

Configuring the YouTube Video Window

If the embedded video window looks the way you want it to, there's no need to do anything else. But if you want to tweak its size, you can.

To do that, you need to make two changes. First you replace your URL with the full web address, by removing the *youtube* portion and substituting *www.youtube.com/ watch?v=* in its place (if you're in any doubt, view the video in a browser and copy the URL from your address bar). Your URL should look something like this:

```
http://www.youtube.com/watch?v=0xKKr0Qrcjg
```

Next, you need to add this URL inside WordPress's [youtube] shortcode, like this:

```
[youtube=http://www.youtube.com/watch?v=0xKKr0Qrcjg]
```

Now you need to tack an extra piece onto the end of the URL to set the size of the video window (Figure 10-19). If you want to change the width, you add *&w=* followed by a number. To change the height, use *&h=*. Here's an example that shrinks down the video window:

```
[youtube=http://www.youtube.com/watch?v=0xKKr0Qrcjg&w=200]
```

NOTE The shape of the video window depends on the video itself. YouTube won't stretch a video out of its normal proportions. For that reason, you should probably specify just the width or height of your video window, but not both. If you do use both, your video window will get the dimensions you specific, but inside YouTube will pad the window with blank space to make sure the video isn't stretched.

If you're using a WordPress.com site, you can tweak two more details, using the YouTube shortcode. You can include YouTube's search box in your video window by adding *&showsearch=1*. To hide YouTube's "related videos" teaser, which usually plays after your video, add *&rel=0*. (Web authors use this feature to make sure their readers won't catch sight of someone else's content, become distracted, and surf away to watch more videos or visit a different site.) Here's an example that changes the width *and* hides related videos:

```
[youtube=http://www.youtube.com/watch?v=0xKKr0Qrcjg&w=200&rel=0]
```

Unfortunately, this trick doesn't work on self-hosted sites. This minor detail can become quite a problem—for example, if you're showing a serious video on a professional site, you don't want YouTube offering visitors wildly inappropriate follow-up videos. Currently, the best way to fix this problem is with a plug-in. Smart YouTube PRO (*http://tinyurl.com/smart-tube*) is one that does the trick. The only hassle is that you need to change the syntax of your YouTube links to match the format the plug-in expects. (The plug-in page's documentation has the full details.)

Dance Battle

Posted on July 20, 2012 by krakatow

If you consider yourself a fan of popping and locking (and I do), the Crazylegs World Classic is an event you cannot miss.

Here, Jutsu breaks out some sick moves against the battle-master Salah. The result probably won't surprise dance masters, but the battle is enjoyable all the same.

 Uncategorized

FIGURE 10-19

You can control the size of your embedded video window. That can come in handy if you want to include more than one video on a page. By specifying small video windows, you can focus readers' attention on your post rather than distract them with a large video.

Showing Videos from Other Video Services

Although YouTube is the most popular video service, it's not the only game in town. Happily, WordPress's auto-embed feature supports a range of media sites, including:

- Hulu
- DailyMotion

- Vimeo

- Viddler

- blip.tv

- Funny or Die

- Qik

- Flickr (for videos as well as pictures)

- Revision3

- WordPress.tv

As with YouTube, you simply need to supply a web address that points to a video on one of these sites, and WordPress does the rest.

When you embed video, WordPress configures the size of the playback window to suit the content and to fit in your post area. However, in some situations you might want to tweak the size to get it just right, using the corresponding shortcode. To do that, you need to be running a WordPress.com site, or you need to have Jetpack installed on a self-hosted site. Here's where things get a bit tricky, because each shortcode has similar but maddeningly different syntax. To see how you need to format the shortcode for a video site, refer to the WordPress documentation at *http://support.wordpress.com/shortcodes*.

Premium Video Hosting

As you learned earlier, it's generally a bad idea to host video files on your own website, unless you're a web development god with a clear plan. But there may be times when a free video-hosting site won't suit your needs. Here are some of the problems you might encounter hosting your files on a free service:

- **Maximum length restrictions.** Free video services won't host your three-hour self-directed *Star Wars* sequel. YouTube, for example, limits videos to 15 minutes.

- **Privacy.** Free video services make your videos visible to the entire world. If you have a video with sensitive material in it, you might not be comfortable exposing it to the public. And forget about limiting your videos to a private blog (page 373) or trying to run a subscription service that lets only paid members watch your videos.

- **Ads.** Video sharing services may try to profit from your free account by including ads. They use two basic strategies: playing a television-commercial-style ad before your video starts playing, or superimposing an irritating banner over your video while it plays. YouTube's advertising policy is good—it won't show ads unless you give it permission to (usually, in a misguided attempt to make a buck) or you post someone else's copyrighted content and *they* ask YouTube to slap on an ad (in which case they collect the money).

Overall, when your video is on a free web hosting service, you're at the mercy of the company that runs the service. You have to follow their rules.

To escape these restrictions, you need to pay. That may be as easy as buying a video hosting package from one of the sites listed on page 340. For example, the popular video site Vimeo (*http://vimeo.com*) offers free basic hosting and a more flexible premium service that costs $60 per year. It offers unlimited bandwidth, no length restriction, and the option to limit your videos to specific people, who must sign in to see them. Vimeo is particularly generous with storage space, allowing premium members to upload 5 GB of video per week. It also gives viewers high-quality streaming right out of the box; by comparison, to get the same quality on YouTube, a viewer needs to click the gear icon in the bottom-right corner of the video window and manually pick a higher resolution.

WordPress also offers its own video hosting service called VideoPress. Like Vimeo, VideoPress offers unrestricted bandwidth and large files. It also integrates well with WordPress.com, letting you limit video viewing to the registered users of your WordPress site. (You'll learn how to create private sites with registered users in Chapter 11.) VideoPress is particularly well-suited to WordPress.com sites, because it's already integrated into the WordPress.com hosting service, and only a simple upgrade away. However, it's far stingier with space than Vimeo. You start with a paltry 3 GB of storage, and if you need more, you need to pay a yearly fee, which rings in at about $20 per 10 GB.

To sign up a WordPress.com site for VideoPress, you buy the VideoPress upgrade. Click Store in the dashboard, look for the VideoPress box, and then click the "Buy now" button. Or, consider buying the value bundle, which is described in the box below.

A Better Choice: The WordPress.com Value Bundle

Instead of buying the WordPress.com VideoPress upgrade (currently $60 per year), you can buy the *value bundle*, which offers VideoPress and several useful extras, for a slightly higher price of $99 per year. These extras include a free domain name, no ads, and the custom design feature for tweaking the styles in your theme (page 439).

Most important of all, the value bundle includes a storage upgrade from 3 GB to 10 GB. This is important, because even though VideoPress offers unlimited bandwidth (meaning it won't charge you for web traffic, no matter how many times people watch your videos), it doesn't offer unlimited storage. And while 3 GB is more than enough to swallow all the pictures you can throw at a site, it may not accommodate the videos you

want to upload. (For comparison purposes, a feature-length HD movie takes up about 4GB of space if it's properly compressed in a video editing program. Raw HD video out of a consumer camcorder is less compressed, and it can chew up 4 GB in 30 minutes or less.) The space upgrade is also important if you want to include an audio player (page 344), because Word-Press.com won't allow you to upload audio files unless you buy at least one storage upgrade.

If you need even more space for giant videos, you can buy separate upgrades. However, more space doesn't come cheap. Currently, it costs roughly $20 per year for each extra 10 GB of space.

Once you sign up for VideoPress, you can upload a new video by clicking the Add Media icon above the post editor box. Uploading a video is more or less the same as uploading a picture, except that there are a few more details you can specify, such as a rating (from a family-friendly *G* to an explicit *X-18*) and the thumbnail (the still image shown in the video box before the video starts playing). The upload process also takes quite a bit longer.

NOTE If you have high-quality HD video, you may need to use a video tool to re-encode it to a leaner, more heavily compressed format before uploading it. Otherwise, you'll be stuck with a gigantic file on your Word Press.com site, eating up valuable space. (This is different from the process you follow when you upload a video to YouTube, which takes any file you can throw at it, and doesn't complain about space.) You may also experience technical troubles if you upload huge files. Although VideoPress officially supports files of up to 1.4 GB, gargantuan uploads can fail, sometimes after hours of waiting.

When you finish uploading a video, you can add it to your post by using the trusty "Insert into Post" button. This embeds a VideoPress shortcode that looks something like this:

```
[wpvideo MTFnELOW]
```

The result is a VideoPress window that looks a lot like a YouTube video player.

FREQUENTLY ASKED QUESTION

VideoPress and Self-Hosted Sites

I need a premium video host, but I'm not using Word Press.com. Should I consider VideoPress?

If you're running a self-hosted WordPress site, you can sign up for VideoPress, but it's probably not the best video-hosting package for you. That's because it uses an awkward hosting model that forces you to get a WordPress.com account and use it to store your videos. VideoPress is also relatively expensive, because you need to pay extra to get additional space (and given the size of video files, you'll probably need more space).

If you're still interested in trying out VideoPress, go to *http://videopress.com*. Enter the address of your WordPress site into the "Get started – enter your blog address" text box, and then click Next. VideoPress walks you through a somewhat convoluted process that involves creating a WordPress.com account and paying the $60 fee (or more if you also need a space upgrade). When you finish, you need to install the VideoPress plug-in (*http://tinyurl.com/vidpress*), which lets you use the [wpvideo] shortcode in your posts.

■ Playing Audio Files

Sometimes, you'll want to give readers a way to play an audio clip (or several) without using a full-blown video window. An obvious example is if you're a music artist promoting your work. However, audio files are equally well-suited to the spoken word, whether that's an interview, talk show, sermon, audio book, or motivational lecture. Audio files are particularly useful if you want to join the Web's thriving community of *podcasters*—sites that provide downloadable long audio files that users can listen to on the go (for example, on their iPods or smartphones).

You might expect that adding audio to your WordPress site is easier than adding video. After all, audio files are smaller and simpler than video files. However, you'll face many of the same issues. In the following sections, you'll consider three strategies for getting audio into a web page.

Adding a Basic Audio Player

The simplest approach to hosting audio is to upload the audio file to your website. You can then provide a link that readers can use to download your audio file or (even better) a tiny audio player that lets them listen without leaving your site (Figure 10-20).

Before you get started, you need to upload your audio file. Ideally, you'll upload an MP3 file to ensure the best cross-browser support. Technically, Internet Explorer, Safari, and Google Chrome support MP3 files, but Firefox and Opera don't. However, most websites get by using Flash to fill the gap. Essentially, the process works like this:

- If the browser you use supports both MP3 files and HTML5 markup, WordPress creates an HTML5 <audio> element that points to your MP3 file. The browser then creates a miniature audio player, like the one shown in Figure 10-20.

- If a browser doesn't support these two standards, WordPress uses a small Flash application that creates a tiny audio player. The end result is the same—your guests see (and hear) a simple music player.

- In the unlikely event that the browser can't meet either of these requirements—in other words, it doesn't support MP3 files with HTML5, and it doesn't have the Flash plug-in—WordPress swaps in an ordinary HTML link. Click the link, and you can download the audio file to your computer, where you can play it using a desktop music player.

The Flash-fallback solution is a good one, but it's a bit too messy to implement on your own. Fortunately, WordPress helps you out with the [audio] shortcode. If you use WordPress.com, this shortcode is always available. If you build a self-hosted WordPress site, you need to install the Jetpack plug-in to get it.

The [audio] shortcode is every bit as straightforward as it should be. You simply put the URL that points to your audio file inside the square brackets. Here's an example that launches an MP3 file on another web server:

```
[audio http://wpcom.files.wordpress.com/2007/01/mattmullenweg-interview.mp3]
```

You can also use the [audio] shortcode to play music files stored on your own website. But before you go any further, there's a significant catch that applies if WordPress.com hosts your site. Unless you buy a space upgrade or the WordPress value bundle (page 342), WordPress.com won't let you upload *any* audio files, even if you have plenty of space left in your initial 3 GB allotment. Instead, you're limited to playing audio files stored on other sites.

Depending on what you're trying to accomplish, this audio file limit might be a minor inconvenience or completely unworkable. If it's the latter, you have two options. You can buy a space upgrade for as little as $20 a year (just click the Store menu in the dashboard to sign up). Or, you can use a music hosting service, as covered on page 347.

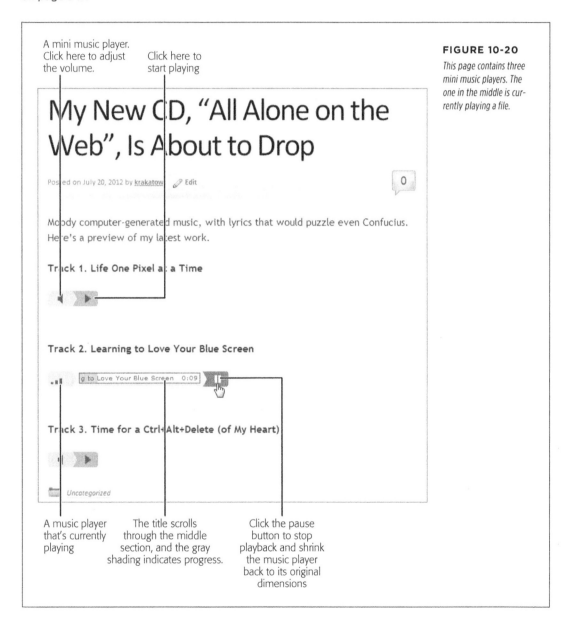

A mini music player. Click here to adjust the volume.

Click here to start playing

FIGURE 10-20

This page contains three mini music players. The one in the middle is currently playing a file.

My New CD, "All Alone on the Web", Is About to Drop

Posted on July 20, 2012 by krakatow   Edit   0

Moody computer-generated music, with lyrics that would puzzle even Confucius. Here's a preview of my latest work.

Track 1. Life One Pixel at a Time

Track 2. Learning to Love Your Blue Screen

g to Love Your Blue Screen   0:09

Track 3. Time for a Ctrl+Alt+Delete (of My Heart)

Uncategorized

A music player that's currently playing

The title scrolls through the middle section, and the gray shading indicates progress.

Click the pause button to stop playback and shrink the music player back to its original dimensions

If you want to use the [audio] shortcode to play one of your own files, you can follow the three-step process of uploading it to the media library, copying the web address, and pasting that into your post (see page 189). But there's a shorter and quicker option that lets you upload your audio and insert the [audio] shortcode at the same time, without forcing you to do any of the typing. Here's what to do:

1. **First, click Upload/Insert link above the post editor.**

   This is the same link you use to upload a picture.

2. **In the Add Media window, pick your audio file.**

   Now, wait for it to upload.

> **NOTE** If you try this on a WordPress.com site that doesn't have the space upgrade, nothing will happen, so don't waste your time.

3. **When you finish uploading the track, fill in its title.**

   The music player displays the title while the track plays (Figure 10-20). If you don't supply a title, the player IDs it as "Track 1."

4. **Copy the URL from the Link URL box.**

   This is what you'll use in the [audio] shortcode.

5. **Now click the small X button in the top-right corner of the Add Media window to close it.**

   This returns you to your post.

6. **Paste the URL inside your [audio] shortcode, just as you would for an audio file on someone else's web server.**

   Make sure the shortcode is on a separate line and that WordPress doesn't turn it into a link. If it does, select the text and click the Unlink button.

7. **Now publish your post.**

   You'll be rewarded with a tiny music player. You can repeat this process to add as many music players as you want to the same page.

> **NOTE** If you build a self-hosted site, you don't need to stick with Jetpack and the [audio] shortcode. There are dozens of other plug-ins that offer similar features—just search for "MP3 player." Examples include oEmbed HTML5 audio (*http://tinyurl.com/oembed*), which automatically replaces any MP3 URL with a music player; and MediaElement.js (*http://tinyurl.com/media-element*), which supports Flash fallbacks with audio files *and* self-hosted video.

Using a Music Sharing Service

If you're serious about sharing a set of audio tracks—for example, you're a band trying to popularize your work—your best bet is to sign up with a serious music-sharing service.

The first advantage is that a good music service increases the exposure of your audio tracks. Casual music browsers may stumble across your work, similar artists may link to it, and just about anyone can add a comment or click "Like," which boosts your buzz. The second advantage is that you'll get a number of extra refinements, like the ability to provide music in different formats for different browsers (without resorting to Flash), and a sleek jukebox-style player that can seamlessly play through a whole list of your songs.

WordPress.com has built-in support for a number of music sharing services through its shortcode system. However, self-hosted WordPress sites won't feel the shortcode love until you install Jetpack.

WordPress.com and Jetpack support the following services:

- SoundCloud
- Spotify
- Rdio
- Bandcamp
- 8tracks

Once again, the actual shortcode syntax varies subtly for each service, so you need to get the exact details from *http://support.wordpress.com/shortcodes*. Figure 10-21 shows a site that uses SoundCloud.

SoundCloud offers a sweet deal: no charge for the first 120 minutes of audio that you upload, and a polished music player that makes almost any music look good. If you need more storage space, you need to pay a yearly fee. (Currently, that's $42 a year for 240 minutes, or $114 per year for a whopping 12 hours.) If you plan to sell your music, a service like Bandcamp may make more sense—they give you unlimited room to store audio but take a percentage of your sales, if anyone buys your tracks.

To sign up with SoundCloud, start at *http://soundcloud.com*, click Sign Up, and follow the instructions. Once you upload some audio files, you can start embedding them in your WordPress posts. SoundCloud gives you the option of a single-track music player, or you can assemble a group of tracks into a playlist (as in Figure 10-21) and upload a player for the set. Either way, click the Share button when you're ready to embed (Figure 10-22). Click WordPress, and SoundCloud gives you the WordPress shortcode you need, which will look something like this:

```
[soundcloud url="http://api.soundcloud.com/users/1664614" iframe="true" /]
```

Paste that into a post, and you'll get the player shown in Figure 10-21.

FIGURE 10-21

The SoundCloud music player is more refined than just about any other plug-in-powered music player. It includes the artist's profile picture, a list of tracks, and a waveform of the song that's currently playing.

FIGURE 10-22

To get a shortcode for WordPress, click Share, and then WordPress, and then copy the link it provides.

Podcasting

So far, you've seen how to let viewers play individual audio tracks or a playlist with a bunch of music on it. *Podcasting* is a similar, but slightly different way to present audio. It gives readers the choice of listening to audio files the normal way (in their browsers, by clicking the Play button) or downloading the audio files, so they can put them on a mobile device.

The central idea with podcasting is that you prepare content that busy people will listen to while they're on the go. Usually, the content is long—30 minutes to an hour is common for an individual podcast file. If your audio file is only a couple of minutes long, it's not worth a visitor's trouble to download it and transfer it to a mobile device.

Podcast creators also tend to organize podcasts in groups—for example, making each audio file an episode in a longer series, and releasing them at regular intervals (say, weekly). Good examples of podcasts include a web show with commentary and interviews, a motivational lecture, a spoken chapter from an audio book, or a 45-minute techno mix for a workout session.

> **NOTE** The word *podcasting* is a mash-up of *pod* and *broadcast—pod* because this form of audio file distribution first gained popularity with the iPod music player, and *broadcasting* because a podcast-creator provides easily accessible, regularly released audio "shows," a concept that's a bit like television broadcasting.

■ CREATING PODCAST-FRIENDLY AUDIO

You don't need any special technique to upload a podcast audio file. You can simply create a post and add an ordinary link to the file. If you want to get a bit fancier, you can use the audio-embedding feature described on page 312 (provided you use WordPress.com or you have Jetpack installed). That way, visitors can play the audio in their browser if they haven't caught the podcast bug.

Podcast audio files should be in the MP3 format, because that gives them the best support over a range of mobile devices. You can also create podcast *video* files, but that process is a bit more complicated. You'll need to first make sure the video is in MP4 format, and then upload it somewhere, and then add a link in your post that points to it.

> **NOTE** If you want to use a video file for podcasting *and* embed it so guests can play it directly inside their browser, you'll need the help of a high-caliber podcasting plug-in, as explained in the box on page 351.

■ GETTING YOUR PODCAST FEED

Although podcast audio is the same as normal audio, there's a slight difference in the way you *present* podcasts. For readers to find your podcasts quickly and download new episodes easily, you need a way to separate these audio files from the rest of your site.

To do that, you create a dedicated category for the posts that contain podcasts. You can give this category a name like "Podcasts" or "Lectures" or "Audio Book." Then, when you create a new post that has an audio file in it, and you want to include that audio as part of your podcast, assign the post your podcast-specific category (Figure 10-23). Depending on the structure of your site (and the way you let viewers browse it), you may decide to set two categories—one to identify the type of post (say, "Sports"), and one to flag this as a podcast ("Podcasts").

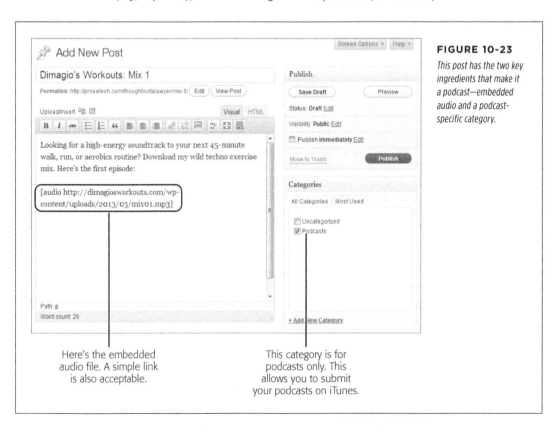

FIGURE 10-23

This post has the two key ingredients that make it a podcast—embedded audio and a podcast-specific category.

Here's the embedded audio file. A simple link is also acceptable.

This category is for podcasts only. This allows you to submit your podcasts on iTunes.

You group audio files into a single podcast category so you can generate a *feed* for that category. As you'll learn on page 408, a feed is a sort of index to your content. In the case of podcasting, your feed tells other programs and websites where to get the podcast audio files on your site. It also lets you notify visitors when you publish a new audio file—say, if they're subscribed to your podcast in iTunes.

NOTE iTunes is one of the favorite tools for podcast-lovers. If your site offers podcasts, and you'd like to use them to attract new visitors (and why wouldn't you?), you need to submit some podcast information to iTunes.

You can get the feed for a category using a URL with this syntax:

```
http://[Site]/category/[CategoryName]/feed
```

So if you have a site named *http://dimagiosworkouts.com*, you can get a feed for the Podcasts category like this:

```
http://dimagiosworkouts.com/category/podcasts/feed
```

This is a valuable link—it's the piece of information you need to supply to iTunes to register your podcast.

To register with iTunes, start by reviewing Apple's instructions at *http://tinyurl.com/podcastspecs*. First, read the "Testing Your Feed" section, which explains how to make sure your feed includes the podcast files you expect, and that the feed works. Then, follow up with the instructions in the "Submitting Your Podcast to the iTunes Store" section to learn how to officially tell iTunes about your feed, and make it visible to a podcast-hungry audience of millions.

Better Podcasting with a Plug-In

Podcasting with WordPress is easy. All you need is the right type of audio file (MP3) and a post category just for podcasts.

However, if you're a power podcaster—meaning you plan to invest serious effort in making podcasting a part of your web presence—it's worth considering a plug-in that can make your life easier. The most popular podcasting plug-in for self-hosted WordPress sites is Blubrry PowerPress (*http://tinyurl.com/wp-podcast*).

Among PowerPress's most useful features is its tight iTunes support. PowerPress can optimize your feeds for iTunes, submit your feed to iTunes, and even help you manage your iTunes cover art. PowerPress is also invaluable if you want to forge into the world of video podcasting, because it lets you embed your video content in your page, using a JavaScript-based video player. (That way, visitors have the choice of downloading it for a mobile device, as usual, or playing it right in their browser, as they would with a YouTube video.) PowerPress also offers statistics that help you gauge the popularity of your podcasts and an optional paid hosting plan for audio and video files.

Collaborating with Multiple Authors

When you start out with WordPress, it's a solo affair. You choose your site's theme, write every post and page, and put every widget in place. Your readers can add their own comments, but you're the one in charge of starting every conversation.

You might like this arrangement (and if so, that's fine). But WordPress also makes it possible for you to have friends, colleagues, family members, and even complete strangers contribute to your site. For example, you can create a site where several people can post content, or you could be more selective, letting some people write content and others review and edit it. You can also implement an approval system so you can check the work of other contributors before it goes live, and you can even create an entirely private site that can be viewed only by the people you approve.

In this chapter, you'll learn how to enable all these features by registering new users—not new *visitors*, but new *users* who have special privileges to use your site. You'll also consider WordPress's more ambitious multisite feature that's open to self-hosters only. With a multisite network, you can let other people create their own sites on *your* web server. For example, big companies can use the multisite feature to give each employee a personal blog. Essentially, the multisite feature lets a whole family of WordPress sites exist side-by-side, on the same domain.

◾ Adding Users to Your Site

A new WordPress website starts with only one user: *you*. You assume the role of administrator, which means you can do anything from write a post to vaporize the entire site.

Eventually, you may decide to make room for company. Usually, you make that decision because you want to work with co-authors, who will write posts for your site.

Before you add another user to your site, though, you need to decide what role they should play. WordPress recognizes five types of user, listed here in order of most to least powerful:

- **Administrator.** Administrators can do absolutely everything. For example, if you add a friend as an administrator to your site, he can remove you, delete all your posts, and switch your site to a Hawaiian beach theme. WordPress strongly recommends that every site have just one administrator, to prevent power struggles.

- **Editor.** Editors have full control over all posts and pages. They can create their own posts, and they can edit or delete any post, even ones they didn't create. Editors can also manage post categories and tags, upload files, and moderate comments. They can't change site settings, tweak the site's layout and theme, or manage users.

- **Author.** Authors have control over their posts *only*. They can create new ones and upload pictures, and they can edit or delete their posts at any time. Everyone else's content is off limits.

- **Contributor.** Contributors are a more limited form of author. They can create draft posts, but they can't actually publish them. Instead, contributors submit their work for review, and an editor or administrator must approve and publish it. Sadly, contributors can't upload pictures, even for their own posts.

- **Follower or Subscriber.** These users can read posts and add comments. Word-Press.com calls them followers, while WordPress.org calls them subscribers. If you run a WordPress.com site, it automatically notifies your followers about newly posted content (and these notifications may be emailed to them, depending on their personal preferences). If you run a self-hosted site, your subscribers won't get any notifications, but they can opt-in to an email subscription service (page 401).

Now that you know what types of user WordPress recognizes, you're ready to start creating new accounts. There's one wrinkle, however. The steps you take for a self-hosted site are significantly different than they are for a WordPress.com site. If you're a self-hoster, continue reading to the next section, "Creating a New User for a Self-Hosted Site." If you're a WordPress.com fan, skip ahead to the section named "Inviting Users to a WordPress.com Site" on page 358.

The Role of a Subscriber

Why would I add subscribers? Can't everyone read my posts and make comments?

Ordinarily, there are no limits to who can read posts and write comments. In that way, subscribers are no different than regular, unregistered guests. Yes, subscribers may get email notifications about your content (if your site is hosted on Word-Press.com, or if you've added the right plug-in to a WordPress.org site). But they certainly won't get any extra privileges.

However, the situation changes in these special cases:

- If you create a private site (page 373), every reader needs a subscriber account. Without one, they won't be able to access any part of your site.

- If you restrict comments with the "Users must be registered and logged in to comment" setting on a self-hosted site, and you don't allow Facebook or Twitter logins (page 259), only subscribers can leave comments. This is a pretty severe restriction, and few sites use it.

- If you add a social plug-in like BuddyPress (*http://buddypress.org*), you'll want to give user accounts to as many people as possible in the hope that they exploit the plug-in's enhanced features, like sharing content with friends and chatting in discussion groups. That'll make your site feel more like a community.

Creating a New User for a Self-Hosted Site

Using the dashboard, you can register new users, one at a time. You supply a few key details (like a user name, password, and email address), and let your users take it from there.

Here's what to do:

1. **Choose Users→Add New.**

   This loads the Add New User page (Figure 11-1).

2. **Choose a good user name for the person you're inviting.**

   The best approach is to use a consistent system that you can apply to every user you add. For example, you might choose to combine a person's first and last name, separated by an underscore (like *sam_picheski*) for all user names.

3. **Type in the user's email address.**

   WordPress uses the address to send the user important notifications, including password resets.

4. **Optionally, specify a user's first name, last name, and website.**

   These are three descriptive details that become part of the user's profile.

Help ▼

👥 Add New User

Create a brand new user and add it to this site.

Username *(required)*	dianejenkins
E-mail *(required)*	diane_j43@hotmail.com
First Name	Diane
Last Name	Jenkins
Website	
Password *(twice, required)*	••••••••••
	••••••••••

Strong

Hint: The password should be at least seven characters long. To make it stronger, use upper and lower case letters, numbers and symbols like ! " ? $ % ^ &).

Send Password?	☑ Send this password to the new user by email.
Role	Subscriber ▾

Subscriber
Administrator
Editor
Author
Contributor

Add New User

FIGURE 11-1

There's nothing mysterious about the Add New User page. Here, the site's administrator has entered the sign-up information for a new user named dianejenkins, and is picking the user type from the Role drop-down list.

5. **Type in a strong password. (See the box on page 37 for tips.)**

When you create a new account, you *must* supply a password—WordPress doesn't let users pick their passwords the first time they log in. However, if you turn on the "Send this password to the new user by email" checkbox, WordPress emails your new user her user name and password, along with a link to your site's login page (Figure 11-2). (And even if you don't ask, WordPress sends you, the administrator, an email with a record of the new user's name and email address.)

NOTE The emails WordPress sends often end up in an email account's junk folder, because they contain links. Therefore, you may need to tell new users to check their junk mail to find the message with their WordPress credentials.

FIGURE 11-2

Here's the message WordPress sends to newly registered users if you tick the "Send this password to the new user by email" checkbox. Sadly, WordPress doesn't let you add a custom welcome message or any extra information.

TIP If a frustrated user arrives at your site but doesn't know his password, he can click the "Lost your password" link on the login page. WordPress emails him a link that lets him pick a new password.

6. **Pick a role from the drop-down list.**

   You can use any of the user types described on page 354.

7. **Click Add New User.**

   WordPress creates the user, sends a notification email (if you chose the "Send this password..." option), and takes you to the Users→All Users section of the dashboard. There, you can review a list of every user you've ever added. Hover over one of them and you'll see two straightforward links—use Edit to change the info in a user account and Delete to remove the account.

   If you choose to edit a user's info, you'll see that user's full profile page, which includes details that aren't in the Add New User page. For example, you can tweak personal preferences like the dashboard's color scheme and proofreading settings. Usually, you won't worry about these details—instead, you'll let invited people configure their own profiles. If you do make any changes, click Update Profile before you move on.

TIP If you're adding accounts for people who have never used WordPress before, you may want to change the "Display name publicly as" setting, so that posts are signed with the person's full name (like Diane Jenkins) rather than the shortened WordPress user name (like *djenkins42*). This makes it easier for readers to tell who's written what content on your site.

Helping Your Users Log In

To log into your site, users need to request the *login* page. That means that if your site is at *http://cantonschool.org*, they need to visit *http://cantonschool.org/login*. Alternatively, users can go straight to the dashboard by requesting the *wp-admin* page (as in *http://cantonschool.org/wp-admin*). In this case, WordPress automatically asks them to log in before they can continue.

If you have a lot of users who haven't used WordPress before, you may need to help them find the login or dashboard page. Here are two good options:

- You can create your own welcome email message that contains a link to the login page, and send it to every

user. Use your favorite email program or get the Email Users plug-in (*http://tinyurl.com/emailusers*), which lets you send a mass email to all your users at once. That's a big help if you don't have their email addresses handy.

- You can add a link that goes to your login page. Put that link in the main site menu, or add the link to a sidebar using a Text widget (page 155) or a Custom Menu widget (page 219). Make sure you give your link some descriptive text that clearly explains why your user needs to log in, like "Log in to write your own posts" or "Log in as a contributor."

Inviting Users to a WordPress.com Site

Before you can register someone as a user on your WordPress.com site, that person must have a WordPress.com account. Some people may already have one (for example, they might have their own site or they may be following other people's blogs). Non-WordPressers will need to sign up, and they need to do it themselves—you can't create a WordPress.com account for someone else.

Instead, your job is simply to *invite* people to become users. For example, imagine you invite two friends, Cathy and Sanjeev. Cathy is already a WordPress.com user, which means that all she needs to do is accept your invitation. WordPress then authorizes her to read, edit, or manage your site (depending on the user role you grant her). On the other hand, Sanjeev isn't a WordPress.com user, so WordPress asks him to create an account. Once he does, Sanjeev can accept your invitation and become a user, just like Cathy.

You can invite one person or several at a time. The only rule is that if you create an invitation for several people, all those people must be the same type of user. That means you can invite a batch of followers all at once, or a group of contributors, but not a mix of the two.

To create an invitation, follow these steps:

1. **Choose Users→Invite New in the dashboard.**

2. **Enter a list of email addresses, one for each person you want to invite, separated by commas (Figure 11-3).**

   If you're inviting someone who already has a WordPress.com account, you can supply the WordPress.com user name instead of an email address (either way, the invitation reads the same).

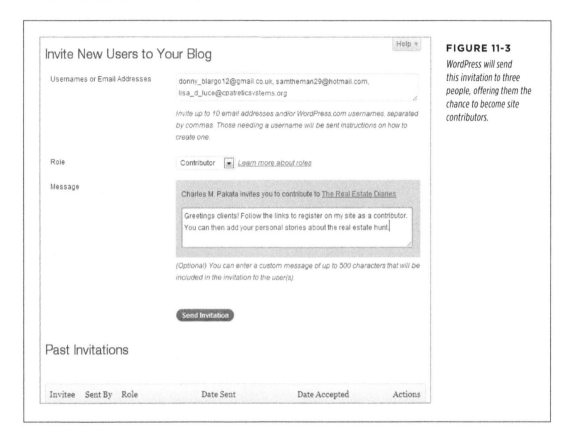

FIGURE 11-3

WordPress will send this invitation to three people, offering them the chance to become site contributors.

3. **Choose the user type from the Role drop-down list.**

   You can use any of the user types described on page 354.

4. **In the Message box, type a short invitation.**

   For example, if you're inviting contributors, you might write "Come share your stories on my blog." This message will become part of the welcome message that WordPress sends to each person you invite (Figure 11-4).

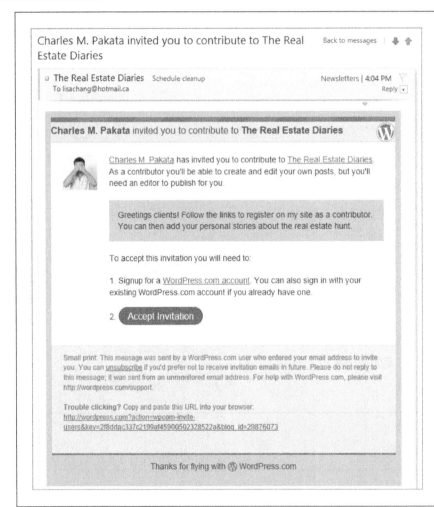

Charles M. Pakata invited you to contribute to The Real Estate Diaries   Back to messages

☐ The Real Estate Diaries   Schedule cleanup   Newsletters | 4:04 PM
   To lisachang@hotmail.ca   Reply ▾

Charles M. Pakata invited you to contribute to **The Real Estate Diaries**

Charles M. Pakata has invited you to contribute to The Real Estate Diaries.
As a contributor you'll be able to create and edit your own posts, but you'll
need an editor to publish for you.

Greetings clients! Follow the links to register on my site as a contributor.
You can then add your personal stories about the real estate hunt.

To accept this invitation you will need to:

1. Signup for a WordPress.com account! You can also sign in with your
existing WordPress.com account if you already have one.

2. Accept Invitation

Small print: This message was sent by a WordPress.com user who entered your email address to invite
you. You can unsubscribe if you'd prefer not to receive invitation emails in future. Please do not reply to
this message; it was sent from an unmonitored email address. For help with WordPress.com, please visit
http://wordpress.com/support.

Trouble clicking? Copy and paste this URL into your browser:
http://wordpress.com?action=wpcom-invite-
users&key=2f8ddac337c2199af45900502328522a&blog_id=29876073

Thanks for flying with ⓦ WordPress.com

FIGURE 11-4

Here, site owner Charles Pakata is inviting Lisa Chang to contribute to his WordPress site, "The Real Estate Diaries." If Chang clicks the Accept Invitation button, WordPress will prompt her to sign in with her WordPress.com account (or to create an account if she doesn't have one). She can then accept the invitation and become a contributor.

5. **Click Send Invitation.**

   WordPress sends the invitation into cyberspace.

   Below, on the same Invite New Users to Your Blog page, WordPress keeps track of who you invited and how they responded (Figure 11-5). These records remain in the list until you delete them (more about that in a moment).

   If you think a previously invited person missed your email, you can ask WordPress to send it again by clicking the Resend link. If you want to revoke an invitation that hasn't been accepted, click Delete. Now, if that person clicks the activation link in the invitation message, WordPress displays an error message.

If a user has already registered, you may choose to click Delete to remove the invitation record so you can focus on the people who haven't responded. Deleting an invitation for an already registered user has no effect on the user—he remains registered on your site. (If you decide that you *do* want to want to take down an existing user, you need to go to the Users→All Users section of the dashboard, and click the Remove link next to the persona non grata.)

> **NOTE** The Users→All Users page shows all the administrators, editors, authors, and contributors you've signed up. It doesn't include mere followers, because they have no special powers on your site.

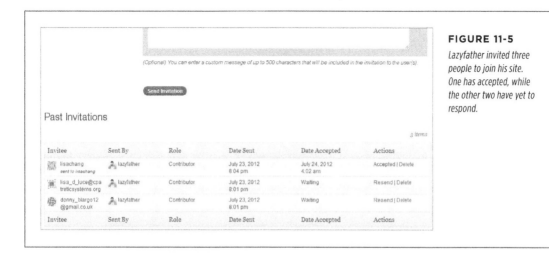

FIGURE 11-5

Lazyfather invited three people to join his site. One has accepted, while the other two have yet to respond.

Working with Authors

The most common reason to add new users to your WordPress site is to get more content from more people. After all, new and interesting content is the lifeblood of any site, and by recruiting others to help you write it, you increase the odds that your site will grow and flourish.

As you already learned, all but one type of WordPress user (followers for WordPress.com sites, subscribers for self-hosted sites) can write posts. Whether you're an administrator, editor, author, or contributor, the first step is the same. To write a post, you must begin by logging into the dashboard.

WordPress tailors the dashboard to the user type, so that each person sees only the menu commands they can use. For example, if you log in as a contributor, you'll see the stripped-down dashboard in Figure 11-6.

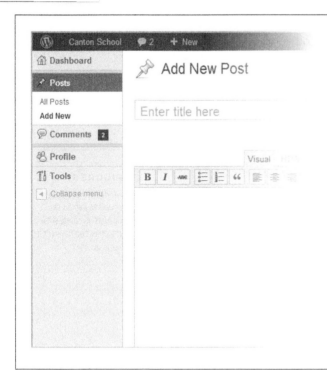

If you run a site on WordPress.com, all users except followers can access the dashboard. That's because, in WordPress.com, a user's profile information isn't tied to your site—it's actually part of that person's WordPress.com user account. Thus, there's no need for followers to get into your site's dashboard to change their profile.

If you run a self-hosted site, every type of user can log in to the dashboard, although subscribers get just one option—the Profile command that lets them change their preferences and personal information.

Either way, the only type of user who can see the full, unrestricted version of the dashboard is an administrator—and, ideally, that's just you.

> **NOTE** To go directly to the dashboard, users can add */wp-admin* to the end of your site URL (as in *http://lazyfather.wordpress.com/wp-admin*). If your site is hosted on WordPress.com, users can also access the dashboard through their WordPress.com account when they log in at *http://wordpress.com*. For example, contributors will see your site in their list of blogs at *http://wordpress.com/my-blogs*, along with handy links for creating a new post, reviewing drafts, or visiting the dashboard.

The Post Approval Process

Administrators, editors, and authors can add posts and pages to your site in the usual way. When they finish writing, they simply click Publish to make the content go live.

As you know, contributors have more limited site powers. They can create posts, but not publish them, which gives you a broad safety net—there's no chance bad content can get on your site, because you get to review it first. When contributors create posts, they have two options: they can save the post as a draft so they can return and edit it later, or they can submit it for review (Figure 11-7).

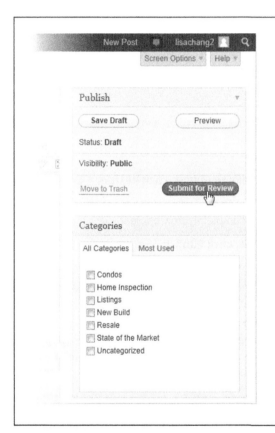

FIGURE 11-7

When a contributor logs in to your site, WordPress changes the familiar Publish button to a "Submit for Review" button.

When a contributor submits a post this way, WordPress assigns it a special status, called *pending*. A pending post won't appear on your site until an editor or administrator approves it. Here's how you do that:

1. **On the dashboard, choose Posts→All Posts.**

2. **Click the Pending link (Figure 11-8).**

FIGURE 11-8

When a contributor submits a post for review, it becomes a pending post.

3. **If you see a pending post you'd like to review, click its title.**

   WordPress opens the post in the Edit Post window. Make any changes you want, from minor corrections to adding completely new content.

4. **If the post is ready for prime time, click Publish.**

   This is the same way you publish your own posts. However, the newly published post's byline will have the original author's name, even if you edited the post.

   If you made changes to the post but you're not quite ready to publish it, click "Save as Pending" to store the edited version. For example, you might use this technique to add your own questions or comments inside someone else's work. You can wrap your comments in square brackets, [like this]. The post author can then make changes and re-submit the post.

NOTE Don't be confused by the way WordPress uses the term "author." Even though WordPress has a specific type of user called *author*, WordPress experts often use the same term to refer to anyone who writes a post on a WordPress site. Thus, administrators, authors, editors, and contributors can all act as post authors.

Browsing an Author's Posts

Just as you can view all the posts in a particular category or all the posts that have the same tag, so you can browse all the posts by an author. The easiest way to do that is to click the author's name, which appears just before or after the post content, depending on the theme (Figure 11-9).

Better Workflow for Reviewing Posts

WordPress includes the basic infrastructure you need to get multiple contributors working together on the same site. However, the process has a few rough edges.

The problem is the *workflow*—the way a task passes from one person to another. Right now, it's up to editors or administrators to go looking for pending posts. WordPress makes no effort to notify you that there's content waiting for review. Similarly, if an administrator edits a post but decides it needs more work, there's no easy way to let the contributor know that you need a rewrite. And when you *do* publish a pending post, WordPress once again fails to notify the original author.

The creators of WordPress are aware of these gaps, and they may fix them in future versions of the program. But because the contributor feature is a bit of a specialized tool, these fixes are low on the list of WordPress priorities.

However, if you run a self-hosted site and want to implement a better system, there's a plug-in that can change everything. It's called Edit Flow (*http://tinyurl.com/editflow*) and it adds everything you need to manage a multistage review process, including:

- **Custom statuses.** Instead of simply designating a post as "Pending" or "Published," you can give it a status that

reflects its stage in your organization's workflow. For example, if you run a news site, you might want posts to go from "Pitched" to "Assigned" to "Pending Review" to "Published." Edit Flow can help manage that sequence.

- **Editorial comments.** Edit Flow lets users attach short notes to a post as it whizzes back and forth between them (as in "I love your post, but can you expand on paragraph 3?")

- **Email notifications.** Edit Flow can send notifications at key points in the review process—when authors submit new posts for review, when an editor publishes a post, when an editor places a comment on a post asking for changes, and so on. On a bustling site, these emails keep the post review process running quickly and efficiently.

- **Calendar.** If you want to make a long-term content plan to spread out your authors' work, and make sure there's always something new on your site, the Edit Flow editorial calendar can help.

Although Edit Flow is stuffed full of features, they're arranged in a logical way, and you can find helpful information at *http://editflow.org*. If you need to coordinate the publishing efforts of a small or mid-sized group of people, don't be afraid to give it a whirl.

NOTE The name that WordPress uses to sign posts is the user's *display name*, which might be the WordPress user name (the default), the person's full first and last names, or a nickname. Users can configure their display names by editing their profile settings (Users→My Profile).

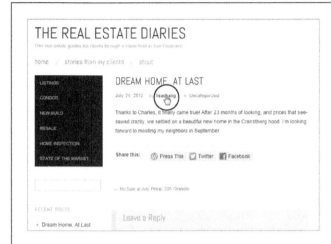

THE REAL ESTATE DIARIES

One real estate guides his clients through a house hunt in San Francisco

home / stories from my clients / about

LISTINGS
CONDOS
NEW BUILD
RESALE
HOME INSPECTION
STATE OF THE MARKET

DREAM HOME, AT LAST

July 24, 2012   By lisachang   in Uncategorized

Thanks to Charles, it finally came true! After 23 months of looking, and prices that see-sawed crazily, we settled on a beautiful new home in the Cransberg hood. I'm looking forward to meeting my neighbors in September

Share this: Press This   Twitter   Facebook

← No Sale at Any Price: 205 Grandio

RECENT POSTS

Leave a Reply

• Dream Home, At Last

FIGURE 11-9

By clicking a user name (in this case, lisachang), you can dig up all the posts that author wrote.

FREQUENTLY ASKED QUESTION

Co-Authoring Posts

What if several people edit the same post? Can they all be credited as authors?

If you're curious to know who has worked on a post, you can use WordPress's revision-tracking feature. First, edit the post. Then, click the Screen Options button (in the top-right corner) and then turn on the checkbox next to Revisions. Now you'll see a Revisions box that lists every time someone has saved the post, the date and time of the save, and the name of the person who saved it.

Revision-tracking is neat, but that information isn't visible to your readers. All they see is the post author—the person who initially created the post. Even when someone else edits a post, it remains the property of the initial author. An editor or administrator can edit a post and attribute it to someone else, but it isn't possible to have two people credited as authors on the same post at the same time—unless you're running a self-hosted site and you're willing to fiddle with your theme, as explained next.

To create true, co-authored posts, you need to take two steps. First, you need to add the Co-Authors Plus plug-in (*http://tinyurl.com/co-authors-plus*), which lets you designate multiple authors for any post or page. The second task is the hard part—getting your posts and pages to display the names of *all* the authors who worked on them. To make that possible, you need to edit your theme, as the Co-Authors Plus plug-in explains (see *http://tinyurl.com/ccr7896*).

WordPress uses a special URL syntax to make it easy to browse posts by author. For example, if you click *lisachang*, WordPress adds */author/lisachang* to the end of the site address, like this:

```
http://therealestatediaries.com/author/lisachang
```

This is essentially the same way that category URLs work (page 113).

Now that you know how to get the posts for a specific author, you can make it easier for visitors to get them as well. For example, you could create a menu that has a link for each author. You could then use that menu in the main menu area of your site (Figure 11-10) or in a sidebar, with the help of the Custom Menu widget (page 219).

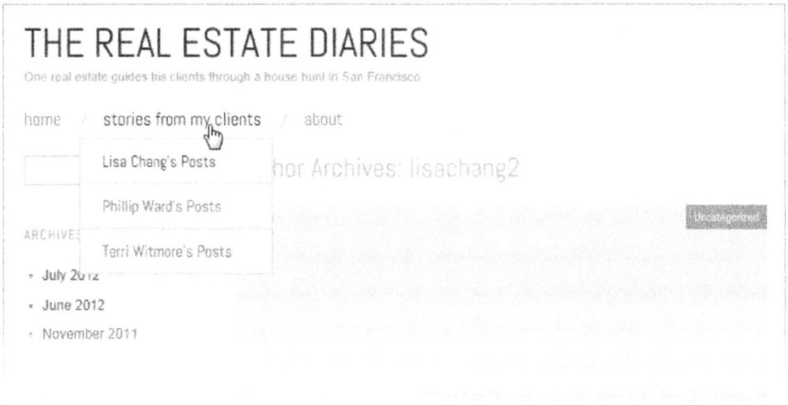

FIGURE 11-10

This menu includes a link for each author, making it easy for readers to browse posts by author.

PLUG-IN POWER

More Ways to Browse Authors

The custom menu approach gives you a great way to create author links. But if you're building a self-hosted site, you may want to check out one of the many author-browsing plug-ins, which give you more display options and may save a bit of effort.

The Authors Widget (*http://tinyurl.com/authorswidget*) is a basic but effective example. It offers two display modes. The first is a list that's not much different from what you'd build with the Custom Menu widget, just slightly more convenient, and with the option of showing the post count next to each

author's name. The second display mode is an author *cloud* that works like the Tag Cloud widget (page 154), creating a jumbled mass of author links, with the most prolific authors' names the biggest.

The Author Avatars List plug-in (*http://tinyurl.com/author avatars*) is one of many author-browsing widgets that use avatars, the tiny headshots that you can pair up with any email account (page 251). As with the more pedestrian author list, you can click an author headshot to start browsing the author's posts.

Adding Author Information

Ordinarily, WordPress keeps author information to a minimum. Even though it stores a few key details in each user's profile—including a basic "Biographical info" box—none of these details show up in a post. All your readers see is the author's name.

In some cases, you might prefer to showcase your author. For example, you might want to add a more detailed byline or include a brief bio that highlights the author's achievements. The low-tech solution is to add this information to the bottom of the post (consider setting it in *italics* to make it stand apart from the rest of the content). But if you run a self-hosted site, this is one more challenge you can tackle with the right plug-in.

The WordPress plug-in repository is overflowing with author info widgets and bio boxes. One decent starting point is the WP About Author plug-in (*http://tinyurl. com/wp-about-author*), which automatically adds an author box to the bottom of every post. The WP About Author plug-in also adds several new text boxes to every user's profile, where authors can enter links to other sites where they have public pages (like Facebook, Twitter, and Pinterest). The author box will then include links to these pages (Figure 11-11).

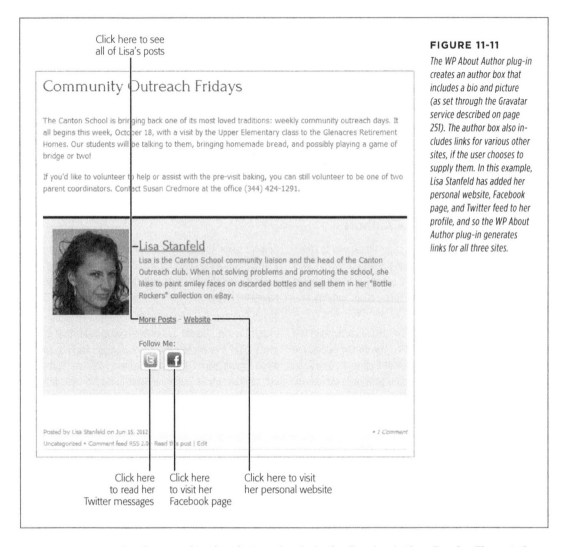

Click here to see all of Lisa's posts

FIGURE 11-11

The WP About Author plug-in creates an author box that includes a bio and picture (as set through the Gravatar service described on page 251). The author box also includes links for various other sites, if the user chooses to supply them. In this example, Lisa Stanfeld has added her personal website, Facebook page, and Twitter feed to her profile, and so the WP About Author plug-in generates links for all three sites.

Click here to read her Twitter messages

Click here to visit her Facebook page

Click here to visit her personal website

Another good author footer plug-in is the Fancier Author Box by ThematoSoup (*http://tinyurl.com/authorbox*). It uses a slightly smaller version of the author picture, fewer links, and a neat-o two-tab view that lets you see the author's recent posts without leaving the current page (Figure 11-12).

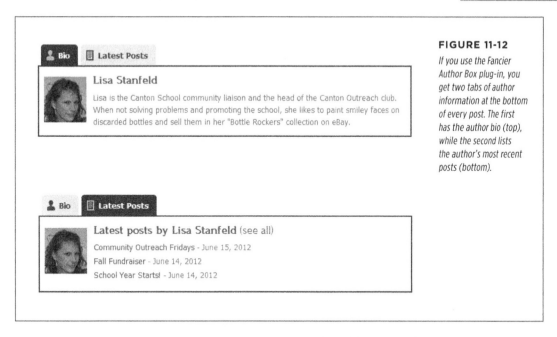

FIGURE 11-12

If you use the Fancier Author Box plug-in, you get two tabs of author information at the bottom of every post. The first has the author bio (top), while the second lists the author's most recent posts (bottom).

Finally, you can use one of several plug-ins that puts author information into a widget. That way, you can take the author details out of a post and tuck them into a sidebar. One such plug-in is Author Spotlight (*http://tinyurl.com/authorspot*). Of course, this idea works only if your theme includes a sidebar in its single-post view. The WordPress standard, Twenty Eleven, includes a sidebar on the main post page, but doesn't include one on single-post pages, so author box widgets aren't much use.

Removing Authors (and Other Users)

As your site evolves, the group of contributors you work with may change. You already know how to *add* contributors, but at some point you may decide to *remove* a user. To do that, you first need to view your site's user list by choosing Users→All Users.

If your site is on WordPress.com, the user list includes all the administrators, editors, authors, and contributors registered on your site (it doesn't include followers). To remove a user, hover over the person's name and click the Remove link. That user's WordPress.com account remains intact, but they no longer have privileges on your site. If you remove a user who has posts on your site, the posts will remain (although you can delete them by going to the Posts→All Posts list).

If you run a self-hosted site, the user list includes everyone who can access your site. Unlike a WordPress.com site, you don't merely remove users, you *delete* them by clicking the Delete link. Deleting a user account is a fairly drastic step, because it completely wipes the traces of that person off of your site. WordPress will ask you what to do with any posts that belong to the newly deleted user (Figure 11-13). You can either delete the posts, too, or assign them to another user.

If you don't want to take such a drastic step, you can simply *demote* a user, so that he remains on your site but doesn't have the same privileges. For example, you could change a contributor to an ordinary subscriber. That way, his existing posts will remain on your site, but he won't be able to create any new ones. And if, some time in the future, you decide to reenlist this person's help, you can simply change his status from subscriber back to contributor.

To change the user type, find the person in the user list and click the Edit link under her name. Then, pick a new type from the Role list, and click Update User.

■ Building a Private Community

So far, you've used WordPress's user registration features to open up your site to new people. Ironically, those same features are also an effective tool for closing the door to strangers. For example, you can prevent unregistered guests from reading certain posts, or even stop them from seeing any content on your site at all.

Before you build a private site, however, make sure you have enough interested members. Transforming an ordinary site into a members-only hideout is a sure way to scare off 99.9% of your visitors. However, a private site makes sense if you already have a locked-in group of members. Your site might be the online home for a group of people who are linked tightly together in the real world—for example, a team of researchers planning a new product, or a local self-help group for cancer survivors. But if you're simply hoping that people will stumble across your site and ask to sign up, you're in for some long and lonely nights.

NOTE The goals of a private site are very different from the goals of the average public site. A public site aims to attract new faces, gain buzz, and grow ever more popular. A private site is less ambitious—it allows certain types of discussions or collaboration in a quiet space.

Hiding and Locking Posts

You don't need to make your site entirely private; WordPress gives you two ways to protect individual posts, so the wrong people can't read them.

The first technique is *password protection*. The idea is simple—when you create a post, you pick a password that potential readers need to know. When someone attempts to read the post, WordPress refuses to display it until the reader supplies the right password (Figure 11-14).

Posted on July 25, 2012   ← Previous

Protected: My Secret Cookie Recipe

This post is password protected. To view it please enter your password below:

Password: ●●●●●●●●●   [Submit]

This entry was posted in Uncategorized by Katya Greenview. Bookmark the permalink.

This post is password protected. Enter the password to view any comments.

FIGURE 11-14

WordPress adds the text "Protected:" to the title of every password-protected post. To read the post, you need to type in the correct password.

The nice part about password protection is that it's straightforward—you either know the password or you don't, and password-protected posts don't require guests to be registered users on the site. Of course, administrators and editors can edit any post and remove its password protection at will, so password-protection doesn't affect them.

> **NOTE** Use password-protected posts sparingly. If your WordPress site includes a mix of public and password-protected posts, frustrated readers are likely to give up on you altogether. Password-protected posts make sense if your WordPress site isn't really on the Web, but is housed on the internal network of a business or organization (a.k.a. an intranet).

WordPress's second post-protection technique is *private posts*. Private posts are hidden from everyone, except logged-in administrators and editors. When other people visit the site, WordPress scrubs every trace of your private posts. They won't be in the post stream, they won't show up in searches, and they won't appear when you browse by category, tag, date, or author.

To see your options, click the Edit link next to a post's Visibility setting (see Figure 11-15).

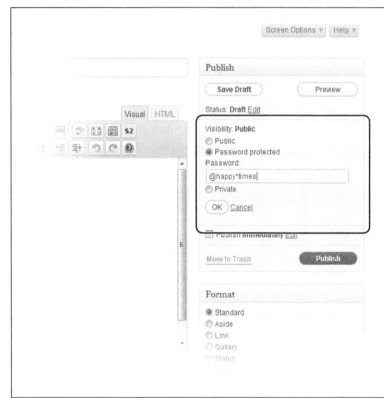

FIGURE 11-15

You can choose from three Visibility options for posts: Public (the standard), Password protected (the post's title is visible to everyone, but the content can be read only by people with the right password), or Private (the title, post, and comments are hidden from everyone except editors and administrators). Once you choose, click OK.

You can also add a password to a private post or make it private using the familiar Publish box, which appears in the Add New Post and the Edit Post page.

PLUG-IN POWER

Creating More Specific Privacy Rules

The problem with private posts is that they're *too* private. You need to be an editor or administrator to view them, and that may be more power than you want to give other people.

If you're developing a self-hosted site, a good plug-in can provide a solution. One is Page Security by Contexture (*http://tinyurl.com/page-security-c*). It lets you create groups of users, and then give that group permission to read specific posts or pages. For example, you could create a group called Managers, add several users to that group, and then give the entire group permission to read your "Tax Evasion Secrets" post.

Be careful about going too far with the Page Security plug-in, however. If you need to set security rules for dozens of pages, WordPress might not be the right tool for the job—you might be better off with a content management system like SharePoint or Alfresco. And although Page Security does a good job of grafting on some basic security features, things can get messy, and there's no guarantee that the complex security rules you set up now will continue to work in future versions of WordPress.

Creating a Completely Private Site

A completely private site is one that forces visitors to log in to view *anything*. If they don't, they can't read a single post or page.

You can turn a WordPress.com site into a private site by flipping a single setting. Choose Settings→Privacy, turn on the "I would like my site to be private, visible only to users I choose" checkbox, and then click Save Changes. Now, new visitors will meet up with the WordPress login page, no matter what content they try to access (Figure 11-16).

Oddly enough, self-hosted sites lack the private site feature that WordPress.com offers. However, there are several simple plug-ins that can fill the gap. One is Page Restrict (*http://tinyurl.com/page-restrict*), which lets you prevent people from accessing specific pages—or your entire site—until they log in. Page Restrict also lets you pick a suitable message that explains the issue to anonymous users, such as "This content is private. To view it, you must log in."

> **NOTE** You've reached the end of the line for WordPress.com sites in this chapter. The following sections cover a few more plug-ins and features that self-hosters can use. So if you run a WordPress.com site, you may as well skip ahead to the next chapter).

Letting People Register Themselves on a Self-Hosted Site

If your site is on WordPress.com, it's WordPress.com that's in charge of registering your users. But if you run a self-hosted site, you're in control, and that gives you a unique ability. If you're feeling a bit daring, you can open the floodgates to your site and let your readers register themselves.

This strategy might seem a bit dangerous—and if you don't think it through, it is. Giving random web users extra powers on your site is an extreme step for even the most trusting person. However, there are several scenarios where WordPress's self-registration feature makes a lot of sense. Here are the most common:

- You're creating a private blog and you want to prohibit anonymous users. However, you don't want to make your restrictions too onerous—you simply want to deter spammers and other riff-raff. Often, the process of signing up is enough to keep out these troublemakers. And if you let readers sign themselves up, you save yourself the task of doing so, and new users don't need to wait for your approval.

- You're creating a site that welcomes community contributors. You're ready to let anyone sign up as a contributor, because you know you'll have the chance to review their work before it goes live. However, this is no small task—reviewing other people's content and sniffing out spam makes comment moderation seem like a day at the spa.

- You've restricted comments with the "Users must be registered and logged in to comment" setting (page 260), but you're willing to let people comment if they go through the trouble of creating an account. Sometimes, site owners take this step in a bid to lock out spam, and typically, it works well, although it also drives away legitimate commenters who can't be bothered signing up. In most cases, it's better to allow Facebook and Twitter authentication (page 259), and to use Akismet to fight spam (page 263).

- Your WordPress site isn't really on the Web. Instead, it's on the internal network of a business or organization. Thus, you can assume that the people who reach your site are relatively trustworthy. (Of course, you still shouldn't grant them anything more powerful than a contributor account without your personal review.)

Flipping on the self-registration feature takes a fraction of a second. In the dashboard, choose Settings→General. Add a checkmark next to the "Anyone can register" setting, choose the user type in the New User Default Role box below, and then click Save Changes to make it permanent.

> **WARNING** The default role for new users should be subscriber or contributor. Use subscriber to welcome new readers to a private blog, and contributor to let potential authors sign themselves up. But you should never allow new users to sign themselves up as authors or editors, unless you want spammers to paste their ads all over your site.

When you turn on self-registration, WordPress adds an extra link to the login page (Figure 11-17).

FIGURE 11-17

This blog lets people register themselves. They simply need to click the Register link (left), enter an email address and password (right), and then wait for the activation link to arrive by email.

If you allow self-registration on a public website, you'll eventually have spammers creating accounts. Usually, the offender is an automated computer program called a *spambot*. This bot searches the Web for WordPress sites and attempts to sign up with every one it finds, in the hope that the site will grant the spambot author or editor permissions. If a site is unwise enough to do so, the spambot immediately gets to work spewing spam into new posts. But as long as you limit new users to the role of contributor or (powerless) subscriber, the spambot won't be able to do anything. (But just to keep your site clean, you should periodically review your user list and delete bad accounts.)

■ Creating a Network of Sites

So far, you've learned how to transform your site from a lonely one-man-band to a collaborative workspace full of authors, editors, and contributors. This transformation keeps you in control of your site, but gets new recruits to help expand your content, extend your reach, and attract new visitors.

Now, you'll take a step in a different direction. Instead of looking at adding multiple users to a crowded site, you'll see how to create multiple WordPress *sites* that co-exist on the same web server. Think of it as a way to empower your users to do even more. Now, each author gets a separate site, complete with its own dashboard, theme, and reverse-chronological list of posts. And your web server hosts all these sites, alongside your own, much like children living in their parent's home.

Each site in a multisite network gets its own distinct address, too. For example, if you create a WordPress multisite network at *http://EvilCompanyOfDoom.com*, an employee named Gareth Keenan might create a site at *http://EvilCompanyOfDoom .com/garethkeenan*. Similarly, another employee might add a site at *http://EvilCompanyOfDoom.com/dawntinsley*. Of course, you don't need to create sites based on individual people—you can just as easily create sites that represent departments, teams, clubs, or any other group of people who need to blog together.

> **NOTE** The multisite feature works well if you have a community of people who need to work independently, keep their content separate from everyone else's, and have complete control over the way their content is organized and presented. For example, the Canton School site might use the multisite feature to give each teacher their own site. Teachers could then use their sites to post assignments and answer student questions. The multisite feature isn't very useful if you want people to team up on the same project, share ideas, or blog together—in all these cases, a single site with multiple users makes more sense.

The multisite feature is particularly convenient when it comes to administration. When you build a network of sites, you become its *network administrator*—a special sort of administrator with sweeping powers over all the sites in the network. Using these powers, you can choose what themes your users can install and what plug-ins they use. And when a new version of WordPress appears, you can update all the sites in a single step.

UP TO SPEED

Websites that Use the Multisite Feature

To really understand the multisite feature, it helps to check out some websites that already use it. Here are some examples:

- **Reuters Blogs** (*http://blogs.reuters.com*). The multisite feature is a great way to handle columnists in a news site. On Reuters, each columnist gets a separate blog that uses the same distinctive theme. But because each site is separate, columnists can create their own categories and tags, and moderate their own comments.

- **Harvard Law School** (*http://blogs.law.harvard.edu*). Harvard Law offers a free WordPress site to anyone in the Harvard University community. Users can even sign themselves up and create a site immediately, as long as they have an email address that ends with *harvard.edu*.

- **Adobe Blogs** (*http://blogs.adobe.com*). Here, different teams of Adobe employees blog about their projects. This example is particularly interesting because it combines

the multisite *and* multiuser features. For example, if you check out just one site, the Adobe Digital Media Blog (*http://blogs.adobe.com/digitalmedia*), you'll find a number of Adobe experts weighing in.

- **Best Buy Stores** (*http://stores.bestbuy.com*). The omnipresent electronics store isn't known for website innovation, but it makes good use of WordPress, giving each store its own WordPress site. For example, visit *http://stores.bestbuy.com/577* to see the latest news for the Best Buy in Fairless Hills, Pennsylvania.

- **WordPress.com**. The largest and most impressive example of a WordPress multisite network is WordPress.com, the free blogging hub for several hundred thousand people. If the multisite feature works for a network this popular and this big, it's a safe bet that it will serve the needs of your users, too.

Before going any further, be aware of one thing: building a network of sites is significantly more complex than simply adding users to an existing one. Expect to spend more time feeling your way around and relearning how to configure sites and users. Furthermore, be careful with the plug-ins you use, because some won't work in a multisite network.

By the end of this chapter, you'll know how to set up a network of sites, add sites, and perform the basic configuration that holds it all together. However, there are significant aspects of the multisite feature that are outside of the scope of this book, like using it with subdomains (see the Note below).

NOTE There are two ways to create addresses for the sites in a network. You can give each site its own subfolder (as in *http://OrilliaBaseballTeams.com/***madcats**), or you can give each site its own subdomain (as in *http://***madcats**.*OrilliaBaseballTeams.com*). The latter approach is the way WordPress.com works. It's slightly more complicated, because it requires some additional settings on your web host. In this chapter, you'll stick to the subfolder approach.

Creating a Multisite Network from Scratch

The best and easiest way to create a multisite network is to start from scratch. Fortunately, the installation process is almost exactly the same as the one you used in Chapter 3. The difference is that somewhere in your installer, you need to find a setting named something like "Enable Multisite" and switch it on (Figure 11-18).

Once you install your site, you can go straight to the dashboard and look around. Skip ahead to the section "Your Multisite Network: A First Look" to see what's there (page 379).

Converting an Existing Site to a Multisite Network

Converting an existing WordPress site into a multisite network is trickier than creating a new network from scratch. If you use subfolders (rather than subdomains) in your network, the conversion process will also disrupt any existing post links you have (see the note on page 379 to learn why). For that reason, it's best to convert a newly created WordPress site, rather than one you've been using (and that other people have been reading) for some time.

NOTE There's one case where it makes good sense to convert a normal WordPress site into a multisite network—when your web host's autoinstaller doesn't support creating a new multisite network from scratch.

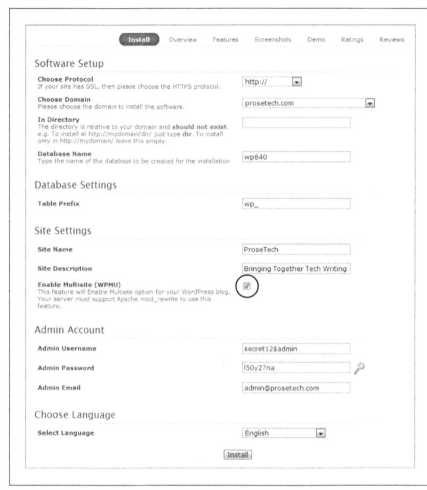

FIGURE 11-18

To tell Softaculous to create a multisite, turn on the corresponding checkbox. In this example, you're creating a multisite network in the root folder of the http://prosetech. com domain.

A network-savvy webmaster can perform the transition from ordinary site to multisite network by using the steps described in the WordPress documentation at *http://tinyurl.com/wp-multisite*. But if you don't want to mess around with network settings, you can get help from a handy little plug-in called Enable Multi-Site (*http://tinyurl.com/e-multisite*). Here's how to use it:

1. **Before you begin, make sure you back up your site (page 299).**

   You're unlikely to run into trouble, but a backup is an important safeguard whenever you change low-level settings that affect your site. Of course, if you just created the site and it doesn't have any important content on it yet, you can skip the backup step.

2. **Install the Enable Multi-Site plug-in and activate it.**

3. **Choose Settings→Enable Multi-Site.**

   This takes you to the Enable Multi-Site plug-in page. Here, you'll see some warnings (imploring you to back up your site before you continue) and some technical information about the changes the plug-in needs to make.

4. **Choose Sub-directories or Sub-domains, depending on the type of address you want to use with your sites.**

   Page 377 explains the difference. The sub-domain option works only if you installed your WordPress site in the root of your website domain (not a sub-folder), and if your web host allows a techy feature called wildcard subdomains. The sub-folder approach is safer, but it has the side effect of changing the links to all the posts you already have on your site (as explained in the Note at the bottom of this page).

   To follow along with the example in this chapter, choose Sub-directories.

WARNING Make sure you really want a multisite network before you go ahead, because there's no easy way to change a multisite network back to a single site after you make the jump.

---

5. **Click Install.**

   In a matter of seconds, the Enable Multi-Site converts your site to a network. Continue to the next section to take a look around.

Your Multisite Network: A First Look

When you create a multisite network, WordPress starts you out with a single home site. This site exists at the root of the installation folder. For example, if you install a multisite network at *http://prosetech.com*, the first site is at *http://prosetech.com*. This is exactly the same as when you create a standalone site. When you create *additional* sites, however, WordPress places them in subfolders. So if you add a site named *teamseven*, WordPress creates it at *http://prosetech.com/teamseven*. (You might think that it makes more sense to write TeamSeven rather than teamseven, but to WordPress it's all the same. No matter what capitalization you use, WordPress shows the site name in all lowercase letters when you manage it in the dashboard.)

NOTE There's one quirk in WordPress's URL naming system. When you view a post or page on your home site, WordPress adds */blog* to the address. For example, WordPress puts a post that would ordinarily be found at *http://prosetech.com/2013/06/peanut-butter-prices-spike* at *http://prosetech.com/***blog***/2013/06/peanut-butter-prices-spike*. This slightly awkward system makes sure that WordPress can't confuse your home site blog with another site in the network, because no other site is allowed to use the name *blog*.

When you finish creating your multisite network, you'll find yourself at the dashboard of your home site. But this dashboard is more limited than what you're used to. For example, even though you'll be able to activate an existing plug-in or theme,

WordPress won't let you install a new one. And on the dashboard home page you'll find another surprise—a storage space limit that restricts how many pictures, documents, and other files you can upload to your site (Figure 11-19).

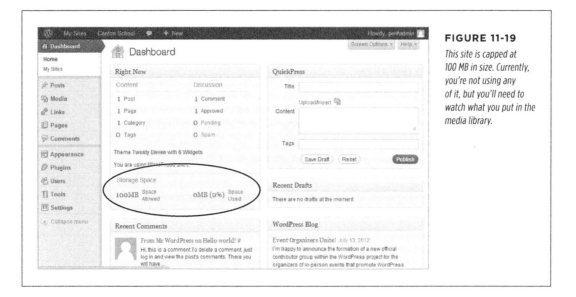

FIGURE 11-19

This site is capped at 100 MB in size. Currently, you're not using any of it, but you'll need to watch what you put in the media library.

If you haven't already guessed, your home site has these new and slightly unwelcome limitations because it's part of your multisite network. Every site in a network faces these safeguards. Without them, you'd be at the mercy of an inexperienced user who uploads a spam-filled theme, or a space-hogger who swallows gigabytes of hosting room, leaving your web server starved for space. However, if these requirements aren't quite right, you can relax them, as you'll see shortly.

Adding a Site to Your Network

To add a site, you need to enter network administration mode. This is a step that only you, the network administrator, can take. Other administrators on your network will be able to manage their own sites, but they won't be able to change the network settings—or even look at them.

> **NOTE** In WordPress parlance, a *network administrator* is the person who manages a multisite network and has full power over all the sites inside. A *site administrator* oversees a single site—the site you create for them.

To start managing the network, hover over the My Sites menu, which sits to the right of the navigation bar (that's the black bar that stretches across the top of the page). Then, click Network Admin (Figure 11-20).

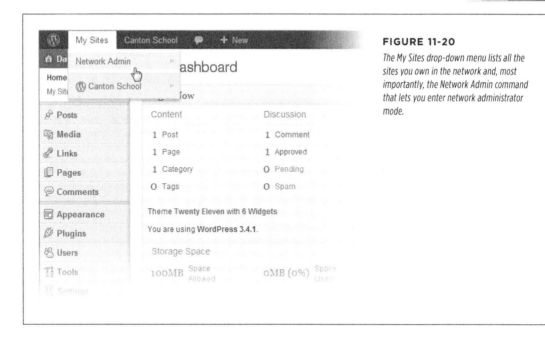

FIGURE 11-20

The My Sites drop-down menu lists all the sites you own in the network and, most importantly, the Network Admin command that lets you enter network administrator mode.

In network administration mode, the dashboard changes. Because you're no longer managing a specific site, the Posts, Pages, Comments, Links, and Media menus all disappear. In their place is a smaller set of commands for managing sites, users, themes, plug-ins, network settings, and updates.

> **TIP** You can go straight to the network administration page by adding */wp-admin/network* to the end of your home site address, as in *http://prosetech.com/wp-admin/network*.

Once you're in network administration mode, you can create a new site:

1. **Choose Sites→Add New from the dashboard.**

   This brings you to the Add New Site page (Figure 11-21).

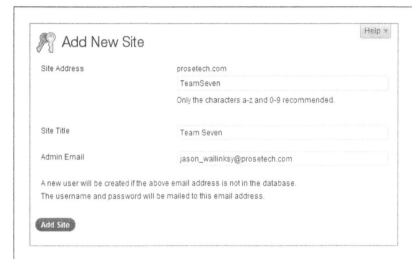

FIGURE 11-21

WordPress knows that a network administrator may need to create dozens of sites. To keep your life simple, it asks for just three pieces of information: the site address, the site title, and the email address for the person who will become the site's administrator. Here, WordPress will create the new site at http://prosetech.com/TeamSeven.

2. **Type the site's folder name in the Site Address box.**

   WordPress adds the folder name to the address of your multisite network. For example, if you use the folder name *drjanespears* and your multisite network is at *http://StMarciMarguerettaDoctors.org*, the new site has the address *http://StMarciMarguerettaDoctors.org/drjanespears*.

3. **Give the site a title.**

   The site administrator can change this detail later.

4. **Supply the email address of the person who will own the site.**

   This person will become the site's administrator.

   Adding users to a multiuser network is different from adding users to a standalone site in one important respect: you don't need to pick the password for new users. WordPress knows you're busy, and it generates a random password and emails it to the new administrator.

5. **Click Add Site.**

   WordPress creates the site, and adds two links to the top of the Add New Site page: Visit Dashboard (which takes you to the new site's dashboard) and Edit Site (which lets you change the site's settings). The dashboard is in its familiar place—just add */wp-admin* to the end of the site address to go straight to its front door.

   Ideally, you won't need to visit the new site's dashboard, because the newly christened administrator will take it from there.

TIP If, at some later point, you need to delete a site, modify it, or assign it to a new administrator, start at the list of sites in the Sites→Add Sites section of the network administration dashboard.

GEM IN THE ROUGH

Letting Users Create Their Own Sites

Ordinarily, it's up to you to create every site in a multisite network. WordPress helps you out by automatically creating a user account for the new administrator, so you can create a site in one step instead of two. But if you have dozens or even hundreds of users who want sites, manually creating each site is tedious. WordPress gives you another option—you can choose to let people create their own sites.

This isn't quite as crazy as it sounds. As you long as you don't allow people to create their own user accounts, WordPress only allows registered users to start site-building. If you're crafty, you can use a WordPress plug-in like Add Multiple Users (*http://tinyurl.com/add-multiple*) to create your users automatically, based on a list of email addresses in a text file or spreadsheet. Then you can let these users build the sites they need on their own. (There's no restriction on the number of sites, so if a user can create one, they can also create 12. If

you notice a power-drunk user creating too many sites, you'll need to step in, delete some, and send them a stern email.)

To allow users to create their own websites, choose Settings→Network Settings in the network administration dashboard. Then, next to "Allow new registrations," choose "Logged in users may register new sites." Make sure the setting "Send the network admin an email notification every time someone registers a site or user account" is also turned on (which it is by default) so WordPress notifies you about newly created sites. Finally, click Saved Changes at the bottom of the page.

New users might not realize that they're allowed to create new sites. WordPress won't tell them unless they ask for the sign-up page, by requesting *wp-signup.php* in the root site (as in *http://prosetech.com/wp-signup.php*). Figure 11-22 shows the page.

Understanding How Users Work in a Multisite Network

You can create as many sites as you want in a multisite network. In each site, you can add as many users as you need.

Sometimes, the same user needs to access more than one site. For example, one person might need to contribute to different blogs maintained by different people. Or, an administrator who manages one site in a network might also want to contribute to another.

To understand how to deal with this, you need to realize that a multisite network maintains a master list of all the users who belong to *every site* in the network. By default, each user has subscriber access to every site. (As you learned on page 354, subscribers are the lowest class of WordPress user—they aren't allowed to do anything more than read posts and write comments.)

In addition, you can give users special privileges for specific sites. For example, you might make a user an administrator on one blog and an author on another. In this case, there's still just one user record, but now it's registered with two different sets of capabilities on two different sites.

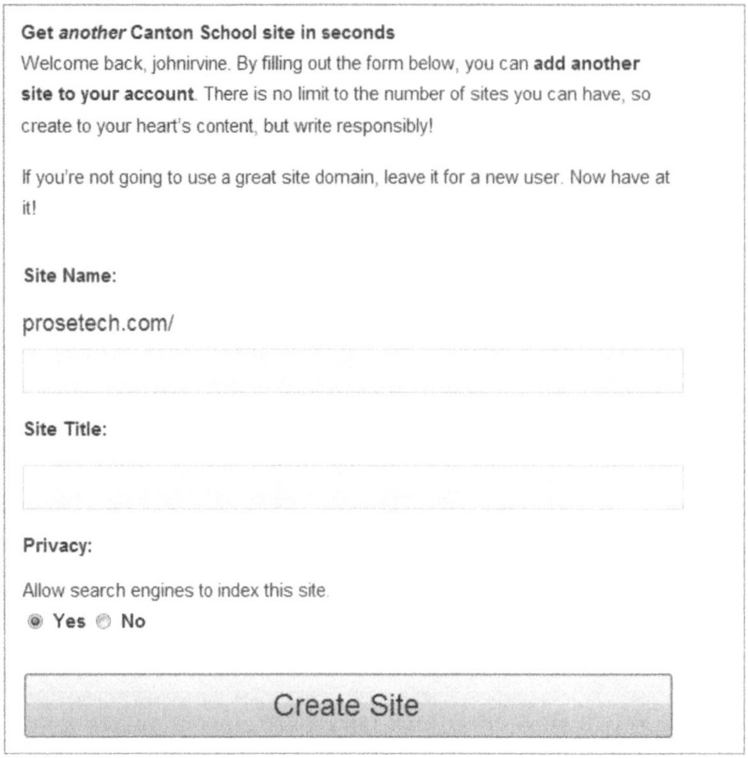

Get _another_ Canton School site in seconds

Welcome back, johnirvine. By filling out the form below, you can **add another site to your account**. There is no limit to the number of sites you can have, so create to your heart's content, but write responsibly!

If you're not going to use a great site domain, leave it for a new user. Now have at it!

Site Name:

prosetech.com/

Site Title:

Privacy:

Allow search engines to index this site.

◉ Yes ◎ No

Create Site

FIGURE 11-22

To create a new site, a logged-in user simply needs to supply the site folder name and the site's title on the sign-up page, and then click the big Create Site button. The sign-up text shown here is WordPress standard boilerplate. One you learn how to edit a theme (page 452), you can customize it.

NOTE Happily, WordPress only forces a person to log in once. When visitors move from one site to another in the same network, WordPress remembers who they are, and determines what privileges they should have on each site.

If you choose Users→Add New on the network administration dashboard, you can add a user to the master list (Figure 11-23, top). However, WordPress won't give new users any special privileges for any site.

Life is different for ordinary site administrators. Consider what happens if an administrator named Suzy logs into her dashboard. When she chooses Users→Add New, she's not given the option to create a new user. Instead, she's allowed to invite an existing user to take on a more powerful role on her site (Figure 11-23, bottom).

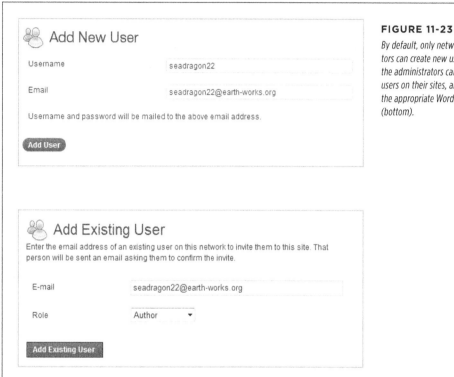

FIGURE 11-23

By default, only network administrators can create new users (top) while the administrators can register existing users on their sites, and assign them the appropriate WordPress role (bottom).

One potential problem with the user registration system is that it can create a lot of extra work. For example, if a site administrator needs to add a new user, the side administrator needs to ask you to create the user account first. To improve this situation, choose Settings→Network Settings, turn on the "Allow site administrators to add new users to their site" checkbox, and then click Save Changes. Now, site administrators can add new people to the master user list.

Another problem occurs if one person needs to contribute to several sites. In this case, someone needs to visit each dashboard and invite the user separately to each site. If you're not the sort of person who likes to spend all weekend tweaking WordPress settings, you may want to enlist the help of the plug-in like Multisite User Management (*http://tinyurl.com/multisite-um*). It lets you set a default role for each site in a multisite network. Every new user you create will automatically be registered on these sites using the default roles.

Rolling Out Updates

One of the advantages of a multisite network is that it streamlines certain management tasks. Updates are an example—once you're at the network administration page, you can push updates out to all the sites in your network in a single operation.

To get started, choose Updates→Available Updates from the network administration dashboard. You'll see, at a glance, what themes, plug-ins, and WordPress system updates are available. If you're not up-to-date, start by installing your updates on this page.

When you update themes or plug-ins, the changes take effect on all the sites in your network immediately. That's because a multisite network stores only a single copy of each theme and each plug-in.

When you install a new version of WordPress, you need to take one more step. Choose Updates→Update Network, and click the Update Network button to upgrade all your sites at once.

Adding Themes and Plug-Ins

In an ordinary WordPress website, the site administrator has complete control over the themes and plug-ins the site uses. But in a multisite network, this approach would be too risky, because a single malicious plug-in could steal sensitive data from any site in the network, or wipe out the database of your entire network.

Instead, multisite networks use a more disciplined system. You, the network administrator, can pick the themes and plug-ins you want to support. Site administrators can then pick from the options you allow.

Initially, your new multisite network begins with just one or two themes. To add more, follow these steps:

1. **Choose Themes→Add New, and search for themes you want.**

   If you need a refresher, page 161 has the full story on theme searches.

2. **When you find a suitable theme, click the Install Now link.**

   This downloads the theme to your multisite network, but it doesn't actually make it available to any sites.

3. **After you install the theme, click the Network Enable link.**

   The Network Enable link takes the place of the Activate link you see when you install a theme on an ordinary, standalone WordPress website. You can click Network Enable immediately after you install a theme, or you can view all your themes (Figure 11-24) and click the Network Enable link next to the ones you want.

FIGURE 11-24

When you click Network Enable below a theme title, WordPress makes that theme available to all the sites in your network.

It's also possible to enable a theme for some sites but not others, although it's awkward. First, make sure your theme isn't network-activated. Then, choose Sites→All Sites, and click the Edit link for the site that needs the theme. When the Edit Site page appears, click the Themes tab. There you'll see a list of all the disabled themes—simply click Enable next to the ones you want to add to the site.

The process for installing plug-ins is similar to the process for adding a theme. First, you choose Plug-Ins→Add New and search for the plug-in you want. When you find the right one, you click Install Now to install it. Then, you can click the Network Activate link to make your plug-in active on all the sites in your network (or click Network Deactivate to turn it off).

NOTE Themes and plug-ins aren't the only restrictions that come into play on a multisite network. You can also set the maximum space allocation (usually 100 MB) and the maximum size for a single file (usually 1.5 MB). To change these settings, choose Settings→Network Settings on the network administration dashboard.

Attracting a Crowd

Now that you know how to build a fantastic WordPress site, you need to show it off to the world. That means you need to spend some serious time *promoting* your site.

Web promotion can be grueling work, and many WordPressers would rather avoid the subject altogether. Not only does it take a significant amount of effort, but the benefits aren't always clear, and you'll often need to pursue a promotional strategy without knowing how well it'll work out. The best approach is to make web promotion as easy and natural as possible. That means weaving it into your daily routine and integrating it into the way your website works. It also means using honest promotional strategies rather than search engine hacks and other trickery. Follow the guidelines here, and you'll still have plenty of time to pursue your real job—publishing fabulous content.

In this chapter, you'll learn how to use a common-sense approach to web promotion. You'll begin with the best type of advertising a site can have, word-of-mouth recommendations. That doesn't mean waiting for your site to crop up in casual conversation. Instead, it involves learning how to help your readers rate, "Like," and tweet your content through social media services such as Facebook and Twitter.

Next, you'll help existing readers bond with your site. You'll notify them when you publish new posts, and alert them when their comments receive a reply. Done right, these steps build long-term loyalty with your fans and increase the number of repeat visitors.

After that, you'll consider a few basics of SEO (search engine optimization). You'll learn how to use plug-ins to make your site more Google-friendly, so web searchers can stumble across your site while hunting for content. Finally, you'll take a look at web statistics so you can assess how well your promotional strategies are working.

Encouraging Your Readers to Share

There's a gaping chasm of difference between commercial promotion and personal recommendations. If you can get your readers to share your posts and recommend your site to their friends, you'll accomplish far more than the average ad campaign.

Usually, sharing means enlisting the help of Facebook and Twitter, two social sites that are all about exchanging information, from gossipy chit-chat to breaking news. With the right WordPress settings and widgets, you can make it easier for your visitors to share your site and recommend it to their friends and followers. In the following sections, you'll see how.

NOTE Most of the features in this chapter require WordPress.com or the Jetpack plug-in for self-hosted sites. So if you're building a WordPress.org site, now's a good time to get Jetpack up and running, if you haven't already; page 284 explains how.

How Sharing Buttons Work

Sharing is often an impulsive act. You stumble across a site, it catches your easily distracted mind for a few seconds, and you pass the word out to a few choice friends. You're more likely to share a site if the process is quick and easy—for example, if the site provides a handy link that does the bulk of the job for you. If a guest has to fire up her email program or log in to another site (like Facebook or Twitter), she might just defer the task for another time—and then forget about it altogether.

The best way to encourage readers to share is to make sharing easy, quick, and convenient. And the best way to do that is to add buttons that make the process as simple as a couple of mouse clicks (Figure 12-1). That way, your readers can share your site before they move on to their next distraction.

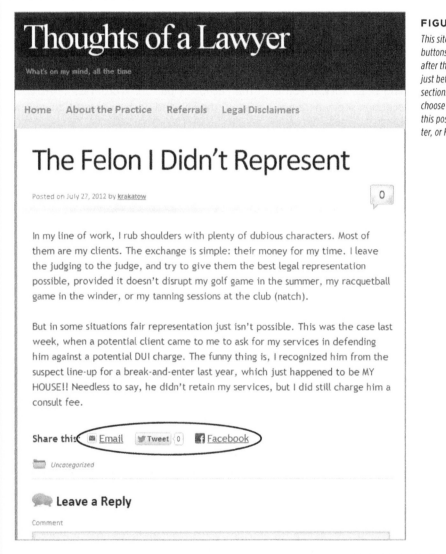

Email sharing is great for guests who may not use social media. Best of all, it works even if your visitor doesn't have an email program handy, because WordPress sends the message on the guest's behalf.

To share a post by email, you start by clicking the Email link. A box drops down so you can type in the recipient's email address, your name, and your email address.

Fill in those details, click Send Email, and WordPress sends a short message that looks something like this:

> Jason Minegra (jackerspan4evs@gmail.com) thinks you may be interested in the following post:
>
> The Felon I Didn't Represent
>
> http://thoughtsofalawyer.net/the-felon-i-didnt-represent/

Facebook sharing is another good option, simply because of Facebook's mind-boggling popularity. If you click the Facebook button, WordPress takes you to the Facebook site, where you can share the link and post an excerpt on your wall (Figure 12-2).

FIGURE 12-2

Two mouse clicks and an optional comment are all it takes to share a post with your Facebook friends.

Twitter sharing is a great way to get the word out into the ever-chattering Twitter-verse. Serious Twitter users are always looking for small tidbits of interesting material, and your Tweet button will be a hard temptation for them to resist. When you click it, WordPress pops up a new browser window, asking you to log in to Twitter and offering to send the link to your followers.

Adding Sharing Buttons

To add sharing buttons to posts or pages, your site needs to run on WordPress.com or use a plug-in. In this chapter, we'll stick to the familiar Jetpack plug-in, which adds the same sharing buttons as WordPress.com. To get started, choose Settings→Sharing to go to the Sharing Settings page. There, you choose the buttons you want to add to your site and decide where they appear.

WordPress divides the Sharing Settings page into several sections. In the Available Services section, you'll see a long list of sharing buttons you can use. To make one of them appear on your site, drag it to the Enabled Services section of a post or page (Figure 12-3).

The sharing buttons you see on a WordPress.com site differ slightly from the ones on a self-hosted site that uses Jetpack. Currently, WordPress.com offers a few more buttons, but Jetpack gives you a few more options for tweaking those buttons.

These are the sharing buttons that you aren't currently using

Drag a sharing button here to use it

Drag sharing buttons you want hidden to this box; WordPress will automatically generate the +Share button that appears on your post or page

FIGURE 12-3

Adding sharing buttons is a lot like arranging widgets. You pick the ones you want (by dragging them into the Enabled Services section) and arrange them in the order you like. Below that, the Live Preview section shows you exactly what the buttons will look like on your site.

Make sure you choose at least one place to show your sharing buttons

Here's what your visitors will see on your site

Email, Facebook, and Twitter aren't your only sharing options, but they're three of the best. Another good choice is the Print button, which gives people an easy way to print out your post and take it to their friends on foot. But the best advice for sharing buttons is to use just a few of the most useful ones (ideally, cap it at four or five). Too many buttons can overwhelm your readers and make you look needy.

Once you pick your sharing buttons, you need to tell WordPress where to display them—on your home page, on posts, and so on. You do that by turning on the checkboxes next to the places listed under "Show sharing buttons on." Here are your options:

- **Posts.** This adds the sharing buttons to single-post pages—the ones with your post content and comments section. You definitely want sharing buttons here.

- **Pages.** This adds sharing buttons to each static page (for example, the About Me page you may have on your site). Static pages usually show content that doesn't change often and isn't as newsworthy as your posts, so you might not want your pages to include sharing buttons.

- **Front Page, Archive Page, and Search Results.** This adds sharing buttons after each post, when it appears in a list of posts—for example, on the front page or in a page of search results. You might choose to put sharing buttons here if your home page shows complete posts rather than just excerpts. In this case, it's reasonable to assume that some visitors will do all their reading on your home page, without clicking through to the single-post page. But if your home page displays excerpts, you definitely don't want to show the sharing buttons, because it'll seem wildly presumptuous to ask your readers to share posts they haven't even read.

> **NOTE** It's unfortunate that WordPress combines the Front Page, Archive Page, and Search Results options into a single setting. When you perform a search, you never see more than an excerpt of the post, so it doesn't make sense to have sharing buttons in your search results, even if you do want sharing buttons on your front page. Sadly, WordPress won't let you make this distinction.

- **Media.** This adds sharing buttons to attachment pages, which display media files. For example, readers can get to this page by clicking a picture in a gallery (page 316). It's not terribly important to add sharing buttons here, because most of your readers won't go to these pages or spend much time on them.

Once you pick your sharing buttons and choose where you want them to appear, click Save Changes. You can now browse to your site and give them a whirl.

FREQUENTLY ASKED QUESTION

How to Hide Sharing Buttons on Some Posts

I don't want all my posts and pages to be the same. Can I show sharing buttons on some but not all?

Yes.

To understand how, you first need to understand that WordPress shows sharing buttons only if your site meets two criteria. First, in "Show sharing buttons on" section, you must turn on the Posts checkbox. Second, when you create or edit a post, you need to turn on the "Show sharing buttons on this post" checkbox. WordPress automatically turns it on for every new post, but you can change that.

Consider an example. Imagine you have a site with 36 posts and you want to allow sharing on all but three. You first make sure you have the Posts checkbox on the Settings→Sharing page turned on. Then, you edit each of the three posts that *shouldn't* have sharing buttons to turn off the "Show sharing buttons on this post" checkbox.

The same technique works for pages, except that WordPress pays attention to the Pages checkbox rather than the Posts checkbox on the Settings→Sharing page.

More Ways to Customize Your Sharing Buttons

WordPress gives you a surprising degree of control over your sharing buttons. Under the Live Preview section, you'll find several options. They include:

- **Default button style.** Choose "Text only" to turn your buttons into text links (ugly) or "Icon only" to turn your buttons into tiny pictures (which are more difficult for people to understand, but do save space).

- **Sharing label.** This is the text that appears just before your sharing buttons. The standard text is "Share this:" but if you want to write "Spread the word!" no one's going to stop you.

- **Open links in.** Some sharing buttons take your reader to another site. For example, the standard Facebook button takes guests to Facebook and asks for a comment (Figure 12-2). Ordinarily, this means your visitor leaves your site. But if you choose "New window" for the "Open links in" option (Figure 12-3), the browser opens a new window when a visitor clicks a sharing button.

If you host your site on WordPress.com, you'll see an additional option that lets you turn WordPress.com "Likes" on or off. You'll learn more about that feature on page 399.

If you use Jetpack, you'll find that some sharing buttons have extra options, like those that let you change how the button looks or works. You'll know that a button has additional options if you see a small drop-down arrow on the right side of the button when you add it to the Enabled Services section. For example, in Figure 12-3 both the Facebook and Twitter buttons have additional options. Click the drop-down arrow in the Facebook button, and you can turn it into a Like button, which streamlines sharing (Figure 12-4).

FIGURE 12-4

When someone on Facebook clicks the Like button under a shared post, the Like count increases. In this example, four Facebook users enjoyed this post.

suspect line-up for a break-and-enter last year, which just happened to be MY HOUSE!! Needless to say, he didn't retain my services, but I did still charge him a consult fee.

Share this: ✉ Email 🐦 Tweet {0} 👍 Like {4}

🗂 *Uncategorized*

NOTE   "Liking" isn't quite the same as sharing. For example, if Victor Gonzales shares a post (using the standard Facebook button), he gets the chance to add a comment on his Facebook page. If he "Likes" a post (using the Like button), Facebook makes a note of the action but doesn't ask Victor to supply a comment. In both cases, Victor's friends will see a link to the post in their news feeds, along with an excerpt.

The Sharing Settings page has one more nifty feature you haven't used: a pop-up panel that reveals extra sharing buttons. So if you feel compelled to stuff your page with a large number of sharing buttons, you can hide some of the less important ones in this panel. That way, they'll be tucked out of sight until a visitor clicks the "+ Share" button, which WordPress adds automatically (Figure 12-5).

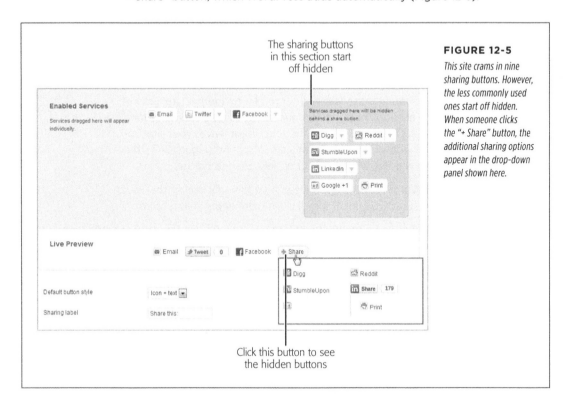

The sharing buttons
in this section start
off hidden

FIGURE 12-5

This site crams in nine sharing buttons. However, the less commonly used ones start off hidden. When someone clicks the "+ Share" button, the additional sharing options appear in the drop-down panel shown here.

Click this button to see
the hidden buttons

Letting People Like Your Site

As you've seen, visitors can use the Facebook button to share and Like your posts. But you might prefer to let Facebookers show their appreciation for your site as a whole, using the sort of Like box shown in Figure 12-6.

FIGURE 12-6

This Facebook Like box sits in a post's sidebar. It lets visitors Like your entire site. It also counts up the total number of Likes you have, and displays profile pics of your most recent Facebook fans.

There are two good reasons to create a site-wide Like box:

- It advertises your *whole* site on Facebook, not just one post. As a result, it's more likely to get people interested in your content.

- It centralizes voting in one place. If your site doesn't attract huge amounts of traffic, your posts may only accumulate a few Likes. But if you include a single Like button for your entire site, your Like count will probably reach a larger, more respectable-looking number.

There's one extra hassle with the Like button: To let people Like your site, you need to create a Facebook Page for it.

A Facebook Page is a public meeting spot you create on Facebook. You use a Facebook Page to promote something—say, a company, a cause, a product, a television show, or a band. You might already have a Facebook Page to promote your business or yourself (for example, musicians, comedians, and journalists often do). Any Facebook user can create one.

A Facebook Page is similar to a personal Facebook profile, but it's better suited to promotion. That's because anyone can visit a Facebook page and read the content, even if they don't have a Facebook account. Those who do have accounts can do the usual Facebook things—click Like to follow the page, post on the Page's wall, and join in any of its discussions. Generally, a personal Facebook profile is better suited for keeping up with friends or networking with business contacts, while a Facebook Page offers a better way to promote yourself, your business, or your cause to masses of people you don't know. If you don't have a Facebook Page and you aren't sure how to create one, see the box on page 399.

Once you have a Facebook Page, it's easy to add a Facebook Like Box to your site. Once again, your site needs to be running on WordPress.com, or you need the Jetpack plug-in. If it meets either of these requirements, follow these steps:

1. **Choose Appearance→Widgets.**

   This brings you to the familiar Widgets page.

2. **Drag the Facebook Like Box into one of the widget areas.**

   Ideally, you should add the widget to your home page (with its list of posts), *and* to your single-post pages. Some themes (like Twenty Eleven) don't include a sidebar on the single-post page. That means you need to put the Like box somewhere else, such as in the footer area.

3. **Type in the Facebook Page web address.**

   The easiest way to do that is to visit your page through Facebook, and then copy the address from your browser.

4. **Optionally, configure the other settings for the Facebook Like Box.**

   Like any widget, you can give the Facebook Like Box a title, but that's really not necessary. You can also set its width, change its color scheme, and choose whether you want to display your fans' faces (as in Figure 12-6), the latest posts from your Page's news stream, or the latest posts from its wall. If you opt out of all these options, you get a very compact box that includes a Like button, the number of Likes you've received, and a tiny thumbnail of the profile picture from your Facebook Page.

5. **Click Save.**

   This adds the Like Box widget to your page.

Creating a Facebook Page

To create a Facebook Page, go to *www.facebook.com/pages/create.php*. You start by clicking the button that best represents the type of page you want—for example, you can create one for a local business, a big company, a band, a product, a public figure, or a cause. Depending on the button you click, Facebook asks you for some more information, like your name and address. Once you fill that in, click the Get Started button.

You now need to either sign in to your Facebook account or create a new one. It's easy—all you need is an email address, a password, and a birth date.

When you finish signing in or registering, Facebook asks for three final ingredients:

- **A profile picture for your page.** You can upload it from your computer or grab it off your WordPress site, if you have a link. Facebook pictures are square-shaped, so don't try to use your WordPress site header picture.

- **A description.** This is a few sentences that describe you or your business (Figure 12-7). It shows up on your Facebook Page, so make sure your description is fun and engaging.

- **A link to another site.** This part is optional, but it makes sense to supply a link to your WordPress site here.

Click Save Info and Facebook creates your Page. Make note of its URL, which appears in your browser's address bar—you'll need to copy it into the Facebook Like Box widget to set the link up in WordPress.

FIGURE 12-7

This is the description for the Magic Tea House's Facebook Page.

Using WordPress.com Ratings

On WordPress.com itself, there's another rating system you can use. It's called (rather unimaginatively) WordPress.com Likes.

By default, WordPress turns WordPress.com Likes on, and a Like button appears in every post, just after the sharing buttons. This button works just like the Facebook Like button, but only WordPress.com users can use it. (WordPress asks everyone else to sign up when they click it.)

WordPress.com tracks all the posts a person likes, just as it tracks the sites they follow (page 48). WordPress users can review their favorite pages in their account—to do that, visit *http://wordpress.com*, log in, click the Reader tab, and choose Posts I Like.

> **TIP** If you don't want to use WordPress.com Likes, you can turn them off site-wide on the Settings→Sharing page. You can also switch them off when you create or edit an individual post, by turning off the "Show likes on this post" checkbox in the Likes and Shares box.

WordPress.com Likes are a good way to engage the very active community of WordPress.com bloggers. Some users get quite fanatical about them. They also work with two nifty widgets:

- **Top Posts & Pages.** This widget shows the hottest pages on your site, based on either the number of times guests have viewed them or the number of times visitors have Liked them. It's a great way to highlight popular content. But don't confuse the Top Posts & Pages widget with the similarly named Top Rated widget. The latter is for PollDaddy ratings, an alternative ranking system described in the box on this page.

- **Posts I Like.** This widget shows the posts *you've* liked, on any WordPress.com site. Similarly, if someone else uses this widget on their WordPress.com site and then Likes one of your pages, a link shows up on their site, inviting readers to check out your content. That makes it a great way to lure new readers.

GEM IN THE ROUGH

Yet Another Ratings System

If you're a WordPress.com user, you can be forgiven for getting confused by the panoply of rating options available. You already know how to integrate Facebook sharing and WordPress.com Likes. In addition to those options, WordPress.com sites can use the PollDaddy rating system. (Self-hosters can get a plug-in that offers the same features at *http://tinyurl.com/wp-polls*. However, it's a bit finicky, and it forces you to sign up for a free PollDaddy account.)

Initially, WordPress has PollDaddy ratings turned off. To add them to posts, pages, or comments, go to the Ratings→All Ratings section of the dashboard. There, you can position the ratings section above or below your content. When you apply the ratings to posts and pages, readers can rate a post from one star (very poor) to five stars (excellent). When you apply the ratings to comments, visitors choose from simple thumbs-up and thumbs-down buttons. And, as with WordPress.com Likes, self-hosters can get a widget that uses the PollDaddy rating

system. It's called Top Rated, and it lets guests link to your top posts, pages, or comments, depending on the options you pick.

It doesn't really make sense to use both WordPress.com Likes and PollDaddy ratings. There's only so much feedback you can request before your readers get tapped out. Both systems have their respective advantages. WordPress.com Likes require guests to sign in, but provide extra features—namely, it lets people log into the WordPress.com home page and see all the posts they've liked. But PollDaddy ratings are more inclusive, because they allow everyone to participate, with no login required. They also include a reporting feature that lets web authors review their most popular posts (to see it, choose Ratings→All Ratings). You may need to play with both systems before you decide which one better suits your site.

Finally, it's worth noting that even if you choose WordPress.com Likes for your posts, you might still decide to use PollDaddy to let readers rate comments (page 247), because there's no overlap between those two features.

Keeping Readers in the Loop

The best sites are *sticky*—they don't just attract new visitors, they also encourage repeat visits.

To make a sticky site, you need to build a relationship between your site and your readers. You want to make sure that even when your readers leave, they can't forget about your site, because they're still linked to its ongoing conversation. One way to do that is to notify readers about posts that might interest them. Another strategy is to tell readers when someone replies to one of their comments. Both techniques use email messages to lure visitors back after they leave your site.

If your site is on WordPress.com or you installed Jetpack on a self-hosted site, you automatically get a convenient opt-in system for email notifications. It starts with two checkboxes that appear in the "Leave a Reply" section (Figure 12-8).

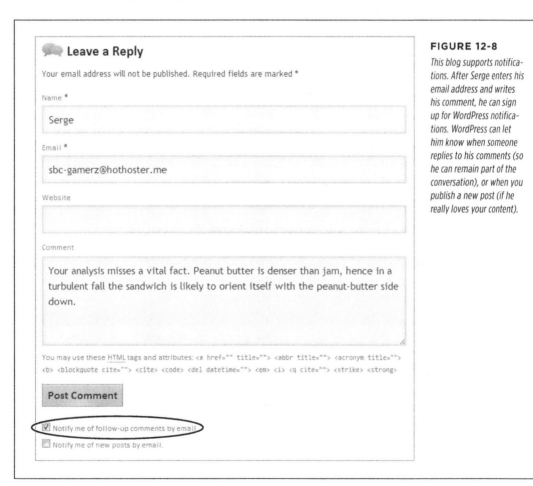

FIGURE 12-8

This blog supports notifications. After Serge enters his email address and writes his comment, he can sign up for WordPress notifications. WordPress can let him know when someone replies to his comments (so he can remain part of the conversation), or when you publish a new post (if he really loves your content).

You can hide the post notification and comment options. Go to Settings→Discussion and then turn off the checkboxes next to "Show a 'follow comments' option in the comment form" and "Show a 'follow blog' option in the comment form." But there's really no reason you'd want to do that, unless you're using a plug-in that adds similar options somewhere else on your site.

Taking Care of Your Peeps

Even on sites with thousands of comments, most readers keep quiet. Whether it's due to laziness, indifference, or the fear of being ignored, the average reader won't leave a comment. So when someone does speak up, you need to do your best to keep them in the discussion.

One way to do that is with the comment-tracking option you just read about (see Figure 12-8). And you can reward commenters and stoke the conversation several more ways:

Comment on your commenter's sites. You already know that, every once in a while, you need to step into a discussion with your own comment. Visitors like to see you involved because it shows you're reading their opinions just as they read yours. However, if you see a particularly good comment, you can take this interaction a little bit further. Follow the commenter's website link. If the commenter has a blog, stick around, read a bit, and add a comment to one of *her* posts. Comments are a

two-way street, and the more you participate with others, the more likely it is that a reader will keep coming back.

Thank commenters. Not every time—maybe just once. If you notice a new commenter with some useful feedback, add a follow-up comment that thanks them for their input. Or, if you want to get fancier, you can use a plug-in like Thank Me Later (*http://tinyurl.com/wp-thank*) to send an email message to first-time commenters, telling them you appreciate the feedback. (But be warned, you need to tweak this plug-in carefully to make sure you don't send out too many emails and annoy both your commenters and your web hosting company.)

Ask for comments. Sometimes, non-commenters just need a little push. To encourage them to step up, end your post with a leading question, like "What do you think? Was this decision fair?", or an invitation, like "Let us know your best dating disaster story."

Making Email Subscriptions More Accessible

Although it makes sense to put the comment notification checkbox in the comments area of your posts, that spot's not as good a place for the checkbox that lets readers subscribe to your posts. Ideally, you'll put a prominent subscription option after every one of your posts *and* on the home page.

There's another problem with the standard post notification checkbox. To sign up for notifications, a reader needs to leave a comment. Not only is this requirement a bit confusing (readers might not realize they need to fill out a comment, tick the site-subscription checkbox, and *then* click Post Comment), it's also unnecessarily limiting.

Fortunately, WordPress offers a better option, with a subscription widget that can sign up new followers any time. If you use WordPress.com, the widget is called Follow Blog. If you use Jetpack, it's called Blog Subscriptions. Both widgets are virtually identical, the only difference being that the WordPress.com version recognizes WordPress.com users, and lets you address them with a customized text message.

WordPress.com users get one other extra feature: they can adjust the frequency of their outgoing emails so their readers get notified only once a day at most, or just once a week.

To use the subscription widget, choose Appearance→Themes, and then drag the plug-in onto one of the widget areas on your site. You can then customize several bits of information, including the widget title, the text that invites readers to sign up, and the text on the Subscribe button (Figure 12-9). (For best results, keep the text in the widget brief.)

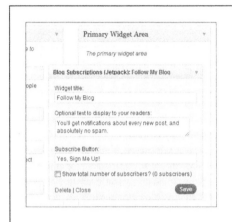

FIGURE 12-9

If you configure the widget like the one on the left, your readers will see a subscription box like the one on the right.

You can also choose to show the total number of subscribers, in which case the subscription box adds a line like "Join 4 other followers."

It's a good idea to include the subscription widget in two places. First, you can add one to your home page sidebar. Second, you can put it in the footer area of each post, with a message like "Liked this article? Subscribe to get lots more."

Emailing Your Subscribers (Without WordPress's Help)

Occasionally, you might want to reach out to your followers and send them an email that doesn't correspond to a post. For example, you might want to offer them a special promotion or solicit their feedback on a website change. If you decide to take this step, tread carefully—if you harass your readers with frequent or unwanted emails, they'll feel like they're being spammed. If you decide to go ahead and email your followers on your own, you first need to get their email addresses. Here's how:

- If you use WordPress.com, you need to visit the WordPress.com home page (*http://wordpress.com*), log in, and choose the Stats tab. Scroll down to the "Totals, Followers & Shares" box. Under the heading "Followers," WordPress counts up the total number of people subscribing to posts and comments. Click the "Blog" link to get their email addresses.

- If you use Jetpack on a self-hosted site, choose Jetpack→Site Stats, and scroll down to the Subscription box. You'll see the total number of people subscribed to your blog (and those who are registered to receive replies to a particular comment). Click the Blog link next to the number to see the full list of email addresses.

PLUG-IN POWER

Even Better Email Subscription Services

Jetpack gives self-hosters a solid, straightforward subscription package. The WordPress.com servers handle all the user tracking and emailing, making your life easy. However, Jetpack doesn't include any settings that let you customize the way it handles subscriptions. More advanced email and newsletter plug-ins (some of which will cost you a bit of cash) offer more features.

One example is the popular Subscribe2 plug-in (*http://tinyurl.com/wp-sub2*). It adds the following useful features:

- **Digests.** Instead of sending your readers an email notification after you publish every new post, Subscribe2 lets you send a single email, periodically, that announces several new posts at once. Subscribe2 calls this message a *digest.* For example, you might choose to send subscribers a weekly digest summarizing the past seven days' posts.

- **Excluded categories and post types.** Perhaps you don't want to send notifications for every new post. Subscribe2 lets you ignore certain categories or post types (like asides and quotes), so they don't trigger a notification email.

- **User-managed subscriptions.** If you're willing to let readers sign up as subscribers on your site (page 354), they can manage their own subscriptions. For example, they can subscribe to just the post categories that interest them, and pick the most convenient digest option.

Publicizing Your Posts on Social Media (with WordPress.com)

As you've seen, one good way to get the word out about your site is to get your readers talking and sharing on social media sites. But you don't need to wait for them to do the work for you—if you have a Facebook or Twitter account, you can use it yourself to announce new content.

This technique is often called *publicizing*, and it's not quite the same as the social sharing you learned about earlier. Sharing is when a visitor introduces new people to your content. Publicizing is when *you* tell your readers about new content. The difference is that the people you tell probably already know about your site. Your goal is to get them interested enough to come back.

Publicizing is an increasingly important way to reach your readers. Twitter fanatics may pay more attention to tweets than they do to email messages. Facebook fans who won't bother to sign up for an email subscription might not mind Liking your Facebook Page and getting notifications from you in their news feed. For these reasons, many WordPressers choose to publicize their posts.

WordPress.com sites get a built-in Publicize feature. You simply need to connect your site to the social media account (or accounts) you want to use. To do that, choose Settings→Sharing. Then click the Connect link under the appropriate social media icon (Figure 12-10).

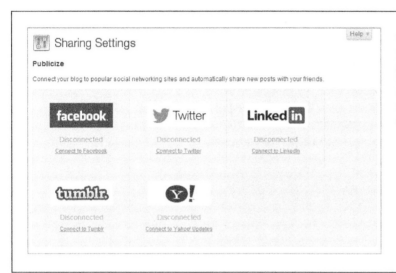

FIGURE 12-10

The WordPress.com Publicize feature supports services like Facebook, Twitter, LinkedIn, Tumblr, and Yahoo Updates. Once you pick one, you need to log in to your social media account to complete the connection.

The Publicize feature springs into action every time you publish a new post. However, WordPress lets you take control of the process using the Publish box.

Once you write your post, look in the Publish box. Next to the word "Publicize," you'll see a list of the services you can use to publicize your post. Click the Edit link and more options appear (Figure 12-11). You can choose to publicize your post on only some services, or none at all. You can also edit the message that WordPress sends out to announce the new post. Ordinarily, WordPress uses the post title for the message, but you can substitute more descriptive text.

FIGURE 12-11

When you publish this post, WordPress will publicize it on Twitter, but not on Facebook.

If you publish the post you set up in Figure 12-11, your subscriber will see the tweet shown in Figure 12-12.

FIGURE 12-12

The tweet that WordPress sends includes your custom message and a link to the full post.

Publicizing Your Posts on a Self-Hosted Site

Many self-hosters are clamoring for the Publicize feature. Unfortunately, it hasn't made it into Jetpack yet.

In the meantime, you may be able to find a plug-in that performs a similar service. One possibility is the Social Networks Auto-Poster (http://tinyurl.com/social-p), but it's a new plug-in that's yet to be truly tested. Otherwise, you'll need to use a plug-in that's specifically suited to the social media service you want to use. For example, you can use Wordbooker (*http://tinyurl.com/wordbooker*) to announce your posts on Facebook, complete with a link and an excerpt. Or you can use the WP to Twitter (*http://tinyurl.com/wp2tw*) to send out a link to your new posts on Twitter.

Showing Your Own Tweets on Your Site

You already learned how to encourage people to tweet about your site. But the integration between WordPress and Twitter runs deeper than that. If you're a Twitter-holic, WordPress has a nifty way to integrate *your* Twitter feed into your own site.

Before you dive into this feature, it's worth taking a moment to ask why you'd use it and how it fits into your site's promotional plans. There are several good reasons:

- **To offer extra content.** If you're an avid Twitterer, you can stuff your feed with news, tiny tips, and micro observations related to your site. Those details might be interesting to your readers even if they aren't worth a full post.

- **To make your site feel *alive*.** Having a Twitter feed can make your site seem more current and dynamic—provided you tweet regularly.

- **To attract new followers.** If you display your Twitter feed on your site, there's a chance that some of your readers will decide to follow your feed. If they do, you'll have another way to reach them. This is particularly useful if you use Twitter to announce your blog posts using WordPress.com's Publicize feature (page 404) or the WP to Twitter plug-in (*http://tinyurl.com/wp2tw*).

To display a Twitter feed on your site, you need the Twitter widget. It's automatically available to WordPress.com sites, but self-hosters need the trusty Jetpack plug-in.

To use the Twitter widget, choose Appearance→Widgets, and then drag it into a widget area, like a sidebar or footer. To properly configure the widget, you need to supply the Twitter user name and the number of tweets you want to appear on your posts and pages (Figure 12-13). You can also choose to hide your tweets if they simply reply to other people's tweets (which readers can find confusing out of context), and to show retweets (which is when a Twitter user takes your tweet and republishes it from his account). WordPress.com gives you the additional option of adding a Follow button, which Jetpack sadly lacks. If you really must have a Follow button, you need to bypass Jetpack's version of the Twitter widget and try out one of the many Twitter plug-ins available in WordPress's plug-in directory.

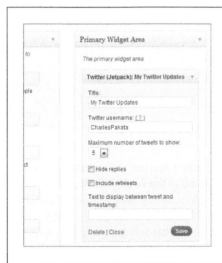 

FIGURE 12-13

If you configure the Twitter widget like the one on the left, your readers will see a Twitter feed like the one on the right. In the feed, each tweet becomes a link that, if clicked, takes readers to Twitter to read the whole conversation.

> **NOTE** WordPress.com truly loves Twitter. Although the Twitter widget may be the only tool you need, WordPress.com sites can get additional Twitter integration by using two shortcodes (page 315) that put Twitter content inside a post. The [tweet] shortcode lets you show a single tweet, and customize its appearance (learn about it at *http://tinyurl.com/cwfa77u*). The [twitter-follow] shortcode lets you add a Follow button anywhere you need it (*http://tinyurl.com/cn29khu*).

▉ Notifying Readers by Using Feeds

A *feed* is a computer-generated document that lists an archive of your posts, and the content they contain, in a computer-friendly format. Feeds are a cool and slightly geeky tool that people use to keep up with their favorite sites. The essential idea is that a site—say, a WordPress blog—provides a feed with recent posts. People who read that blog can use another program—say a browser, or a feed reader—to *subscribe* to this feed.

Here's the neat part. Once you subscribe to a feed, your browser or feed reader automatically checks the sites you signed up with for new content. This saves you from visiting the same site 47 times a day, or digging through an endless stream of spammy notification messages in your email inbox. Best of all, one feed-reading program can track as many sites as you want.

NOTE Feeds have been around a long time—they're far older than social networking sites like Twitter. The advantage to them is that the feed-reading program does all the work—you don't need to check sites for new posts, read your emails, or click a link in a tweet.

All WordPress sites automatically support feeds. In fact, you can take a look at the feed *your* site sends out by adding */feed* to the end of your website address. So if you have a WordPress site at *http://lazyfather.wordpress.com*, you can see its feed by requesting *http://lazyfather.wordpress.com/feed*.

NOTE In a self-hosted site, the */feed* syntax works only if you use post titles in your permalinks, which you definitely should (page 117). Otherwise, you'll need to replace */feed* with the more convoluted code */?feed=rss2*.

Depending on the browser you use, you might see the raw feed document when you request it, or your browser might turn the feed into a lightly formatted list of posts (Figure 12-14).

Most browsers provide some sort of feed-reading feature. For example, Internet Explorer keeps a list of feeds you've bookmarked in the Feeds tab of the Favorites panel. Hover over one of these links, and it automatically tells you how many new posts have been published since your last visit. Firefox has a slightly different feature—subscribe to a feed and it adds a *live bookmark* that automatically collects every new post behind the scenes. Google Chrome works similar magic with a tiny icon in the search box that, when you click it, pops open a list of new posts. However, you have to install a small browser extension to activate it (*http://tinyurl.com/28q8dth*). Safari is the lone holdout—it recently removed its feed-reading features.

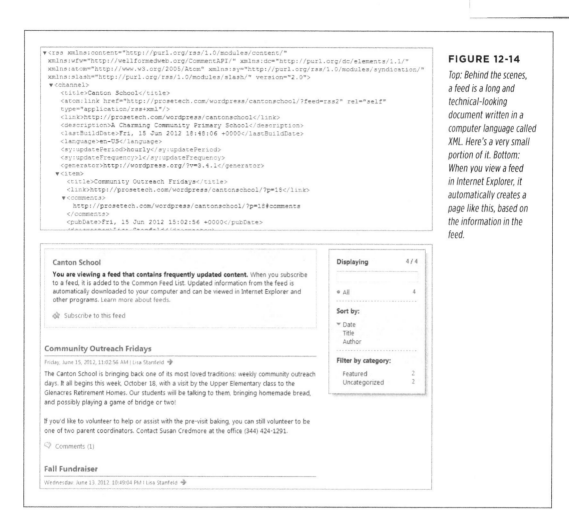

FIGURE 12-14

Top: Behind the scenes, a feed is a long and technical-looking document written in a computer language called XML. Here's a very small portion of it. Bottom: When you view a feed in Internet Explorer, it automatically creates a page like this, based on the information in the feed.

To make feeds truly convenient, you need to use a specialized feed-reading program (or a feed-reading app, if you want to check feeds on a smartphone or tablet). Good options include FeedDemon (*www.feeddemon.com*, Figure 12-15) for Windows, NetNewsWire (*http://netnewswireapp.com*) for Mac addicts, and Google Reader (*www.google.com/reader*) for online feed reading. Tablet lovers can use feed-reading apps like Flipboard (*http://flipboard.com*) and Feedly (*www.feedly.com*) to stay current. All these programs let you read posts right inside your feed reader, without making a separate trip to the website that publishes the feed.

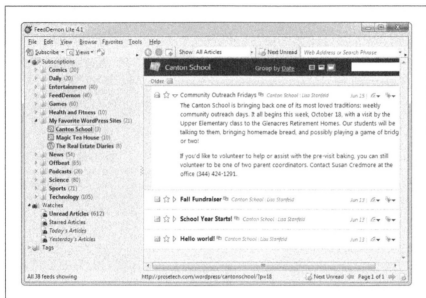

FIGURE 12-15

In a feed-reading program, you can see all the new posts for all the sites you follow. With FeedDemon, it's like checking your inbox for new email.

Getting Customized Feeds

Adding */feed* to the end of your site address gets you the standard feed, the one with all your posts. However, sites provide different feeds if you tweak the URL slightly.

For example, you can get a feed that provides all the posts in a specific category, like this:

```
http://www.magicteahouse.net/category/green-tea/feed
```

Or all the posts with a certain tag:

```
http://www.magicteahouse.net/tag/promotions/feed
```

Or all the posts by a specific author:

```
http://www.magicteahouse.net/author/katya_g/feed
```

But the most interesting type of feed just might be the one that grabs the comments from a post (on crystal jasmine tea in this example):

```
http://www.magicteahouse.net/crystal-jasmine-named-tea-of-the-year/feed
```

Or the comments from your entire site:

```
http://www.magicteahouse.net/comments/feed
```

Try plugging all these variations into a feed reader to see what posts show up. Or, check out the WordPress feed documentation at *http://tinyurl.com/64lmdo* to learn about a few more exotic feed expressions, such as the ones that exclude a specific category or tag, and those that return all the posts that match a search expression.

Using a Feed Widget

Here's a universal truth of the web publishing world: even if your site supports a feed, visitors aren't likely to subscribe to it unless you display a big, fat Feed button.

Some themes automatically include one. Usually, it looks like an orange-colored square with radiating semi-circles that suggest transmission (see Figure 12-16). If your theme doesn't offer a Feed button—and the standard Twenty Eleven theme doesn't—you can add one using the RSS Links widget, which is available to all Word-Press.com sites and included with Jetpack. (If you're wondering, RSS is the name of the standard that feeds must follow.)

FIGURE 12-16

When you add a Feed button to your site, it tells readers they can easily keep up with your posts. Clicking the button launches your feed document, although this isn't much help unless you click that button in a feed-supporting browser, or copy it to a genuine feed reader, like FeedDemon.

When you add the RSS Links widget, you need to choose whether to include a link for the posts feed, the comments feed, or both. If you want a more specialized feed, like one for a specific category, you need to create the link yourself and put it in the Text widget, as described on page 155.

You also need to choose the format for the feed button (text only, image only, or image and text). If you use an image, you need to specify its size and color. Once you finalize these details, you'll be rewarded with a button like the medium-sized text-and-image feed link shown in Figure 12-16.

NOTE Don't confuse the RSS Links widget with the similarly named but completely different RSS widget. The RSS Links widget provides links to your feeds. The RSS widget looks at someone *else's* feed, finds the most recent entries, and displays links for them on your site. In other words, the RSS Links widget tells visitors that your website provides feeds. The RSS widget lets you display links on your site that lead to someone else's content.

■ Search Engine Optimization

As you've seen, you have an exhaustive range of options for getting the word out about your site. You can share your posts, publicize them, use email notifications, and tweet the heck out of everything. All these techniques share something in common—each one is a type of *social networking*, where you use connections to people you already know to reach out just a bit farther.

There's another way to get people to your site, but it's more difficult and less fun. You can try to attract complete strangers through the magic of a search engine. To perform this trick, you need to understand *search engine optimization* (SEO), which is the sometimes cryptic art of getting web search engines like Google to notice you.

The goal is to make your site appear in a highly ranked position for certain searches. For example, if your WordPress site covers dog breeding, you'd like web searchers to find your site when they type *dog breeding* into Google. The challenge is that for any given search, your site competes with millions of other sites that share the same search keywords. If Google prefers those sites, your site will be pushed farther down in the search results, until even the most enthusiastic searcher won't spot you. And if searchers can't find you on Google, you lose a valuable way to attract fresh faces to your site.

Next, you'll learn a bit more about how search engines like Google work, and you'll consider how you can help your site rise up the rankings of a web search.

> **NOTE** In the following sections, you'll spend a fair bit of time learning about Google. Although Google isn't the only search engine on the block, it's far and away the most popular, with a staggering 80 percent (or more) of worldwide web-search traffic. For that reason, it makes sense to consider Google first, even though most of the search engine optimization techniques you'll see in this chapter apply to all major search engines, including Bing, Yahoo, and even Baidu, the kingpin of web search in China.

PageRank: Scoring Your Site

To help your site get noticed, you need to understand how Google runs a web search.

Imagine you type *dog breeding* into the Google search page. First, Google peers into its gargantuan catalog of sites, looking for pages that use those keywords. Google prefers pages that include the keywords "dog breeding" more than once, and pages that put these keywords in important places (like headings and page titles). Of course, Google is also on the lookout for sites that try to game the system, so a page that's filled with keyword lists and repetitive text is likely to get ignored at best, and blacklisted at worst.

Even with these requirements, a typical Google search turns up hundreds of thousands (or even millions) of matching pages. To decide how it should order these pages in its search results, Google uses a top-secret formula called *PageRank*. The basic idea behind the PageRank system is that it determines the value of your site by the community of websites that link to it. Although the full PageRank algorithm is incredibly convoluted (and entirely secret), its basic workings are well known:

- The more sites that link to you, the better.

- A link from a better, more popular site (a site with a high PageRank) is more valuable than a link from a less popular site.

- A link from a more selective site is better than a link from a less selective site. That's because the more outgoing links a site has, the less each link is worth. So if someone links to your site and just a handful of other sites, that link is valuable. If someone links to your site and *hundreds* of other sites, the link's value is diluted.

■ FINDING YOUR PAGERANK

Because of the power PageRank scores have over websites, it's no surprise that web authors want to know how their pages are doing. However, Google won't give out the real PageRank of a web page, even to its owner.

That said, Google does allow website owners to see a *simplified* version of the PageRank score, which gives you a general idea of your site's performance. This simplified PageRank is based on the real PageRank, but it's updated just twice a year, and it only provides a value of from 1 to 10. (All things being equal, a website rated 10 will turn up much higher in someone's search results than a page ranked 1.)

There are two ways to find your website's simplified PageRank. First, you can use the free Google Toolbar (*www.google.com/toolbar*), which snaps onto your browser window and provides a PageRank button. However, you need to explicitly turn on this feature, as described at *http://tinyurl.com/64bjmtd*. A simpler approach is to use an unofficial PageRank-checking website, like *www.prchecker.info* (Figure 12-17).

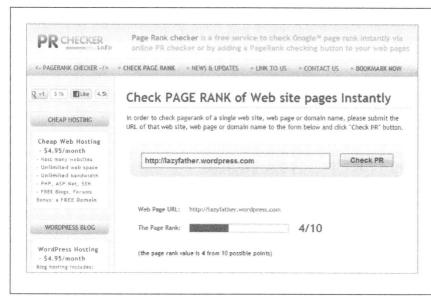

FIGURE 12-17

To see the PageRank for your home page, type in your site's address and click Check PR. Here, http://lazyfather .wordpress.com scores a middle-of-the-road 4 out of 10.

The simplified PageRank score isn't always accurate. If you submit a site that's very new, or hasn't yet established itself on the Web (in other words, few people are visiting it and no one's linking to it), you may not get a PageRank value at all.

> **TIP** Don't worry too much about your exact PageRank value. Instead, use it as a tool to gauge how your website improves or declines over time. For example, if your home page scored a PageRank of 4 last year, but earns a PageRank of 6 this year, your promotion is clearly on the right path.

Getting More Links

The cornerstone of search-engine ranking is links—the more people connect to you, the greater your Web prestige, and the more trustworthy your site seems to Google. Here are some tips any WordPresser can use to build up their links:

- **Look for sites that are receptive to your content.** To get more links, you need to reach out and interact with other websites. Offer to guest-blog on a like-minded site, join a community group, or sign up with free website directories that include your type of business. Or, if your site has a broader reach, search for your topic in Google Blogsearch (*http://blogsearch.google.com*) to find similar sites.

- **Keep sharing.** The social sharing techniques you learned about in the first part of this chapter are doubly important for PageRank. Although tweets and Likes aren't as powerful as website links, Google still counts them in your favor when respected people talk about your content on social media sites.

- **Add off-site links (that point to you).** You don't need to wait for other people to notice your content. It's perfectly acceptable to post a good comment on someone else's

blog, with a link that references something you wrote. Or, post in a forum, making sure your signature includes your name *and* a link to your site. The trick is to find sites and forums that share the same interests as your site. For example, if you're an artisanal cheesemaker in Chicago, it makes sense to chat with the people running organic food co-operatives. But be careful. There's a thin line between spreading the word about your fantastic content and spamming other people. So don't post on a forum or someone else's site unless you can say something truly insightful or genuinely helpful. If you're not sure whether to post, ask yourself this question: "If this were my site, would I appreciate this comment?"

- **Research your competitors' links.** If you find out where other people are getting their links from, you may be able to get links from the same sites. Google has a nifty feature that can help, called *link.* turn on put *link:* in front a full website address in a search to find the other sites that lead to that site. For example, searching for *link:www.magicteahouse.net* will show you all the sites that link to the home page on *www.magicteahouse.net*.

Making Your Site Google-Friendly

You can't trick Google into loving your site, and there's no secret technique to vault your site to the top of the search page rankings. However, you can give your site the best possible odds by following some good habits. These practices help search engines find their way around your posts, understand your content, and recognize that you're a real site with good content, not a sneaky spammer trying to cheat the system.

Here are some guidelines to SEO that don't require special plug-ins or custom coding:

- **Choose the right permalink style.** Every WordPress post and page gets its own permalink. If you're creating a self-hosted site, your permalinks should include the post title, because the search engine pays special attention to the words in your URL. (Page 116 explains how to change your permalink style.) If you're using a WordPress.com site, you already have the right permalink style.

- **Edit your permalinks.** When you first create a post, you have the chance to edit its permalink. At this point, you can improve it by removing unimportant words (like "a", "and," and "the"). Or, if you're using a cute, jokey title for your post, you can replace the title in the permalink with something that's more topical and includes the keywords you expect web searchers to use. For example, if you write a post about your favorite cookware titled "Out of the Frying Pan and Into the Fire," you ordinarily get a permalink like this *http://triplegoldcookwarereview.com/out-of-the-frying-pan-and-into-the-fire*. If you remove some words, you can shorten it to *http://triplegoldcookwarereview.com/out-of-frying-pan-into-fire*. And if you substitute a more descriptive title, you might choose *http://triplegoldcookwarereview.com/calphalon-fry-pan-review*.

- **Use your tags.** Google pays close attention to the tags you assign to a post. If they match a web searcher's keywords, your post has a better chance of showing up in the search results. When choosing tags, pick just a few, and make sure that they clearly describe your topic and correspond to terms someone might search for (say, "artisanal cheese," "organic," and "local food"). Some search-obsessed bloggers scour Google statistics to find the best keywords to use in attracting web searchers, and use those as their tags in new posts. However, that's too much work for all but the most fanatical SEO addicts.

- **Optimize your images.** Google and other search engines let people search for pictures. When someone searches for an image, Google attempts to match the search keywords with the words that appear near the picture on a web page, and the alternate text that describes the picture. That means people are more likely to find your pictures if you fill out all the details in the Add Media window, including a title, the alternate text, a caption, and a description (page 180). Remember to use descriptive, searchable keywords when you do.

GEM IN THE ROUGH

Hiding from Search Engines

You don't *have* to let search engines find you. If you want keep a low profile, choose Settings→Privacy, and then turn on the radio button beside "Ask search engines not to index this site." That way, your website won't appear in most search engine listings.

People will still be able to find you if they click a link that leads to your site, or if they know your site address. For that reason, you shouldn't rely on this trick to conceal yourself if you're do-

ing something dubious or risky—say, planning a bank robbery, cursing your employer, or trying to sell someone else's pirated software. In cases where you need utmost privacy, you can use WordPress's private site feature (page 373), or just keep yourself off the Web.

Boosting SEO with a Plug-In

If you run a self-hosted site, you can make it even more attractive to Google and other search engines by using an SEO plug-in. But be warned, most SEO plug-ins are an extreme case of overkill for the casual WordPress site-builder. Prepare to be swamped by pages of options and search settings.

If you search WordPress's plug-in repository for "SEO," you'll discover quite a few popular plug-ins. One of the best is WordPress SEO by Yoast (*http://tinyurl.com/ seo-yoast*). Its creator is WordPress über-guru Joost de Valk, who also blogs some useful (but somewhat technical) SEO articles at *http://yoast.com/cat/seo*.

Once you install and activate the WordPress SEO by Yoast plug-in, you'll see a new SEO menu in your dashboard, and it's packed with a dizzying array of options. You can ignore most of them, unless you want to change the way the plug-in works. The following sections explain a two useful features you can tap into right away..

■ CREATING AN XML SITEMAP

After installing the SEO plug-in, your site gets one immediate benefit: an *XML sitemap*. This is a document that tells Google where your content resides on your site. It ensures that all your posts get indexed, even if they aren't all accessible from your home page. Although you don't need to give your XML sitemap another thought, you can take a look at it by choosing SEO→XML Sitemaps, and then clicking the XML Sitemap button. Needless to say, the WordPress SEO by Yoast plug-in updates your sitemap every time you publish a new post or page.

> **NOTE** The XML sitemap feature works only if you're using descriptive permalinks that include the post name (as explained on page 116). If you're using the stock ID-based permalinks, the plug-in won't create an XML sitemap.

■ TWEAKING TITLES AND DESCRIPTIONS

The WordPress SEO by Yoast plug-in also gives you control over two important details: the title and *meta description* of each post or page. These details are useful—even to SEO newbies—because Google displays them when it lists a page from your site in its search results. Figure 12-18 shows an example.

The title and description are also important because Google gives more weight to keywords in these places than keywords in your content. In other words, if someone searches for "dog breeding" and you have those words in your title, you can beat an equally ranked page that doesn't.

Ordinarily, the WordPress SEO by Yoast plug-in picks a good title when you create a new post, based on a title-generating formula that's set in the SEO→Titles & Metas section. This formula puts your post name first, followed by your site name, like this for the "crystal jasmine" post:

```
Crystal Jasmine Named Tea of the Year - Magic Tea House
```

However, you can customize the title before you publish the post using the Word-Press SEO by Yoast box, which appears on the Add New Post page (Figure 12-19). For example, it's a good idea to shorten overly long post titles, and replace cutesy titles with ones that clearly describe your content. You can also use the WordPress SEO by Yoast box to type in a meta description.

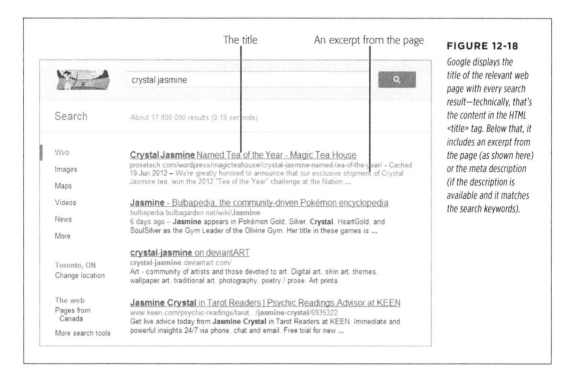

The title An excerpt from the page

FIGURE 12-18

Google displays the title of the relevant web page with every search result—technically, that's the content in the HTML <title> tag. Below that, it includes an excerpt from the page (as shown here) or the meta description (if the description is available and it matches the search keywords).

The WordPress SEO by Yoast box also lets you perform a pretend Google search so you can see how your newly chosen title and description perform. To do that, simply type the search keyword you want to test in the Focus Keyword box. Figure 12-20 shows an example.

> **TIP** For even more ways to optimize your site for search engines using the WordPress SEO by Yoast plug-in, check out his detailed tutorial at *http://yoast.com/articles/wordpress-seo*.

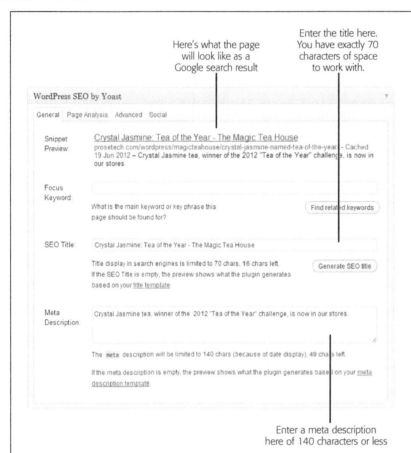

Here's what the page will look like as a Google search result

Enter the title here. You have exactly 70 characters of space to work with.

Enter a meta description here of 140 characters or less

FIGURE 12-19

In this example, the post has a new title and a meta description. The WordPress SEO by Yoast plug-in shows a preview of what the page will look like in a Google search. Compare it to the original version in Figure 12-18.

FIGURE 12-20

The keyword combination "crystal jasmine" occurs in the heading of your post, the title of your page, the permalink, the actual post content, and your meta description for the page. All these details increase the odds that a visitor searching for these words will find your page. Of course, all these efforts are for naught if you haven't written a decent post.

WordPress Site Statistics

Once you have some solid promotion tactics in place, you need to evaluate how well they're performing. There's no point in pursuing a failed strategy for months, when you should be investing more effort in a technique that actually *is* working. The best way to assess your site's performance, and see how it changes over time, is to collect *website statistics*.

There are a number of popular statistics packages that work with WordPress, and a range of plug-ins that automatically add tracking code to your site. In this section, you'll focus on WordPress's own statistics-collection service, which it automatically provides to all WordPress.com sites and which is available to self-hosted sites through the Jetpack plug-in.

Viewing Your Statistics

The best place to view your site statistics is on the WordPress.com home page. Go to *http://wordpress.com*, log in, and click the Stats tab. If you have more than one site, you need to pick just one from the drop-down menu in the top-right corner (Figure 12-21).

NOTE Jetpack users can see the same statistics by choosing Jetpack→Site Stats in the dashboard. However, WordPress encourages everyone to view statistics on the WordPress.com home page, and it may remove the statistics link from the dashboard in the future.

The obvious question is now that you have all this raw data, what can you do with it? Ideally, you'll use site statistics to focus on your strengths, improve your site, and keep your visitors happy. You should resist the temptation to use it as a source of endlessly fascinating trivia. If you spend the afternoon counting how many visitors hit your site from Bulgaria, you're probably wasting time that could be better spent writing brilliant content.

The following sections present four basic strategies that can help you find useful information in your statistics, and use that insight to improve your site without wasting hours of your time.

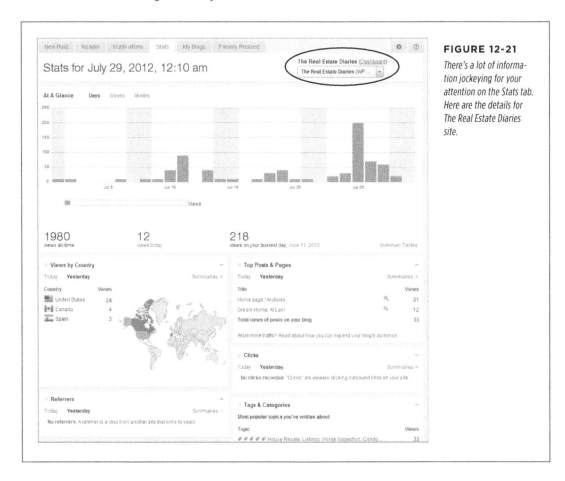

Strategy 1. Find Out What Your Readers Like

If you know what you're doing right, you can do a lot more of it. For example, if you write a blog with scathing political commentary, and your readers flock to any article that mentions gun control, you might want to continue exploring the issue in future posts. (Or, to put it less charitably, you might decide to milk the topic for all the pageviews you can get before your readers get bored.)

To make decisions like these, you need to know what content gets the most attention. A Facebook Like button (page 396), a WordPress.com Like button (page 399), or PollDaddy ratings (page 400) may help you spot popular posts, but a more thorough way to measure success is to look at your traffic. On the Stats page, focus on the Top Posts & Pages box, which shows you the most read posts and pages over the past couple of days (Figure 12-22).

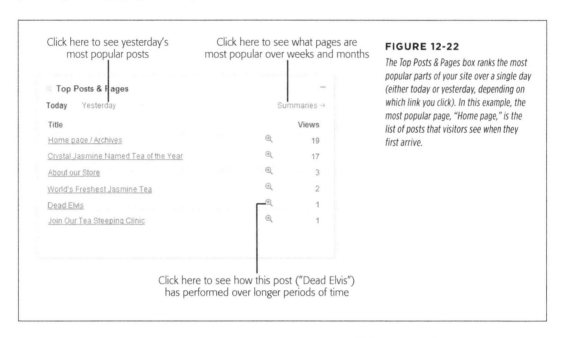

Click here to see yesterday's most popular posts

Click here to see what pages are most popular over weeks and months

Click here to see how this post ("Dead Elvis") has performed over longer periods of time

FIGURE 12-22

The Top Posts & Pages box ranks the most popular parts of your site over a single day (either today or yesterday, depending on which link you click). In this example, the most popular page, "Home page," is the list of posts that visitors see when they first arrive.

The Top Posts & Pages box gives you a snapshot of the current activity on your site, but to make real conclusions about what content stirs your readers' hearts, you need to take a long-term perspective. To do that, click the Summaries link. Now Word-Press lets you compare your top pages over the past week, month, quarter, year, or of all time. Just keep in mind that bigger timeframes are often biased toward older articles, because they've been around the longest.

If you analyze a site on WordPress.com, you can also check out the Tags & Categories section. It shows you the categories and tags that draw the most interest. You can form two conclusions from this box—popular categories may reflect content your readers want to keep reading, and popular tags may indicate keywords that align with popular search terms (see Strategy 3 on page 422).

Strategy 2. Who's Giving You the Love?

There are three ways a visitor can arrive at your site:

- By typing your address into their browser (or use a bookmark—it's the same thing).

- By following a link from another site that points to you.

- By performing a search, and following a link in a search results page.

The first type of visitor already knows about you. There's not much you can do to improve on that.

The second and third types of visitor are more difficult to predict. You need to track them so you can optimize your web promotion strategies. In this section, you'll focus on the second type of guest. These people arrive at your site from another website, otherwise known as a *referrer.*

If you followed the link-building strategies laid out on page 414, the social sharing tips from page 390, and the publicizing techniques described on page 404, you've created many different routes that a reader can take to get to your site. But which are heavily traveled and which are overgrown and abandoned? To find out, you need to check the Referrers box, which ranks the sites that people come from in order of most to least popular (Figure 12-23).

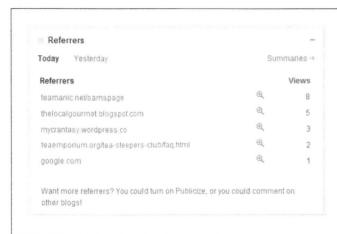

Referrers

Today   Yesterday   Summaries →

Referrers   Views
teamanic.net/samspage   8
thelocalgourmet.blogspot.com   5
mycrantasy.wordpress.co   3
teaemporium.org/tea-steepers-club/faq.html   2
google.com   1

Want more referrers? You could turn on Publicize, or you could comment on other blogs!

FIGURE 12-23

Use the Referrers box to see where your visitors came from. It shows you the referring sites from a single day. You can click a specific referrer to get more information, or you can click Summaries to examine your top referrers over longer periods of time.

Once you know your top referrers, you can adjust your promotional strategies. For example, you may want to stop spending time and effort advertising your site in places that don't generate traffic. Similarly, you might want to spend more effort cultivating your top referrers to ensure you keep a steady stream of visitors coming to your site.

Strategy 3. Play Well with Search Engines

In any given minute, Google handles well over a million search queries. If you're lucky, a tiny slice of those searchers will end up at your site.

Webmasters pay special attention to visitors who arrive through search engines. Usually, these are new people who haven't read your content before, which makes them exactly the sort of person you need to attract. But it's not enough to know that visitors arrive through a search engine. You need to understand what *brought* them to your site, and to understand that you need to know what they were searching for.

The Search Engine Terms box can help answer this question (Figure 12-24). It lists the top queries that led visitors to your site for a single day (or, if you click Summaries, over a longer period of time).

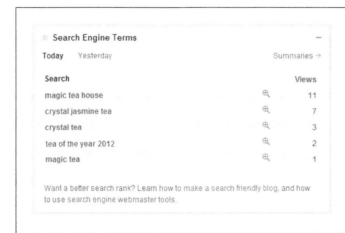

FIGURE 12-24

Here are the keywords that led different searchers to the Magic Tea House. Notice that you may not see the common, short keywords that you expect (like "tea," by itself). That's because the more general a keyword is, the more sites there are competing for that keyword, and the less likely it is that a searcher will spot your site.

If you use SEO to find what you think are the best keywords for tags, titles, or descriptions (see, for example, page 416), the Search Engine Terms box helps you determine if your efforts are paying off. And even if you aren't, it gives you insight into hot topics that attract new readers—and which you might want to focus on in the future.

Strategy 4. Meet Your Top Commenters

If WordPress.com hosts your site, you can tap one more set of useful statistics. Take a look in the Comments box to see which of your visitors left the greatest number of comments, and which posts stirred the most conversation (Figure 12-25).

FIGURE 12-25

Comments are the lifeblood of a WordPress site. A site with a thriving Comments section is more likely to attract new visitors and to keep existing ones. By examining the Comments box, you can see who deserves the most credit for keeping your conversations alive.

The most interesting information is the top commenters. These people are particularly valuable, because their input can start discussions and keep the conversation going.

Once you identify your top commenters in the past week or month, you can make an effort to strengthen your (and therefore your site's) relationship with them. Make an extra effort to reply to their comments and questions, and consider making a visit to their blog and commenting on their posts. If they stick around, you might even offer them the chance to guest post on your site, or become a contributor (page 354).

From Blog to Website

Editing Themes: The Key to Customizing Your Site

As you've traveled through this book, you've taken a look at every significant feature that WordPress offers, and used those capabilities to build a variety of sites. However, you've always played by the rules, picking themes from the theme gallery, installing plug-ins from the plug-in directory, and sticking to the safety of the WordPress dashboard. But there's a whole other world of possibilities for those who can color outside the lines.

The key to unlocking more flexibility and building a truly unique WordPress site is to create your own theme. As you know, a theme is a mash-up of HTML markup, formatting rules, and PHP code. Ordinarily, these details are hidden from you—the people who create the themes and plug-ins your site uses handle all this, while you focus on writing fab content and adjusting settings in the dashboard. But if you decide to cut loose and become a theme customizer (or even a theme *creator*), you step into a different world. Be forewarned: this world can seem dizzyingly complex. But you don't need to understand every detail. Instead, you simply need to find the parts of a theme you want to change, and work on those.

In this chapter, you'll start your journey to becoming a theme customizer. You'll take a close look at how themes work, and you'll learn how to make small alterations that can have big effects. First, you'll try modifying styles. Then, you'll crack open the theme files to change the code stored inside. All this is preparation for the next chapter, where you'll build a new theme for a completely customized website.

◼ The Goal: More Flexible Blogs and Sites

Before you begin fiddling with themes, you need to have a clear idea of *why* you'd want to do so. In other words, what do you hope to gain by changing a theme that you can't get by using a good, preexisting theme with just the right combination of WordPress settings and plug-ins?

There are several good answers:

- To get something *exactly* the way you want it

- To make your site unique

- To create a site that doesn't look "bloggy" (see the next section)

Custom themes are the key to unlocking WordPress and to building any sort of website you can imagine. Your task might not be easy, but custom themes make it *possible*.

> **NOTE** Often, WordPressers first delve into a theme to make a tiny alteration. But it rarely stops there. The ability to transform a site, often by changing just a single style rule or modifying a single line of code, is addictive. If you catch the bug, you'll want to customize every theme you touch, and you'll be unable to rest until you get exactly the result you want out of every site.

WordPress Sites (That Aren't Blogs)

One reason to customize a theme is to create a site that looks and feels less like a blog. It's a bit difficult to pin down exactly what this means, because no one can agree on exactly what a blog is (see the sidebar on page 430).

That said, most sites built with WordPress have some characteristics that make them feel more bloggish and less like the sort of complex, traditional websites that rule the world of business and e-commerce. For example, WordPress sites usually display dated posts in reverse chronological order. But what if you want to build a product showcase where the posts are actually product profiles, and you don't want them to show any date information at all?

Another limitation is the fact that WordPress treats all its posts the same way. But what if you want create an e-magazine with a custom-made home page for each news category you cover (Sports, Current Affairs, Lifestyle, and so on)? You can't make those kinds of changes unless you're willing to step away from WordPress's blog origins and customize your theme. Do that, and you can build a WordPress site that behaves like almost any other type of site you've seen on the Web.

Before you get there, you need to learn a bit more about the way WordPress themes work—and lucky for you, that's the point of this chapter. Figure 13-1 shows the final goal—a completely customized website, which you'll learn to build in Chapter 14.

FIGURE 13-1

Top: Not many clues tell you that Word-Press's blogging engine actually powers this e-commerce store. Bottom: Here's the same site, without a custom theme. It still functions (more or less), but it's back to feeling like a blog.

When Is a Blog Not a Blog?

Originally, WordPress was designed to be the world's best tool for building a blog. To most people, the word blog (short for *web log*) meant a personal journal made up of dated posts.

No sooner were blogs created than the definition of what a blog could do began to expand. Bloggers began to create more topical blogs—for example, ones that provided political commentary, chronicled cooking exploits, or deconstructed popular television shows. For the most part, blogs were still intensely personal, but they were no longer restricted to covering people's personal lives.

Since then, the definition of *blog* has continued its aggressive expansion. Now, blogs aren't necessarily written by a single person in the first-person voice. They include sites that were never described as blogs before—for example, magazine-like news sites and picture-focused photoblogs or portfolio sites. Businesses often create "bloggy" sites rather than traditional

websites, especially if they want to build social buzz or emphasize news and events. (For example, that hot restaurant setting up shop down the street might feel, legitimately so, that a blog's a better way to get people talking than a boring brochure site.)

This discussion raises an important question: When do blogs stop being blogs? Usually, you'll recognize a blog because it contains dated entries you can read (usually) in reverse chronological order, and browse by category or tag. However, depending on the theme you pick and the content you use, these blog-like characteristics can be deemphasized to such a point that many people won't consider your blog a blog at all. Throughout this book, you've seen several examples of "blogs" that stretch the definition of the word blog in this way, such as the Canton School site (page 186) and the Pernatch Restaurant site (page 221).

NOTE If you're curious to get more ideas for non-bloggish sites that WordPress can create, visit the gallery of examples at *http://tinyurl.com/9dvpn3y*.

Getting Ready

Before you can move from WordPress-the-blogging-platform to WordPress-the-site-design-tool, you need to satisfy a few conditions. First, you need to self-host WordPress—WordPress.com doesn't give you the flexibility you need to stretch your site-design wings. Second, you need to be ready to crack open the template files that run the WordPress show.

NOTE While it's true that, to edit a theme, you need a self-hosted site, WordPress.com users aren't completely left out. If you bought the custom CSS upgrade, you can use many of the theme customization techniques described on page 439. You just won't be able to edit templates, change the PHP code, or build a complex site like the one demonstrated in Chapter 14.

You should also be familiar with the basics of HTML markup—comfortable enough to find your way through the tangle of angle brackets and elements that lives in every web page.

It also helps to know some CSS (that's the Cascading Style Sheets standard that formats every modern page). If you don't, you'll still be able to feel your way around with the quick introduction you'll get on page 440, but be prepared for a steep learning curve.

If you need more help, here are two good places to go:

- If you've never edited a web page before, or you need to brush up on your HTML skills, consider *Creating a Website: The Missing Manual*, which covers the HTML and CSS standards (and plenty more besides). Or, you can read a barebones HTML tutorial at *http://tinyurl.com/4mwq8*.

- If you want to learn about CSS only, consider *CSS: The Missing Manual* by David Sawyer McFarland. Or, you can try an online CSS tutorial at *http://tinyurl.com/mlqk7*.

NOTE You don't need to understand *everything* about HTML and CSS to change a WordPress theme. Often, you can google your way to the style rule or PHP code you need to implement a feature you want. You can then copy and paste that code into the right theme file, without worrying about any other details.

■ Taking Control of Your Theme

Before you can create a brilliantly customized WordPress theme, you need to know a bit more about how themes work, behind the scenes.

When you first met themes in Chapter 5, you discovered that every theme consists of a combination of files. These files work together to create all the pages on your WordPress site. The files in a theme fall into three basic categories:

- **Style sheets.** These files contain style rules that format different parts of your site, such as headlines, sidebar headings, and links. These use the much-loved CSS standard, which will be familiar to anyone who's dabbled in web design.

- **Templates.** These files contain a mix of ordinary HTML and PHP code. Each template is responsible for creating a different part of your site—for example, there's a template for the list of recent posts, the page header, the footer, the single-post view, and so on.

- **Resources.** These are other files that your theme's templates might use, often to add a bit of pizzazz. Examples include image files, like the one Greyzed used to create its dirty stone background (page 157); and JavaScript code, like the stuff the Brightpage theme used to run its featured image slideshow (page 186).

At a bare minimum, every theme needs two files: a single style sheet named *style.css*, which sets the colors, layout, and fonts for your entire site; and a template named *index.php*, which creates the list of posts on your home page. Most themes have a few more style sheets and many more templates, but you'll get to that in a moment.

How WordPress Stores Themes

On your WordPress site, the *wp-content/themes* folder holds all your themes. For example, if your website address is *http://magicteahouse.net*, the Twenty Eleven theme will be in the following folder:

```
http://magicteahouse.net/wp-content/themes/twentyeleven
```

Each theme you install gets its own subfolder. So if you install seven themes on your website, you'll see seven subfolders in the *wp-content/themes* folder, even though you use only one theme at a time.

All the related style sheets and template files reside inside a theme's folder (Figure 13-2). Most themes also have subfolders. For example, they might tuck JavaScript files into a subfolder named *js* and image files into a subfolder named *images*. You don't need to worry about these details as long as you remember that themes are a package of files and subfolders you need to keep together in order for your site to function properly.

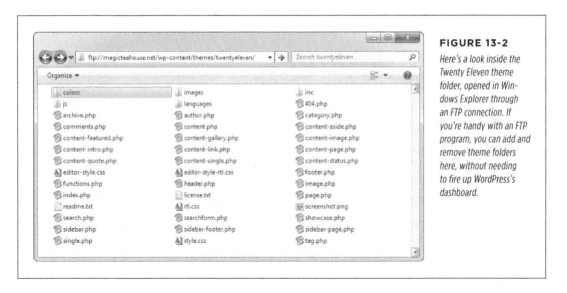

FIGURE 13-2

Here's a look inside the Twenty Eleven theme folder, opened in Windows Explorer through an FTP connection. If you're handy with an FTP program, you can add and remove theme folders here, without needing to fire up WordPress's dashboard.

Style.css: How a Theme Identifies Itself

The *style.css* file is the starting point of every theme. In most themes, it's a huge file packed with formatting instructions. For example, the Twenty Eleven theme's *style .css* file weighs in with more than *two thousand* lines of formatting magic.

The *style.css* file also defines a few essentials pieces of information about the style itself. It does that using a *theme header* at the beginning of the file. Here's a slightly shortened version of the header that starts the *style.css* file in the Twenty Eleven theme. Each distinct bit of information is highlighted in bold:

```
/*

Theme Name: Twenty Eleven
Theme URI: http://wordpress.org/extend/themes/twentyeleven
Author: the WordPress team
Author URI: http://wordpress.org/
Description: The 2011 theme for WordPress is sophisticated, lightweight, ...
Version: 1.4
License: GNU General Public License v2 or later
License URI: http://www.gnu.org/licenses/gpl-2.0.html
Tags: dark, light, white, black, gray, one-column, two-columns, left-sidebar,
...

*/
```

WordPress brackets the header with two special character sequences: it starts with /* and ends with */, the CSS comment markers. As a result, browsers don't pay any attention to the header. But WordPress checks it, and extracts the key details. It uses this information for the theme description you see in the Install Themes tab (page 162). WordPress also tracks the version number and checks the theme URL for new versions. (Although it says "URI" in the theme file, a URI is the same as a URL when you're dealing with content on the Web, as in the case of themes.)

If your theme lacks these details, WordPress won't recognize that it's a theme. It won't show it in the Appearance→Themes section of the dashboard, and it won't let you activate it on your site.

NOTE Many themes include style sheets beyond *style.css*. However, these style sheets are for extra features or specialized cases—for example, to provide alternate color schemes, to deal with old browsers, to handle languages that write text from right-to-left, and to format the content in the editing box when you create a new post, so it provides the most realistic preview possible.

The Theme Editor

If you want to edit a theme, choose Appearance→Editor in the dashboard. This brings you to the Edit Themes page, with your current theme loaded.

WordPress splits the Edit Themes page into two parts. On the right is a sidebar that lists all the files in your theme. And in the center of the page is a giant editing box that lets you edit your theme, one file at a time (Figure 13-3).

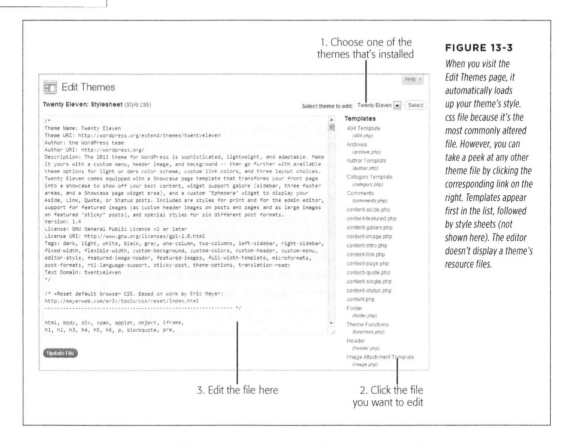

1. Choose one of the themes that's installed

FIGURE 13-3

When you visit the Edit Themes page, it automatically loads up your theme's style. css file because it's the most commonly altered file. However, you can take a peek at any other theme file by clicking the corresponding link on the right. Templates appear first in the list, followed by style sheets (not shown here). The editor doesn't display a theme's resource files.

3. Edit the file here

2. Click the file you want to edit

Once you finish making changes to a file in your theme, click Update File to save it. You can then choose a different file to edit.

If you want to make extensive changes to a theme, you might not want to do all the work in the cramped environment of the dashboard. You might prefer to download your theme files and edit them on your computer. Some web editing programs, like Dreamweaver, even have built-in theme-editing features for WordPress.

One way to do this is to pick the file you want to edit, copy its content, and paste it into a text editor (like Notepad on Windows PCs or TextEdit on Macs). Then, after you make your changes, you can copy the edited content back into the editing box. But assuming you want to edit multiple files, it's easier to download the whole theme folder. To do that, browse your website with an FTP program (as shown in Figure 13-2) and then drag the theme folder to your computer's desktop. When you finish making changes, delete the original folder from your website and drag the new version back to your website to upload it.

■ Protecting Yourself with a Child Theme

Before you start mucking around with one of your themes, you should think about the long-term effects. Someday, probably not long from today, the person who created the theme you're editing will release a new and improved version that you'll want to use on your site. Here's the problem: if you install a theme update, you wipe out all the edits you made to your theme files. Editing themes is enough work without having to do it over and over again.

Fortunately, there's a solution. You can create a *child theme*, which takes the current theme as a starting point, and lets you slap your customizations on top. You don't change the original theme (known as the *parent theme*) at all. Instead, you selectively edit the templates and style sheets and save those altered files in the child theme folder. These new files override the same-named templates and style sheets in the parent theme, so you get the features you want in your site. And when you update the *parent* theme at some future date, your customizations stay in place, because WordPress stores the child theme as a separate group of files.

To customize a theme, you should *always* start by creating a child theme. However, if you want to create a completely new, original theme, you *shouldn't* use a child theme. You might still use an existing theme as a starting point for your work, but there's no need to create a child theme. Your changes will be so significant that future updates and fixes won't be relevant to your tricked-out theme.

> **NOTE** All the examples in this chapter use child themes. Creating a complete theme on your own is a significant undertaking for even the best propeller heads among us, although you'll get an introduction to the practice in Chapter 14.

Creating a Child Theme

To create a child theme, you need to create a new theme folder in the *wp-content/ themes* section of your website. Name the folder whatever you want. However, unlike a normal theme folder, you don't need to fill this folder with files. Instead, all you need to do is put a new *style.css* file inside the folder—one that links itself to the parent theme via the theme header.

If this sounds like a slightly intimidating challenge, don't worry. Rather than go to the hassle of creating the folder for your child theme and creating the *style.css* file with the right header, you can use a tiny plug-in, called One-Click Child Theme (*http://tinyurl.com/child-theme*), to help you out. Here's what to do:

1. **Install and activate the One-Click Child Theme plug-in.**

   You do this the usual way—by choosing Plugins→Add New, and searching for it by name.

2. **Activate the theme you want to customize.**

The Once-Click Child Theme plug-in assumes you want to create a child theme for the theme that's active on your site. If this isn't the case, activate the right theme now in the Appearance→Themes section.

3. **Choose Appearance→Child Theme.**

This is a new menu command, courtesy of the One-Click Child Theme plug-in. It leads you to the Create a Child Theme page (Figure 13-4).

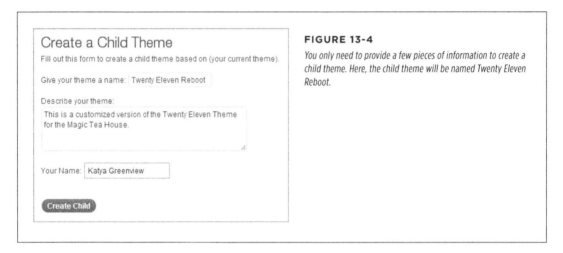

Create a Child Theme
Fill out this form to create a child theme based on (your current theme).

Give your theme a name: Twenty Eleven Reboot

Describe your theme:

This is a customized version of the Twenty Eleven Theme for the Magic Tea House.

Your Name: Katya Greenview

Create Child

FIGURE 13-4

You only need to provide a few pieces of information to create a child theme. Here, the child theme will be named Twenty Eleven Reboot.

4. **Supply a name for the theme, a brief description, and your name.**

The header of the *style.css* file stores all these details in your new child theme. Your name will be recorded as the theme author.

5. **Click Create Child.**

The One-Click Child Theme plug-in creates the folder on your web server, and creates a new *style.css* file inside it. It then activates the child theme on your site.

In this example, the theme is named Twenty Eleven Reboot, so the newly created folder will be named *twenty-eleven-reboot*.

6. **To verify that your child theme is working, choose Appearance→Themes.**

You'll see your new child theme at the top of the Manage Themes tab (Figure 13-5).

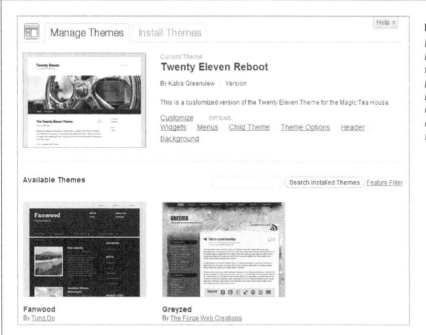

FIGURE 13-5

Right now, the Twenty Eleven Reboot child theme is identical to its parent theme, Twenty Eleven. The One-Click Child Theme Plug-In even gives it the same thumbnail picture.

Within the figure:

Manage Themes | Install Themes

Help ▾

Current Theme

Twenty Eleven Reboot

By Katya Greenview | Version

This is a customized version of the Twenty Eleven Theme for the Magic Tea House.

Customize   OPTIONS:
Widgets   Menus   Child Theme   Theme Options   Header
Background

Available Themes

Search Installed Themes | Feature Filter

Fanwood
By Tung Do

Greyzed
By The Forge Web Creations

7. **Customize your header and background, if necessary.**

When you switch to a new theme, even a child theme, you lose your previous header and background settings. You don't lose your layout choices, your menus, or your arrangement of widgets. These are the only signs on your site that you switched from the original theme (in this example, Twenty Eleven) to the new child theme (Twenty Eleven Reboot). The formatting doesn't change, because the templates and the style files are all the same—for now.

How Child Themes Work

If you check out the newly created folder for your child theme, you'll find it holds just three files. The first is the all-important *style.css* file. The second is a supplementary style sheet for right-to-left languages named *rtl.css*. The third is an image named *screenshot.png* that WordPress copied from the parent theme; it uses this image for the thumbnail in the Manage Themes tab (Figure 13-5).

To start editing your child theme, choose Appearance→Editor. You'll start with the *style.css* file (Figure 13-6), as you do when you edit a normal theme.

Click here to load the Twenty Eleven theme in the editor

FIGURE 13-6

A child theme starts life as little more than stripped-down style.css file that refers back to its parent theme. As you edit the child theme, you'll need to visit the parent theme frequently (click the link shown here) because it's the starting point for many of your changes.

The key to a child theme is its *style.css* style sheet. Unlike the *style.css* file in the parent theme, the *style.css* in the child theme contains just a few lines of text. Here's the complete *style.css* file in the Twenty Eleven Reboot theme (as defined in Figure 13-4):

```
/*
Theme Name: Twenty Eleven Reboot
Description: This is a customized version of the Twenty Eleven Theme for the
Magic Tea House.
Author: Katya Greenview
Template: twentyeleven
*/

@import url("../twentyeleven/style.css");
```

You've already seen the first three details (theme name, description, and author). However, the template setting is new—it points to the parent theme's folder. When WordPress sees this setting, it knows to look in a folder named *twentyeleven* (in the themes section of your site). When it does, it finds the files for the familiar Twenty Eleven theme.

Unlike the original version of the *style.css* file in the Twenty Eleven theme, the child theme contains just a single line after the header. This line grabs all the styles from the Twenty Eleven theme and applies them to the child theme:

```
@import url("../twentyeleven/style.css");
```

If you're foolish enough to delete this line, your site will lose all the styles from the parent theme. (You can try it out, just remember to add the @import statement back when you finish.) Suddenly, all your text will switch to the generic Times New Roman font, your nicely formatted headings will disappear, and the layout of your headers, footers, and sidebar will get scrambled together in a mess.

TIP Child themes are a great way to customize your site permanently, but they're also a handy tool for *temporarily* changing your formatting. For example, the Magic Tea House might decide to run a special winter promotion. During this promotion, they plan to make sweeping changes to the color scheme of their site. If they use a child theme to make these changes, they can quickly go back to the original theme when the promotion is over. (They simply need to choose Appearance→Themes and activate the parent theme.)

■ Editing the Styles in Your Theme

There are a number of reasons you might crack open your theme's styles and make changes:

- **Unique-ify your theme.** You might change your theme to make sure your site doesn't have the same look as other sites that share that theme. After all, there are only so many themes, and if you pick a good one, it's a safe bet that you're following in the footsteps of thousands of other webmasters.

- **Branding.** Perhaps you need your theme to match the official corporate colors of your business. Or you might want it to more closely resemble another website, run by the same business, that doesn't use WordPress.

- **Highlight certain design elements.** By changing a theme, you can emphasize details that are important to you. For example, maybe you want to use a style that makes author comments stand out (page 446).

To make changes to any theme, you follow two steps. First, you create a child theme (page 435). Then, you add one or more style rules to the *style.css* file in your child theme. These rules will selectively override the original theme, letting you change whatever you don't like.

However, it's not quite as easy as it sounds. To cook up the right style rule, you need to know a bit more about the CSS standard and the styles your theme uses. Every theme is slightly different, but most include a gargantuan *style.css* file stuffed full of formatting instructions. Finding the exact detail you want to override may take some digging. In the next section, you'll take your first look at the sort of instructions the *style.css* file contains.

> **NOTE** If you're already well-versed in the CSS standard, you can skip the next section and continue on to the one after that, called "Changing the Twenty Eleven Theme."

Taking a Look at the Style Rules in Your Theme

Reading the average *style.css* file is not for the faint of heart. As explained earlier, the typical theme includes hundreds or thousands of formatting instructions. Understanding any one of them isn't too difficult, but finding the exact one you want can be a challenge.

■ DECODING A BASIC RULE

The first step to understanding CSS styles is to take a look at a few style rules and get familiar with their syntax.

Every style sheet is a long list of rules, and every rule follows the same format, which looks like this:

```
selector {
  property: value;
  property: value;
}
```

Here's what each part means:

- The selector identifies the type of content you want to format. A browser hunts down all the elements on a web page that match the selector. There are many ways to write a selector, but one of the simplest (shown next) is to identify the elements you want to format by their element name. For example, you could write a selector that picks out all the level-1 headings on a page.

- The property identifies the type of formatting you want to apply. Here's where you choose whether you want to change colors, fonts, alignment, or something else. You can have as many property settings as you want in a rule—the example above has two.

- The value sets a value for the property. For example, if your property is *color*, the value could be light blue or queasy green.

Now here's a real rule from the Twenty Eleven theme:

```
body {
  background: #fff;
  line-height: 1;
}
```

This tells a browser to find the web page's <body> element, which wraps all the content on the page. The browser applies two formatting instructions to the <body> element. First, it changes the background color. (You'll be excused for not knowing that #fff is an HTML color code that means white.) Second, it sets the line spacing to a normal value of 1. (A higher value would add more space between each line of text.)

You need several skills to decode a style sheet rule like this. First, you need to know the basics of HTML, so you understand what the <body> element is, and what it does in a web page. Second, you need to know what style properties are available for you to tweak. In this case, for example, you have to be aware that editing the background property lets you change the color behind an element. Style rules let you change color, typeface, borders, size, positioning, and alignment. Third, you need to know what values are appropriate for setting a property—for example, you set a page's background color using an HTML color code. (In the case of colors, you can pick the color you want and get its HTML color code from a color-picking site like *www.colorpicker.com*.)

> **TIP** You can get style sheet help from a book like *CSS: The Missing Manual*. Or, if all you need is an overview of the style properties you can change and their acceptable values, check out the style sheet reference at *http://tinyurl.com/bz5tcp*.

■ OTHER TYPES OF SELECTORS

The style sheet rule in the above example targeted the <body> element specifically. Such a rule is called an *element rule*, because it applies to a specific element on a page. For example, if you write a rule that formats <h1> headings, every first-level heading on the page gets the same formatting.

CSS supports other types of selectors, and WordPress themes use them heavily. One of the most popular is the *class selector*, which starts with a period, like this:

```
.entry-title {
  color: #222;
  font-size: 26px;
  font-weight: bold;
  line-height: 1.5em;
}
```

This rule formats any element that has a class named *entry-title* applied to it. It's important to realize that the word "entry-title" doesn't mean anything special to WordPress or to a browser. It's simply a naming convention the Twenty Eleven theme decided to use. Somewhere in one of the Twenty Eleven theme files, there's an element tagged with the entry-title class, like this:

```
<h1 class="entry-title">
  <a href="http://magicteahouse.net/closing-for-christmas/">Closing for
Christmas</a>
</h1>
```

This is a snippet from the Twenty Eleven home page, the one with the list of posts. Here, the theme uses the entry-level class for each post title in the list. So if you want to change the way post titles appear in the post stream, this is the style you want to change.

NOTE Sometimes, you'll see a CSS rule that combines element selectors and class selectors. So the selector *h1.entry-title* refers to any <h1> element that uses the entry-title class.

There's one more selector that's similar to class selectors, called an *ID selector*. It starts with a # character:

```
#site-title {
  margin-right: 270px;
  padding: 3.65625em 0 0;
}
```

And here's a snippet of HTML that gets its formatting from this rule:

```
<h1 id=id="site-title"><a href="http://magicteahouse.net/"
title="Magic Tea House">Magic Tea House</a></h1>
<h2 id="site-description">Tea Emporium and Small Concert Venue</h2>
```

The difference between class selectors and ID selectors is that a class selector can format a number of elements (provided they all have the same class), while an ID selector targets just a single HTML element (because two elements can't have the same ID). A WordPress page will have only one site title, so it makes sense to use an ID selector for it, even though a class selector would work just as well.

◼ COMBINING SELECTORS

You can *combine* selectors to create even more powerful formatting rules. For example, you can chain selectors together so long as you separate them with a comma. WordPress then applies the style rule to any element that matches any *one* of the selectors.

Here's an example that changes the alignment of three HTML elements—the <caption> element used with figures and the <th> and <td> elements used with tables.

```
caption, th, td {
    text-align: left;
}
```

You can also create more complex rules that match elements *inside* other elements. This is called a *contextual selector*, and you build one by combining two ordinary selectors, separated by a space. Here's an example:

```
.comment-content h1 {
  ...
}
```

This selector matches every <h1> element inside the element with the class name *comment-content*. It formats the heading of every comment.

WordPress loves contextual selectors—in fact, most of the Twenty Eleven theme's style rules use contextual selectors. If you haven't seen them before, they may take some time to decipher. Just remember that a browser works on the selectors one at a time. It starts by finding an element that matches the first selector, and then it looks inside that element to match the second selector (and if the rule includes another selector, the browser searches inside *that* element, too).

Here's another example to practice your CSS-decoding skills:

```
.one-column #content {
  ...
}
```

Got it? This selector looks for an element with the ID name *content* inside an element with the class name *one-column*. This is a useful rule, because WordPress uses the class name *one-column* for the <body> element of a page when you use a single-column layout. Inside that, the main content region uses the ID *#content*. The end result is a rule that targets the content section, but only becomes active when you use a single-column layout.

This is where things can get a bit head-spinny. Understanding the syntax of CSS is one thing, but editing the styles in a theme means knowing which class and ID names that theme uses, and what elements are associated with those names. You'll get some pointers in the box on page 448.

Changing the Twenty Eleven Theme

The Twenty Eleven theme is filled with styles, and you can override any of them. For example, say you don't want to include the search box that normally appears in the Twenty Eleven header. The box isn't a widget; it's a built-in, nonconfigurable part of the Twenty Eleven theme. But here's where your child theme and CSS knowledge pay off, because you can hide the search box with the right style rule.

To do that, choose Appearance→Editor to start editing the *style.css* file in your child theme (Figure 13-7). Then, add this rule:

```
#branding #searchform {
  display: none;
}
```

This works because *#branding* represents the header section of the Twenty Eleven theme (the header's ID is *branding*), and *#searchform* corresponds to the search box inside (its ID is *searchform*). The *display: none* instruction tells browsers to collapse this element into nothingness.

FIGURE 13-7

Here's the style.css file from Twenty Eleven Reboot, the Twenty Eleven child theme. The style rules you place here override the parent theme's formatting instructions for same-named classes and IDs. Right now, Reboot adds just a single style rule.

NOTE When you add a style rule to a child theme, it *overrides* the parent theme. However, your child theme won't wipe out style settings that don't conflict. For example, if you change the *color* of your post title in the child theme, that won't affect the *font* applied to the post title by the parent theme.

If you're comfortable with CSS (or you're using one of the CSS resources mentioned on page 431), you'll have no trouble understanding the *display* property. However, you might have more trouble finding the ID and class names of the elements you want to change. Table 13-1 provides a cheat sheet to some of the key elements in the Twenty Eleven theme. (Other themes may use a similar structure, but there's no guarantee.)

TABLE 13-1 *Class and ID Names in the Twenty Eleven Theme*

STYLE SELECTOR	CORRESPONDS TO...
#branding	The header section at the top of every page; it includes the site title, the side description, and header image.
#branding img	Just the header image. Use this rule to change its size or position.

STYLE SELECTOR	CORRESPONDS TO...
#site-title	The site title in the header (for example, "Magic Tea House").
#site-description	The byline that appears under the site title in the header (for example, "Tea Emporium and Small Concert Venue").
#primary	All the content between the header and footer, including the sidebar (if it appears on the page).
#secondary	The sidebar area, with its widgets. You might want to use this style, in conjunction with #primary, to change the widths of the columns in your layout.
.widget	Any widget in a widget area.
.widget-title	The optional title that appears above a widget.
#access	The navigation menu at the top of each page (which is also known as a navigation bar).
#access a	An individual link in the navigation menu.
#featured-post-1	On a showcase page, the first featured post. Remember, featured posts are sticky posts that are called out for extra love and attention when you use the showcase template (page 225). Use featured-post2 for the second featured post, and so on.
#colophon	The footer area on every page, starting with the solid horizontal border line.
.entry-title	The title of any post. Post titles appear in several places (including the home page, the single-post page, and the search page). You probably don't want to format titles all the same way, so you need to combine a class name with another selector, as shown in the next three examples.
.blog .entry-title	The title of any post in the main post stream.
.singular .entry-title	The title of any post on the single-post page.
.page-template-showcase-php .entry-title	The title of any post on a showcase page.
.entry-content	The content in the post. As with the entry-title class, this applies to the post content no matter where it appears, unless you combine this selector with another one.

STYLE SELECTOR	CORRESPONDS TO...
.entry-meta	The information about the post, which appears before it (for example, "Posted on January 14, 2013" and after it ("This entry was posted in Uncategorized by Katya Greenview. Bookmark the permalink")
#comments	The comments area after a post.
.comment-meta	The byline of information about a comment, such as "Salah on April 26, 2013 at 11:00 pm said:"
.comment-content	The comment text, after the byline.
.commentlist li.bypostauthor	A comment left by you (the author of the post).
.commentlist li.byuser	A comment left by someone other than you.
.logged-in	A class added if the current visitor is logged in as a website user (page 353). For example, you can use the selector .logged-in body to change the formatting of the <body> element for people you know.

Once you get the right class or ID name, you can target the exact visual ingredient you want to alter. For example, to change the font, color, and size of the text in a blog post in a single-post page, you can add a style rule like this:

```
.singular .entry-content {
  font-family: "Times New Roman";
  color: red;
  font-size: 1.7em;
}
```

Type it into the editor (Appearance→Editor), hit Update File, and refresh the website to see the change (Figure 13-8).

It's a simple recipe: find the class name or ID name for the element you want change, add some style properties, and you have an instant change.

Here's another example that makes your comments ridiculously obvious, with a yellow background, bold text, and a blue border:

```
.commentlist li.bypostauthor {
  background-color: yellow;
  font-weight: bold;
  border:2px solid blue;
}
```

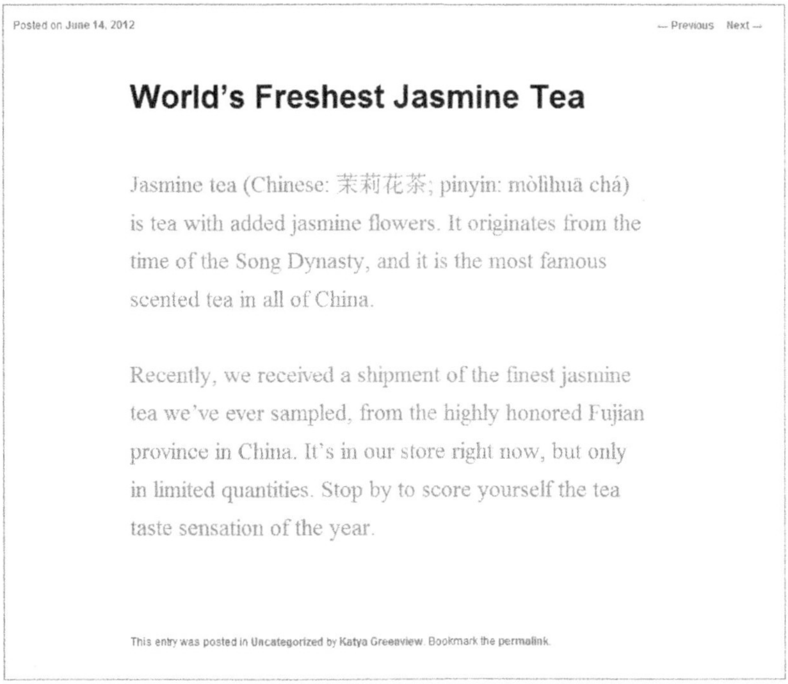

FIGURE 13-8

This revamped post, with its large red-lettered text, doesn't exactly look better, but it does look different.

In this case, it isn't enough just to use the *.bypostauthor* selector on its own. That's because the *style.css* file in the original Twenty Eleven theme uses a more specific version of *.bypostauthor*. CSS won't allow a more general selector (like .bypostauthor) to override a more specific one (like .commentlist li.bypostauthor)) if their properties conflict. For that reason, you need to use longer selector *.commentlist li.bypostauthor* in your child theme if you want to banish the dark-gray background (which is the normal way the Twenty Eleven theme distinguishes your comments).

Puzzling Out the Styles in a Theme

Half the battle in editing the *style.css* file is figuring out how to write your selector. Often, you won't know the class or ID name of the section you want to change. Instead, you'll need to do a bit of detective work.

The best starting point is to scour the HTML that WordPress generates for your page. You can do this in any browser by visiting the page, right-clicking it, and choosing a command with a name like "View Source." This shows you the complete HTML, so you need to search for the section of content you want to change. To get started, hit Ctrl+F (or Command+F on a Mac), and type in a bit of the text that's near the part of the page you want to change. For example, if you're trying to figure out how to change the comments section, you might search for "Leave a Reply" to jump to the heading that starts it off. Many browsers make this process easier with a feature for homing in on the HTML in a specific part of the page (Figure 13-9).

Once you find the right place—roughly—the real hunt begins. Look at the elements just before your content, and check the *class* and *id* attributes for names you recognize, or that seem obvious. Pay special attention to the <div> element, which HTML pages use to group blocks of content, like sidebars, posts, menus, headers, and footers. And you'll often find one <div> nested inside another, which lets the theme apply a layered tapestry of style settings (which is great for flexibility, but not so good when you're trying to understand exactly what rule is responsible for a specific formatting detail).

Once you have a potential class or ID name, it's time to experiment. Pop open the theme editor and add a new style rule that targets the section you identified. Do something obvious first, like changing the background color with the *background-color* property. That way, you can check your site and immediately determine if you've found the right element.

Using Fancy Fonts

One of the most common reasons to edit the styles in a template is to change an element's font. In fact, it's often the case that all you need to do to turn a popular theme into something uniquely yours is to change some of the typefaces.

Originally, HTML pages were limited to a set of *web-safe fonts*. These are the typefaces every web surfer has seen, including stalwarts like Times New Roman, Arial, and Verdana. But web design has taken great strides forward in recent years with a CSS feature called *embedded fonts*. Essentially, embedded fonts let you use almost any typeface on your web pages—you just need to upload the font to your web server in the right format.

The embedded fonts feature has a few quirks. First, older browsers don't support it, so you need to make sure that your pages look respectable even if your visitor's browser can't load the embedded fonts. Second, although every modern browser supports embedded fonts, they don't all understand the same font files. For that reason, web designers often have to upload several copies of the fonts they want to use, each one in a different format. And third, the CSS rule you write to use embedded fonts is a bit convoluted, which can make for a few unnecessary headaches.

FIGURE 13-9

In Google Chrome, you don't need to search through all the HTML on a page to find a class name or ID. Instead, right-click the part of the page you want to examine and choose "Inspect element." A panel pops open with the corresponding bit of HTML markup selected. That quickly tells you that the post title is an <h1> element with the class name entry-title (but you already knew that).

In Firefox, you can right-click the page to use a similar "Inspect element" command. In Internet Explorer, you need to first press F12 to show the Developer Tools panel. Then choose Find→"Select element by click" at the top of the Developer Tools panel and click the part of the page you want to examine.

Happily, you can sidestep all these problems by using a web font service like Google Web Fonts. There, you can pick from a huge gallery of attractive typefaces. When you find a font you want, Google spits out the CSS style rule for you. Best of all, Google *hosts* the font files on its high-powered web servers, in all the required formats, so you don't need upload anything to your site.

TIP If you want to learn everything there is to know about web fonts, including how to host them on your website, write the CSS rules yourself, and webify your own fonts, check out *HTML5: The Missing Manual*, which has a section all about embedded fonts.

To use a Google font on a WordPress site, follow these steps:

1. **Go to *www.google.com/webfonts*.**

Google displays a long list of available fonts (Figure 13-10). At the time of this writing, there were more than 500 typefaces to choose from, which is more than double the font count of just last year.

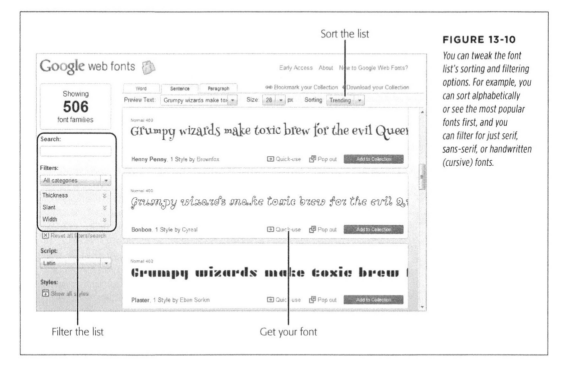

Sort the list

Filter the list

Get your font

FIGURE 13-10

You can tweak the font list's sorting and filtering options. For example, you can sort alphabetically or see the most popular fonts first, and you can filter for just serif, sans-serif, or handwritten (cursive) fonts.

2. **When you see a font you like, click the "Pop out" link to take a closer look.**

   Google opens a font preview page that shows the font at different sizes.

3. **If you like the font, click the "Quick use" link.**

   Google shows you a page with information about how to use the font. It consists of a style sheet link (which you must add to your web page) and an example of a style sheet rule that uses the font.

> **TIP** Google also lets you add a personalized collection of fonts. If you do, Google gives you a few added features, like the ability to download a copy of the font to install on your computer for print work. Google also remembers the fonts you store in your collection when you return to the Google Web Fonts site.

4. **Scroll down the page until you find the blue set of tabs with the caption "Add this code your website" (Figure 13-11). Click the @import tab.**

   Google has created a ready-made style sheet for every font on its site. To use the font, you need to link this style sheet to a web page, or import it into *your* style sheet (that's the *style.css* file in the child theme). With WordPress, the second approach is easier.

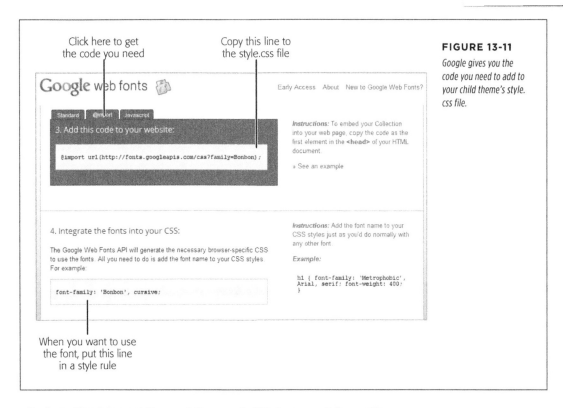

Click here to get the code you need

Copy this line to the style.css file

Google web fonts

Early Access   About   New to Google Web Fonts?

Standard | @import | Javascript

3. Add this code to your website:

`@import url(http://fonts.googleapis.com/css?family=Bonbon);`

Instructions: To embed your Collection into your web page, copy the code as the first element in the **<head>** of your HTML document

» See an example

4. Integrate the fonts into your CSS:

The Google Web Fonts API will generate the necessary browser-specific CSS to use the fonts. All you need to do is add the font name to your CSS styles. For example:

`font-family: 'Bonbon', cursive;`

Instructions: Add the font name to your CSS styles just as you'd do normally with any other font.

Example:

`h1 { font-family: 'Metrophobic', Arial, serif; font-weight: 400; }`

When you want to use the font, put this line in a style rule

FIGURE 13-11

Google gives you the code you need to add to your child theme's style. css file.

5. **Copy the @import line and then paste it into your *style.css* file.**

Put it right after the @import line that accesses the standard Twenty Eleven styles.

> **TIP** If you use several embedded fonts, you can add more than one @import command. However, there's a slightly more efficient approach—create a font collection, and Google will give you a single @import line that grants you access to all the fonts you've picked.

6. **Create a style that uses the font.**

Once you import the Google style sheet, you can use your new font, by name, wherever you want. Just set the *font-family* property, as you would with a normal web-safe font. But remember to add a true web-safe font name after it as a fallback, in case you're dealing with an old-school browser that doesn't support embedded fonts or can't download the font file.

Here's a complete *style.css* file that uses this technique. The newly added parts are highlighted in bold.

```
/*
Theme Name: Twenty Eleven Reboot
Description: This is a customized version of the Twenty Eleven Theme for the
Magic Tea House.
Author: Katya Greenview
Template: twentyeleven
*/

@import url("../twentyeleven/style.css");
@import url(http://fonts.googleapis.com/css?family=Bonbon);

.singular .entry-title {
  font-family: 'Bonbon', 'Times New Roman';
}
```

Figure 13-12 shows this font in action in a post.

FIGURE 13-12

The Bonbon font is perhaps not the best for this site, but it's impossible to deny that it makes for eye-catching post titles.

Editing the Code in Your Theme

When you want to customize the appearance of a theme, the first place you should look is the *style.css* file. But if you need to make more dramatic changes to your site's appearance, you have to go further. Your next step is to consider the theme's *template files*.

A typical theme uses anywhere from a dozen to 50 templates. If you crack one of them open, you'll see a combination of HTML markup and PHP code. The PHP code is the magic ingredient—it triggers the specific WordPress actions that pull your content out of the database. Before WordPress sends a page to a visitor, it runs all the PHP code inside.

Writing this code is a task that's well beyond the average WordPress website owner. But that's not a problem, because you don't need to write the code yourself, even if you're building a completely new theme. Instead, you'll take a ready-made page template that contains all the basic code, and *edit* that file to your liking. Here are two ways you can do that:

- **Change the HTML markup.** Maybe you don't need to change the code in the template file at all. You might just need to modify the HTML that wraps around it. After all, it's the HTML (in conjunction with the style sheet) that determines how your content looks and where it's placed.

- **Modify the PHP code.** You'll start with a template full of working code. Often, you can carefully modify this code, using the WordPress documentation, to change the way it works. For example, imagine you want the list of posts on the home page to show fewer posts, include just post titles or images instead of content, or show posts from a specific category. You can do all this by adjusting the code that's already in the home page template.

Of course, the more thoroughly you want to edit the PHP, the more you'll need to learn. Eventually, you might pick up enough skills to be an accomplished PHP tweaker.

Learning PHP

The actual syntax of the PHP language is beyond the scope of this book. If you'd like to develop your ninja programming skills, there are plenty of great resources for learning PHP, whether you have a programming background or are just starting out. However, don't rush off just yet, because while learning PHP will definitely help you customize a WordPress theme, it may not help you as much as you expect.

Learning to customize a WordPress template is partially about learning PHP (because it helps to understand basic language details like loops, conditional logic, and functions). However, it's *mostly* about learning to use WordPress's functions in PHP code (see the Note on page 460 for more about WordPress functions). For that reason, you'll probably get more practical value out of studying WordPress functions than learning the entire language, unless you plan to someday write web application of your own.

To get started with WordPress functions, you can dip your toe into the function reference at *http://tinyurl.com/func-ref*. To learn more about PHP, you can start with the absolute basics with the tutorial at *http://tinyurl.com/ctzya55*.

Introducing the Template Files

Every theme uses a slightly different assortment of templates. The WordPress staple Twenty Eleven uses a fairly typical set of 30 templates.

You can recognize a template by the fact that its file name ends with *.php*. Although template files hold a mix of HTML and PHP, the *.php* extension tells WordPress that there's code inside that the WordPress engine needs to run before it sends the final page to a browser.

Even though a template is just a mix of HTML and PHP, understanding where it fits into your site can be a bit of a challenge. That's because every page WordPress stitches together uses several template files.

For example, imagine you click through to a single post. WordPress has a template, called *single.php*, that creates the page on the fly. However, *single.php* needs help from a host of other templates. First, it inserts the contents of the *header.php* template, which sits at the top of every page in a WordPress site. The *header.php* file takes care of basics, like linking to the style sheet, registering some scripts, and showing the header section, complete with the top-level menu. (Some themes farm out the menu-creation work to yet another template file, but Twenty Eleven doesn't go that far.)

Next, the *single.php* file adds the Previous and Next navigation links to the post, and then it calls out to another template to display the actual post. If it's a regular post, it uses *content-single.php*, but the Twenty Eleven theme has a number of specialized alternatives. For example, an "aside" post (page 177) uses the *content-aside .php* template, a featured post (page 226) uses *content-featured.php*, and so on.

Then, the *single.php* template ends by calling two more templates into action: the *comments.php* template creates the comment section, and the *footer.php* template ends the page. Remember, Twenty Eleven's single post page doesn't have a sidebar (or so it seems). The creators of the theme actually treat the widget area in the footer as a sidebar. To create this ingredient, *footer.php* calls yet another template, named *sidebar-footer.php*.

If you're going cross-eyed trying to follow this six-template assortment, Figure 13-13 shows how it all breaks down.

At first glance, this system seems just a bit bonkers. How better to complicate life than to split the code for a single page into a handful of template files that need to work together? But in typical WordPress fashion, this design is actually pretty brilliant. It means that a theme designer can create a single template file that governs a repeating site element—like a header—and use it everywhere, without needing to worry about duplicating effort or being inconsistent.

When you edit theme styles, your first challenge is finding the right style rule to change. When editing *templates*, the first challenge is finding the right template file to modify. Table 13-2 can help you get started. It describes the fundamental templates that almost every theme, including Twenty Eleven, uses.

Keep in mind, however, that themes will commonly add extra templates to create the formats for different types of posts and pages, and to handle special formatting (for example, to create different layouts that move the sidebar around). You may also decide to add extra templates of your own (for example, to change the way your site presents specific categories or authors, a technique you'll see in Chapter 14).

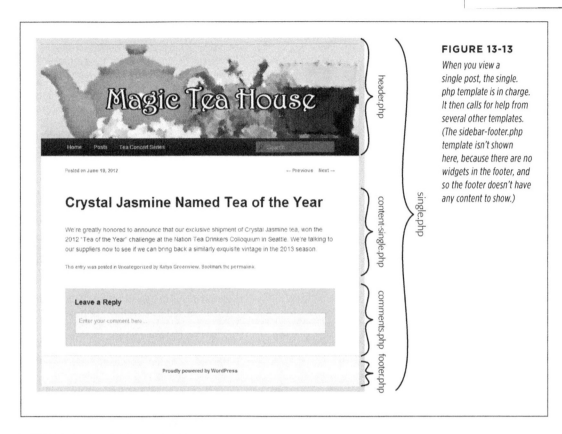

FIGURE 13-13

When you view a single post, the single.php template is in charge. It then calls for help from several other templates. (The sidebar-footer.php template isn't shown here, because there are no widgets in the footer, and so the footer doesn't have any content to show.)

TABLE 13-2 *Essential WordPress Templates*

TEMPLATE FILE	DESCRIPTION
index.php	This is a theme's main template, and the only one that's absolutely required. WordPress uses it if there's no other, more specific template to use. Most themes use *index.php* to display a list of posts on the home page.
header.php	Displays the banner that appears across the top of every page.
footer.php	Displays the footer that stretches across the bottom of every page. Often, header.php includes a navigation menu.
sidebar.php	Shows the sidebar widget area. Twenty Eleven also has a more specialized *sidebar-footer.php* template that creates the widget areas in the footer.

TEMPLATE FILE	DESCRIPTION
single.php	Displays a single post.
page.php	Shows a static page. Themes often have additional templates that let you create different "flavors" of pages. For example, Twenty Eleven adds a *sidebar-page.php* template that creates a page that also includes a sidebar (page 224).
content.php	Displays the content of a post or page. Some themes create many different content templates, for different types of posts and pages. Twenty Eleven, for instance, has 11 content templates. An ordinary post uses *content-single.php*, a page uses *content-page.php*, and special post formats (page 177) use a corresponding template (for example, asides use *content-aside.php*).
comments.php	Displays the comment section after a post or page.
showcase.php	Creates a showcase page in the Twenty Eleven theme (a page that includes a sidebar and a featured post section; see page 225).
attachment.php	Shows the attachment page—what you see when you click a media file (page 317). Themes can include specialized attachment pages for different types of media, such as *image.php* and *video.php* for pictures and video.
archive.php	Lists posts when you browse by author, category, tag, or date. Or, you can use one of the four more specific templates listed next.
category.php	Lists posts when you browse a category. You can also create templates that target specific categories, like *category-tea.php* for a category with "tea" as its slug, or simplified name (page 113).
tag.php	Lists posts when you browse by tag. You can also create templates that target specific tags, like *tag-promotion.php*.
author.php	Lists posts when you browse by author. You can also create templates that target specific authors, like *author-grabinksy.php*.
date.php	Lists posts when you browse by date.
search.php	Lists posts after you execute a search.
404.php	Displays an error message when the requested post or page can't be found.

A Basic Editing Example

By this point, you've digested a fair bit of WordPress theory. It's time to capitalize on that by editing a template file.

You'll begin with an example that seems simple enough. You want to remove the "Proudly powered by WordPress" message that appears at the bottom of every page on your site, just under the footer widgets (Figure 13-14). (It's not that you're embarrassed by WordPress. You just can't help notice that none of the other big-gun WordPress sites have this message slapped onto their pages. Sometimes, being professional means being discreet.)

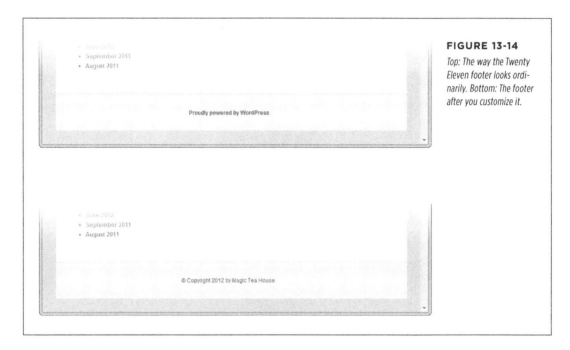

FIGURE 13-14

Top: The way the Twenty Eleven footer looks ordi-narily. Bottom: The footer after you customize it.

June 2012
- September 2011
- August 2011

Proudly powered by WordPress

June 2012
- September 2011
- August 2011

© Copyright 2012 by Magic Tea House

▓ STEP 1. FIND THE TEMPLATE FILE

To find the template file you need, start by examining the list of templates in Table 13-2. In this case, the *footer.php* file is the obvious candidate. It creates the entire footer section, widgets and all, for every page.

▓ STEP 2. CREATE A COPY OF THE TEMPLATE FILE

Once again, you need to start with a child theme (page 435). If you don't, you can still customize the footer, but your hard-won changes will be vaporized the moment you install a theme update.

Here's where things get a bit more awkward. As you know, WordPress templates are really a collection of many template files. To change a template, you need to figure out the changes you want to make to your pages, and then find the template file (*single.php*, *comment.php*, and so on) responsible for that part of the page. Then you add a new version of that template file to the child theme. That new template will override the one in the parent theme.

You do this by copying the template file you want to edit from the parent theme to your child theme, and then making your changes. In this example, that means you need to copy the *footer.php* file in the *twentyeleven* folder and paste it into the *twenty-eleven-reboot* folder.

Unfortunately, the dashboard doesn't have any tools to help you copy a template. You can get the job done relatively quickly using an FTP tool. But if that's not comfortable for you, it's plug-in time. This time, the solution is the Theme File Duplicator plug-in (*http://tinyurl.com/dup-theme*). Install it, activate it, and then choose Appearance→Add Page Template (Figure 13-15).

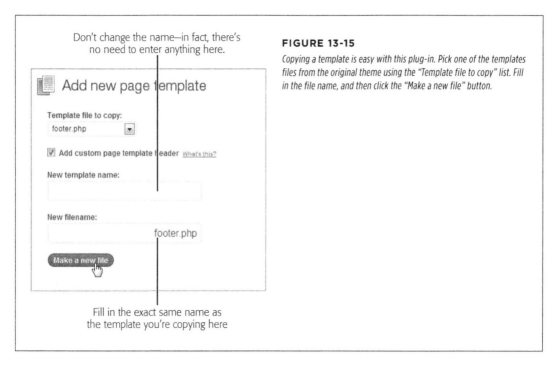

Don't change the name—in fact, there's no need to enter anything here.

FIGURE 13-15

Copying a template is easy with this plug-in. Pick one of the templates files from the original theme using the "Template file to copy" list. Fill in the file name, and then click the "Make a new file" button.

Fill in the exact same name as the template you're copying here

When you use the Theme File Duplicator, it copies the template file you pick to your child theme folder. You can then return to the editor (choose Appearance→Editor) where you'll see the newly copied file in the list.

NOTE The child theme's version of a template completely overrides the parent theme's copy of the template. In this example, that means WordPress ignores the original version of the *footer.php* file, which is in the original theme folder (*twentyeleven*). You can refer to it any time to check the code or copy important bits, but WordPress won't run the code anymore.

Since the changes you need to make to the *footer.php* template are relatively small, it's easy enough to do all your editing here, in the dashboard. For more significant changes, you probably want to copy the theme file content to a text editor on your computer, work with it there, and then copy it back to the Edit Themes page when you're done.

TIP If you decide to edit a theme file on your computer, it's worth considering a text editor that has a few more frills. For example, Windows users can grab the free Notepad++ program (http://notepad-plus-plus.org), which uses color-coded text to distinguish the different ingredients in PHP code. (For example, it uses different colors for keywords, comments, and variables.)

■ STEP 3. EXAMINE THE TEMPLATE FILE

Footer.php is one of WordPress's simpler template files. But even simple templates have a fair bit of boilerplate to wade through.

In this section, you'll look at the entire contents of *footer.php*. You don't always need to take this step, but it's a good practice when you're just starting out and still trying to make sense of WordPress's template system.

If you've written web pages before, you probably know that programming code, like JavaScript, needs to be carefully separated from the HTML in the page. The same is true for PHP, although it has its own special syntax. Every time a block of PHP code appears, it starts with this:

```
<?php
```

Similarly, the following character sequence marks the end of a block of PHP code:

```
?>
```

You can see this system at work at the very beginning of every template file, where there's a block of PHP that has no real code at all, just a long comment. This comment lists some basic information about the template. Here's what you'll see in *footer.php*:

```
<?php
/**
 * The template for displaying the footer.
 *
 * Contains the closing of the id=main div and all content after
 *
 * @package WordPress
 * @subpackage Twenty_Eleven
 * @since Twenty Eleven 1.0
 */
?>
```

The next line is the first one that actually does anything. It's a puzzling bit of HTML that looks like this:

```
</div><!-- #main -->
```

Even seasoned HTML veterans will be a bit thrown off here. The </div> tag closes a <div> element. But you haven't seen an opening <div> tag, so this code snippet seems a bit strange.

It makes more sense when you remember the way WordPress stitches together a page, as shown in Figure 13-13. The <div> element *was* opened, but it happened earlier, when WordPress processed another template file. The HTML comment (<!-- #main --> here) that appears immediately after the </div> element is WordPress's way of reminding you what this <div> is for. Here, it indicates that it's the closing </div> for an element with the ID *main*, which holds the main content of the page.

The next line of HTML is easier to interpret. It identifies the beginning of the footer content. This section has the ID *colophon*, which you might remember from Table 13-1.

```
<footer id="colophon" role="contentinfo">
```

After that is another block of PHP code:

```php
<?php
  /* A sidebar in the footer? Yep. You can can customize
   * your footer with three columns of widgets.
   */
  if ( ! is_404() )
    get_sidebar( 'footer' );
?>
```

This code isn't what you're after. Its job is to create the footer's widget area, by calling the *get_sidebar()* function. If the *get_sidebar()* function succeeds, it inserts the content from the *sidebar-footer.php* file here. If the function can't find the file (which results in what's known as a *404 error*), WordPress ignores the problem and keeps processing the footer.

NOTE A *function* is a block of programming code stored somewhere other than the page it appears on. WordPress is full of useful functions, and *get_sidebar()* is one of many. To browse the full catalog of functions and find out what they do, visit *http://tinyurl.com/func-ref.*

The next section of the *footer.php* file starts a new <div> element, and gives it the ID *site-generator*. The creators of the Twenty Eleven theme chose that name because this is the section that indicates how the site was generated (i.e., with the help of that fantastic piece of software called WordPress).

```
<div id="site-generator">
```

The next bit is another block of PHP code, but it's compressed into a single line:

```php
<?php do_action( 'twentyeleven_credits' ); ?>
```

The *do_action()* function is a WordPress feature found throughout its template files. The idea is that you can register an action you'd like to take place at a certain point (using some code). WordPress triggers that action for you at the right time. In this example, the *do_action()* function isn't much help because it won't allow you to edit the "Powered by" message in the footer. You could use *do_action()* to add information to the footer, but it can't remove what's already there.

After *do_action()* is the part of the footer template you've been looking for. It's a link that displays the "Proudly powered" message:

```
<a href=
 "<?php echo esc_url( __( 'http://wordpress.org/', 'twentyeleven' ) ); ?>"
 title= "<?php esc_attr_e( 'Semantic Personal Publishing Platform',
 'twentyeleven'); ?>" rel="generator">
 <?php printf( __( 'Proudly powered by %s', 'twentyeleven' ),
 'WordPress'); ?>
</a>
```

The markup looks a bit complicated, because there are three PHP code statements embedded inside the <a> element. The first one generates the actual link address, the second one generates the title, and the third generates the text inside the <a> element. You don't need to understand exactly how these statements work to realize that this is the part you want to remove. But first, scan through the rest of the footer template to make sure you understand what's going on.

It's pretty straightforward. First, *footer.php* closes the <div> and <footer> elements. Then it closes another <div> that represents the entire page.

```
    </div>
   </footer><!-- #colophon -->
  </div><!-- #page -->
```

Next, the footer template launches WordPress's *wp_footer()* function.

```
<?php wp_footer(); ?>
```

This is a bit of WordPress infrastructure. Many plug-ins wait for this call and then do something important. Removing this line can cause those plug-ins to break, so it's best to leave it in, even though it isn't doing anything right now.

Finally, the template closes the <body> and <html> elements, proving that you have really and truly reached the end of the page. No more templates will be called into action, and no more content will be added after this point.

```
</body>
</html>
```

■ STEP 4. MAKE YOUR CHANGE

Now you found the culprit—the piece of the WordPress template that you want to change. In this example, it's a single <a> element.

You could delete the <a> element completely, or you can replace it with some text of your own, like this:

```
&copy; Copyright 2013 Magic Tea House
```

The *©* code is a character entity, an HTML code that inserts a special character—in this case, a copyright symbol.

If you consider yourself a bit of a PHP whiz, you can get fancier in your footer. For example, instead of sticking in the current year for the copyright notice, you could ask PHP to *do that for you*.

First, you need to explicitly tell WordPress that you need PHP's help. You do that by adding the *<?php* and *?>* character sequences. You'll put your code inside.

```
<?php [ Your code goes here. ] ?> by Magic Tea House
```

Next, you need a PHP command. In this case, it's the trusty *echo* command, which means (in PHP language) "take the result of the next statement, and spit it out onto the page."

```
<?php echo ?> by Magic Tea House
```

But what exactly do you want to spit out? That's the current date, which you can fetch with the help of a function built into the PHP language, called *date()*. Unsurprisingly, the *date()* function displays the current date. But by supplying a capital letter *Y*, you tell the *date()* function that you're only interested in getting the current year.

```
<?php echo date('Y'); ?> by Magic Tea House
```

Like every line of PHP code, you indicate you finished the end of a statement by adding a semicolon at the end (;)

This completes the example, and drives home a clear point: even the most straightforward theme-editing tasks require a bit of slogging.

FREQUENTLY ASKED QUESTION

Updating a Child Theme

What happens when I update a theme that uses customized templates?

Child templates don't work in exactly the same was as child styles. Child styles extend style rules already put in place by the parent theme. Even if the parent gets a new, updated *style.css* file, the child styles remain, and WordPress applies them on top of the parent styles.

But page templates don't extend parent templates, they *replace* them. As soon as you add *footer.php* to your child theme,

WordPress starts ignoring the *footer.php* in the original theme. That means that if you update the parent theme and change the original *footer.php* file, no one really notices.

This is probably the safest way to handle theme updates, because there really isn't a way that WordPress could combine two versions of a template. However, it means that if you plan to customize all the templates in a theme, you probably shouldn't create a child theme. Instead, you may as well build a completely separate theme of your own.

Delving into the Loop

WordPress experts talk in hushed tones about "the loop," which is the heart of WordPress. Its job is to fetch content from your website's database, one piece at a time, until it reaches the post limit (that's the "Blog pages show at most" setting in the Settings→Reading section of the dashboard).

The loop appears in many templates. WordPress uses it to create the main list of posts on the home page (*index.php*), the list of results after a search (*search.php*), and the list of articles when you browse by category, tag, author, or date (*category. php*, *tag.php*, *author.php*, and *date.php*, or *archive.php* when one of the former is missing). The loop even appears on Twenty Eleven's showcase page (*showcase.php*), twice—first to grab the featured posts that it puts up top, and again to grab the recent posts that it shows underneath. (Showcase pages are explained on page 225.)

In the following example, you'll take a look at the loop in the *index.php* file, and you'll change the way it works by adding a new feature: the ability to highlight recent posts (Figure 13-16).

FIGURE 13-16

The first post ("Tea Sale") in this list of posts was published today. To advertise this fact, it's given a bigger headline, a border, and a bright yellow background. Tomorrow, it will revert back to normal and look like any other post.

■ STEP 1. PREPARE THE TEMPLATE FILE

Your first task is to prepare your template. You can copy the *index.php* file into your child theme folder, using an FTP program, or you can use the Theme Duplicator plug-in to copy it for you.

■ STEP 2. EXAMINE THE TEMPLATE FILE

The next step is to dig through the *index.php* template and try to get a handle on what's going on and what area you need to change. Overall, *index.php* has this structure:

```php
<?php get_header(); ?>

<div id="primary">
  <div id="content" role="main">

    [ The stuff for displaying posts goes here. ]

  </div><!-- #content -->
</div><!-- #primary -->

<?php get_sidebar(); ?>
<?php get_footer(); ?>
```

This boils the template down to its essentials. As you can see, the template calls other templates to create the page's header, sidebar, and footer. In the middle of this action are two <div> elements, and inside them is the heart of the *index.php* template and the loop. This is the part you'll focus on.

The first ingredient here, inside the <div> elements, is a block of *conditional logic*—code that tests a condition, and takes different actions depending on whether that condition is true or false. Essentially, the template here uses PHP to ask a question: Are there any posts?

Here's how the template structures the conditional logic:

```php
<?php if ( have_posts() ) : ?>

    [ If there are posts, you end up here. ]

<?php else : ?>

    [ If there are no posts, this section shows the "sorry" message.]

<?php endif; ?>
```

The *have_posts()* function gets the answer to the question, "Are there any posts?" If there are, the condition is true, and the first section springs into action. That's the part you're interested in. (If there aren't any posts, the condition is false, and you can let the template handle it in the usual fashion, by showing an apologetic message.)

So what takes place inside the first section, which runs only when posts are available? The code starts by adding a navigation link, if necessary. This is the link that appears before the post list, and lets visitors step forward to newer posts. (If your guest is already viewing the most recent posts, this link doesn't show up.)

Then the code triggers the loop (shown here in bold), and ends by inserting another navigation link—the one that lets readers step back to see older posts.

```php
<?php twentyeleven_content_nav( 'nav-above' ); ?>
<?php while ( have_posts() ) : the_post(); ?>
  <?php get_template_part( 'content', get_post_format() ); ?>
<?php endwhile; ?>

<?php twentyeleven_content_nav( 'nav-below' ); ?>
```

The actual loop comes down to just three lines. The *while* and *endwhile* commands delineate the start and end of the loop. As long as you have posts, the loop keeps running. Every time it runs, it grabs a new post, using the WordPress function *the_post()*, and feeds it to the single line of code inside. This code is less exciting—it simply farms out the work of displaying the post to one of the content templates you learned about earlier, using the *get_template_part()* function.

Although the code doesn't seem that exciting right now, there's a lot you can do if you wedge yourself inside the loop, between the *while* and *endwhile* lines. Currently, there's just a single line of code there, but you can expand it to suit your needs. For example, before the code calls *get_template_part()* to display a post, you can run some extra code that does something more clever, like change the post's formatting based on one of the post details. Examples include making the post look different based on its category, author, or publication date. The latter is what this example does.

■ STEP 3. ADD NEW CODE

The final step is to add the code that checks the post's date and decides whether or not to highlight it. Here it is, inside the loop you saw earlier. The new code is boldfaced:

```php
<?php while ( have_posts() ) : the_post(); ?>

  <?php
    $postdate = get_the_time('Y-m-d');
    $currentdate =
      date('Y-m-d',mktime(0,0,0,date('m'),date('d'),date('Y')));

    if ($postdate == $currentdate) {
      echo '<div class="newpost">';
    } else {
      echo '<div>';
    }
  ?>

  <?php get_template_part( 'content', get_post_format() ); ?>
  </div>
<?php endwhile; ?>
```

To understand what's taking place, you need to examine the code one line at a time. First, it uses a WordPress function named *get_the_time()*, which returns the date and time that the current post was published.

```
$postdate = get_the_time('Y-m-d');
```

WordPress takes the result from *get_the_time()* and puts it into a variable (a named storage slot in memory) named *$postdate*. That's so the code can use the date stored there at a later time, when the function compares dates.

> **NOTE** It doesn't matter what you call your variables, as long as you're consistent. (So you can't call the variable *$postdate* in one place and *$date_of_post* in another, because you'll end up creating two separate variables.) However, your variable names must start with the dollar sign ($), which has the side effect of making them easily recognizable.

The next line of code creates a second variable, named *$currentdate*. It stores the current date, as retrieved by the PHP *date()* function, which you saw earlier (page 462). Only now the date is returned in a slightly different format, so it matches up with the publication date format WordPress uses with posts.

```
$currentdate =
    date('Y-m-d',mktime(0,0,0,date('m'),date('d'),date('Y')));
```

The moment of drama occurs next. An *if* statement compares the two variables to see if the current date matches the publication date (in other words, to see if the post was published today). If the answer is yes, the code adds a new <div> element, with the class name *newpost*.

```
if ($postdate == $currentdate) {
    echo '<div class="newpost">';
```

If the answer is no, the code adds a <div> that doesn't use any class name.

```
} else {
    echo '<div>';
}
?>
```

And either way, the code tacks on the closing </div> element at the end of this block of content, after it inserts the post content into the page.

```
<?php get_template_part( 'content', get_post_format() ); ?>
</div>
```

> **NOTE** This code may seem slightly magical, because it relies on a tight combination of PHP commands and WordPress functions that you haven't seen before. Obviously, you wouldn't be able to cook up this sort of code on your own. However, you *will* be able to grab this sort of code from one of the many WordPress recipe sites (page 470), and insert it into your templates when you need it. And the more you do that, the more comfortable you'll be adjusting code to suit your site and recognizing when you've found the bit of code that can solve the problem you're facing.

■ STEP 4. ADD A NEW STYLE

Right now, the revised template doesn't have much of an effect. All it does is add a `<div>` element around the post content. However, this `<div>` gives you a new way to apply customized formatting. You do that by creating a style rule for the *newpost* class.

Here are the style rules that create the effect shown in Figure 13-16. The first rule adds the border, spacing, and background color around the post. The second rule targets the link in the heading, which holds the post title, and gives it large red text.

```
.newpost {
  padding: 8px;
  border: 2px solid darkgray;
  border-radius: 10px;
  background-color: lightyellow;
  margin-bottom: 50px;
}

.newpost h1 a {
  font-size: 2.5em;
  color: red;
}
```

This two-part approach—using the PHP code to add a style, and then applying the formatting through the style—is a common technique in theme customization. It gives you the most flexibility, because you can change the formatting anytime, without editing the template and wading through the PHP again.

Extending WordPress with Functions.php

Some WordPress themes contain one PHP file that isn't a template, named *functions.php*. Experienced theme designers place important parts of their code in here, and then call it from their template files when they need it. WordPress gurus also use the *functions.php* file to add other features, like new shortcodes and widgets, so they don't need to create a complete plug-in.

All these tasks are advanced operations best kept to WordPress gurus. However, even people with no PHP experience can use the *functions.php* file to unlock extra WordPress features. Usually, you do that by copying a few lines of code that you've read about online (or in a book), and pasting them into the *functions.php* file in the theme editor.

For example, in Chapter 10, you learned how WordPress's auto-embed feature lets you turn certain types of website addresses into embedded objects, like Flickr slideshows and YouTube videos. However, WordPress turns off this handy feature in widget areas, like the sidebar. But those in the know can enable shortcodes and embeds in widget areas with just a couple of lines in the *functions.php* file. Figure 13-17 shows the result.

The *functions.php* file works a bit differently from the template files you've learned about so far. The key quirk is that the *functions.php* file in your child theme *extends* the *functions.php* file in your parent theme; it doesn't replace it. For that reason, you can't use the Theme Duplicator plug-in to copy the *functions.php* file.

Instead, you need to create a new, empty text file on your computer, change its name to *functions.php*, and then upload that new *functions.php* file to your child theme folder. In the customized Twenty Eleven example you've considered in this chapter, that's a folder named *twenty-eleven-reboot*.

> **WARNING** If you use Theme Duplicator to copy the *functions.php* file from your parent theme to your child theme, your site will stop working. That's because the *functions.php* is full of important routines that Twenty Eleven uses, and having two copies of this code is enough to blow WordPress's mind. The only fix (if you disregard this warning and put the full *functions.php* file in your child theme folder) is to log in to your site with an FTP program and delete the copied *functions.php* file.

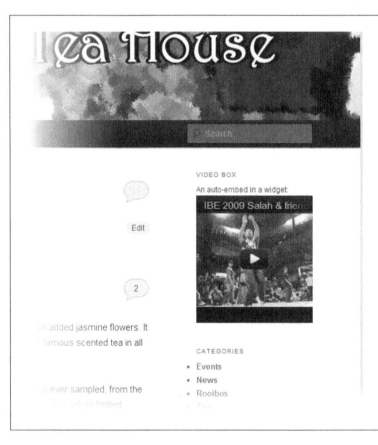

FIGURE 13-17

This sidebar holds a miniature YouTube video, courtesy of the Text widget and the auto-embed feature.

Once you add the blank *functions.php* file to your site, you can edit it in the Edit Theme page, as you do with any other theme file. To enable widget-embedding, as shown in Figure 13-17, you simply need to add these lines:

```php
<?php
  add_filter( 'widget_text', array( $wp_embed, 'run_shortcode' ), 8);
  add_filter( 'widget_text', array( $wp_embed, 'autoembed'), 8 );
?>
```

Now you can put an auto-embed URL in a Text widget, just as you can put it in a post (Figure 13-18).

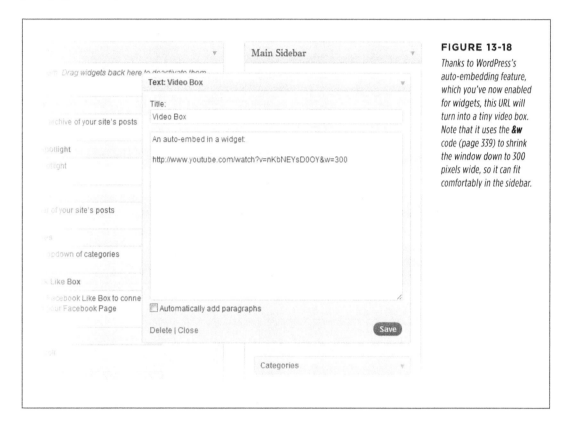

FIGURE 13-18

*Thanks to WordPress's auto-embedding feature, which you've now enabled for widgets, this URL will turn into a tiny video box. Note that it uses the **&w** code (page 339) to shrink the window down to 300 pixels wide, so it can fit comfortably in the sidebar.*

Learning More About Theme Customization

This chapter offers a glimpse of the styles, templates, and PHP code that underpins WordPress. Even if you don't understand how it all works (and most people don't), you still know enough to start making template changes. You may need trial-and-error experimentation to get the result you want, and you may need to search for other people's hacks and tricks to help you out (Google is your friend). But as long as you're not afraid to open a template file, look inside, and make changes, you have the potential to change anything.

In the next chapter, you'll methodically explore a complete end-to-end site example. In the meantime, it's worth pointing out some resources you can use to develop your theme-tweaking skills:

- **Simple style changes.** If you want to start small, you can try the examples at *http://tinyurl.com/7dalazv*, which let you customize the Twenty Eleven theme through its styles.

- **Template recipes.** There's a grab bag of simple theme tricks to practice at *http://tinyurl.com/templatetrix*. They're divided into short, practical chunks. The more you try out, the more comfortable you'll become navigating

the tangled maze of templates that constitute a theme. Need to fill in the sites with ready-to-roll customization here.

- **Blogs by WordPress pros.** Lorelle van Fossen (*http://lorelle.wordpress.com*) has acres of practical content about customizing WordPress sites, including many adventures in theme customization.

- **Smashing Magazine.** If you're looking to get more serious, Smashing Magazine (*http://wp.smashingmagazine.com*) has hardcore articles about every aspect of WordPress site development. They often go far beyond ordinary features and deep into theme customization.

- **Theme frameworks.** Theme frameworks create a whole extra layer on top of WordPress to add new features. The cost is extra complexity, although you won't need to fiddle with low-level details and PHP code anymore. Popular examples include Thematic (*http://tinyurl.com/themat*), which is free, and Genesis (*http://tinyurl.com/gen-theme*), which isn't.

Building an Advanced WordPress Site

In the previous chapter, you learned how to stretch WordPress's capabilities by editing your theme files. You saw how a few small changes—like adding a style rule or changing a section of PHP code—let you customize details that would ordinarily be out of reach.

Tinkering with a WordPress theme is a great way to get started, and, as you saw, it opens the door to a number of small but genuinely useful tweaks. But once you start poking around the inner workings of a theme, it's just a small jump to a more ambitious endeavor: reworking the entire theme to create a completely customized site.

In this chapter, you'll learn how to customize a theme by creating a furniture-selling site called Distinct Furnishings. You'll see how to put together a browsable product catalog, custom archive pages, and a fully functional shopping cart (with the help of PayPal). The lessons you'll learn will apply whenever you want to adapt WordPress's post and page system to work with different types of content, like the online product catalog you'll create in this chapter.

TIP Many parts of this chapter introduce useful snippets of code that you can take and adapt to suit your own site. Rather than type this code in by hand, you can download these excerpts from the Missing CD page for this book (*http://missingmanuals.com/cds/wpmm*). You can then modify them and paste them into your own template files, wherever you need them. And if you want to browse the example site that's created in this chapter, visit *www.prosetech.com/wordpress*.

■ Planning Your Site

The first step to building an advanced, completely customized site is to get out a notepad and start planning. Before you set fingers to keyboard and start customizing templates, you need to answer a few questions:

- What type of content will your site showcase?

- How will your content be arranged, and how will visitors browse your site?

- Will your content use posts or pages or both?

It's important to think about these questions early on because you need to consider how visitors will interact with your site. And that, in turn, will determine the kind of changes you need to make to your theme files. In the case of Distinct Furnishings, for example, the site's job is to display information about the different pieces of furniture the company sells. Visitors will arrive at the site, browse through the pieces that interest them, and maybe even make a purchase. Essentially, the Distinct Furnishings site is a product catalog, which is a common type of advanced WordPress site.

The easiest way to structure a product catalog is to put each item on a separate page or in a separate post (but not both). That way, your visitors have the flexibility to search or browse products according to different groupings (for example, by category). They can also drill right down to the specific item that interests them, and even bookmark its page in a browser.

So far, this design is fairly obvious. The first real decision you need to make is whether you want to put each product in a WordPress post or a WordPress page.

Deciding Between Posts and Pages

Behind the scenes, posts and pages are similar. Both are blocks of content, which are stored as HTML and placed in individual records in your website's database. Both support comments, sharing buttons, featured images, and custom fields.

WordPress stores a bit more information about posts. It includes the post's category, tags, and excerpts. It also assumes that you want to see posts grouped together, in a reverse chronological list that's usually on the home page. However, once you start editing a template and customizing the look of your site, the distinctions between posts and pages start to fade, and the decision between using one or the other becomes at least partly a matter of preference.

There are advantages to both posts and pages. The page system gives you a simple, clean way to arrange items that works particularly well when you have a small amount of content (for example, just three pages describing the breakfast, dinner, and lunch menus for your restaurant). Instead of letting readers browse by category or tag, you can let them go from one page to another by clicking the links in a menu, as you saw with the Pernatch Restaurant site (page 221).

If you don't want to use the features the post system offers, the page system is a reasonable approach. But in the Distinct Furnishings example developed in this chapter, the extra WordPress conveniences are worthwhile. For example, you can use categories to separate your products into meaningful subgroups (like Chairs and Sofas), so visitors can browse them more easily. You can also give each product a shortened description called an excerpt (page 195), which is handy if you need to summarize your product catalog in a small space.

> **NOTE** Most sites use both posts *and* pages. For example, a post-centric site usually has a few pages with additional information that doesn't change very often. Similarly, a page-centric site might include a news section that features a stream of short, time-sensitive postings. But right now, the decision is whether to use posts or pages to represent *products*.

Adding Content

If you plan to create a completely customized WordPress site, you run into a bit of a chicken-and-egg dilemma. The problem is that your site content won't look right until you customize your templates, but you can't test your template changes unless you have some sample content to work with.

The best way to deal with this is to begin by adding some content, in the form that you think will be most useful, based on the planning you did in the previous section. In the case of Distinct Furnishings, that means adding sample posts with product information (Figure 14-1).

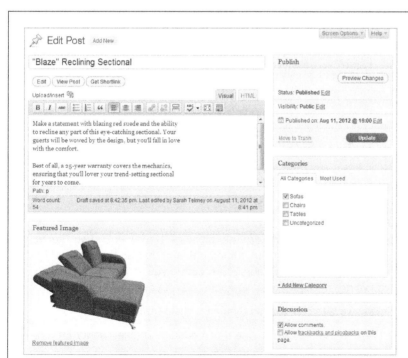

FIGURE 14-1

On the Distinct Furnishings site, each post represents a single product. To create the post, all you need to provide are the product name (actually the post title), the product description (the content), a featured image, and a category. The posts don't use tags or excerpts, so they aren't shown here. (Remember, you can customize the Edit Post page to hide the stuff you don't need, as explained on page 123.)

NOTE In the Distinct Furnishings example, each post represents a piece of furniture, but the posts could just as easily represent something different, like a movie review, how-to article, celebrity biography, employee resume, recipe, or any other kind of content (so long as it comprises text and pictures). No matter what type of content you have, you're performing essentially the same task—hijacking the WordPress blogging system for your own ends.

GEM IN THE ROUGH

Avoid Confusion with a Test Site

It may take some time to transform your new site from a few good ideas into a final, polished product. This raises a risk—while you're hard at work, your half-finished, slightly broken site will be on the Web, visible to potential visitors and slightly embarrassing.

If you're creating a brand-new site where none existed before, this might not be an issue. Because no one knows about your site, there won't be many people stopping by (and anyone who stumbles across your work by chance won't expect much). But if you're replacing an old, traditional-style website with a new WordPress site, you'll want to avoid the potential disruption of a work-in-progress.

One way to do this is to create your website in a subfolder on your web server, and then transfer it to the real location once it's finished. For example, say you own the domain *super-chic.com*. You could create your new WordPress website in a subfolder (page 53), like *super-chic.com/v1.*. Then, when your site is ready to go, you change the configuration of your root site (super-chic.com) so that it actually uses the files from super-chic.com/v1.

The WordPress documentation has the full instructions to make this sort of changeover happen (see *http://tinyurl .com/89wochm*). Here's a slightly compressed overview:

1. Go to the Settings→General section of the dashboard in your test site, and change the "Site Address (URL)" setting to the root of your website. For example, you would replace *http://super-chic.com/v1* with *http://super-chic .com*. (But don't change the "WordPress Address (URL)" setting.)

2. Using an FTP program, copy the index.php and .htaccess files from the test site folder (in this example, that's v1) to your computer.

3. Edit the index.php file (the copy you downloaded to your computer) using a text editor. Find the command that says require('./wp-blog-header.php') and insert your folder name before the file name, like this: require('./v1/ wp-blog-header.php').

4. Upload the modified index.php file and the untouched .htaccess file to the root folder of your website.

5. If your root folder has any other default pages that load up automatically (like index.htm), rename or remove them now.

That's it—your test site is now live. Don't forget to delete any posts or pages you created for testing purposes.

Picking a Theme

Every WordPress theme has similar underpinnings. However, no two themes are quite the same, and if you start out editing a theme that isn't well-suited to your site, you'll create extra work for yourself. So before you commit to a theme, make sure that you've got the best, most workable one for your needs.

There are many ways to pick a good theme for customization:

- Some WordPressers pick a theme they understand (like Twenty Eleven) and use that in all their customization projects.

- Some web designers pick a theme that's as close as possible to the final result they want. This means they'll have much less customization to do, but it also forces them to spend time learning the subtly different workings of a new template.

- Some WordPress pros use a heavily stripped-down theme, which provides very little beyond the core WordPress code. This way, they don't need to worry about removing built-in features and embellishments they don't want. It also means they need to supply the majority of the markup and styles that format the site, which takes time and requires some serious web design skills.

- Some WordPressers favor theme frameworks, which are simple, foundational themes that have been designed for other developers to extend. The drawback is choice and complexity: there are many theme frameworks to choose from, and they all have their own subtly different extensibility model. (To learn more, read what WordPress has to say at *http://tinyurl.com/theme-f.*)

The Distinct Furnishings site follows the second approach. It uses the PinBlack theme (*http://tinyurl.com/pinblack*), which already has most of the right layout and formatting in place (Figure 14-2).

FIGURE 14-2

PinBlack is a portfolio theme (page 330) that arranges posts in a grid of packed-together tiles. Each one includes the title of the post (that's the product name in this case), its featured image, and its category ("Filed Under"). This makes PinBlack an almost perfect theme for browsing products, except that it orders the posts based on their publication dates.

Before you go any further, you need to decide whether you want to create a child theme (page 435). As you learned in Chapter 13, child themes are always the right choice for making cosmetic changes to a theme you love. They're also a good idea if you plan to make targeted changes to specific aspects of a theme, while leaving the rest of it alone.

If you're making more extensive changes that will require you to modify most of the template files in a theme, a child theme doesn't make as much sense. Since you'll override almost all the functionality in the original template, there's little reason for your child theme to keep up a relationship with its parent.

Once again, there's no clear-cut answer for all situations. It all depends on how complex a theme you're starting with, and how heavily you plan to customize it.

- If you decide to create a child theme that *extends* the original theme, follow the instructions on page 435.

- If you decide to create a completely new theme that *replaces* the original theme, continue reading the next section. This is the approach that the Distinct Furnishings example follows with the PinBlack theme.

Creating a Custom Copy of a Theme

In theory, you can edit any theme in the dashboard without taking any special steps. But doing so is risky. Eventually, the creator of the original theme will distribute an update, and it's all too easy to accidentally install the update and wipe out all your carefully crafted customizations.

To protect yourself, create a copy of the theme that WordPress won't ever try to update. Here's how:

1. **Download the theme files to your computer.**

   There are two ways to do this. One option is to use an FTP program, and drag the appropriate theme folder (say, *pinblack*) from your site's */wp-content/ themes* area to your computer.

   The other option is to visit the WordPress themes directory at *http://wordpress .org/extend/themes*. Search for the theme you're using, view it, and then click the Download button. WordPress downloads the theme files in a ZIP file; you need to pull the theme folder out of the ZIP and place it somewhere on your computer so you can edit it.

2. **Open the theme's *style.css* file in a text editor.**

   Usually, that means Notepad on a Windows computer and TextEdit on a Mac.

   At the top of the file, you'll see the header comment with basic information about the theme.

3. **Change the theme name.**

   For example, where it says this:

   Theme Name: PinBlack

   You can change it to this:

   Theme Name: PinBlack_Custom

   This is the name WordPress will use in the dashboard for the copied theme.

NOTE PinBlack_Custom is a good theme name, because it clearly communicates that this is a customized version of the original PinBlack theme. PinBlack2 would be a bad choice, because the person who created PinBlack might use that name to denote a significant revamp of the original theme.

---

4. **Remove the theme URL.**

   That's the line that starts with "Theme URI." Find it and delete it. This severs the link between your theme and the original one, ensuring that any theme update won't overwrite your customized files.

5. **Rename the theme folder to match the theme name.**

   For example, if you used the name PinBlack_Custom, you might rename the theme folder *pinblackcustom*. It doesn't really matter what name you use, as long as you change the folder name from the original (*pinblack*) in some way.

6. **Upload the new theme to your site.**

   There are two ways to do this.

   The most direct is with an FTP program, where you drag the new theme folder (say, *pinblackcustom*) from your computer to your site's */wp-content/themes* area.

   The other option is to ZIP up your theme folder, and then upload it, using the dashboard. Once you create the ZIP file, choose Appearance→Themes, click the Install Themes tab, and click the Upload link. Select your ZIP file (click Browse or Choose File—the button's name depends on your browser), and send it off to your site (click Install Now).

   Either way, once you upload the custom version of your theme, you can start using it.

7. **Choose Appearance→Themes, and click the Activate link under your new theme copy.**

   Figure 14-3 shows the PinBlack_Custom theme being activated.

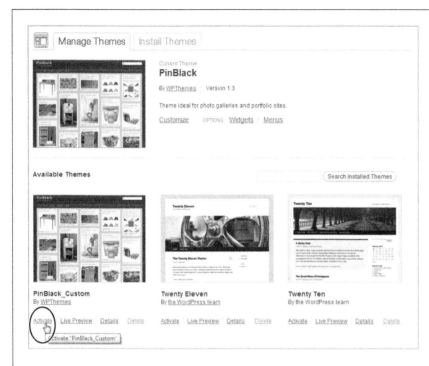

FIGURE 14-3

The only difference between a copy of a theme and a child theme is the information in the header of each one's style.css file. In a child theme, the style header has a reference that links the child theme to the parent theme. But a theme copy is completely self-sufficient; it has its own version of every template, style sheet, and resource file, and no link to the original theme.

■ Creating Custom Category Pages

Now that you've picked a theme and added a bit of sample content, you're ready to start reengineering your site. Your goal is to remove the "bloggish" details that don't really fit, and make your site feel like a fine-tuned custom creation.

The first challenge is to give your visitors a decent way to browse Distinct Furnishing's products. Right now, WordPress sorts the products the same way that it sorts the posts in every site—in reverse chronological order, based on the date you published the post. This makes sense for a blog, a news site, and many other types of sites, but it isn't terribly useful in a product catalog. Visitors who arrive at Distinct Furnishings probably won't want to see every item crowded into a somewhat disordered single page of tiles (Figure 14-2). Instead, they'll want to focus on the *type* of furnishing they need—such as a sofa, chair, or table.

This is clearly a job for the WordPress category system. As you already know, you can browse posts by category by putting the category name in the URL, like this:

`http://distinctfurnishings.net/`**sofas**

Of course, you won't expect your visitors to type this sort of address on their own. Instead, you'll supply links in a post or page, in the Categories widget, or in a menu. Menus are the most common way that visitors navigate sites (Figure 14-4).

FIGURE 14-4

The easiest way to organize a product catalog is to create links that let your visitors focus on one category of product at a time.

The menu approach is probably the best browsing experience you can create without hacking your theme. However, it's not perfect. Some of its shortcomings include:

- You can't display different categories in different ways. For example, you might want the sofa-browsing page to look different from the tables-browsing page.

- You can't display additional information about a category.

- You can't control the order of products *within* a category—WordPress still puts them in reverse chronological order by publication date.

However, you *can* control all these options by customizing the category page (also known as a *category archive page*). This is the template that creates the page shown in Figure 14-4. For example, when you visit a URL like *http://distinctfurnishings.net/sofas*, the category page grabs the products in the Sofas category and displays them.

The stock category page does a decent enough job, but theme-hackers can do better. Figure 14-5 shows a revamped version of the category page that adds a number of refinements. In the following sections, you'll learn how to make all these improvements.

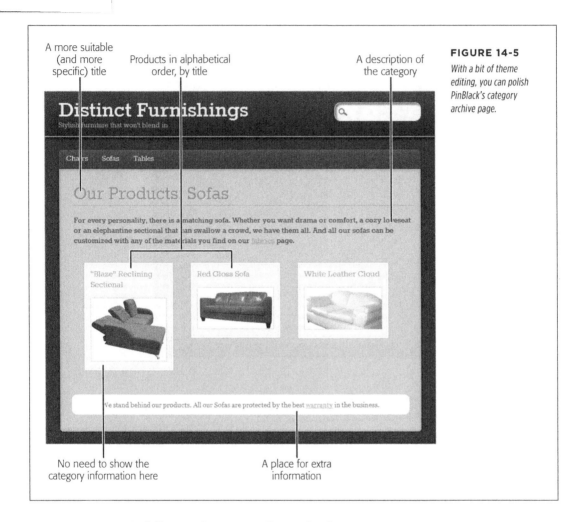

A more suitable (and more specific) title

Products in alphabetical order, by title

A description of the category

No need to show the category information here

A place for extra information

Adding a Category Description

The first and easiest change you can make is adding a category description. Many themes, including PinBlack, automatically show the category description on the category page. You don't even need to edit your theme.

When you first create a category, it doesn't have a description, but you can easily add one by editing the category record. Start by choosing Posts→Categories to see a list of all your categories, and then click the Edit link under the category you want to edit. Then, type the category description in the Description box.

Here's the description for the Sofas category shown in Figure 14-5:

```
For every personality, there's a matching sofa. Whether you want drama
or comfort, a cozy loveseat, or an elephantine sectional that can swallow
a small crowd, we have them all. And all our sofas can be customized
with any of the materials you find on our
<a href="http://distinctfurnishings.net/fabrics">fabrics</a> page.
```

When you finish editing the category description, click Update to save your changes.

Finding the Right Template File

If you want to add any more information to the category archive page, or change any other detail—or if your theme doesn't support category descriptions—you need to edit the theme's template files. But first, you have to find the right files.

When WordPress assembles a page, it prefers to use a specific template (say, one designed for browsing categories) rather than a more general one (one designed for browsing any group of posts, for example). To pick a template, WordPress goes through this list, from top to bottom, and stops when it finds a match:

1. **category-slug.php.** This template matches a specific category (say, the category-browsing page for sofas). The slug is a URL-friendly version of the category name, which replaces spaces with dashes. For example, if you're browsing the Sofas category, the slug-specific template is *category-sofas.php*.

2. **category-ID.php.** This template also matches a specific category, but it uses the category ID to find its match. For example, it might be *category-4.php* if you're browsing the Sofas category, and the Sofas category has an ID of 4. You can get the ID of a category by editing the category record and looking carefully at the URL in your browser's address bar. But you don't need to, because the category-*slug* naming system is easier to understand and has the same effect as the older category-*ID* approach.

3. **category.php.** This is the standard archive page for all categories that don't have specialized formatting. If you haven't customized your theme, this is probably the template that's doing all the work.

4. **archive.php.** This is a more general template for browsing by category, tag, author, or date when there isn't a more specific archive page that does the work.

5. **index.php.** This is your home page, and the final fallback if every other template file is missing.

Almost no theme uses either of the first two types of template (*category-slug.php* and *category-ID.php*) out of the box. That's because these templates are for you, the website creator, so you can add category-specific formatting when you need it, to suit the types of posts on your site.

Most themes include a *category.php* page. But a few don't, relying on *archive.php* instead. In such a case, the *archive.php* template may use more complex code that spits out different text or formatting depending on whether your visitor browses by category, tag, author, or date.

PinBlack includes the *category.php* file, so this is the one you want to edit. Choose Appearance→Editor and click the "Category Template (category.php)" link to get started. Inside, you'll find several dozen pages of interwoven HTML markup and PHP code. The overall pattern will be familiar from the previous chapter (page 454). First, a *get_header()* command starts the page and inserts the header, and then the loop displays all your posts, and finally a *get_footer()* command adds the footer and ends the document.

Changing the Title

Once you crack open the category template, there's nothing you can't change. The first target is the title of the archive page. Most themes use something generic, if they use a title at all.

The PinBlack theme shows a heading with text like this: "Category Archives: Sofas" (Figure 14-4). To quickly home in on this part of the template, press Ctrl+F (or Command+F on a Mac) and type in "category archive." That takes you to a part of the template that looks like this:

```
<h1 class="archive-title">
<?php
    printf( __( 'Category Archives: %s', 'pinblack' ), '<span>' .
      single_cat_title( '', false ) . '</span>' );
?>
</h1>
```

It may take a second to puzzle out this markup, because it relies on some hard-working PHP code. Inside the code block, the *printf()* function inserts some formatted text into the current page. Here's where things get a bit tricky. The *printf()* function actually stitches together several pieces of text, using quotation marks to delineate them and periods to link them together. The final result is a bit of HTML that looks like this, which the template spits out onto the page (Figure 14-4):

```
Category Archives: <span>Sofas</span>
```

The words "Category Archives" sound a bit jargony. Imagine you're shopping through Amazon.com, and you browse to a list of recent bestsellers, and see "Category Archives: Bestsellers" at the top.

To replace this heading with the more suitable text shown in Figure 14-5, you need to make the simple edit shown here:

```
<h1 class="archive-title">
<?php
    printf( __( 'Our Products: %s', 'pinblack' ), '<span>' .
      single_cat_title( '', false ) . '</span>' );
?>
</h1>
```

As always when editing a template, click Update to save your changes and then take a look at your site to see the effect of your modification.

Adding Extra Information

One of the most common ways to soup up a category page is by adding extra bits of useful information. You've seen how to add a category description (page 480), which the archive page picks up automatically. However, you can also add content elsewhere on the page. One example is the white, rounded box in Figure 14-5, which provides a reassuring message about the furniture warranty, and a link to the relevant page.

To add this sort of detail, you need to find the right spot in the template and insert your own HTML. To place something right at the end, you need to scroll down until you're nearly at the end of the template, where you find a line like this:

```
</div> <!-- end #content -->
```

This is the closing </div> tag that ends the content section of the page. After this line, the template adds the final footer.

To add more content, you simply add a section before the closing </div> tag. Here's the markup that creates the white box in the Distinct Furnishings example:

```
<div id="WarrantyBox">
    We stand behind our products. All our
    <?php single_cat_title(); ?> are protected by the best
    <a href="http://distinctfurnishings.net/warranty">warranty</a>
    in the business.
</div>
    </div> <!-- end #content -->
```

Notice that the new content doesn't include the word "Sofas." That's because you want this template to work for *all* your categories. So it uses the *single_cat_title()* function to grab the name of the current category. This is the same trick you saw above, where you added the category name to the title of the category page.

> **NOTE** This code assumes there's a page with warranty information at *http://distinctfurnishings.net/warranty*. You can create the warranty page in the usual way, using the Pages→Add New command.

There's another important detail in this example—the box applies custom formatting by using the same technique you saw in Chapter 13. First, you need to make sure your new section has a unique ID (if it occurs just once in the page) or a unique class name (if you use it multiple times). In the Distinct Furnishings example, the new section has the ID *WarrantyBox*. But the exact name doesn't matter, as long as you follow up by adding a corresponding style rule in the *style.css* file (page 432).

Here's the style rule that makes the warranty box look pretty by setting the right colors, spacing, and border:

```
#WarrantyBox {
    color: #708090;
    background: white;
    margin: 25px;
    padding: 10px;
    text-align: center;
    border-radius: 10px;
}
```

TIP As you start adding new rules to your *style.css* file, make sure you keep them all in one place, either at the beginning or the end of the file. That way, you won't mix up the new and old rules, and forget what formatting you added and what formatting is part of the original theme.

Reordering Posts

By now, you're well aware of WordPress's fascination with fresh content. Whenever you have a list of posts, WordPress puts the newest ones first, leaving the older entries to languish at the end. This makes sense if you're showing a series of news bulletins, but it's less helpful for a product catalog. To fix this problem, you need to tweak the loop in the category page. (The loop is the crucial bit of code that creates the list of posts in a WordPress site. You first considered it on page 462, where you learned to highlight new posts. Now you'll modify the loop to put posts in a different order.)

The first step is to find where the loop starts. In most well-designed themes—including Twenty Eleven and PinBlack—a comment clearly signals the start of the loop so you don't need to waste time sniffing around. It looks like this:

```
<?php /* Start the Loop */ ?>
```

To change the order of posts, you need to spring into action at this point in the code, before the loop starts pulling posts out of the database. The easiest way to do that is with a handy WordPress function called *query_posts()*, which runs a database query to grab the posts you want. (A *query* is a database operation that fetches a group of records that meets the criteria you specify.) To alter the order of your posts, you need to alter the database query that the category page uses to get its posts.

Before you look at the solution, it helps to consider the simplest operation the *query_posts()* function can perform. It looks like this:

```
<?php
    $posts = query_posts( $query_string );
?>

<?php /* Start the Loop */ ?>
```

This code takes the query that WordPress wants to run, which is stored in the *$query_string* variable, hands it to the *query_posts()* function, and stuffs the result (the group of matching posts) into the *$posts* variable. The important thing to understand here is that the code hasn't changed the query, so the end result (the way the category page looks in a visitor's browser) remains the same.

To get a different result, you need to stick some extra text onto the end of the query command in the *$query_string* variable. For example, if you want to sort posts by their title, in alphabetical order, you need to modify *$query_string* like this:

```php
<?php
    $posts = query_posts( $query_string . '&OrderBy=title&Order=asc' );
?>

<?php /* Start the Loop */ ?>
```

Here, it helps to understand the SQL language that database engines love, because that's the syntax *$query_string* uses. But even if you're not a database god, you can still decipher the modified query command. The *&OrderBy=title* portion of the command tells WordPress "and by the way, sort the posts by title." The *&Order=asc* portion adds "and when you do that sort, use ascending alphabetical order, just like a dictionary does." Together, these two instructions override the reverse-chronological order that WordPress would otherwise apply.

This is just one way to edit the loop that creates a post list. You'll see a similar but slightly different example later in this chapter. In the meantime, you can explore the *query_post()* function in more detail in WordPress's function reference, at *http://tinyurl.com/yhjtze5*.

GEM IN THE ROUGH

Different Category Pages for Different Categories

In some situations, you might decide to have significantly different content on your category pages, depending on the category. In that case, you need to create more than one copy of your category template, using names like *category-sofas.php*, *category-tables.php*, and *category-chairs.php*. This approach obviously requires more work, so don't go down this road unless it clearly benefits your site.

One type of site that frequently needs category-specific archive pages is a news site structured like an online magazine. In a site like that, it's often important to emphasize the difference between topics, and to give each category a distinct, compelling identity. For example, if you create an online magazine that includes posts in the categories Politics, Sports, and Lifestyle,

you'll probably want to give each category a slightly different style. And if you have multiple contributors, you may want give each columnist their own archive page, by augmenting the *authors.php* template with author-specific templates like *author-rami.php*, *author-grabinsky.php*, and so on.

In a product catalog site like Distinct Furnishings, category-specific formatting is less useful. That's because the goal of the site is to help visitors browse through the product selection as quickly as possible, so they can find the items that interest them. And to do that, it helps to minimize the differences between categories and keep your formatting and layout consistent.

Removing the Post Footers

The final detail to adjust on your catalog page is the footer that appears under every product tile. This footer details the category information (for example, "Filed Under Sofas"). But because every product in Distinct Furnishings has a single category, and because all the posts on a category archive page already share the same category, this information doesn't help anyone.

To remove it, look for and delete this markup:

```
<footer>
  <p class="cat"><?php _e("Filed Under", 'pinblack'); ?>
  <?php the_category(', '); ?>
  </p>
</footer> <!-- end article footer -->
```

■ Building a Better Home Page

The Distinct Furnishings site now has a first-rate browsing system, which lets potential customers hunt through the product catalog one category at a time. However, new visitors still arrive at the standard home page, which features every product in one big jumble.

The easiest way to fix this is to add a static page and set that as the home page for the site. This new home page can provide a welcome message, and invite visitors to dig into the content by offering a navigation menu. If this solution suits your needs, you can follow the instructions on page 210. There's no need to customize any template, or look at any PHP code.

But the home page also presents an opportunity to do more. Instead of using a plain page, you can add links that take visitors straight to specific products. You could hard-code these links (meaning you type them in, exactly the way you want them), but that's not flexible, and it forces you to make frequent page edits to keep your home page current. A more ambitious approach is to use some clever PHP to create links that appear on your home page *automatically*.

Figure 14-6 shows this technique in action. Here, the home page includes a welcome message and links to every product category, sorted by title.

Creating a page like this is easier than it appears. It's a technique worth learning even if you don't want the exact result shown in Figure 14-6, because you can easily adapt it to display other product links—for example, for featured products, new products, or products on sale (see the box on page 493).

The following sections show you how to create a custom home page like this one.

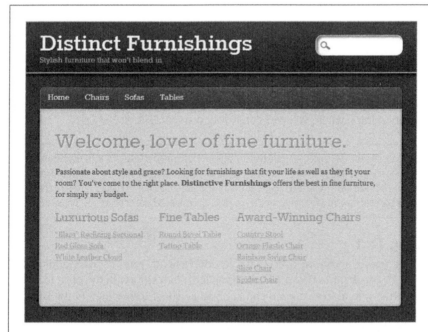

FIGURE 14-6

The links in this custom
home page give readers
a bird's-eye view of
the products Distinct
Furnishings offers. But
because the page is short
and well-organized,
the links don't become
overwhelming.

Cleaning Out the Template

The first step in creating this sort of custom home is to find the template you want, and prepare it for editing. In virtually all modern themes, the *index.php* template is the one you want. It creates the home page, with the standard list of posts. (The only exception is if your theme has a *home.php* file—if it does, edit that template instead.) To get started, choose Appearance→Editor and pick "Main Index Template (index.php)."

In many ways, the *index.php* template is like the *category.php* template you considered in the first part of this chapter. The heart of both is a loop that extracts and displays posts. The most significant difference is that *category.php* uses a narrower query that includes the posts in a single category.

You could keep the standard loop in the *index.php* template and simply change the way it displays each post. You've seen examples that use this technique to highlight new posts (page 462) and change the post order (page 484). However Figure 14-6 makes a more radical change—it grabs several separate post lists, by category, and then displays them. The easiest way to make this happen is to remove the existing loop entirely and add all new code. In most themes, that means deleting everything inside the content <div>.

In the PinBlack theme, deleting the loop leaves you with this exceedingly simple skeleton:

```
<?php get_header(); ?>

  <div id="content" class="clearfix">

  </div> <!-- end #content -->

<?php get_footer(); ?>
```

All this template does is add a header and the footer to a page. In between is a great big empty section where you can slot in your own content.

> **NOTE** Remember, the header template (*header.php*) isn't just a header. It has the HTML markup that starts each page, including the title, style sheet links, background, and menu. Similarly, the footer template (*footer.php*) includes the HTML markup that ends every page. So even in a simple stripped-down template like the one shown above, your site ends up with a fully formatted home page, albeit one that doesn't have any content inside it.

Adding Text

Now that you've removed everything you don't need, you can start adding the content you *do* want to the *index.php* template. First, start with the plain text and HTML. Wrap it in a <div> so you can apply style sheet formatting. In the Distinct Furnishings page, the main section is in a <div> that has the ID *WelcomePageMain*. Inside is a heading and a single paragraph of text:

```
<?php get_header(); ?>

  <div id="content" class="clearfix">

    <div id="WelcomePageMain">
      <h1 class="archive-title">Welcome, lover of fine furniture.</h1>
      <p>Passionate about style and grace? Looking for furnishings that
fit your life as well as they fit your room? You've come to the right place.
<b>Distinct Furnishings</b> offers the best in fine furniture, for simply
any budget.</p>
    </div>

  </div> <!-- end #content -->

<?php get_footer(); ?>
```

The specific ID you use isn't important, as long as it doesn't clash with the names that already exist in your theme's *style.css* file, and as long as you create a matching rule in your style sheet. In the Distinct Furnishings example, the style sheet rule adds some margin space around the main content area, so it isn't smushed up against the edges:

```
#WelcomePageMain {
    margin: 30px;
}
```

You can also use existing styles where appropriate—in this example, the <h1> heading uses the ready-made *archive-title* class, the same one that formats the title in the category page. (Keen eyes may have noticed this detail when editing the category page on page 482.) Every theme uses different class names, and if you can't find the one that adds the formatting you want, you'll need to create a new style rule and add the formatting on your own.

Creating the Links

The next step is more interesting. Immediately after the main text on Distinct Furnishing's home page, you want to create three sections, each with a heading and a list of links. You can decide exactly how you structure this markup—and if you're an HTML whiz, you may already have a plan. The Distinct Furnishings example places each column of links in a separate <div> element, as explained in the box below.

UP TO SPEED

The Multiple-Column Effect

There are several ways to create the multicolumn layout shown in Figure 14-6. Possible approaches include using the <table> element, or putting each column in a separate <div>, which is what the Distinct Furnishings example does.

The trick to the <div> approach is to use a CSS feature called *floating layout*. This technique is commonly used with images, because it lets you put a picture on one side of a page while the rest of the content (the text) flows around it. The same technique lets you create multiple columns, by floating each column to the left side of your page. That way, the first column goes hard up against the left side of the page, the second column goes right up against the first column, the third column goes up against the second, and so on. If the browser runs out of width, it bumps the next column further down the page, starting again on the left side.

To put this effect into practice, you need a style rule that sets the *float* property. Here's an example that uses the class name *FloatingColumn*:

```
.FloatingColumn {
    float: left;
    margin-right: 30px;
    margin-bottom: 30px;
}
```

You can then create a <div> for each column, and use the same style rule for each one:

```
<div class="FloatingColumn">
    ...
</div>
```

This is a standard technique in the style sheet world, and it works as well in WordPress as it does in any other website. If you'd like to polish up your CSS skills, consider a good book like *CSS: The Missing Manual*, by David Sawyer McFarland.

Here's how the first column starts:

```
<div class="FloatingColumn">
    <h2>Luxurious Sofas</h2>
```

Next, you need to add the links that belong in this category. The best tool for getting the links is a miraculously useful WordPress function called *get_posts()*.

The *get_posts()* function is similar to the *query_posts()* function you learned about on page 484. The difference is where and when you use them.

The *get_posts()* function lets you grab a bunch of posts (and all their information) whenever you need it. (This is the operation that database nerds call *querying*.) You can use *get_posts()* anytime, in any template file. However, to gather just the posts you want, you need to do some of the work. In other words, you need to write the code that examines each post, pulls out the information you want, and shows it on the page.

The *query_posts()* function does the same post-grabbing work as *get_posts()* does, but it was developed for archive pages, where it *replaces* the standard query. In other words, you can use *query_posts()* to change what posts an archive page shows. You don't need to write any more code, because the code that's already in the archive page does the rest of the work.

In this example, the original loop has been removed. Furthermore, the page needs to use several queries to get several separate lists of results (one for each category). For both of these reasons, the *get_posts()* function is the right choice.

If you've never programmed before (and we assume you haven't), using *get_posts()* is a sizeable task. Not only do you need to create the database query that gets your posts, you also need to step through the results, looking at each one and extracting the information you want to display on the home page. Fortunately, you don't need to write this logic from scratch. You can start with one of snippets from WordPress's function reference, which are featured at *http://tinyurl.com/yhjtze5*. There, you'll see examples that display post titles, display posts in random order, and get the posts that belong to a specific category. You can copy one of these examples into the *index.php* page to try it out. Or, start with this very basic code:

```
<?php
  global $post;
  $args = array( [ Your search and sort criteria go here. ] );
  $myposts = get_posts( $args );
  foreach( $myposts as $post ) :
    setup_postdata($post); ?>

    [ This is where you display the post data you want. ]

<?php endforeach; ?>
```

This is an all-purpose function that can handle any post-querying task. All you need to do is replace the two square-bracketed sections with the right details. (If you want to use this handy pattern in your own templates, you can get it as a text file on the Missing CD page at *http://missingmanuals.com/cds/wpmm*.)

The first detail you need to supply is the *$args* variable. Think of this as an all-in-one package that tells WordPress how to perform the database query. Although WordPress lets you retrieve content by using a lot of sorting options (see *http://tinyurl.com/yhjtze5* for the full list), this example uses just three: You want to specify the category that holds the posts, the way you want the posts sorted (by title), and the order you want the posts listed (*asc* for ascending or *desc* for descending). Here's the result:

```
$args = array( 'category' => 4, 'orderby' => 'title', 'order' => 'asc' );
```

To specify the category you want, you need to enter the category ID, not the category name. This code grabs posts in the Luxurious Sofas category, because it has an ID of 4.

TIP To find the ID for your categories, go to the Posts→Categories section, and edit the category. Then, examine the URL in the browser's address bar for the *tag_ID* code:

```
http://distinctfurnishings.net/wp-admin/edit-tags.php?action=edit&taxonomy=cat
egory&tag_ID=4&post_type=post
```

In this example, the category ID is 4.

The second detail you need to supply is the HTML markup you want to add to the page. WordPress copies your content to the page multiple times, once for each post it finds. This is more or less the same way that the standard loop works.

In your HTML markup, you use WordPress's oddly named "the_" functions to get information about each post. For example, to get the post title, you use *the_title()*, like so:

```
foreach( $myposts as $post ) :
  setup_postdata($post); ?>

  <?php the_title(); ?>
  <br />

<?php endforeach; ?>
```

This inserts a list of post titles into the page. After each title, the <br /> element adds a new line. The result is something like this:

```
"Blaze" Reclining Sectional
Red Gloss Sofa
White Leather Cloud
```

The example in Figure 14-6 is a bit more practical. It creates an <a> link for each post. The post title becomes the link's label. The target of the link is the post address. To get the title of the post, you use the function *the_title()*, which you just saw. To get the post address, you use the function *the_permalink()*. Here's how the code fits into the markup:

```
<a href="<?php the_permalink(); ?>"><?php the_title(); ?></a>
</br>
```

Extracting Information from a Post

The current example uses two well-worn WordPress functions to get information about each post: *the_title()* and *the_perma-link()*. But WordPress has many more useful functions that let you extract even more information from a post. You can determine the post's ID, publication date, publication time, category, and tag using the functions *the_ID()*, *the_date()*, *the_time()*, *the_category()*, and *the_tags()* respectively. There are also some WordPress information-extracting functions that, for historical reasons, start with "get_the_" instead of "the_".

These include *get_the_excerpt()*, *get_the_post_thumbnail()*, *get_the_author()*, and *get_the_content()*.

All these functions are terrifically useful in different loop-customization scenarios. For example, the PinBlack theme's tile-based display relies on *get_the_post_thumbnail()* to get the featured image for every post. It then inserts that image into a fluid, style-based layout. WordPress describes all these information-gathering functions on its function reference page at *http://tinyurl.com/func-ref*.

Just to make sure you haven't lost you place, here's the complete markup that creates the list of products in the Luxurious Sofas category. The customized details are in bold.

```
<div class="FloatingColumn">
  <h2>Luxurious Sofas</h2>
  <?php
    global $post;
    $args = array( 'category' => 4, 'orderby' => 'title', 'order' => 'asc' );
    $myposts = get_posts( $args );
    foreach( $myposts as $post ) :
      setup_postdata($post); ?>
      <a href="<?php the_permalink(); ?>"><?php the_title(); ?></a>
      <br />
  <?php endforeach; ?>
</div>
```

To create the other two columns (Fine Tables and Award-Winning Chairs), you can copy this section (twice), and adjust the heading and the category ID accordingly:

```
<div class="FloatingColumn">
  <h2>Fine Tables</h2>
  <?php
    global $post;
    $args = array( 'category' => 5, 'orderby' => 'title', 'order' => 'asc' );
    $myposts = get_posts( $args );
    foreach( $myposts as $post ) :
      setup_postdata($post); ?>
      <a href="<?php the_permalink(); ?>"><?php the_title(); ?></a>
      <br />
```

```php
  <?php endforeach; ?>
</div>

<div class="FloatingColumn">
  <h2>Award-Winning Chairs</h2>
  <?php
    global $post;
    $args = array( 'category' => 3, 'orderby' => 'title', 'order' => 'asc' );
    $myposts = get_posts( $args );
    foreach( $myposts as $post ) :
      setup_postdata($post); ?>
      <a href="<?php the_permalink(); ?>"><?php the_title(); ?></a>
      <br />
  <?php endforeach; ?>
</div>
```

The final result is a page that looks up posts from three different categories and combines them into one compact, perfectly organized page of links.

GEM IN THE ROUGH

Highlighting Products on Sale

In the current example, the Distinct Furnishings site uses three loops, and offers a link to every product in its catalog. This works well in a site that has a few dozen products, but it's not workable in one that has hundreds.

Of course, there's no need to fetch posts from every category. Instead, you can highlight just *some* of your posts. Using this technique, you can create even more interesting home pages, such as ones that highlight recently added products, clearance products, or new promotions. The only challenge is writing a query that gets the posts you want.

The easiest approach is to create an *additional* category, and apply it to the items you want to highlight. For example, you could create a category named Featured. Then, if you have a loveseat that warrants special attention, you assign it two categories: Sofas and Featured. Because it's in the Sofas category, visitors will find it when they click Sofas in the menu. And because it's in the Featured category, your home page can retrieve it with a category-specific query, and display it prominently. (Just remember not to add the Featured category to your menu, because having the same product appear in more than one place can confuse visitors.)

From Post to Product Page

The changes you've made so far have transformed the Distinct Furnishings site into a sleek, browsable product catalog, with no trace of its WordPress blog roots—at least, not until you click on a product. Once you do, you see the standard post-viewing page that includes plenty of unnecessary information, like the author name and publication date, and a sidebar of mostly useless widgets (Figure 14-7).

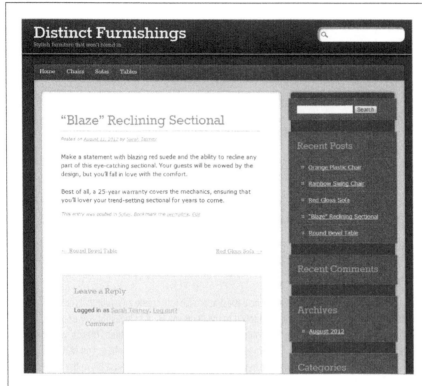

FIGURE 14-7

On close inspection, the products pages on the Distinct Furnishings site still look like posts.

Fortunately, it isn't hard to change the product posts. Once again, the task involves editing a template, but this time the work involved is significantly less. You don't need to tamper with loop code or change your query. In fact, most of the work involves removing the post details that don't apply to your product listings.

Figure 14-8 shows the goal: a cleaned-up post that showcases the current product.

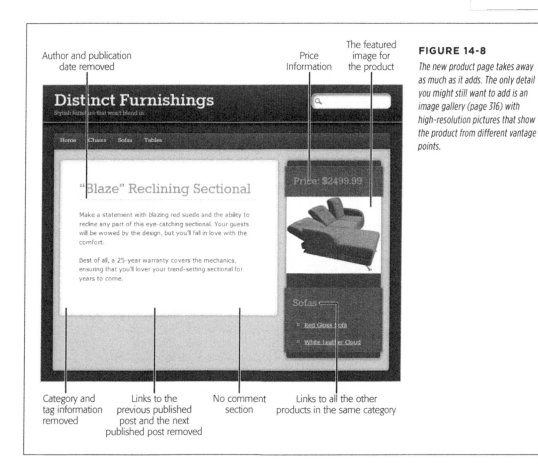

Author and publication date removed

Price Information

The featured image for the product

FIGURE 14-8

The new product page takes away as much as it adds. The only detail you might still want to add is an image gallery (page 316) with high-resolution pictures that show the product from different vantage points.

Category and tag information removed

Links to the previous published post and the next published post removed

No comment section

Links to all the other products in the same category

Cleaning Out the Template

To change the way WordPress displays your posts, you need to alter two template files. As you may remember from Chapter 13, *single.php* creates the single-post view for every post and page. However, it gets help from another template, depending on what type of content it's displaying. In the case of an ordinary post, *single.php* asks *content-single.php* to do the real work of showing the post content (page 454) explains the process).

TIP Before you edit these templates, it's a good idea to make a backup copy of each. The easiest way to do that is to launch an FTP program and drag the templates to your computer to download them. A backup is important because you might decide later that you need to display some posts in a more typical single-post page. If so, you have a copy of the unedited template ready to roll. (For example, on page 500, you'll consider how you might add ordinary posts with news alongside your catalog of products.) Keeping a backup is also a good idea, in case you get carried away with your template surgery and accidentally lobotomize your page.

Once again, you can choose Appearance→Editor and do all your editing in the dashboard. Start by choosing "Single Post (*single.php*)." Here, you need to remove the navigation links that let readers step from one post to another. These don't make sense when you profile products, because the links are based on the publication date, which is a completely arbitrary order for furniture items.

The navigation links appear just under the call to the *content-single.php* template. Here's the section as it appears in the PinBlack theme. You need to remove the second line (in bold below).

```
<?php get_template_part( 'content', 'single' ); ?>
<?php pinblack_content_nav( 'nav-below' ); ?>
```

Immediately after that is the comment section. You can remove the entire thing. Here's the comment you don't need:

```
<?php
  // If comments are open or we have at least one comment, load the template
  if ( comments_open() || '0' != get_comments_number() )
    comments_template( '', true );
?>
```

GEM IN THE ROUGH

Repurposing the Comments Section

Instead of deleting the comments section, you can put it to a new purpose: product reviews. All you need to do is alter the wording around the comment form, by editing the *comments .php* template.

In the *comments.php* template, almost at the end, you'll find a line like this:

```
<?php comment_form(); ?>
```

This creates the complete comment form, using WordPress's default settings. If you edit this line, you change the comment form, and WordPress details the many possible customizations you can make at *http://tinyurl.com/26qf74x*. For example, here's how you rename the heading (from "Leave a Reply" to "Review This Product":

```
<?php comment_form(array( 'title_
  reply'=>'Review This Product' )); ?>
```

And here's how you rename the heading *and* change the text on the comment submission button from "Post Comment" to "Submit":

```
<?php comment_form(array('title_
  reply'=>'Review This Product',
  'label_submit' => 'Submit' )); ?>
```

If you decide to let people review your products, you might also want to consider adding ratings with a plug-in like GD Star Rating (*http://tinyurl.com/gd-star-rating*).

After you finish editing *single.php*, move on to *content-single.php*. Here, you want to remove two sections. First, find the section just under the post title, which has the publication author and date. It looks like this:

```
<div class="entry-meta">
  <?php pinblack_posted_on(); ?>
</div>
```

Remove this completely.

Next, find the section that adds the category and tag information after the post content. The PinBlack theme wraps this section in a massive <footer> element. You can delete the whole thing, from the opening <footer> tag to the closing one (</footer>).

Adding the Sidebar Content

Now that you cleaned out the stuff you don't want, it's time to add some extra content to the sidebar. You *could* do this by fiddling with the *sidebar.php* template, but that approach can get a bit awkward, because you need to make sure that your new content doesn't interfere with the space your theme reserves for widgets. It's also extra work that you don't need to do, if you can find suitable widgets to do the job.

The revamped page in Figure 14-8 is composed entirely of widgets. They are:

- **Get Custom Field** (*http://tinyurl.com/get-field*). This widget grabs the price for each product. You'll learn how to set that up in the following section.

- **Featured Image** (*http://tinyurl.com/featured-i*). This widget displays the featured image for the current post. This saves you from adding the same picture twice (once as a featured image, and once as an image inside the post). However, you can still improve your product posts by adding more pictures, or—even better—a picture gallery (page 316).

- **Post by Same Categories** (*http://tinyurl.com/postbysame*). This widget adds links to all the posts in the same category, sorted the way you want (in this case, by title). That means that when a visitor takes a look at the "Blaze Reclining Sectional," they automatically see a list of other sofas they might want to consider.

Using these widgets is easy. You simply install the plug-in, activate it, and choose Appearance→Widgets. Then, drag the corresponding widget into the sidebar area.

Custom Fields: Adding Extra Pieces of Information to a Post

As you probably know, WordPress stores the information for every post in a separate record in a database on your website. That record includes obvious details like the post title and post content, along with a slew of extra info about the author, the publication date, the last modified date, the excerpt, and so on. (Database nerds can get the full, behind-the-scenes details at *http://tinyurl.com/3a88qt*.)

The post records don't include price information, and why would they? Price is one of many additional possible details that apply only to certain sites in certain scenarios. Of course, you're free to put the price information in the post content, but that's a bit sloppy. There's no way to make sure that every post puts its price in the same place and formats it the same way. There's also no guarantee that every post includes a price, and there's no easy way to extract it if you need it (for example, if you want to create a query that pulls out posts in a certain price range).

You're probably prepared to live with this limitation, but WordPress has a surprisingly flexible feature that can help you out. It's called *custom fields*, and it lets you bolt extra pieces of information to any post.

Here's how:

1. **Start editing one of your product posts.**

   The quickest approach is to choose Posts→All Posts, and then click the Edit link under the first post in the list.

2. **Click the Screen Options button in the top-right corner of the Edit Post page, and then turn on the checkmark next to Custom Fields.**

   If you haven't used any custom fields on your site, the Custom Fields box is tucked away out of site (Figure 14-9). But once you change the screen options, it appears under the editor box that holds the post content.

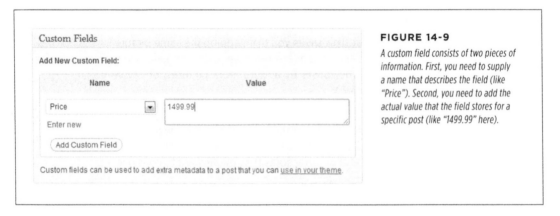

FIGURE 14-9

A custom field consists of two pieces of information. First, you need to supply a name that describes the field (like "Price"). Second, you need to add the actual value that the field stores for a specific post (like "1499.99" here).

3. **In the Custom Fields box, fill in a name for your custom field.**

   In the Distinct Furnishings example, that name is "Price."

   If you see the word "— Select —" in the Name box, your theme already has one or more custom fields that it uses for its own purposes. To add a new field, you must first click the "Enter new" link. That clears the text box so you can type in a name.

4. **Type in a value for your custom field.**

   The value applies to this particular post. For example, if you add a custom field named Price, the custom field value is the price of the current product (say, "1499.99"). Enter the number only—don't include a currency symbol or any additional text.

5. **Click the Add Custom Field button.**

6. **Click Update to save the changed version of your post.**

You're done. WordPress creates a new custom field for your posts, and attaches the value you supplied to the current post.

Next you need to set the price of every other product. You already created the custom field you need, but you need to supply the correct value for each product.

7. **Choose Posts→All Posts to see your list of posts, and then click the Edit link under the post you want to change.**

8. **In the Custom Fields section, select "Price" from the Name box (Figure 14-10).**

FIGURE 14-10

Once you add a custom field, WordPress makes it available to every other post. All you need to do is select it and fill in suitable values.

9. **Type in the appropriate price in the Value box, and then click Add Custom Field.**

10. **Click Update to save the post.**

11. **If you have posts left to edit, return to step 7.**

Continue editing posts until you assign a price to each one.

Creating a custom field doesn't change what your posts look like. In fact, WordPress carries on exactly as it did before, displaying the post content and ignoring the extra information. To change this state of affairs, you need to extract the information from your custom field and show it in the right place.

There are several ways to do this. The most straightforward is to edit the *content-single.php* template, fetch the price information, and show it somewhere on the page. To do this, you use *the get_post_meta()* function, like this:

```
This product is available for
$<?php echo get_post_meta( get_the_ID(), 'Price', true ); ?>.
```

The revised post page in Distinct Furnishings (Figure 14-8) doesn't use this approach. Instead, it displays the price information in the sidebar, with the help of the handy Get Custom Field plug-in (*http://tinyurl.com/get-field*). To use this plug-in, install it, activate it, and then drag the Get Custom Field widget into the sidebar. To configure the widget, you need to enter the key for your custom field (that's "Price" in this example), and optionally supply some extra text to put before and after the custom field.

In the Distinct Furnishings example, this text precedes the custom field:

```
<div class="Price">Price: $
```

And this markup follows it:

```
</div>
```

The only step left is to add a style rule for the Price class in the *style.css* file. This lets you apply the formatting you need to your custom field.

POWER USERS' CLINIC

Classifying Your Posts with Custom Taxonomies

Custom fields let you attach additional information to any post, which is ridiculously useful. However, WordPress has another post-extending trick that's more specialized, but also more powerful. It's called *custom taxonomies*, and it lets you create a completely new classification system for your posts.

To understand custom taxonomies, it helps to remember the two staples of post organization: categories and tags. These themselves are examples of taxonomies—ways to organize posts. With a *custom* taxonomy, though, you set up other ways to group posts.

For example, the Distinct Furnishings site might add a taxonomy called Color. You could then create a list of color choices, including Black, White, Red, and so on. When you create a product post, you would pick one of these color choices, and visitors could browse products by color (to check out all the red furniture, for example). Other possible taxonomies that Distinct Furnishings might use include Size (Full, Luxurious, Apartment-Sized) and Material (Fabric, Leather, and so on). As with custom fields, custom taxonomies let you add extra information. The difference is that custom taxonomies are *browsable*.

For a small or medium-sized product catalog, custom taxonomies add extra work with no obvious benefit. But if you have a gargantuan catalog, they can give visitors more flexible ways to look around and find what they want.

Unlike custom fields, the WordPress dashboard won't help you add a custom taxonomy. To do that, you need to run some code (which is ugly) or use a plug-in (which is much nicer). One plug-in option is the Ultimate Taxonomy Manager (*http://tinyurl.com/ultimate-t*). Of course, you'll also need to extend the single-post template to show the information from your custom taxonomy.

For a more detailed overview of custom taxonomies, with examples, you can read a tutorial on the subject at *http://tinyurl.com/8slqbkn.*

Sites with More than One Type of Post

You just learned how to create a custom template to make your product posts appear just right. This is a time-tested WordPress technique with one stumbling block—what happens if you need to show more than one type of post?

In the Distinct Furnishings example, every post represents a product, so this isn't a problem. But consider what happens if you want to use posts to display store news in a separate section of the site. Keeping the news separate from the furniture products isn't too hard, provided you give each set of posts a different category (and create a category-specific template for browsing, as explained on page 481).

But what happens when a visitor clicks through to read a news post, and gets the customized single-post template with price information?

What you need in this situation is a way to tell WordPress to use a different single-post template depending on the post's category. WordPress doesn't have this feature built in, but you can add it with relatively little trouble. The basic technique requires three steps:

1. **Take your existing *single.php* file, which you currently use for product posts, and rename it to *single-product.php*.**

2. **Create a template to use for your other posts.**

   For example, you can copy the old version of *single.php* (grab it from the original PinBlack theme folder if you don't have it any longer) and name it *single-news.php*.

3. **Now, create a new *single.php* master template.**

   This template has the job of deciding when to use the *single-product.php* template, and when to use the *single-news.php* template.

Creating the new *single.php* file is the key step. This template requires one ingredient—a block of PHP that examines the category and tells WordPress which of your two single-post templates to use.

If you want to use the two-template model for Distinct Furnishings, which lets the site distinguish between products and news items, this is the code you need :

```php
<?php
  $post = $wp_query->post;
  if (in_category('news')) {
      include(TEMPLATEPATH.'/single-news.php');
  }
  else {
      include(TEMPLATEPATH.'/single-product.php');
  }
?>
```

The first line grabs the current post. The second line starts a block of conditional logic, much like the one you saw on page 464. It asks the critical question—is this post in the "News" category?

```php
  if (in_category('news')) {
```

If so, the code tells WordPress to find the *single-news.php* template and inject all its content into it. Essentially, this is where the *single.php* template hands over the job to *single-news.php*.

```php
      include(TEMPLATEPATH.'/single-news.php');
  }
```

The final section deals with every other condition, using the *else* keyword. In other words, if a post isn't in the News category, it's assumed to be a product, and so it needs the *single-product.php* template:

```
else {
    include(TEMPLATEPATH.'/single-product.php');
}
```

If you need to distinguish between even more types of posts, you add extra conditions in between the first *if* and the final *else*. These are called *elseif* conditions, and here's an example of what they look like:

```
<?php
$post = $wp_query->post;
if (in_category('news')) {
    include(TEMPLATEPATH.'/single-news.php');
}
elseif (in_category('suppliers')) {
    include(TEMPLATEPATH.'/single-suppliers.php');
}
elseif (in_category('people')) {
    include(TEMPLATEPATH.'/single-people.php');
}
else {
    include(TEMPLATEPATH.'/single-product.php');
}
?>
```

In this example, the News, Suppliers, and People categories get their own special templates, while every other type of post uses the *single-product.php* template.

Once again, if this is the first time you've seen conditional code, it may look a bit strange. But you should be able to copy this block of code (grab it from the Missing CD page at *http://missingmanuals.com/cds/wpmm*) and modify it to use your category names. And to see this code in action, visit the sample sites at *www.prosetech.com/wordpress.*.

■ Adding E-Commerce

A product catalog is a great way to advertise your wares to the world. But some sites go further by giving visitors the ability to *buy* products.

E-commerce isn't suited for every site. For example, a furniture store like Distinct Furnishings might prefer to let salespeople handle all the selling, in person. If your business has items that are difficult to ship, available to local buyers only, or one-of-a-kind (for example, individual items in an antique warehouse), you might make a sensible decision to pass on any type of e-commerce.

Of course, there are even more sites that *will* want to take advantage of e-commerce. Some will need to ship items (for example, a shop that sells handcrafted jewelry), while others will be able to deliver the goods right away (like an indie band that lets purchasers download high-quality audio tracks). And although e-commerce features aren't a part of the WordPress software, they are available through a wide range of plug-ins. In the rest of this chapter, you'll consider one that lets you integrate a PayPal shopping cart into your site.

PLUG-IN POWER

The Many Ways to Make Money

Shopping carts are only one way that your site can start making bank. Here are three more money-earning methods, along with the plug-ins that will help you implement them.

- **Donations.** Begging for coin is awkward, but it may work. If your site offers genuinely useful advice, you can ask for tips with something like this: "Like what you read? Buy me a coffee!" If you're writing in support of a charitable cause or if your writing entails danger or significant sacrifice, you can ask for support, as in "Donate today to support independent journalism." Whatever the case, the easiest approach is to set up a PayPal account and add the PayPal Donations plug-in (*http://tinyurl.com/paypal-d*) to your site.

- **Advertising.** If you get masses of traffic reading the posts on your site, you might be able to accumulate some click-through money with the right advertising program. One popular choice is Google AdSense (*www.google.com/adsense*), which automatically shows ads that match the

content on your site, and pays you every time someone clicks one of them.

If you decide to incorporate ads, the Ad Injection plug-in (*http://tinyurl.com/ad-injection*) can help. It supports Google AdSense and other advertising programs, and it lets you customize exactly when and how you show your ads.

- **Subscription services.** This is probably one of the hardest ways to make money, because potential customers need to be completely convinced about the value of your content before they sign up to read it. Subscription services are also quite complex because you need to register every reader. But if your site offers one-of-a-kind information that has real financial value to other people, it's an option worth exploring. The powerful subscription plug-in s2Member (*http://tinyurl.com/s2member*) can help you get started.

Signing Up with PayPal

PayPal strikes a simple but compelling deal: You tell it the name and price of your product, and it gives you a shopping cart that you can drop into your website, with little (if any) customization.

When a customer buys one of your products, PayPal handles the checkout process, and then notifies you by email. At this point, you need to deliver the goods (for example, by sending them electronically or shipping them out). Shortly after the transaction, the money appears in your PayPal account. You can then transfer it to a bank account, or use it buy stuff on other PayPal-equipped websites.

You might already have a PayPal account, but odds are that it's a personal one—suitable for buying other people's goods, but not much else. Before you can set up a PayPal shopping cart, you need a premier or business account (see the box below).

NOTE All PayPal accounts are free to set up. PayPal makes its money on the commission it takes when you make a sale, as detailed below.

The Three Types of PayPal Accounts

The first decision you need to make when you sign up with PayPal is the type of account that's right for you. PayPal gives you three options:

- **Personal account.** This type of account lets you use PayPal to buy items on sites like eBay. You can also *accept* money transfers from other PayPal members without having to pay any fees. However, there's a significant catch—personal accounts can't accept credit card payments, so they won't work on an e-commerce site.

- **Premier account.** This type of account gives you an easy way to run a small business. You can still make payments to others, and you can accept any type of payment that PayPal accepts, including both credit and debit cards. However, PayPal charges you for every payment you

receive, an amount that varies by sales volume but ranges from 1.9 percent to 2.9 percent of the payment's total value (with a minimum fee of 30 cents). That means that on a $25 sale, PayPal takes about $1 off the top. If you accept payments in another currency, you surrender an extra 2.5 percent. To get the full scoop on fees and to see the most current rates, refer to *www.paypal.com/fees*.

- **Business account.** This type of account has the same features and fees as a premier account, with two key differences: First, it lets you do business under your business name (instead of your personal name). And second, it supports multiple users. For that reason, a business account is the best choice if you have a large business with employees who need to access your PayPal account to help you manage your site and its finances.

If you already have a personal PayPal account, you can upgrade to a premier or business account quickly by visiting *https://www.paypal.com/upgrade*. If you don't have an account, you need to sign up for one by following these steps:

1. **Head to the PayPal website (*www.paypal.com*) and click the Sign Up link.**

   This takes you to PayPal's Sign Up page.

2. **Choose your country and language.**

3. **Choose the type of account you want to create (Personal, Premier, or Business), and click the Get Started button in the corresponding box.**

   PayPal takes you to a new page to fill in your account information.

4. **If you're creating a business account, PayPal will ask you to pick your "payment solution." Choose the first option, Website Payments Standard, and then click Continue.**

5. **Enter your email address and choose a password, and then fill in your name, address, and phone number.**

Make your password complex—you don't want a malicious hacker guessing it and using your PayPal account to go on an electronic buying binge.

If you're creating a business account, you have two pages of information to fill out. The extra information you need to supply includes the type of business you run, the business name, and the business address.

6. **Finally, click "Agree and Create Account" to complete the process.**

PayPal sends you an email confirmation immediately. Once you click the link in the message, it activates your account, and you can create your first PayPal shopping cart.

Installing the Shopping Cart Plug-In

PayPal has a shopping cart feature that lets you put a shopping cart on *any* website. If you're building a traditional site, you need to use the PayPal interface to create a form, which you can then cut and paste into a web page. But if you're building a WordPress website, the job gets significantly easier, because you can install a plug-in that does all the form-generating work for you.

There's no shortage of PayPal-powered shopping cart plug-ins. Overall, they fall into two categories:

- **Simple PayPal shopping carts.** These no-nonsense plug-ins give you the quickest, easiest way to add the standard PayPal shopping cart to your site. One popular example is the WordPress Simple PayPal Shopping Cart (*http://tinyurl.com/paypal-c*).

- **Custom shopping carts.** The best example is the wildly popular WP e-Commerce plug-in (*http://tinyurl.com/wp-ecom*), which lets you build your own, painstakingly customized shopping cart experience. It doesn't use PayPal to build the shopping cart, but it does use the service to process payments (unless you use another payment service that the plug-in supports, like Google Checkout).

And if WP e-Commmerce doesn't quite do it for you, there's no shortage of competitors, including WooCommerce, JigoShop, DukaPress, and Cart66 Lite. All are free, but they usually have premium versions that add more features.

In this chapter, you'll use the first approach, using the WordPress Simple PayPal Shopping Cart plug-in. To get started, choose Plugins→Add New, and search for "simple paypal." When you find the plug-in, install and activate it.

To configure the plug-in, choose Settings→WP Shopping Cart. At a minimum, you need to enter your PayPal email address at the top of the Settings form. The other details are optional; they let you customize the text in the shopping cart pages, the default currency, shipping costs, the threshold for free shipping, and the web address the customer is sent to after making a purchase, among other details.

Adding the Shopping Cart

PayPal doesn't care about the details of your products. All it needs to know is the name of your product and its price. With these two pieces of information, you can create an "Add to Cart" button, and PayPal takes it from there.

The WordPress Simple PayPal Shopping Cart plug-in adds a shortcode (page 315) that makes it easy to create Add To Cart buttons. The shortcode uses this syntax:

```
[wp_cart:ProductName:price:Price:end]
```

So if you want to sell the Blaze Reclining Sectional for $2,499.99, you need to edit the post for the Blaze Reclining Sectional and add the shortcode to the end of the post, after your content. Here's what the shortcode should look like:

```
[wp_cart:Blaze Reclining Sectional:price:2499.99:end]
```

Now, when you view this product, the shortcode turns into an "Add to Cart" button (Figure 14-11).

"Blaze" Reclining Sectional

Make a statement with blazing red suede and the ability to recline any part of this eye-catching sectional. Your guests will be wowed by the design, but you'll fall in love with the comfort.

Best of all, a 25-year warranty covers the mechanics, ensuring that you'll lover your trend-setting sectional for years to come.

FIGURE 14-11

Although you can't tell by looking at it, this is customized so that one click adds the Blaze Reclining Sectional sofa to a PayPal shopping cart.

You can click the Add To Cart button, but you won't know what's going in your shopping cart (and you won't be able to complete your purchase). To properly test the "Add to Cart" button, you need a way to display the current contents of the cart. The WordPress Simple PayPal Shopping Cart plug-in gives you two options: by adding another shortcode to your product posts, or by using a widget.

Using the shortcode approach, you can create a shopping cart that appears at the bottom of the post. To try this out, begin by editing a product post (say, the Blaze Reclining Sectional). Scroll to the bottom, after the shortcode that creates the "Add to Cart" button, and add this shortcode:

```
[show_wp_shopping_cart]
```

Now, update the product post and take a look. The first time you view the product you'll see the "Add to Cart" button, same as before. But once you click it, the shopping cart becomes visible underneath (Figure 14-12). Click "Check out with PayPal," fill in some credit card details, and voilà!—your first e-commerce sale.

The only problem with the shopping cart shortcode is that you need to add it to *every* product post. This extra work is understandably necessary for the shortcode that creates the "Add to Cart" button, because every product has a different price. But it's needless extra work for the shopping cart.

There are two solutions that can save you the effort of pasting the [show_wp_shop ping_cart] shortcode in all your posts. One is to add the shopping cart shortcode to a template file (as explained in the box on page 510). A simpler approach is to use the handy shopping cart widget described next.

To use the shopping card widget, choose Appearance→Widgets. Then, drag the WP PayPal Shopping Cart widget to right place. (Common choices include a sidebar or footer.) Figure 14-13 shows the shopping cart in a sidebar.

FIGURE 14-12

If your visitor's shopping cart is empty, WordPress doesn't display it on the page. But once your guest clicks Add To Cart, he'll see something like this.

"Blaze" Reclining Sectional

Make a statement with blazing red suede and the ability to recline any part of this eye-catching sectional. Your guests will be wowed by the design, but you'll fall in love with the comfort.

Best of all, a 25-year warranty covers the mechanics, ensuring that you'll lover your trend-setting sectional for years to come.

Add to Cart

Your Shopping Cart

Item Name	Quantity	Price	
Blaze Reclining Sectional	1	$2,499.99	
	Total:	$2,499.99	

Check out with **PayPal**
VISA

FIGURE 14-13

The sidebar is a great place to put your shopping cart (as long as it fits). That way, it remains visible but doesn't look like part of the post.

TIP If you want to tweak the formatting around the shopping cart (for example, to change its margins, background color, or border), write a style rule that targets the *shopping_cart* class.

The shopping cart follows your visitor around your site. For example, visitors can visit several product pages and add several items to their cart before making the final checkout. When a visitor clicks "Check out with PayPal," the PayPal service takes over, asking for a shipping address and credit card information. You'll get an email that confirms the purchase when the checkout process is done.

TIP Make sure your customers leave with a good feeling. After someone's placed on order, take them to a thank-you page. All you need to do is create this page (like any other WordPress page), and type the page's URL into the "Return URL" box in the Settings→WP Shopping Cart page.

Putting the Shopping Cart in Your Template

It might occur to you that the Simple PayPal Shopping Cart plug-in forces you to do some extra work. After all, you need to edit *every* product post to add an "Add to Cart" button and, optionally, to add the shopping cart. Surely it would be better to add these details to the product post template (*single.php*)—the same file that you customized on page 495—and save yourself some time?

The answer is yes, but only partially. That's because templates aren't designed to deal with shortcodes, and they do it a little unevenly at best.

You *can* add the shopping cart to your post template, so that the cart appears after every product listing automatically. To do that, you need to insert some code that triggers the [show_wp_shopping_cart] shortcode in the *single.php* template file, creating the shopping cart display. Here's what you need:

```php
<?php
  echo do_shortcode(
    '[show_wp_shopping_cart]');
?>
```

You can place this code wherever you need it, but it makes sense to put it after the post content, before the </article> tag that closes the final section.

Unfortunately, this trick doesn't work with the "Add to Cart" button. You might think that a genius piece of code should be able to grab the title and the current price information for each product and create a matching "Add to Cart" button. But, sadly, the button doesn't currently work in templates, even with the *do_shortcode()* function shown above. That means you still need to hand-create a separate "Add to Cart" button for each product post, which works, but is a bit messy. You'll need to be extra vigilant when you change product names or prices, and make sure you change both the details in the post *and* the details in the "Add to Cart" button.

Appendixes

Migrating from WordPress.com

WordPress.com is a great place to start your WordPress venture, and many fans stay there forever. But there are several reasons that you might decide to strike out on your own and set up a self-hosted WordPress site. Most commonly, it's because you want to customize your site beyond what WordPress.com allows.

Here are the two features that can compel otherwise happy WordPress.com users to move on:

- **Themes.** WordPress.com site owners can choose from a collection of barely 200 themes, while self-hosters get to pick from well over a thousand themes in the WordPress theme repository (and still more if you're willing to trawl the Web). More important, you can *modify* any theme without restrictions, which lets you do everything from swapping in your favorite Google Web Font for headlines (page 448) to redesigning the site so that it works like a product catalog (Chapter 14).

- **Plug-ins.** You can't add plug-ins to a WordPress.com site. Instead, you're limited to a very small set of preinstalled plug-ins, chosen by Automattic. But on a self-hosted site, you have your choice of thousands of plug-ins that can extend your site with useful features, like better search optimization (page 416), new tools for multi-author collaboration (page 365), and money-making options like ads and donation buttons (page 503).

Making the jump from WordPress.com to a self-hosted site can be awkward, but it's nothing you can't handle. Happily, WordPress has an import/export tool that does most of the work. In this appendix, you'll learn how to make the shift, and deal with some of the inevitable hiccups.

Before You Begin

Before you do anything, it helps to get an overview of the whole migration process. You need to complete several steps, in this order:

1. **Sign up for a new site with a web host (for a monthly or annual fee).**

   This is also the point where you register a custom domain name (like *www .supernovatattooparlor.com*) if you don't already own one. If you already bought a domain name through WordPress.com, don't worry—you can have it point to your new site when you finish the transfer process, as explained on page 521.

2. **Install a fresh copy of WordPress on your new site.**

   Unfortunately, you can't move a complete WordPress site, as-is. Instead, you need to start with a basic blank shell of a site, and then load it up with the data from your old site.

3. **Export the data from your old site.**

   You'll download this data to your computer, as a single compact file.

4. **Import the data into your new site.**

   In this step, you add the downloaded content to the empty WordPress site on your web host.

5. **Configure and clean up your new site.**

   This is the part where you fiddle with your theme and install Jetpack, all in an attempt to make your new site function as much as possible like the old one.

6. **Reroute your web visitors from the old WordPress.com site to your new self-hosted site.**

   This is optional, but you don't want your visitors going to an out-of-date copy of your site, missing your new posts. Ideally, visitors will be seamlessly redirected to your new site, without needing to click a link or type in a new web address.

The first two steps are covered in Chapter 3. Make sure you complete them before you continue any further in this appendix, because there's no use in trying to transfer a WordPress.com site if you don't have a self-hosted site ready and waiting to receive it. The rest of this appendix covers everything else you need to do, beginning with step 3 above.

Guided Transfers

If this transition sounds like altogether too much work—or the thought of configuring anything to do with web hosting is enough to wake you, screaming, in the middle of the night—there's an easier option. You can pay WordPress.com to perform a *guided transfer*, in which a nerd-for-hire at Automattic sets up your domain, transfers your site, and configures a few plug-ins that make the site run more like a standard WordPress.com site.

Unfortunately, there are two significant caveats: you need to cough up a one-time fee of $129, and you need to use one of WordPress's recommended web hosts. To learn more, read up at *http://tinyurl.com/guidedtransfer*. To sign up, visit the Store section of the dashboard for your site, find the Guided Transfer box, and click Buy Now.

Transferring Your Data

Assuming you signed up with a web host and installed WordPress on your new site, the next step is to copy all the information from your WordPress.com site. That includes the posts and pages you wrote, the menus you created, and all the comments your readers submitted.

Transferring this data takes two steps. First, you download it from your WordPress.com site to your computer. Then, you upload it from your computer to your new site.

Exporting Your Data from WordPress.com

Here's how to get information out of your original WordPress.com site:

1. **Log in to your WordPress.com site's dashboard and choose Tools→Export.**

   You'll see the Export page, which gives you the option to export your data (described here) or to opt for the guided transfer process (described in the box above).

2. **Click Export.**

   Now WordPress.com asks you what data you want to extract (Figure A-1).

FIGURE A-1

WordPress.com's "All content" export option includes every exportable piece of site data: posts, pages, and comments.

Export Help ▾

When you click the button below WordPress will create an XML file for you to save to your computer.

This format, which we call WordPress eXtended RSS or WXR, will contain your posts, pages, comments, custom fields, categories, and tags.

Once you've saved the download file, you can use the Import function in another WordPress installation to import the content from this site.

Choose what to export

⦿ All content

This will contain all of your posts, pages, comments, custom fields, terms, navigation menus and custom posts.

⦿ Posts

⦿ Pages

⦿ Feedbacks

(Download Export File)

3. Choose "All content."

If you want to create a significantly different site from your current one, you may want to bring over just some data; if so, choose one of the other options. Usually, though, you'll want to export everything.

4. Click Download Export File.

Depending on your web browser, you may be asked for a file name, or the exported file may be automatically placed in your Downloads folder. The file will have a name like this:

```
therealestatediaries.wordpress.2013-01-17.xml
```

The first part is the name of your WordPress.com site (*therealestatediaries*), the second part is the date you performed the export (January 17, 2013), and the final part is the file extension that indicates it's an XML file, which is a format computer programs often use to store structured data.

Where Are the Pictures?

My site uses plenty of pictures, but they aren't in the export file.

WordPress doesn't attempt to put pictures and other post attachments in the export file. (If it did, the export file could easily balloon to a gargantuan size). Instead, WordPress adds a *link* for each picture that belongs to an exported post or page. When you import your WordPress.com site to your new site, the import tool processes these links. It then fetches the associated file from your old site, and copies it to your new one. Problem solved!

Importing Your Data into a Self-Hosted Site

Although the export file doesn't look like much, it holds the nucleus of your site—the raw text of every post you've ever written. To add it to your new site, you need an import operation, as described in the following steps:

1. **Log in to the dashboard of your new site, and choose Tools→Import.**

   WordPress lists the sites from which it can import data, including Blogger, LiveJournal, MovableType, Tumblr, and several more.

2. **Click the WordPress link to import the data you exported from your WordPress.com site (or another self-hosted WordPress site).**

   The "Install importer" window pops open (Figure A-2).

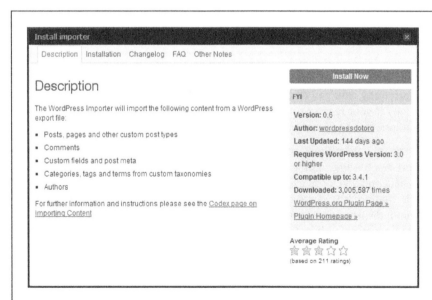

FIGURE A-2

WordPress self-hosters need to install the Importer plug-in before they can suck in any data. The first time you try to import something, you'll see this window, which describes the plug-in and lets you install it.

3. **Click the Install Now button.**

WordPress installs the plug-in in a few fractions of second.

4. **Click the "Activate Plugin & Run Importer" link to start the import process.**

The Import WordPress window appears (Figure A-3).

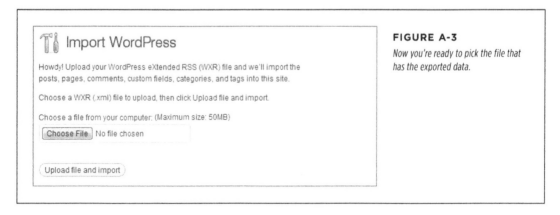

FIGURE A-3

Now you're ready to pick the file that has the exported data.

5. **Click Browse or Choose File (the exact name of the button depends on your browser). When the file selection window appears, browse to the exported XML file and select it.**

That's the file you created in the previous section, like *therealestatediaries .wordpress.2013-01-17.xml*.

6. **Click the "Upload file and import button."**

If your export file is large, it'll take a while for your web browser to transfer it to your WordPress site. When the upload finishes, WordPress shows you a few more options (Figure A-4).

7. **Optionally, you can change the author information for your posts.** (This is handy if your new site already has some or all of the user accounts for your authors, and you want to keep using them.)

Ordinarily, WordPress creates a new user for every author it finds in the export file. In the example in Figure A-4, it creates a user record for Charles M. Pakata and one for lisachang2. WordPress keeps some of but not all the author information. It imports the essential details for each author—his or her user name, display name, and email address. However, each author from the old site becomes a *subscriber* in the new site. (As you may remember from page 354, subscribers are severely limited users who can add comments but can't do anything else—including create new posts or make changes to the site). Of course, you can change a person's user type after the import process by following the steps on page 357.

In some cases, you might want to assign imported posts to a different author. For example, if you import data into a live WordPress site that already has posts on it, you might already have a user account for your authors. In this case, you can choose the user name from the "assign posts to an existing user" list. Or, if you want to create a new user with a different user name, you can type the name you want in the "create new user with login name" text box.

TIP If you're the only author on your site, you should assign all the posts you import to your administrator account on the new WordPress site. This is the account that you use to log in to the dashboard and write new posts.

---

8. **Turn on the checkbox next to the setting "Download and import file attachments."**

   This way, the WordPress importer will copy all your old pictures and other media files from your old site to your new one. However, this copy process doesn't include videos—if you've got any, they're hosted by VideoPress, and you'll need the VideoPress plug-in to display them on your new site (page 342).

9. **Click Submit.**

   WordPress gets to work updating your site. If it needs to transfer a large number of pictures, it may take a bit of time before it finishes.

■ Cleaning Up Your New Site

Congratulations, your website is now under new management! As a self-hosted WordPress site owner, you're in complete control of every setting, plug-in, and line of code in your theme.

However, life isn't perfect yet. Right now, your new site probably doesn't look a lot like your old site. Even though the same data is there, your new site sports the standard Twenty Eleven theme. And its features and permalinks don't quite match what you used in the old WordPress.com world, either. Read on to find out how to get your site closer to its previous incarnation.

Migrating Your Theme

Unfortunately, you can't transfer a WordPress.com theme to a self-hosted site. However, most WordPress.com themes are also available to self-hosters. To check for your favorite theme, start by looking in the WordPress theme repository. Choose Appearance→Themes, click the Install Themes tab, and then search for your theme by name.

If you can't find the theme you want in the WordPress theme directory, you may be able to hunt it down online. Load up a web search engine like Google, and search for the exact theme name, followed by the word "wordpress." For example, the slick Imbalance2 theme is included with WordPress.com but it's not in the self-hosters' theme directory. But if you search for "imbalance2 wordpress" you'll stumble across the freely downloadable theme files at *http://wpshower.com/themes/imbalance-2*.

Unfortunately, if you purchased a premium WordPress.com theme you can't port it over to your self-hosted site. However, you can buy a second copy for your self-hosted site (usually, for the same price). To look into this option, start at the WordPress.com theme showcase at *http://theme.wordpress.com*. Search for your theme, then click it to see a page with more theme information. Now scroll down to the "Stats & Info" section (which is in the right-side sidebar, near the bottom). There, you'll see a link to the company that created the theme. Click that link, and you'll go to the theme-creator's site, where you can pay for the theme, download it, and then upload it to your self-hosted site (page 161).

If you're unlucky, you might not be able to find a version of your theme for your self-hosted site. In this case, you need to start over by choosing a new theme and customizing it to get the look you want. Chapter 5 has plenty of information that can help you find a good theme.

Even if you do find the theme you want, you may need to redo some of the basic customization you did before, when your site was running on WordPress.com. For example, you'll probably need to resubmit your site header (choose Appearance→Header) and add the widgets you want to the appropriate widget areas (Appearance→Widgets). And even though WordPress transfers your old menus, you'll need to reattach them to the right part of your theme (Appearance→Menus).

Missing WordPress.com Features

Although self-hosted sites and WordPress.com sites have most of the same features, they're not identical. The chief culprit is WordPress.com's built-in plug-ins, which provide features like slideshows, Facebook comments, web statistics, and sharing buttons. Throughout this book, we note what plug-ins you need to duplicate different WordPress.com features. However, the best way to fill most of the gaps at once is to install the Jetpack plug-in. In fact, Jetpack was specifically created by the fine folks at Automattic to help level the playing field between WordPress.com sites and self-hosted sites. You can learn more about it on page 284.

Permalinks

By default, a new self-hosted WordPress site uses ID-based permalinks. That means that when you click through to a specific post, you get sent to a page with a URL like this:

```
http://therealestatediaries.net/?p=299
```

WordPress.com uses a different permalink style. It avoids IDs, instead combining the date and the post names. It looks like this:

```
http://therealestatediaries.wordpress.com/2012/07/30/know-the-law-before-it-
knows-you
```

As a result, when you transfer posts to your new site, they won't have the same permalinks. You can easily fix this inconsistency. Choose Settings→Permalinks and pick a new permalink style. Page 117 describes all the options that self-hosted sites have, but if you choose "Day and name" you'll get the same URL structure that WordPress.com uses. Click Save Changes to make your selection permanent, and all your posts will automatically use the style you picked.

Redirecting Your Address

The last thing you want is to have two copies of your site on the Web. Not only will this thoroughly confuse visitors, it'll also baffle search engines. Instead, your website needs a single identity and a single web address.

The exact steps you follow depend on your original website address—that's the one you used with WordPress.com before the transfer process. If you bought a custom domain name from the start, you can read the next section ("Keeping Your Custom Domain"). If your old site used a *.wordpress.com* address, you need to jump to the second section ("Moving from .wordpress.com").

■ KEEPING YOUR CUSTOM DOMAIN

If you followed the good advice in Chapter 2 (page 32) and bought a custom domain name when you first signed up with WordPress.com, the transfer process is easy. You can keep the same domain for your new site.

If you bought the custom name through a domain registrar, you already know what to do—log in to your account and point your domain to the new site.

If you bought the custom name through WordPress.com, you have two choices:

- Transfer your domain from WordPress.com to your new web host.

- Keep it registered with WordPress.com, but point it to your new site.

Both of these options have exactly the same effect. The only difference is who charges you the yearly domain registration fee (either your web host or Automattic, the people who run WordPress.com). You might choose to transfer your domain if your web host charges you less, or if they offer a free domain with your website package. But other than that, there's no advantage to making the change.

No matter which option you choose, you need to configure your WordPress.com domain. To do that, log in to your old WordPress.com site and go to the Store→Domains section of the dashboard. WordPress has the full instructions you need to follow at *http://tinyurl.com/8ese4cp*.

■ MOVING FROM .WORDPRESS.COM

If your original site uses a *.wordpress.com* domain, you need to redirect guests to your new domain. Your best bet is to buy the Site Redirect upgrade, which costs $13 per year. To get it, log into your old WordPress.com site, visit the Store section, find the Site Upgrade box, and click Buy Now. Tell WordPress.com about your new site, and it will handle the redirection automatically, serving out a special sort of notice called an HTTP 301 code, which clearly tells search engines that you've moved on to a new home (so they can update your listing).

In a year or so, when your readers (and the search engines of the world) have gotten used to your change, you can cancel the upgrade and delete your WordPress.com site using the Tools→Delete Blog command in the dashboard.

NOTE Instead of buying the Site Redirect upgrade, you *could* try to redirect traffic on your own. The basic technique is to change the home page on your old site to a static page with a message explaining that you moved your site and a link to the new site. But this technique is fraught with problems, because readers may enter your site through bookmarks and miss your message, and search engines will continue funneling people to the wrong site (because it will have a higher ranking than your new site). So don't do this, unless your site has virtually no readers or search engine traffic to worry about.

Useful Websites

Throughout this book, you learned about a number of great websites where you can get valuable information or download WordPress plug-ins. Odds are, you'll want to revisit some of those sites. To save you the effort of leafing through hundreds of pages to find the link you want, this appendix provides those links, grouped by chapter.

If just the thought of typing in these links gives you carpal tunnel syndrome, you can use the online version of this appendix, located on the *WordPress: The Missing Manual* Missing CD page at *http://missingmanuals.com/cds/wpmm*. That way, once you find a site you want to visit, you're just a click away.

■ Chapter Links

The following tables list the links found in each chapter. Each table lists the links in the same order they appear in the text.

CHAPTER 1 *The WordPress Landscape*

DESCRIPTION	URL
Paul Krugman's blog	*http://krugman.blogs.nytimes.com*
Technorati	*http://technorati.com/blogs/top100* (top 100 blogs) *http://bit.ly/rqGfCs* (state of the blogosphere report)
FAIL Blog	*http://failblog.org*
Damn You Autocorrect!	*http://damnyouautocorrect.com*

DESCRIPTION	URL
How to plan your blog	*http://learn.wordpress.com/get-focused*
The Sartorialist blog	*www.thesartorialist.com*
Wappalyzer	*http://wappalyzer.com*
WordPress-powered Ford site	*http://social.ford.com*
Examples of self-hosted WordPress sites	*http://wordpress.org/showcase*
WordPress.com WordAds	*http://wordpress.com/apply-for-wordads*
WordPress.com upgrades	*http://support.wordpress.com/upgrades*
WordPress.com popular subjects	*http://wordpress.com/tags*
Digg	*http://digg.com*
WordPress.com complaints	*http://wordpress.com/complaints*
WordPress support forums	*http://wordpress.org/support* (self-hosted sites) *http://forums.wordpress.com* (WordPress.com sites)
WordPress.com VIP hosting	*http://vip.wordpress.com*
WP Engine	*http://wpengine.com*
Synthesis	*http://websynthesis.com*

CHAPTER 2 *Signing Up with WordPress.com*

DESCRIPTION	URL
WordPress.com signup page	*http://wordpress.com/signup*
Worst passwords	*http://onforb.es/v2rdOb*
Examples of self-hosted WordPress sites	*http://wordpress.org/showcase*

CHAPTER 3 *Installing WordPress on Your Web Host*

DESCRIPTION	URL
Web Hosting Talk forum	*http://bit.ly/vQ7tkH*
WordPress-recommended hosts	*http://wordpress.org/hosting*
WordPress software (to download)	*http://wordpress.org/download*

CHAPTER 4 *Creating Posts*

DESCRIPTION	URL
Wayback Machine	*http://web.archive.org*

CHAPTER 5 *Choosing and Polishing Your WordPress Theme*

DESCRIPTION	URL
Twenty Twelve demo site	*http://twentytwelvedemo.wordpress.com*
Stock.XCHNG	*www.sxc.hu*
My Link Order (plug-in)	*http://tinyurl.com/7ds4o4*
WordPress reference for *wp_tag_cloud()*	*http://tinyurl.com/wptagcloud*
WPtouch (plug-in)	*http://tinyurl.com/wptouch*
Onswipe (plug-in)	*http://tinyurl.com/onswipe*

CHAPTER 6 *Jazzing Up Your Posts*

DESCRIPTION	URL
WordPress reference for Smilies	*http://codex.wordpress.org/Using_Smilies*
WordPress plug-in directory	*http://wordpress.org/extend/plugins*
TinyMCE (plug-in)	*http://tinyurl.com/tinyeditor*
WordPress mobile apps	*http://wordpress.org/extend/mobile*
Windows Live Writer	*http://tinyurl.com/24h2x65*
WordPress themes	*http://wordpress.org/extend/themes* (self-hosted sites) *http://theme.wordpress.com* (WordPress.com sites)
WordPress reference for *wp_link_pages()*	*http://tinyurl.com/wplinkpages*
Excerpt Editor (plug-in)	*http://tinyurl.com/csudedx*
WordPress reference for *the_excerpt()*	*http://tinyurl.com/the-excerpt*

CHAPTER 8 *Comments: Letting Your Readers Talk Back*

DESCRIPTION	URL
Comments Cleaner (plug-in)	*http://tinyurl.com/cleancomments*
Rich Text Editor For Comments (plug-in)	*http://tinyurl.com/richcomments*
WP Content Filter (plug-in)	*http://tinyurl.com/wpcontentfilter*
Better WordPress Recent Comments (plug-in)	*http://tinyurl.com/wprecentcomments*
GD Star Rating (plug-in)	*http://tinyurl.com/gd-star-rating*
Gravatar	*http://gravatar.com*
Antispam Bee (plug-in)	*http://tinyurl.com/spambee*
AVH First Defense Against Spam (plug-in)	*http://tinyurl.com/avhspam*
Defensio Anti-Spam (plug-in)	*http://tinyurl.com/defensio*

DESCRIPTION	URL
FV Antispam (plug-in)	http://tinyurl.com/fvantispam
Akismet	http://akismet.com/wordpress
Growmap Anti Spambot (plug-in)	http://tinyurl.com/growmapspam
Captcha (plug-in)	http://tinyurl.com/wp-captcha
Anti-Captcha (plug-in)	http://tinyurl.com/wp-anticaptcha

CHAPTER 9 *Getting New Features with Plug-Ins*

DESCRIPTION	URL
WordPress reference for writing a plug-in	http://codex.wordpress.org/Writing_a_Plugin
Smashing Magazine	http://wp.smashingmagazine.com
WP Plugins	http://wpplugins.com
CodeCanyon	http://codecanyon.net
WordPress plug-in directory	http://wordpress.org/extend/plugins
Jetpack	http://jetpack.me
LaTex tutorial	http://tinyurl.com/latexmath
LaTex equation generator	http://tinyurl.com/latexequation
WordPress documentation for LaTex	http://support.wordpress.com/latex
WPtouch (plug-in)	http://tinyurl.com/wptouch http://tinyurl.com/wptouchpro (Pro version)
Google AdSense	http://google.com/adsense
Onswipe (plug-in)	http://tinyurl.com/onswipe
VaultPress	http://vaultpress.com http://vaultpress.com/jetpack (sign up page)
BackupBuddy (plug-in)	http://ithemes.com/purchase/backupbuddy
DropBox	www.dropbox.com
Google Drive	http://drive.google.com
Amazon S3	http://aws.amazon.com/s3
WP-DB-Backup (plug-in)	http://tinyurl.com/wp-db-backup
WP-DBManager (plug-in)	http://tinyurl.com/wp-dbmanager
BackWPup (plug-in)	http://tinyurl.com/backwpup
Online Backup for WordPress (plug-in)	http://tinyurl.com/wponlinebackup
Gmail	www.gmail.com
WP Super Cache (plug-in)	http://tinyurl.com/wpsupercache
BuddyPress (plug-in)	http://buddypress.org

CHAPTER 10 *Adding Picture Galleries, Video, and Music*

DESCRIPTION	URL
WordPress embeds	*http://codex.wordpress.org/Embeds*
WordPress.com shortcodes	*http://support.wordpress.com/shortcodes*
Reference for [gallery] shortcode	*http://tinyurl.com/cfc29n*
Regenerate Thumbnails (plug-in)	*http://tinyurl.com/rthumb*
Portfolio Slideshow (plug-in)	*http://tinyurl.com/port-show*
Photonic (plug-in)	*http://tinyurl.com/wp-photonic*
YouTube	*www.youtube.com*
Smart YouTube PRO (plug-in)	*http://tinyurl.com/smart-tube*
Vimeo	*http://vimeo.com*
VideoPress	*http://videopress.com* *http://tinyurl.com/vidpress* (plug-in)
oEmbed HTML5 audio (plug-in)	*http://tinyurl.com/oembed*
MediaElement.js (plug-in)	*http://tinyurl.com/media-element*
SoundCloud	*http://soundcloud.com*
Instruction for submitting podcasts to iTunes	*http://tinyurl.com/podcastspecs*
Blubrry PowerPress (plug-in)	*http://tinyurl.com/wp-podcast*

CHAPTER 11 *Collaborating with Multiple Authors*

DESCRIPTION	URL
BuddyPress (plug-in)	*http://buddypress.org*
Email Users (plug-in)	*http://tinyurl.com/emailusers*
Blogs you own or write for on WordPress.com	*http://wordpress.com/my-blogs*
Edit Flow (plug-in)	*http://tinyurl.com/editflow* *http://editflow.org* (documentation)
Co-Authors Plus (plug-in)	*http://tinyurl.com/co-authors-plus* *http://tinyurl.com/ccr7896* (theme changes)
Authors Widget (plug-in)	*http://tinyurl.com/authorswidget*
Author Avatars List (plug-in)	*http://tinyurl.com/authoravatars*
WP About Author (plug-in)	*http://tinyurl.com/wp-about-author*
Fancier Author Box (plug-in)	*http://tinyurl.com/authorbox*
Author Spotlight (plug-in)	*http://tinyurl.com/authorspot*
Page Security (plug-in)	*http://tinyurl.com/page-security-c*

DESCRIPTION	URL
Page Restrict (plug-in)	*http://tinyurl.com/page-restrict*
Examples of multisite networks	*http://blogs.reuters.com* *http://blogs.law.harvard.edu* *http://blogs.adobe.com* *http://stores.bestbuy.com* *http://wordpress.com*
Converting a site to a multisite network	*http://tinyurl.com/2835suo*
Enable Multi-Site (plug-in)	*http://tinyurl.com/e-multisite*
Add Multiple Users (plug-in)	*http://tinyurl.com/add-multiple*
Multisite User Management (plug-in)	*http://tinyurl.com/multisite-um*

CHAPTER 12 *Attracting a Crowd*

DESCRIPTION	URL
Facebook	*www.facebook.com*
Twitter	*http://twitter.com*
PollDaddy (plug-in)	*http://tinyurl.com/wp-polls*
Thank Me Later (plug-in)	*http://tinyurl.com/wp-thank*
Subscribe2 (plug-in)	*http://tinyurl.com/wp-sub2*
Social Networks Auto-Poster (plug-in)	*http://tinyurl.com/social-p*
Wordbooker (plug-in)	*http://tinyurl.com/wordbooker*
WP to Twitter	*http://tinyurl.com/wp2tw*
Information about the [tweet] shortcode	*http://tinyurl.com/cwfa77u*
Information about the [twitter-follow] shortcode	*http://tinyurl.com/cn29khu*
Chrome extension for feeds	*http://tinyurl.com/28q8dth*
FeedDemon	*www.feeddemon.com*
NetNewsWire	*http://netnewswireapp.com*
Google Reader	*www.google.com/reader*
Flipboard Feedly	*http://flipboard.com* *www.feedly.com*
WordPress feed reference	*http://tinyurl.com/64lmdo*

DESCRIPTION	URL
Google Toolbar	www.google.com/toolbar http://tinyurl.com/64bjmtd (how to enable PageRank)
Check PageRank online	www.prchecker.info
Google Blogsearch	http://blogsearch.google.com
WordPress SEO by Yoast (plug-in)	http://tinyurl.com/seo-yoast http://tinyurl.com/seo-yoast2 (tutorial)
SEO articles by Yoast	http://yoast.com/cat/seo

CHAPTER 13 *Editing Themes: The Key to Customizing Your Site*

DESCRIPTION	URL
Gallery of non-blog WordPress sites	http://tinyurl.com/9dvpn3y
HTML tutorial	http://tinyurl.com/4mwq8
CSS tutorial	http://tinyurl.com/mlqk7
One-Click Child Theme (plug-in)	http://tinyurl.com/child-theme
CSS property reference	http://tinyurl.com/bz5tcp
WordPress function reference	http://tinyurl.com/func-ref
Basic PHP tutorial	http://tinyurl.com/ctzya55
Theme File Duplicator (plug-in)	http://tinyurl.com/dup-theme
Notepad++	http://notepad-plus-plus.org
Twenty Eleven customization examples	http://tinyurl.com/7dalazv
Template recipes	http://tinyurl.com/c2o288h
Blog with WordPress tips	http://lorelle.wordpress.com
Smashing Magazine	http://wp.smashingmagazine.com
Thematic	http://tinyurl.com/themat
Genesis	http://tinyurl.com/gen-theme

CHAPTER 14 *Building an Advanced WordPress Site*

DESCRIPTION	URL
How to create a test site	http://tinyurl.com/89wochm
Theme frameworks	http://tinyurl.com/theme-f
PinBlack theme	http://tinyurl.com/pinblack

DESCRIPTION	URL
WordPress theme directory	http://wordpress.org/extend/themes
WordPress reference for *query_posts()*	http://tinyurl.com/yhjtze5
WordPress reference for *get_posts()*	http://tinyurl.com/23km6q5
WordPress function reference	http://tinyurl.com/func-ref
Information for customizing the comment form	http://tinyurl.com/26qf74x
GD Star Rating (plug-in)	http://tinyurl.com/gd-star-rating
Get Custom Field (plug-in)	http://tinyurl.com/get-field
Featured Image (plug-in)	http://tinyurl.com/featured-i
Post by Same Categories (plug-in)	http://tinyurl.com/postbysame
Information about WordPress databases	http://tinyurl.com/3a88qt
Ultimate Taxonomy Manager (plug-in)	http://tinyurl.com/ultimate-t
Article about custom taxonomies	http://tinyurl.com/8slqbkn
PayPal Donations (plug-in)	http://tinyurl.com/paypal-d
Google AdSense	www.google.com/adsense
Ad Injection (plug-in)	http://tinyurl.com/ad-injection
s2Member (plug-in)	http://tinyurl.com/s2member
WordPress Simple PayPal Shopping Cart (plug-in)	http://tinyurl.com/paypal-c
WP e-Commerce (plug-in)	http://tinyurl.com/wp-ecom

Index

WordPress

THE MISSING CD

There's no CD with this book; you just saved $5.00.

Instead, every single Web address, practice file, and piece of downloadable software mentioned in this book is available at *missingmanuals.com* (click the Missing CD icon). There you'll find a tidy list of links, organized by chapter.

Don't miss a thing!
Sign up for the free Missing Manual email announcement list at missingmanuals.com. We'll let you know when we release new titles, make free sample chapters available, and update the features and articles on the Missing Manual website.

Lightning Source UK Ltd.
Milton Keynes UK
UKOW06f2358111213

222820UK00001B/2/P